THE VESTIBULE OF HELL

Why Left and Right Have Never Made Sense in Politics and Life

Hugh Graham

Published in Canada in 2001 by
Stoddart Publishing Co. Limited
895 Don Mills Road, 400-2 Park Centre, Toronto, Ontario M3C 1W3

Published in the United States in 2002 by
Stoddart Publishing Co. Limited
PMB 128, 4500 Witmer Estates, Niagara Falls, New York 14305-1386

www.stoddartpub.com

To order Stoddart books please contact General Distribution Services
In Canada Tel. (416) 213-1919 Fax (416) 213-1917
E-mail cservice@genpub.com
In the United States Toll-free tel. 1-800-805-1083 Toll-free fax 1-800-481-6207
E-mail gdsinc@genpub.com

10 9 8 7 6 5 4 3 2 1

Canadian Cataloguing in Publication Data

Graham, Hugh, 1951–
The vestibule of hell: why left and right have never made sense in politics and life

Includes bibliographical references and index.
ISBN 0-7737-3285-3

1. Right and left (Political science). I. Title.

JA83.G736 2001   320.5   C00-932950-1

U.S. Cataloguing in Publication Data
(Library of Congress Standards)

Graham, Hugh.
The vestibule of hell: why left and right have never made sense
in politics and life / Hugh Graham. — 1st ed.
[376] p. : cm.
Includes bibliographical references and index.
Summary: Dissecting the extremes of left and right in politics, economics,
and social theory, and their impact on world political history.
ISBN 0-7737-3285-3
1. Right and left (Political science). 2. Political science — History.
3. Ideology. 4. Social psychology. I Title.
320.5091 21   2001   CIP

Jacket design: Angel Guerra
Text design and typesetting: Kinetics Design & Illustration

THE CANADA COUNCIL | LE CONSEIL DES ARTS
FOR THE ARTS | DU CANADA
SINCE 1957 | DEPUIS 1957

*We acknowledge for their financial support of our publishing program the Canada Council, the Ontario Arts Council,
and the Government of Canada through the Book Publishing Industry Development Program (BPIDP).*

Printed in Canada

Contents

Introduction

Where does the symbolism of left and right come from? How has it endured the span of civilization, passing ultimately into a political distinction that even in our own day retains an archaic, numinous force — haunting enough to mark two sides of the globe each with the power to annihilate the other? Left and right are unquestioned in the Myth of Er, which Plato included in *The Republic* as a sanction to the uneducated lest Reason alone fail to persuade them to lead a life according to the Good. When they died, he warned them, their souls would be presented to judges who sat between a deep abyss on their left hand and a way upward to the sky on their right. At the junction, each soul's record in life was presented. The saved would be sent on the right-hand path to heaven, the damned along the left-hand path to suffer damnation in the abyss. Unlike many other influential ideas, this one did not begin with Plato. His forked road is anticipated in the much older Vedic myth of the Cinvat Bridge, upon which the God Mithra stands, sending the saved across by his right hand and throwing the damned downward upon his left. But even the Vedic myth is drawn from an idea which, if traced backward, seems to disappear into the steppes of Central Asia.

The left and right hands as symbols of damnation and salvation crop up in myths in other civilizations also. The profane left hand and

1

the sacred right appear in Middle Eastern myth and custom, in the Old and New Testament as the left and right hands of the Lord, and, forward into European civilization, as the left and right hands of the king. The right hand was the king's sacred hand, the side on which those he preferred were seated. When France's Louis XVI was dethroned, the right-left distinction passed into the republican assemblies that replaced him. Those who had favoured the monarch or the older ways sat on the right of an empty throne, while the more revolutionary sat on the left. This division has lasted into our own time, where it has come to define two halves of the globe, not to mention opposing sides of town councils. It seems somehow fitting that a dualistic determination, which increasingly clouds policy, generalizes to the point of untruth, and applies an old procrustean bed to a changing world, is still arranged around an absent monarch.

At some point before the end of the Cold War, the political terms "Left" and "Right" began to lose their force. But even now they retain a certain aura that is unstable, haunted. The terms can pinion, damn, insult. They still carry a whiff of accusation — when they are only referring, say, to something as worldly as higher or lower taxes. I would argue, in fact, that they retain some of the taboo power of sexuality — for as sacred and profane sides of the body, they are likely as old as consciousness of the body. And I will attempt to show that the two-handed politics they describe — our politics — is indeed based on a religious idea that has slipped into secular life, and, having done its damage in two world wars, continues to dampen the political imagination and distort reality. It is finally outliving its relevance.

Nevertheless, Left and Right have been slower to die than other concepts at this turn of the century, a time that has brought about talk of Ends, Deaths, Obsolescences, Apocalypses. The sense is always monolithic, the mood foreboding: "the end of history," "the end of the Left," "the end of industrial society," "the end of the modern," "the end of freedom." But the substantial end of an old war between Left and Right with the dissolution of the Soviet Empire was the most timely of all the finales — taking place, in one of Clio's rare feats of chronological neatness, in 1989 — exactly two hundred years after it had begun in Paris. And yet the end came, as Eliot might have said, "not with a bang but a whimper"; indeed, it had little that was monolithic about it and less that was clearly foreboding. It was an "end" leading rather to exhaustion, a loss of bearings, and the prospect of uncharted seas ahead. Hardly what we would expect of a duality as stark as Left and Right.

This opaque, disoriented, new world had already started to appear toward the end of the old. The two superpowers had something tired about them. Like punch-drunk boxers, both were shadows of their former selves. Each had vaguely begun to take on the other's characteristics. The United States was less individualistic than it had been, and the Soviet Union less collective. Capitalist commercial culture had achieved an oddly amorphous collectivism — at the very least a cultural homogeneity; and much of the old individualist self-reliance had given way to reliance on the state or on professionals. Moreover, individualism had lost much of its shine to drug abuse, crime, and the erosion of the small community. Meanwhile, in the USSR, a class system had developed, with special department stores and privileges for state functionaries and Party members. Soviet collectivism was embarrassed by poor agricultural yields, low work productivity, and bureaucratic incompetence. It was hardly that the tired individualist had triumphed. A more exhausted collectivist had simply hit the mat.

The capitalism that drives America today is not the capitalism upon which it was built. The individualistic values of the small community are now more talked about than practised. The same was true of the ragged banner of collectivism that fluttered over a tottering Soviet Union. Each had made of individualism and collectivism an exclusive absolute in a changing world that contradicted absolutes. When absolute principles have to bear the weight of multicultural and multi-ethnic change, those principles get worn out and the nation begins to live a double life — of how things ought to be and how they really are.

As the values of Right and Left weakened within the two camps, their daily usage became vague and uneasy. In the West, after the 1960s, people objected more to being called "Right" or "Left" because of the terms' increasing radicalization by the counterculture. Many did not want their opinions categorized. Nor did they want one opinion to define them in all other matters. Many conservatives did not like being labelled "Right" because the linear spectrum of Left and Right aligned even the gentlest of conservatives with Hitler. But that is the very nature of the paradigm — a paradigm that is bound to wear out, perhaps even break.

There are a number of reasons why this political duality persists, but the main one is that we are still haunted by fears of Communism and Fascism — which people continue to style as "far left" and "far right." Those who call themselves Left or Right use the opposite extreme to position their enemies, especially to unmask supposed impostors. Such name-calling serves a rhetorical purpose but also meets an archaic need to feel that one is standing on holy ground. This need to place the other on a charted landscape is at least as much a sign of the moral insecurity of the observer as a desire for decipherability. That is why, as the terms weaken, they are held up with all the more vigour.

Indeed, the beast fights most furiously when it is wounded, politicians being more vocal than ever about Left and Right on smaller and more confined issues that have little to do with egalitarianism or individualism. People apologize for the terms even as they continue to use them, or they qualify what they *really* mean by "Right" or "Left." If we can't talk about the "end" of Left and Right quite yet, we can watch as the terms become increasingly rhetorical, contributing less and less to their decipherability. It is precisely because the terms persist that they must be questioned. This can be done through a critique of present politics, through logical analysis, or through history. I have chosen to use history because it is the only region of inquiry that includes all the others. The terms Left and Right have grown over the centuries from religious simplicity to political, philosophical, and cultural complexity. As a result, they have become overburdened and begun to collapse — for example, when the Left tries to contain environmentalism as well as labour, or when the Right tries to contain libertarianism as well as fundamentalism. They are each "accretions" of meanings gathered over time.

The best way to understand them is to see how they have been built up — because when things begin to fall apart, as with poorly constructed buildings, their dissolution reveals the weakness in their construction. The "deconstructive" approach of the present work has given it something of the appearance of a large-scale cultural history. If it sometimes seems a little too wide-ranging, I can say only that Left and Right tend to ramify all over the place and if I have not been successful in containing the scope it is not for lack of trying.

Still, to tell the early parts of this story as a linear, chronological history would deprive us of seeing their continuing relevance to the modern world. And isolating the modern sequence would make it too easy to forget the living relevance of the past. So I have chosen, perhaps at some risk, to look at Left and Right in the two centuries since the outbreak of the French Revolution (1789–1999); and from within that period to reach back into their ten-thousand-year history to provide an ongoing background. That is, I will tell an ancient and a modern story at the same time in an effort to illustrate the influence of anthropology and culture on modern politics.

Such a strategy gives emphasis to the age-old conflict between *mythos* and *logos* as means of access to truth. The politics of Left and Right has the obvious claim to being logical. The original distinction inherent in the word *logos* was drawn by the Ionian Greek philosopher Heraclitus, who defined it as a *way* or *route* determined by reasoning. As I follow the development of *logos* in politics, I propose to confront it continually with the critique of *mythos*; that is, to show that even though *logos* implicitly believes itself logical, it often develops distinctions based on the prejudices of myth and taboo. What has happened in Western civilization is that *mythos* has come to determine *logos*, and religion, via philosophy, has influenced the development of politics. Perhaps the most perniciously influential figure in this confounding of *mythos* and *logos* was the Greek philosopher Parmenides.

Parmenides declared, roughly, that the over-arching idea of Being in itself is more real than the individual things of which Being is apparently composed. This distinction between a real, conceptual world of mind and an illusory world of individual things — corresponding, say, to collective ideas and material individuality — is, he would have held, a distinction inherent in *logos*. But its terrible rigidity came when it was imbued with a religious, mystical nature; it would ramify, as in a hall of mirrors, down through time into the inchoate, formative concepts of Left and Right, as idealism and realism respectively, as collectivism and individualism, and so on. It was not a tidy, perfect descent, but the pattern is evident all the same.

This is a simplification, but, I think, a truthful one. And so, I have tried to show that when we impose a dualistic structure on the world, we unconsciously impose a religious duality not just on society, but on time, giving it, for example, the dynamic of a battle, with periods of separation, polarity, combination, progress, and retreat. The oldest instance of this pattern can be seen in the Zoroastrian division of its sacred history into three sequences of a battle between Good and Evil. It begins in a period of "Purity," when humankind is in its innocence; it passes into a phase of "Mixture," when the forces of Good and Evil fight over humanity; and it ends with an apocalyptic "Separation," when Good is separated from Evil, the "grain from the chaff" (a biblical idea for which, it appears, Zoroastrianism was responsible).

Zoroastrian sacred history does have a certain existential logic to it; and in terms of real history it is prophetic — especially if we include the transition of good and evil into Right and Left. And so I have used it as a structural motif for setting out this account. A primal epoch of "Purity," I will suggest, corresponds to the age of polytheism, when clear-cut and universal ideas of good and evil have not yet set in. With the advent of the world religions such as Zoroastrianism, Judaism, Christianity, and Islam, Good and Evil appear as something quite new. The conquests, persecutions, and doctrinal struggles that grow out of these intolerant monotheistic creeds constitute an age of "Mixture" — the war between Good and Evil that lasts throughout the Middle Ages. Its culmination is the chaos of the religious wars of sixteenth- and seventeenth-century Europe. An age of Separation begins during the same conflict, as notions of Good and Evil become organizing forces in a socio-political conflict of classes. At the time of the French Revolution, the religious ideas of Sacred and Profane, Good and Evil, have finally passed into the social and spatial separation of Left and Right as they take up, literally, opposite sides of assemblies all over Europe, and, eventually, all over the world. Separation reaches its most extreme expression, of course, with the Cold War — two halves of the globe, figuratively Right and Left, each conceiving of itself as Good and the other as Evil.

More than just an account of a political process, my effort to relate what has been a complex and often disorderly development of ideas has required reference to philosophy. Philosophers in the West quite involuntarily contribute to the development of dualistic thinking while making other, unrelated points. This is partly because their thought systems are built on the heritage of Plato and, perhaps more important, on the heritage of Plato's precursors Parmenides and Pythagoras.

The legacy of Parmenides is one motif of this book. A second is the earlier concept of the sacred and the profane — the primordial sense of inhibition and taboo hidden in dualities of only limited rationality. A third theme is the idea of the Sacred itself, a sensation or feeling that, I will argue, has always moved just ahead of political change and remains a factor in politics today. I refer to the Sacred not in any religious sense but only as an enduring and primordial feeling of desire combined with loss. It is protean, finding many expressions — economic, philosophical, spiritual, and artistic, to name only a few. I use it, especially in the later chapters, to represent feelings that now seek to express themselves in politics but remain unsatisfied by any politics. In history, it begins as an idea of the Good and, especially in Christian medieval history, it forms the earliest ideas of a Left (in its modern usage) as an idea of order and safety and as moral critic of an older, less moral, and more dangerous "rightish" pagan principle. In that sense we will see that the modern Left is heir to the Church. The modern Right, by contrast, is heir to the aristocracy from the time it began to shake off its role as sacred protector of the poor and embrace a more solitary self-interest. And so we will see the early modern era as a knotty transitional period when popular protest begins to wrest the role of the Left from the Church, loses its aura of profanity, and begins to become sacred in the guise of the moral crusades of the lower classes and the bourgeoisie. And the old ruling class, the Right, by now defined more by wealth and less by a sacred, protective stewardship, begins to be associated with the egoistic and the profane — the former paganism.

So this is really a story of the gradual movement of a sacred morality away from the realm of the sacred into the domain of the secular. And I place the centre, the very nexus, of this history in the High Middle Ages, when the sacred as moral restraint begins its migration from the auspices of the Church into the secular world. The poet who symbolically documents this move is Dante. In his *Divine Comedy*, he represented the disjunction, or "limbo," in this transfer between the holy and the profane fallen world as the First Circle of Hell. This "Vestibule of Hell" in the *Inferno* is reserved for those souls who have been rejected by God and not accepted into Hell because they refused to commit themselves to God or Satan in life. Metaphorically — and with some irony — I pose the refused choice as the choice of Left and Right (or vice versa), and I locate human nature itself between them, in the Vestibule, a place of abstention which, in loyalty to humanity itself, protests the choice as spurious.

A fourth theme is the Left as "most recent moral critic" — the only unassailable definition I have been able to discover for what has been called "Left." A moral protest in the midst of the corrupt collectivism of the Soviet Union, for example, would describe free-market reformers as "Left"; it would be a new protest and a moral one. Fundamentalism, by contrast, is a moral critic, but since it is not a new one, it remains "Right." In this sense Left and Right are terms relative *only* to the idea of *new* moral reform, whether it be individual or collective, egalitarian or libertarian. In proposing this new and very general minimum definition of Left, I am contrasting it with the conventional definitions of Left and Right more or less as collective and individual, egalitarian and inegalitarian. In proposing that the only stable definition is (paradoxically) relative and changing (not qualitative), I hope I am taking a step toward doing away with the terms altogether.

This "most recent moral critic," as I will try to show, always refers to something just beyond itself, the idea that I call the Sacred. The Sacred refers to whatever significant numbers of people tend to feel they are lacking at any given time. For example, people may at times feel materially deprived, lacking in individual autonomy, disenfranchised from nation or community, or bereft of connection with a healthy natural world. This sense of the sacred is a positive rather than a negative term and does not oppose anything except its natural opposite: fascism. Fascism may itself challenge, even attempt to destroy, Left and Right, but it does so only to replace them with a false idea of the Sacred that is linked with a particular people, a particular nation, or a particular ideology. It attempts to eliminate the distinction between Left and Right only so that its narrow interest might have no competitors; in so doing, it merely creates a new dualism. Precisely the same might be said for Left and Right themselves, since their pure manifestations are inevitably anti-democratic. Each can only hold that a better world would no longer have a Left and Right because it and it alone would be the true way.

Right and Left have each claimed the idea of the sacred as their justification. The Right has brought it from the past; the Left, as most recent moral critic, places its ideal in the future. But I will argue that, since the political polarities are wearing themselves out, the sacred is effectively orphaned, unclaimed and unrecognized in their wake, a little like a child or non-combatant who survives unnoticed after a battle of mutual extermination. And indeed it presents a point of departure.

One thing we can say clearly is that the Sacred did not exist as a single, transcendent value in early polytheistic religions. It was dispersed in wells and doorways, in wombs and phalluses, in marshes, deserts, and fire: since it was not in any one place it could not be fought over. Even in hunting societies where the sacred floated in opposition to the profane, it was mobile and subject to interpretation by the shaman. It began to appear as a static concept only with the ritualization of the natural cycles of birth and death. For it is in them that dual ideas are perhaps first systematized with any complexity — in the mystery rites of Osiris, Dionysus, and Orpheus. The sacred is rationalized, "corralled" into a ritual cycle. But even there, good and evil remain cyclical and do not take up permanent residence in an eternal Heaven or an eternal Hell. This latter, more rigid dualism begins to coalesce with Gnosticism.

Gnosticism, as the continuing religious reference and source of Left and Right, constitutes my fifth theme. It coalesced in the centuries just before Christ, in the first monotheistic religions that arose out of the irregular, scattered, and haunted landscape of polytheism and mystery rites. The idea of the sacred gradually became embodied in a sovereign man- or woman-god around whom ideas of good and evil were determined. For a time, monotheisms such as Zoroastrianism and Judaism coexisted with Greek, Roman, and other, more local polytheisms. Across the three centuries before Christ there gradually occurred a startling convergence of all these religious currents with Greek Platonic philosophy — much as it was determined by Parmenides. It emphasized the simple rationalism of *logos* over the irrationality and complexity of polytheistic *mythos*, the abstract over the real. (*Mythos*, after all, was only a divine expression of that material world, condemned as an illusion by Parmenides.) A new, if somewhat dispersed, spiritual background developed, stretching from the Eastern Mediterranean to Persia and from the upper Nile northward into Thrace. It was in this region that religious and philosophical currents began to be reduced to a set of common denominators that responded to new popular needs.

Social stresses caused by the expansion of the Roman Republic into an empire brought about a loss of confidence in the gods of polytheism. With the breakdown of communities, people resorted to an embodiment of all that one had held dear but had lost, a perfect version of one's lost self that could, through ritual discipline, be regained in the next life. That lost self lay in a great beyond. That great collective beyond was an unknown God conceived as the *All*, unknown precisely because we had fallen away from it: we had, literally, *lost* ourselves. The present situation in the world was, effectively, a fall from that original blissful state into an evil, forgetful, and false world of matter — the Parmenidean product of an inferior, malign god, the "World Creator" or *Demiurge* (from *demiurgòs*, Greek for "craftsman"). Even the body was composed of the same corruption. So Good and Evil emerged as fixed ideas corresponding psychologically to true self and lost self. This is the primary concept of alienation, which will reappear in Marx, among many others. Likewise, Left and Right each will come to have its own idea of authenticity, of gain, loss, recovery, and its own inherited ideas of itself as good and the other as the imprisoning Demiurge, or evil.

In its ancient, mythical form, this belief held that a spark that had fallen away from the fire of the original man-god — our primal, perfect state — was preserved in the soul. The goal was to reunite one's spark in the unknown God. But since fallen humanity drifted in a state of forgetfulness, those who realized they had the divine spark possessed a secret. They called this secret the *gnosis*, Greek for "knowledge." Gnosis, although prior to Christianity, remains analogous to modern ideas of ideology — of "true" as opposed to "false" consciousness.

Although many variations of this new, simplified, and rationalized religious mood would emerge, among them Christianity, its general profile is indeed Gnosticism itself. Since the rites and structures of Gnosticism were extremely various, it is better to call it a spiritual attitude or mood rather than a religion. Its many different myths all have the dual motif of above and below: a fall, an entrapment in evil, and a rescue leading to reunification with the original state. One such myth is the myth of the Messiah, the messenger from the unknown god, who imparts to the lost souls the truth of their origin before the messenger himself is murdered by the forces of the Demiurge. Christianity is only one version of this myth. In the Gnostic attitude we find the entire paradigm not just of the modern religions of the West but of Western morality as well. For the Gnostic attitude is, literally, existential: it is the first really articulate analogue for the human condition. The separation of the fetus from the womb is precisely the falling away of the spark from the primal fire of the All. The tearing away from the bliss of the uterus, the birth into a cold and alien world, the unconscious desire to return to the undifferentiated prenatal condition (Freud's infantile "oceanic state"), and the consequent attempts to reproduce that state "above" in love relationships, utopias, communities, or religion are all part of the simple motif of being "thrown" from nothing into something and trying to return into the bliss of nothing — *nirvana*. Politics, as it has developed, suggests there is a "Right" way and a "Left" way of doing this.

Though Gnosticism began as a general pool of belief, Gnostic attitudes survived alongside Christianity, returning from the past to irritate the Church as movements of reform — or heresies, as the Church would have it. Sometimes Gnosticism was manifested in very tightly closed sects, sometimes in general inclinations. However it appeared, the urge toward Gnostic thinking tried to rekindle, by means of dual contrasts, a sense of simplicity and purity, to recover an authentic foundation. In that sense, even Christianity itself emerged as a gnostic reform of Judaism, and Protestantism as a gnostic reform of Christianity.

I frequently refer to Gnostic motifs because it is in Gnosticism that we first find the idea of utopia as an intellectual abstraction (not as a picturesque Greek Arcadia or a Norse Valhalla) and a universal paradigm. Left and Right both, for example, have had a tendency to complain of decline (a "fall"). Both have ideas of a primal state. Both believe that the future can be known through glimpses of things in the past, whether of the medieval village, the pre-industrial workshop, or the harmonious workman's Soviet of 1917. Both hold promises for social salvation in the ideal of the truest personal expression of the individual (the All): as patriot, as labour, or as woman, whether that world is collective or individual, communist or capitalist. This is true not just of radical ideologies but of moderate conservative and liberal ideologies as well, since all are dependent on progress — social, economic, or technological. They are in flight, as it were, from the Demiurge, and in desire for the All.

The idea that the modern political ideologies have really been secular forms of gnostic thinking was first conceived by Eric Voegelin. I am indebted to his work for its clarification and confirmation of gnostic motifs in ideology. But of course the common foundation in political and religious thinking presents itself as soon as one starts to look at the two phenomena. What Voegelin suggests is that the *radical* forms of Left and Right, in Communism and Fascism (when conceived as "Right"), replaced a revered and unknown cosmos with a *known* image of man himself. After the abolition of God and His replacement with Man, what had been an *ethical* relationship to a greater power was transformed into a narcissistic relationship of man to his own reflection. The Cosmic, a voice that whispered the *logos* out of darkness, was reduced to a mirror. What had once been the mysterious "Son of Man" becomes, quite literally, the Worker or the Aryan German himself. For the first time, humanity as a class or as a race — or even as a gender — claims that he or she *is* the cosmos, and it is her primal, perfect reflection upon that cosmos that must be realized here on earth. Of course, we are speaking in metaphors, but the blind and verbatim repetition of certain religious motifs in secular projects is inescapable. The motif of two principles, universally opposed and locked in a dialectical conflict defined as progress is, in short, Gnostic.

The Gnostic sequence in Western historical development is relatively recent. It occupies the last two-and-a-half millennia of six thousand years of civilization. It is a contingent and specific expression of morality and the human condition, quite different, say, from animism, polytheism, or Confucianism. It is characterized by a collective striving toward social and utopian ideals that are never quite graspable. That striving *toward* some end has been supported by rationalizing and justifying ideas such as emancipation, equality, progress, liberty, and fraternity; and it has been carried forward by both the Left and the Right. All of these ideas have been questioned by the more radical critics in the "Deconstruction" school as mere "legitimations" of "the project of the Enlightenment." Thus framed, the Enlightenment is a specifically Western and European (I would say, Mediterranean and Gnostic) idea that has enlisted those legitimations in war, racism, persecution, and potential mutual annihilation, and so it has fallen into question — even into disrepute. It is not my intention to demolish the

Enlightenment — only to remark that it compromised itself in a civil war between its Left and Right manifestations.

In the ruins, the *striving* remains. I don't mean that it persists in a Messianic or Christian sense, only that loss and desire still drift just beyond one's grasp. This is what I call, with some hesitation, the Sacred. It is the wildflower that still blows among the ruins. It is not rooted in salvation, heaven, or perfection, but rather in the present, in immediate surroundings. In its individual and its collective nostalgicism, it is a venerable idea, closer to an older polytheism, and not to some abstract electronic image of a brave new world. It is defined by propinquity, neighbourliness, and intimacy, and a desire for an effortless consciousness of the world. Like the *Monad* of Leibniz, it is the self-contained social entity that reflects the cosmos. In short, the Sacred is the desire for community.

Breaking down Left and Right has brought about a problem of language: to take the terms apart, it is necessary to continue to use them — like the paradox of using language to deconstruct language. In talking about the idea of a "Right wing" for example, one must use "Right" and "Left" as people have conceived of them. This has required using the terms "Left" and "Right" in various strengths. First, in order to show that they are not to be taken for granted, I have capitalized them throughout. Occasionally when a term takes on one possible meaning out of several, or when the usage is ironic, (as, for example, "Mussolini might be styled 'Left'") the word Left or Right has been placed in quotation marks. At other times I will refer to trends or ideas as "leftish" or "rightish" to convey a weaker or more commonly recognized sense in which they apply to certain phenomena. Another term that will appear is "Left-Right," which refers to "centrist" combinations of the two tendencies. By no means does "Left-Right" always point to some ideal synthesis or to their successful elimination. It usually means only that the polarity has been temporarily suspended in a combination, or that a mundane provisional amalgamation has been achieved that is still fully conscious of its "Left" and "Right" elements (as in the phenomenon of Napoleon, in Robespierran Bonapartism, in Liberal Parties, in humanism, or in Liberal Democracy in general).

Left and Right are monolithic ideas — colossal, abstract, and, as their religious origins suggest, cosmic. They are part of the darker side of humanity that replaces the specific with the general, the personal with the impersonal. If you wanted to find a way of making certain that people would have as little as possible in common, there would be no better way than to divide them — not into ten or three or four — but into two. Dual division turns the largest possible sections of humanity against one another, often causing neighbours and compatriots to have nothing to say to one another. No regeneration of community can begin without a careful demolition of Left and Right; nor can this tearing down be relinquished to academic abstraction, technical philosophy, government, corporations, or ideology. Nothing can be built without a new politics — least of all with a politics that refers outward to ideas of heaven and hell rather than inward to the experience of daily life.

PART

UNITY

I

Oneness:

Enlightened and Ancient

Left and Right were manifested physically before they were uttered as political terms — the vague groupings of a crowd on the evening of Friday, August 28, 1789 — in the *Salle des Menus Plaisirs*, a theatrical storage hall converted into a ceremonial throne room in the town of Versailles.

On that day, little more than a month after the fall of the Bastille, the issue of divergence was a certain Article One proposed by the assembly's Constitutional Committee. When it was read, around nine that morning, it asserted — boldly and without precedent — that the monarch must be subject to the law. Pandemonium broke loose. In the ruckus that wore on late into the day, the young deputy Robespierre tried to recommend practical limitations to the debate and was furiously shouted down in the name of free speech. It may have been then, when he relented and descended from the bar into the mob of waiting speakers, that some sort of coalescence appeared in the crowd. The group to which he returned was a floating knot of about thirty deputies who argued most ardently for the prevalence of the law over the king; and they were probably already discernible on the left of the president's table — which was also to the left of the empty throne behind it. If it wasn't by chance, it was because their monarchist opponents had already begun to gather on the right — as if the ghost of the absent king still somehow presided behind the president. For the right hand of the king, traditionally the place of privilege and the sacred, still carried numinous force.[1]

While some wanted a provisional vote subject to further discussion, others insisted upon an immediate question: should the king have the right of absolute veto over laws passed by the nascent assembly? Indeed, a royal veto, which would have to be decided before the prevalence of the law over the monarch could even be established, turned out to be the whole point. Voting for an absolute royal veto put one in favour of the monarchy; its denial would result in the monarchy's effective abolition — a choice that had somehow evolved without quite being intended. The rancour and intensity of the debate at the day's adjournment guaranteed that from the following morning, so a witness tells us, the assembly "separated itself for good into a left side and a right side. All the partisans of the veto would seat themselves to the right of the president; all those opposed to the veto would form an opposition. This separation made it easier to count votes by the system of sitting or standing, which had been conserved."[2]

Firsthand accounts also tell us that on that following morning, Saturday, August 29, 1789, during the ensuing debates over the veto and then over a bicameral legislature, the room was filled with "cries of opposition," and that in the midst of the tumult there suddenly arose a spirit of party rancour, "injury, suspicion, and from the people's tribune a voice directed to the president's right, *toward the seats of the nobility*, pronounce[d] the words, 'bad citizens.'"[3]

King Louis XVI, in arranging a convocation of the Estates General the previous May, had meant only to discuss the terrible state of the nation's finances. The First Estate comprised the delegates of the clergy; the second, the delegates of the nobility. The members of the Commons, or Third Estate, had been in the minority despite representing nine-tenths of the nation. Even after the court reluctantly consented to double their number to 600 members, they made up only half the entire delegation. But they no longer saw themselves as an estate. They now saw themselves as the root and substance of a nation.

There is some irony in the fact that this sense of popular unity was a result of the seventeenth-century royal absolutism of Louis XIV, whose bureaucratization and standardization of many aspects of life and law had begun to pull France out of feudal chaos. As a consequence, by the eighteenth century the French had begun, more than any other people, to resemble one another. Conventions and attitudes appeared to embrace everyone from the top down, stopping only at the lowest classes, where feudal habits were still reinforced by ignorance and poverty. The result was the growth of a class mobility whereby aristocrats fell into the middle class and members of the bourgeoisie rose into the aristocracy, picking up each other's habits as they passed. Indeed, as Alexis de Tocqueville observed, "both had been educated on literary and philosophic lines, for Paris, now almost the sole fountainhead of knowledge for the whole of France, had cast the minds of all in the same mould and given them the same equipment . . . Basically all who ranked above the common herd were of a muchness; they had the same ideas, the same habits, the same tastes, the same kinds of amusements; read the same books and spoke in the same way. They differed only in their rights."[4]

The intellectual vehicle of this great homogenization was the grassroots political body of the Third Estate, the local philosophical society, a putative microcosm of the nation: "a form of social life based on the principle that its members, in order to participate in it, must divest themselves of all concrete distinctions and of their real social existence."[5] This indeed was an idealized equality — perhaps more spiritual and cultural than economic — and a fool's paradise in which the polarizing chasm that lay ahead was scarcely imaginable.

After our own century of total ideological warfare, it is perhaps hard to see that the effort to reduce differences, which has repeatedly asserted itself in Communism, in the global market, and even between the genders, has preoccupied the greater part of human history. Even though monumental social opposites such as Left and Right are still deemed eternal, they are relatively recent. One thing the French Revolution was trying to do in its fight for equality was to reassert a sense of unity, a quest which is in fact as old as history.

For millennia, it seems, the earliest peoples were without the rigid oppositions and taboos that we associate with the primitive. Even in the acts of sex and childbearing they were prosaically practical; in hunting and gathering there was little specialization between the genders. Their mythologies were likewise fluid, practical, and unthreatening.[6] There seems indeed to have been little identification apart from that most practical for survival — identification with the group. And what was then the primal human duality, that of male and female, hardly carried the starkness, say, of night and day, cold and heat. In fact, the female herself was a force of unity.

Even before the last ice age, each paleolithic hunting group carried a carved stone woman as a sustaining symbol of universality. Around 20,000 BCE there had appeared among the Cro-Magnon, wrought in stone from some diffuse, remembered idea, not the symbol of woman as a separate gender, but rather woman as idea, as communal *force*. The tiny sculptures, round with fertility, were endowed with the inexplicable power to reproduce life and perpetuate the tribe with a sureness as haunting as lightning or an earthquake. They represented woman not as partner, wife, opponent, or any other kind of obverse reflection or dual counterpart, but as the amulet of the tribe. Above all, they seem to have implied the awareness of some kind of *collective dependence* on womanhood neither envied by one sex nor brandished by the other.

In later neolithic times, tribes of northern Asian hunters, still paleolithic, had begun to descend southward into Mesopotamia. In the riverine region of the Tigris and the Euphrates, an agricultural world had gradually developed as planting cultures from North Africa migrated northward. There, in the Fertile Crescent, around 10,000 BCE, there seems indeed to have been an intersection between the hunters, self-sufficient members of an individualistic, paleolithic, northern hunting world, and the planters, representatives of a more complex collective society from the south.

The self-sufficient individualism of the hunters and the specializing collectivism of the farmers anticipate very roughly the principles underlying modern Right and Left respectively wherever they are most deeply held. The first aristocracies seem to have developed when hunter-herders invaded, enslaved, and then protected planters.[7] But these peoples were innocent of ideology, and war tended to be a solvent rather than a force of cultural absolutism. So it was that when this Mesopotamian planting culture had its own diffusion around 7000

BCE, it slowly absorbed the sea of hunters and herders that boiled on its frontiers. By 5000 BCE, the symbolic little stone woman of the Asian steppe region had been accepted to reinforce the planters' view of woman as principle of life.[8] There was as yet only a vague idea of male and female as opposed concepts, and the unity of the world, though challenged by contrasting modes of survival, remained intact. Opposites were not yet informed by ideas of good and evil.

But Left and Right, as we will see, are the children of Good and Evil. And scales of judgement for concepts such as good and evil and political Left and Right tend to be linear. But the straight line — the figure by which Left and Right are measured or separated — is a more recent mental construct — more recent at least than the circle, which encloses or describes a cyclical process. Already in Mesopotamia, in about 4000 BCE, highly structured designs and patterns[9] appear to be inspired by the invisible cycles of vegetal nature and the extension and organization of agricultural space outward from the village. Their tendency is to encompass rather than to divide, and local gods take no part in any disruptive duality — but are merely descriptive life symbols like the nurturing Mother or the nurturing Bull. They are almost literally "down to earth," as is the corn God, Adonis, for whose worship, "hunger felt or feared was the mainspring."[10] And they are practical: even the worship of the mother-goddess is only provisional, for a local god could be male if necessary, "the qualifying form itself being merely the mask of an ultimately unqualified principle, beyond, yet inhabiting all names and forms."[11]

The cyclical principle is not related to eternal or ideological reward, but to present life. Life knows no opposition because it sustains itself by passing generations in spite of death. Without opposition, the sense of justice is descriptive and not prescriptive: ordained by the overwhelming cycle of night and day, rain and sun, flood and fire, suffering and pleasure, the waxing and waning of the moon, and the menstrual cycle. "Death and life appear as transformations of a single, superordinated indestructible force."[12]

In the planter's world of the ancient Near East, even if there is a garden there is still no perfection, and hence no hell or paradise, no eternal duality. For neolithic peoples, what came to be considered evil was not a question of morality: it was a fluid state pervading everything.

"Hell" was likewise a passing condition, a temporary discomfort perhaps, rather like winter or melancholy. It was not eternal damnation but a place of passage — even for the gods; for "under the names of Osiris, Tammuz, Adonis, and Attis, the peoples of Egypt and Western Asia represented the yearly decay and revival of life which they personified as a god who annually died and rose again from the dead."[13]

Scales of judgement begin with morality, and morality begins with a peculiar idea of guilt. Neolithic civilization came to suspect that every time it ate, it killed; that the entire process of survival was a process of murder, a destruction of the living stuff of eaten roots or trodden grass. The inevitable tragedy would be lessened if we could at least demonstrate some consciousness of it and some readiness to make public reparation before the gods, by offering sacrifice.[14] Unconsciously, the disagreement between individual and collective, between modern Right and Left, is a disagreement about the extent and nature of the sacrifice; about reparation for the symbiosis between murder and survival. And in their disagreement is the wound of rational civilization. In theory, there is no overcoming, no mending. And yet, "neolithic" tropical peoples who have survived in the shadow of civilization still do all they can to overcome the abyss of guilt and discord in the image of an ideal, or mythological, age that "is supposed to have anteceded the precipitation of this pair-of-opposites, when there was neither birth nor death but a dream-like state of essentially timeless being."[15] This sort of idea was preserved in myth, ritual, and art; without such witnesses to some pre-existing conciliatory state, duality appeared fatal to civilized humanity.

In civilization, opposed ideologies have much to support their contest. They can claim it is existential. From the primordial "this and not that" and then both "this and that" it is a short move to "I and thou," and then to "your village and my village," "this people and that people"; and finally, "you and I both are red people, and they are not."

Even myth itself betrays ingrained dualities of language: for myth "is a form of language and language itself predisposes us to attempt to understand ourselves and our world by superimposing dialectics, dichotomies or dualistic grids on data that may in fact be entirely integrated. And underneath language lies the binary nature of the brain, right and left, good and evil, life and death — these are inevitable dichotomies produced by the brain that has two lobes and controls two eyes, two hands."[16] But after studying myriad intersecting and mutually qualifying dualities in tropical, neolithic peoples — among them concentric dualities and linear dualities — anthropologist Claude Lévi-Strauss could only conclude that "the study of so-called dual organization discloses so many anomalies and contradictions in relation to extant (dualistic) theory, that we should be well advised to reject the theory and treat the apparent manifestations of dualism as different and vastly more complex."[17] Primitive peoples knew this before anthropologists did, and while "many cultures have been and are aware of dualism as a cognitive fact," they "see it as a problem to be transcended through various techniques and practices. Such doctrines are to be found not only in the sophisticated philosophies of the East or in the esoteric traditions of European mysticism and magic but also in small-scale non-literate society."[18]

When the tendency to separate and oppose was seen to be fraught with danger, myth intruded to make duality compensatory and cyclical. Even after such polarities had become socialized and the resulting conflicts between people became irresolvable, there were still no eternal principles to be exalted or condemned. Tribal wars and personal animosities lacked the sort of opposition that can be sustained indefinitely by philosophical or conceptual differences.

This is primordial anarchism, and anarchism, ideally, is neither Right nor Left; it is self-regulation. Left and Right are less interested in self-regulation than in regulation of the other, whom each perceives as eternally malign, omnivorous.

But the anarchist knows that in neolithic conflict there is only blood and never extermination: that in that primal balance, when the planter had only just risen to pre-eminence, absorbing the best ways of the invading hunters, and "the discipline of the hunting band decayed, the political institutions of the earliest village settlements perhaps approximated the anarchism which has remained ever since the ideal of peaceful peasantries all round the earth."[19] It is in defence of this very ideal that Jung warns us that it is "the dammed-up instinctual forces in civilized man [that] are immensely destructive and far more dangerous than the instincts of the primitive, who in a modest degree is constantly living out his negative instinct."[20] Perhaps the largest reservoirs in which such forces are locked up are the political ideologies themselves.

Although the Garden of Eden is our most famous fiction, agricultural life may in fact have brought to humanity, however briefly, an inclination toward a stable combination of freedom and collectivity. But only as long as this collectivity was practical — and not polemical — would it work in the spirit of interplay and exchange that is the natural equanimity of the vegetal world. The first step toward the end of this balance may well have been the appearance of the state; for the state mistrusts its own as well as the Other; and it will come to seek security not in balance but in absolutes.

In ancient Sumer the state materialized with the need to organize masses for the work of irrigation and harvest, and to defend it all through the union of tribes and villages. And since undertakings such as war, harvest, and irrigation are too vital to leave to squabbling, uncooperative hands, the monarchy was born. And rule by a single person will project its own reflection both in monotheism and philosophy with a single idea: "the word." The Sumerian monarch's far-reaching verbal command was the first expression of "the word" before it was represented as "the *logos*" in Greece and in Christianity. At once injunction and principle of unity, the "word" was also the intellectual principle upon which a god ordered all of being.[21] *Logos*, however, was doomed to deteriorate from being a guide for a way of life to being a search for assurance in absolutes.

The maintenance of order was sustained by the lessons of excess — learned from the suicidal effects of self-indulgence. This required humanity to exist for something outside itself: in the service of the gods and heavens.[22] The city and the populace had to reflect that celestial order. How else were we to avoid eating ourselves to death, spending our reserves, or destroying our own, once the agricultural surplus that was the root of civilization gave us the power to do so? The implied opposite of this new world of heavenly and human architecture is chaos; and a new duality of order and chaos soon began to dominate the ancient world. This was no longer the cyclical, interdependent world of nature, of life and death.

Modern ideologies promote competing philosophies; in Sumer the universal duality of order and chaos applied itself to daily life. The

Sumerian gods were perhaps the first gods who were morally and ethically exemplary.[23] At first laws are their utterances and habits. It is when they are codified that they break radically from mythological personification into limitless abstraction. In Sumer, order was *rita* and disorder was *anrita* in the cosmos and in social life — and now also in law. Custom, instinct, and the laws of the dream world were no longer sufficient, for there was no longer trust in any *internal* natural order. Law by its nature suspects either the self or the other of transgression; and so it becomes absolute, untrusting. And the legal instinct is the foundation of ideology — although ideology will one day place itself above the concept of law.

Order and chaos continued to represent the moral and ideological poles of most of the ancient riverine civilizations; civilizations ruled by priesthoods, for in the face of disaster there remained, for the whole society, the promise of recovery. But the riverine utopia was not otherworldly. It lay in the restoration of a past order[24] that tended to preserve rather than abolish the natural dualities.

As Sumer and Egypt entered their decline, the seeds of moral ideology were sewn anew and in a new fashion — westward — on the shores of the Aegean. Northern invaders, only recently emerged from the paleolithic world, once again bring an individualistic ethic — but one that now verges on anarchy. The Indo-Europeans, a Eurasian people, spread south-westward into the Balkans about 1900 BCE and then southward into Greece about 1300 BCE, destroying the vegetal mother-gods and the playful animal worship of the Aegean civilizations of Minos and Mycenae. And around 1150 BCE, as order began to reassert itself in this land already chopped into a patchwork of mountain ranges, poor pasture, and inhospitable winter, a succeeding invasion threw old and new waves of settlers alike into a time of dark chaos that would last two hundred and fifty years until around 900 BCE. This was not a setting conducive to the easy distinction between order and disorder enjoyed by the agrarian mass societies of the old riverine civilizations.

In this bleak world of rock and high barren ground, it seems that humans loomed larger than anything they could coax from the soil. And so a mythology sprang up, neither from earth nor from heaven but from the struggle of settlers in isolation: from civil strife, rape, fratricide, matricide, parricide, and starvation. A mythology not of monsters

of nature but of Heroes: outsized men. This world of the deeds of warriors became the world portrayed by Homer. If the Homeric world
provided little cosmic reassurance, it found models in human rather
than in natural forces. Humanity was spectator of a tragi-comedy of
Olympian quarrels not wholly different from the vendettas he had lived
in the mountain pastures. So it was, in the words of Hannah Arendt, that
"impartiality and with it, all true historiography came into the world
when Homer decided to sing the deeds of the Trojans no less than those
of the Achaeans and to praise the glory of Hector no less than the greatness of Achilles."[25]

Impartiality is almost inconceivable in modern times. The ability
to watch, indeed to judge, the most remote political struggle without
taking sides is alien to ideological thought. An objective sense of tragedy,
or a feeling of joy in acceptance is replaced by a drive for correctness
and perfection. And it remains a paradox that the impartiality of the
tragic sense was inspired not by nature but by strife among men. Here
there is no ineluctable vegetal or heavenly cycle, not even the cataclysm
of flood. The anarchic humanity of the improvident mountain valleys
and squeezed coastal plains takes centre stage, and with it battles of
will, sulking, pride, lust, and courage, leaving us not with any stable
duality, but with the peculiar stability of no duality at all.

The motif remains struggle, and the story of the Olympian pantheon
is still the furious, broken family, a world once again without favourites
or fixed oppositions, a place where woman is as treacherous as man;
where incipient alliance is sundered by incest, treachery, and adultery;
where heaven and earth do not even remain distinct principles since
Gods and men continually trespass.[26] A world where, ultimately —
and in contradistinction to the riverine civilizations — there is no clear
boundary between chaos and order. Again, from the stance of our own
times, we can't help but remark that in the ancient world, there are
never only two, mutually exclusive choices. There are many, and they
exist alongside of one another. This pluralism is called polytheism, and
its narratives, unlike the edicts of law, are kinetic, dramatic. It is precisely what Max Weber and the critics of modernity call the "enchanted"
world, a place alive with tensions, irreconcilable yet coexisting values,
and mystery.[27]

The first Greek thinkers developed as much in reaction to this tradition as in sympathy with it. It is not surprising that their ideas seemed to suggest a more harmonious worldview akin to that of Middle Eastern civilizations or that they lived a more stable life on the Ionic coastline of Asia Minor. These Greeks were perhaps the first people to understand opposites conceptually: that is, without reference to the human, natural, or divine models like those of Homer and Hesiod. But still, they did not place them in permanent apposition. In Asia Minor, at the port of Miletus, a thinker called Thales dispensed with narrative entirely. He discovered opposed concepts in the One and the Many and not with a single underlying substance uniting both — water, admittedly a natural substance — but the beginning of conceptual thinking. However primitive, this was the first of a series of philosophers to whom permanent opposition or the triumph of any single principle remained inconceivable. Chaos was not perdition. Indeed, there was no chaos. Here, surely, was a reaction against the Olympian interpretation of existence.

Anaximander, a pupil of Thales, immediately attracted by the direct apprehension of his teacher, developed it further. To him, plurality — the many — is nevertheless stubborn: the separate things keep emerging out of this flat sea of existence. And so, "It is neither water nor any of the other so-called elements," he says, "but some different, boundless nature from which all the heavens arise, and the earth with them." And it must include motion, force. And so he calls it the *boundless*, or *apeiron*. It is formless and it is suffused both with matter and mind and energy and with oblivion and existence. Above all, it contains all known opposites and a scheme for their interaction: "Out of those things whence is the generation for existing things, into these again does their destruction take place, according to what must needs be; for they make amends and give reparation to one another for their offense, according to the ordinance of time."[28]

Here suddenly is a law of transformation. Like the command of a Sumerian king, it is a system, *the word*: to the Greeks the immortal *logos*, though it is not yet so named. Anaximander uses the term *adikia*, justice, but he means a mysterious justice that functions in constant interplay with injustice, which is the overstepping of bounds. Intense heat is set to rights by cold; heavy rains are corrected by drought. No single principle is to prevail beyond *adikia* itself. However darkly suspended in its contradiction, it was this insistence on plurality within unity that made

Anaximander and Thales apostles of the *single principle*, whether it be water or *apeiron*; in other words, they were Monists. The essence of the *apeiron* was its defiance of reductive opposition.[29]

■

At Versailles in May of 1789, in the *Salle des Menus Plaisirs*, the fatal division of August 28 was still three months away. But even on that May morning, only the diffuse light that shone from the great oval sky-light might have recalled some sense of impartiality in the cosmos, or primordial unity down below.

The throne still commanded the hall from its raised dais at one end, and the clergy and the nobility sat respectively on the right and left hands of the king — facing one another from benches lining opposite sides of the hall. After Louis arrived with arrogant tardiness, the queen was given a seat a few steps below him to his left. (And here we must remark that the right hand remained primordially the side of the sacred, and the left the side both of the profane and feminine — of the Queen and the historically troublesome nobility.) The Third Estate, or Commons, which would soon be split by that very scheme, was not even included. A third wheel and too numerous at 600, they had to be content to sit in bleachers laterally placed across the rear of the hall. What was more, the table of the president supervising the session was in the centre of the floor, at the confused intersection of all three estates, and so he always had his back to half of the assembly whenever he spoke.

The rest is the genesis of a new, putatively homogenous, democratic body from the ancient tripartite relic, and of the subsequent split of that new body. Over the following days, the Third Estate had to be content with the *Salle* for their private meetings, while the other two estates were given their own halls. Without ado, it summarily rejected the estates system and called for a single assembly of all deputies. From their own halls, sympathetic nobles and clergy heeded the call and began to trickle over to the Commons in the *Salle des Menus Plaisirs*.

On June 20, the king retaliated by locking the Third Estate out of the *Salle des Menus Plaisirs*. Its members proceeded to occupy a local indoor tennis court, took a collective oath naming themselves the National Assembly, and swore to remain active and united until the nation had a constitution. That ought to have been the first and last "Left." But it wasn't. On June 23, at the *séance royale*, the king adamantly reasserted the ancient divisions of estates, and a plan of financial reform was watered down to favour the aristocracy.[30] After the session the first two estates filed out, but the Third Estate, the Commons, refused to leave. Over the next few days, the Commons, effectively occupying the *Salle des Menus Plaisirs* as a single assembly in the name of the nation, was joined by yet more of the clergy. No sooner had the guards begun to intervene than many of them were called off by yet more liberal nobles who had arrived in solidarity, while other guardsmen began to fraternize with the growing National Assembly. Soon, all but the most resistant of the nobles and clergy filled the hall. The institutional essence of the revolution was complete. Unity had triumphed.

The Commons' humiliation had been their salvation; expeditiously shunted into an empty throne room, they had occupied it and drawn the nation in their wake. On June 27, Louis XVI reluctantly conceded this massive and spontaneous sea change as a *fait accompli*. He accepted the new assembly and formally ordered the three estates to unite. On June 30, the Estates moved as a single body into the *Salle des Menus Plaisirs*. The surly compliance of the more reluctant members of the nobility and clergy would turn out to be the genesis of the modern "Right." Now, even when the throne sat empty under its towering canopy, its ghostly presence would prove divisive.

But for the time being the order of the day remained national unity in revolution. The fall of the prison of the Bastille ensued a few days later, but the attack was symbolic, directed against tyranny itself rather than against any person or institution. Three days later, the king was persuaded to go to Paris to reassure the French of his loyalty to the revolution itself. And unity held. Throughout this time the new assembly continued to meet at Versailles in the *Salle des Menus Plaisirs*, and in many ways it was still as innocent as the Paris crowd that pleaded with it, threatened it, and tried to influence it. The delegates still behaved, outwardly at least, as a single interest. It was the vanguard — mostly from the streets of Paris — that beseeched the entire nation to follow — from the Royal family down to the poorest of the poor.

To understand the significance of these events from our vantage point at the beginning of the twenty-first century, we must place ourselves inside those crowds and processions and be, for the moment, as blind of the future as they were — or at least entertain the idea that things might subsequently have been otherwise. We must think in terms of the homogeneous mass in which they desired to see themselves. In the *Salle des Menus Plaisirs*, the new Constituent Assembly was a milling crowd with no policy, no rules, an ad hoc committee of over a thousand men. There was in the room no government, no opposition. The deputies moved ahead by feel. Quoting the English diarist Arthur Young, Carlyle tells us, "a hundred members are on their feet at once [with] the president, appointed once a fortnight, raising many times no serene head above the waves."[31]

So persisted the anarchy left behind by the old flat floor of the Estates General. Robespierre, in a mood of idealistic reassurance, seemed to see in this free and healthy chaos a flux of opinion unhindered by the shackles of party or bloc, and stated: "There is no permanent majority because it does not belong to any party, it reforms every time there is a free debate."[32] Here was the brief and tragic glimmer of an ideal. Of course circumstances would bully the crowd of deputies into factions. No sooner had the crisis of the Bastille been put to rest than in October the women of Paris marched on Versailles demanding bread. The lower classes erupted, and violence followed. And when the crowd invited Louis back to Paris, to be under their protection and scrutiny despite their murder of a few of his palace guards, he acceded.

The fact was that this spiritual homogenization and levelling, the conceptual simplification that French society was undergoing in the wake of feudalism, had begun to form a *tabula rasa* for new structures — of class as well as ideology. And such theoretical atomization in society, as in geometry, inclines toward the simplest of divisions — the eternal temptation to divide in two. But before such a split was even anticipated, the new groupings that formed and dissolved in the *Salle des Menus Plaisirs* contained members from all three Estates, and the ideological landscape to most observers was chaos. At some point, however, the Marquis de Ferrières observed a divergence between those who thought the revolution had already gone far enough from those, led by the king's radical cousin the Duc d'Orléans, who felt it had only begun: respectively "Constitutionals" and "Orleanists." "The two factions hated each other and savaged one another equally. The Constitutionals treated the Orleanists as factionalist enemies of the monarchy, and the Orleanists said that the Constitutionals had sold themselves to the government and the aristocracy."[33] And then, five days before the fatal twenty-eighth of August, Duquesnoy, a noble deputy, noted in his journal: "One part of the assembly has been determined only by the fact that they put their case for religious tolerance with intolerance." The room divided in such a way that in the same area "are men with extreme opinions but who nevertheless hold a very elevated view of liberty and equality, who feel that they're inseparable and you can't have a nation where one class rules the other . . . The other part is occupied by those who have less elevated ideas and are less clear in their opinions, which gives them an impression of weakness and pusillanimity."[34] The latter, it seems, were the inchoate, still timid, Right.

On the day of the twenty-eighth, the split that was about to occur was already latent in the issue of procedure. In an attempt to clarify the adoption of Article One about the precedence of Law over the king, the Comte de Mirabeau proposed that amendments be passed by roll call and not by sitting or standing. Another deputy countered that speakers be divided into lists of negative and affirmative on each topic, to which Mirabeau promptly responded that this procedure would lead to the division of the very body intended to make the Constitution, thus destroying the spirit of *fraternité*. He was, of course, absolutely right, and no sooner had he spoken than the noble Deprémenil attempted to involve all of France in an affirmative and negative by proposing that each deputy simply report the consensus of his constituency — and Mirabeau quickly quashed him. But it was too late.

By the following day, the groupings familiar to us everywhere today had arranged themselves in the *Salle des Menus Plaisirs*. To the president's right, and up behind him in the back benches gathered the out-and-out royalists, who mostly jeered and snickered and eventually abandoned the proceedings. Below them and also on the right were the centre-right "Liberal Monarchists," comprising clergy, nobles, and conservative commoners, who supported the government and a royal veto but advocated an English-style bicameral legislature. The centre itself was clustered close around the president by timid default to the seating of the two radical wings. On the president's left were the thirty or so deputies who had gathered the day before on the left side of the room; and above them in the top benches were the deputies who comprised the radical Left, among whom sat Robespierre. But the fault line that would open into an abyss was not down the middle; it was between the Left and Mirabeau's people, throwing the centre in with the right. And so the nation that gave the world the geometrical abstraction of Descartes also gave it, in final, ineradicable form, "the spatial sanctification of immaterial ideas" in the terms Left and Right.[35]

As deputies of the diverging left and right of the revolutionary Constituent Assembly began every day to seat themselves on their respective sides of the *Salle*, it would have been hard to believe that the entire purpose of their first gathering between those very walls had been to declare their unbreakable unity.

2

Division:
The King's Right Hand, the Hunter's Left

On August 30, the day after the *Salle des Menus Plaisirs* had formally divided into Left and Right, the chasm widened further; the monarchist Right thought it might secure for itself an upper house by proposing a bicameral legislature on the English model. The Left saw this proposal as a plot by the Right to preserve aristocratic privilege and insisted that the assembly, like the people it represented, be one and indivisible. On September 10, the threat of violence from Paris urged indissoluble unity and cut short the debate. The idea of a single legislature was carried by a large majority, and it seems that haste and urgency in the face of mob disorder had caused many in the centre and perhaps a few on the Right to throw their votes in with the Left.

When the assembly prepared to vote on the veto the following day — whether to be "suspensive" to the king's detriment or "indefinite" in his favour — the pressure from Paris was present throughout the gallery surrounding the *Salle*. When the president shouted the word "indefinite" a chorus of opprobrium arose from the mob. At "suspensive" the cheer erupted and the majority, this time extending from the left side of the room, stood up to be counted. Again, most of the centre voted with the left, and one might then have asked — what was the Left? Was it the left side of the room or did it include those who had voted with it on only one or two issues? It is a question that might still be asked today, especially as ideology begins to break down into single issues and one can quite rationally be "left" on one question and "right" on another. By now, of course, the meaning has begun more than ever to sag and fray.

But in 1789 it was perhaps natural that, as the spectre of hunger and violence worsened, symbol and gesture acquired increasing importance. Not only was it crucial which side of the assembly you sat on but the location of the assembly itself assumed greater solemnity, and it was decided that king and legislature ought to be in the capital with the people both claimed to represent.

The new hall was the *Manège*, in the heart of Paris, an arena built in the gardens of the Louvre as a riding school by Louis XV. As if to symbolize the stark reality into which events would descend, the *Manège* was a rather murky reflection of the heavenly hall at Versailles — the scheme identical but inferior. The public galleries provided space for a mere 300, making it easy to commandeer by extremists. It was, literally, an arena: the oval ring designed for dressage but perfectly suited for combat. The president's desk bisected one side and the speaker's tribune the other. To the right of the president were the royalists, and to the left the patriots. And as at Versailles, the moderates of each wing sat below, closer to the floor with the radicals up behind them.[1] By then, Right and Left had begun to lay the foundations for a political topography; like folded tectonic plates, their formations would determine every hillock in the landscape of the future.

Reinforcement of what was still a dual abstraction came, significantly, from *outside* the assembly, through other institutions with strategic addresses. The old philosophical societies, athough generally favouring some sort of revolution, had been joined in the non-partisan if short-lived spirit of unity. But after they had set up at Versailles on the margins of the *Salle des Menus Plaisirs*, the societies transformed themselves into political clubs. By the time they had followed the assembly back to Paris, they distinguished themselves according to the arrangements in the *Manège*. Thenceforward, the political clubs, in their halls around the neighbourhood of the *Manège*, evolved from being spectator of the assembly to being its monitor and eventually its dictator. Something as wonderfully lucid and clear-cut as Left and Right, it seemed, could not be abandoned to the vagaries of democracy behind the walls of the *Manège*.

The dominant clubs were of the centre and left. Adjoining the *Manège* was the terrace of the *Café des Feuillants* where the "centrist" *Club des Feuillants* had its meetings. Its formal enemy was the *Club Breton*, named for the café where it had gathered at Versailles. But the *Bretons* were now the driving force behind the left side of the *Manège* and they set up across the rue St Honoré in the old monastery of "the Jacobins" and soon changed their name to the Jacobin Club.

The chapel in the Jacobin Club, it so happened, was set in an oval amphitheatre whose seating was almost identical to that of the assembly halls at Versailles and the *Manège*. And indeed, the choreography of the events there would be similarly blocked out: it had its own speaker and president, its own Left and Right, as if to invite some sort of infinite subdivision of Left and Right within the Left. With its dominant lectern, the schema was pedagogical right down to the rule-book rationalism.

The abstractions of geometry are not conducive to compromise, and it was almost a foregone conclusion that the constitution to which the king finally acquiesced would be too monarchical for the democratic left and too democratic for the monarchist right. But the tendency to align, categorize, and divide was perhaps natural. It was easier to impose paradigms on society in literature than in actual fact — and literature came more naturally to the French of 1789 than did politics. Abstraction had arisen, in the words of historian François Furet, "precisely from the very lack of political experience that characterized the individual in society, whether nobleman or bourgeois. Deprived of true liberty . . . incapable of collective experience . . . they unwittingly set their course toward a revolutionary utopia; without professional politicians, they turned toward men of letters. Literature took on the role of politics . . . France then went from a debate about how to run the country to the discussion of ultimate values, from politics to revolution."[2] Utopia and revolution were projected in abstractions, which use the language of number for their expression. The hold over us that abstraction has gradually taken is called rationalization, and rationalization is the main instrument of modernity.

Rationalization began with cultivation in the neolithic riverine civilizations. The calculation of the growing season was derived from the order of the heavens, as was the volume of food stores and their duration in days and months. Geometry arose in ancient Egypt, where it was needed to work out the area of fields under cultivation and the volume of harvest. The engineering of irrigation and the distribution of work forces gave birth to arithmetic. And if there was still no overriding duality, the conditions for division into two had already been laid in the field of number. The catalyst for actual division had already descended with the nomads from the north some time after 10,000 BCE.

Duality as mutual exclusivity — as opposed to complementarity — was a paleolithic reality. In Central Asia after the last ice age, nomadic hunters occupied the forest lands and the open steppe. The climate was slow to warm, and the old paleolithic hunt persisted; there were still few if any visual, geometrical models and the only dualities were cold and heat, night and day, and, most elemental of all, death and life. Since the southern planters saw death as part of life in the eternal vegetal cycle, they bridged duality and smoothed the way to renewal with transitional objects. The hunter, however, saw the animal carcass rot away to nothing and produce nothing. Death was absolute, and fear was compounded by the fact that the decaying body could be a source of disease. And so the corpse came to symbolize the opposite to life — everything that was bad. What it represented was not new vegetal life in the soil of this world but rather passage out of this world.

Death was darker to the hunter, and the most universal contrast — that between life and death — would come to be preserved in the abrupt, asymmetrical, mutual exclusivity of the sacred and the profane — a distinction universal among pre-literate peoples.[3] The profane was an active negative concept permanently opposed to life.[4] Herein lay the genesis of Evil as an aggressive force, equal and opposite to Good. It was not long before all that was bright, lucky, clean, and prosperous fell under the rubric of the sacred, and all that was dark, hostile, dangerous, and unclean was aligned with the profane. The hunter's ambivalent suspension between the light and the dark made objects that were sacred and profane equally untouchable — the sacred for fear of defiling them, the profane for fear of contagion. Paleolithic perceptions, even as they continued in the hunter-herder, would bring a permanent split to civilization.

The crucial aspect of sacred and profane was their socialization. There followed from life and death, sacred and profane, the simplification of natural differences and disparities in people within tribes — in endowment, ability, and gender — into sacred upper and profane lower castes, so that "from this religious polarity [arose] a reflection in the form of social polarity."[5] Whole social groups would come to be so distinguished that "two phratries or parts of a whole tribe [would] oppose reciprocally as sacred and profane"[6] — the profane for women, enemies, sacrificial victims, and grave-diggers. While neolithic planters maintained a unified world through the vegetal cycle, their lagging contemporaries, the paleolithic hunters, held on to a unified cosmos in their own way. The hunter regarded his game not as an enemy but rather as an aspect of himself — a quarry with whose prowess he identified, whose qualities he tried magically to assume. Whether through the transitional object of the planter[7] or through the hunter's identity with his prey, hunter and planter both held together a world that was about to fly apart. And, although both had their mechanisms of wholeness, both would also play a role in dividing the world irreparably.

With cultivation came domestication and, for the hunter-herder, the consequent separation of animal from man through a new opposition between "wild" and "tame" that sharpened the distinction between "self" and "other." And with agriculture the analogous distinction arose between domestic "edible" and wild "inedible." In sum, "domestication was a profound redirection of human reason, from the subtle to the coarse . . . from polymorphous and kaleidoscopic thinking to binary, mechanical, ideological."[8] As the sacred and profane of the hunter were transferred to the neolithic world of the south, the *transitional objects* of the older, planter's civilization began to disappear until "all that is uncertain or ambivalent [was] aligned with that which [was] outright evil."[9]

Even though they reflected different worldviews, however, the individualism of the hunter and the collectivism of the planter were not conceptually opposed. It is true that the modern Right derives a sort of pedigree from the primordial individualism of the self-sufficient hunter; and the Left (especially in Russia and the East) is seen to reflect ancient agrarian collectivism. But these current political distinctions do not really correspond to their supposed ideological ancestors. The versatility and self-sufficiency of the individual hunter — far from anticipating the hierarchies of the modern individualistic Right — brought into the barbarian Bronze Age a primitive egalitarianism, that is, equal versatility.[10] Conversely, the agrarian city state's collectivism had little of the equality claimed in principle by modern collectivism; on the contrary, its dependence on the specialization of tasks bred hierarchy. By contrast, the equality of rights (as opposed to wealth) that we associate with democracy — both primitive and modern — tends to be rooted in the hunter's north rather than in the planter's south. It might even be argued that the rigid hierarchies that have qualified nominally egalitarian modern regimes are a precondition of collectivist egalitarianism, ancient and modern. Historically, the collectivist Left and the individualistic Right each has its own mixture of egalitarian and hierarchical tendencies.

Nor are private property and collective ownership — Right and Left — neatly aligned with individual and collective cultures. Primitive collective ownership was more natural to the individualist hunter in situations where communal property suited a nomadic existence and protected the group from the harsh conditions of the steppe. It was in agrarian society during periods of prosperity that individual enterprise took hold. Private title to land arose when it was discovered that a plot of soil was more productive when worked by the family unit. Private property increased when agrarian overpopulation drove settlers to clear land and claim it as the product of their labour. The paradox that individualism is in some ways more conducive to egalitarianism, and a collective society more grounded in hierarchy, must account for many of the anomalies that endure in modern Left and Right.

How, then, did we get the talent for simplistic division into two? Dual division appears initially to have been strongest among the paleolithic hunters of continental Asia. On the steppeland margins of the more fertile farming areas of Central Asia, pastoralism developed with the discovery that some animals could be trapped at waterways and husbanded rather than hunted.[11] The vast grasslands of the inner plain were devoid of natural defences, and their hunting and herding populations were subject to migrations and violent displacements from east to west. Tribe faced tribe in open competition for unmarked territory — which already evoked the primal awe of open space, the absence of limits. Here Sacred and Profane served to bound and contain something as terrifying as it was primordial — the concept of the void. As the historian of religion Mircea Eliade tells us: "It is because of man's vertical posture that space is organized in a structure inaccessible to the prehominians: in four horizontal directions, radiating from an 'up-down' central axis. In other words, space can be organized around the human body as extending forward, backward, to right, to left, upward and downward. It is . . . this original and originating experience — feeling oneself 'thrown' into the middle of an apparently limitless, unknown and threatening extension . . . [t]his experience of space oriented around a 'centre' . . . [that] explains the importance of paradigmatic divisions and their distributions of territories, agglomerations and habitations and their cosmological symbolism."[13]

The frightening cosmos of the steppe was at least marked by the sun — welcomed upon its arrival, leaving apprehension in its wake. The principle of heliotropism fills out our understanding of the early sense of the Sacred and the Profane. The biological influence of the sun's "tonic energy" causes inclination of the body toward the sun, from dark toward light, from cold to heat.[13] From here it would have developed that "the slight physiological advantages possessed by the right hand are merely the occasion of a qualitative differentiation the cause of which lies beyond the individual, in the constitution of the collective consciousness. An almost insignificant bodily asymmetry is enough to turn in one direction or the other."[14] The fear and relief associated with the cycle of the sun's setting and rising would gradually orient consciousness into an alignment with the left and right hands.[15]

The fact that in the north the sun follows a flatter cycle closer to the horizon than it does in its more tilted orbit to the south may have led to the hunter's vision of the cosmos as a four-part circle.[16] It appears that to face the East in reverence at sunrise is primordial and universal. From that stance, with the sun rising into noon, heat is associated with the right hand, and the cold and darkness of the north with the left hand. This is the primal religious orientation that established the right and left hands as sacred and profane. With the right hand now sacred, the sun's eastern rising must happen on the right also, its western setting or "death" on the left hand. Thus east, south, light, life, and all that is sacred are associated with the right; and north, west, death, darkness, and the profane are symbolized by the left.

It is not surprising that the hands reinforce their status and that "in tribal ceremonials . . . one finds groupings on the right and on the left."[17] In the end, "the axis which divides the world into two halves, the one radiant, the other dark, also cuts through the human body and divides it between the empire of light and that of darkness. Right and left transcend the limits of our body to embrace the universe."[18] Language too will develop "left" terms that are unstable, or euphemistic, ambivalent, recessive;[19] and "right" terms which are tidier, true, sacred, and consistent. This rationalization will calcify into "binary thinking which will replace the *transitional object* with paradox and dialectic."[20] It is interesting to notice how this primitive contingency continues to express itself in modern distinctions of respectable and disreputable, authoritarian and egalitarian, straight and hip.

In the herding life of the steppeland, sacred and profane played as much into scorching summer and frigid winter as into violent tribal division, and so "the steppe nomads of inner Asia created their own spiritual world . . . a rich dualistic mythology based on heavenly gods of light and the evil gods of the underworld."[21] In the Lake Baikal region of Siberia, there survive petroglyphs that decorate sanctuaries for spring fertility rites "to assure the victory of the universal forces of light over darkness, the conquest of winter by summer, the victory of life over death."[22] This was not the vegetal world of assured cyclical passage. Sacred and profane represented spiritual warfare: effectively, an invisible anti-world that controlled the visible world of daily struggle. The tribe required a guide to this invisible world, an individual possessed of the requisite powers and even some of the oddness of the profane itself. Such a guide, who seems to have originated in northern Asia, was the *shaman* — from the Tunguso-Manchurian word *saman*, "he who knows."[23]

Unlike the priest of the later city state, the shaman belonged to no caste and guarded no tradition; his power was personal and came from ecstatic visions, spontaneous or induced. With the visible world interpreted as the middle world, the shaman navigated two distinct realms: a lower "Left" world of evil and an upper "Right" world of good. This invisible world was not far from the conceptual world of philosophical abstraction; and the haunted steppe of Asia passed on something southward that emerged in the thought of pre-Socratic Greece. What has been said of Greek thought had long been true of the Asian shaman: "that behind the changing phenomena presented by the universe to our senses there lies a reality which is unchanging, and that the pursuit of true knowledge consists in seeking out this reality is the basic axiom of metaphysics."[24] So the origin of the axiom, the concept of an unquestioned founding premise, seems to lie with the seminal shamanic vision.[25]

Now it is tempting to discern in the ecstatic paleolithic shaman and in the rational priest of the city state additional precursors, respectively, of Right and Left. Thought of in this way, Right can be identified as the inspired, emotional shamanic "tender-minded" type; and Left as the rational "hard-headed" type.[26] If we use this psychological distinction, coined by William James, the former is inclined to deal with injustices by interpreting them; the latter by resolving them. This genealogy has with some success traced soft-hearted shamanic mysticism to the modern romantic far-Right and rationalistic priestly hard-headedness to the authoritarian Left; and in this sense the shaman and the priest — with qualifications — will provide useful ancestors. But here we must keep an asymmetry in mind. Dual thinking was initiated by the northern shaman and only later abetted by the priest. It follows that dualism itself, whether of sacred and profane or right and left, tends more to be inspired than rational. By this we mean axiomatic, that is to say, in purely rational terms, arbitrary.

Who, then, were these hunter-herders who brought this "wild and irrational" dualism of the shaman to the Mediterranean? Archaeology gives a clue with the discovery in Central Asia of human remains which it calls "Europoid."[27] If they were "Europoid" they were at best a hybrid, for they seem to have drawn on everyone: from Turko-Mongolian to Caucasoid to Middle Eastern.[28] What unites them is linguistic and cultural, and in reference to the wide dispersal of their language they have come to be known as the Indo-Europeans.

Although historians do not agree on their homeland or precisely who they were, since their origin is as obscure as their assimilation, the

41

Indo-Europeans' influence on Western culture down to the modern day has arguably surpassed that of any other culture.[29] The Indo-European homeland is more or less agreed to have been in the steppelands of eastern Europe and western Russia, where archaeology seems finally to disclose all the characteristics of a proto–Indo-European culture of about 4000 BCE. In response to the instability of the open steppe, their ethic was "warlike because the herder's wealth is movable wealth, an open invitation to enemy raiders."[30] Moreover, their deep, indeed pale-olithic, consciousness of the profane encouraged the proclamation of a missionary war against evil. Their culture and their moral ethic of sacred and profane were disseminated through their vast invasions: they brought the world the highest development of bronze metallurgy, the domesticated horse, the battle-axe, the wheel, and the chariot. That they were patriarchal is shown by the ranking in their graves and by family structure.

The spread of Indo-European culture seems to have been accompa-nied by an increase in the influence of shamanism.[31] In turn, patriarchal, shamanic tradition was characterized by an increasingly abstract polar-ization of opposites, especially in social class and in religion.[32] In contradistinction to the old, matriarchal world, the Indo-Europeans practised the subordination of women and the allocation to the sexes of specialized tasks. The destruction by Indo-Europeans of the more integrated matriarchal culture in eastern Europe around 1500 BCE seems indeed to attest to the sudden arrival of the new ethic.[33] The new, Indo-European class system was tripartite, likely following the shaman's tripartite division of the cosmos into an upper, a present, and a lower world.[34] But the ruling warrior and priestly classes, supported by a pro-ducing class of farmer-stock-breeders, also divided, on a less symbolic level, into a duality of rulers and workers.

The Indo-European pantheon as well was distinctly dualistic, and it is here especially that abstraction enters the field. The new gods of the north were not patrons of villages or rivers; they were expressed as abstract qualities such as "courage," "war," "honesty," and "generosity." These "psychotheistic" qualities fell easily into a binary pattern: the sun and moon gods, Mithra and Varuna, having opposing qualities of male and female, day and night, dry and moist, hot and cold, and so on. In addition, the beacon of morality was upheld in daily habit where dirt, tarnish, or decay was profane; cleanliness was sacred, and rites involved purification.

In the open danger of the steppe, such a schematic duality was ready to receive all kinds of other oppositions. The difficulties of allocating tribal pasture in the open unmarked plain encouraged the forging of treaties to curb incursions and rustling.[35] The treaty, itself an abstraction and a corollary of dual division, had its own guardian, the sun-god Mithra.[36] And so there arose a distinction between those who upheld order in treaty or contract and the marauders who defied it, and thus herdsman and bandit become prototypes of Good and of Evil respectively.[37] For here there began also to appear the sanctions of Heaven and Hell — from the upper and lower worlds of the shaman.

In its developed form, this division into upper and lower worlds becomes the Asian, Vedic religion. The paleolithic figure of the line of division, the vector, now begins to supersede the neolithic circle. The boundary is indeed the most vivid expression of Vedic dualism: a single sacred furrow ploughed in open steppe to mark the temporary altar of the nomad. Outside this line, all is dangerous and profane; within, all is sacred.[38] And if anything could marshal chaotic reality into an abstract alignment of sacred and profane, it was not so much religion itself as the rationalizing force of language.[39]

The early Indo-European language Sanskrit is the ancient Indo-Iranian tongue that lies near the root of Hindi, Latin, Greek, and all the European romance and Germanic languages. *Sramana*, for example, is the Sanskrit root of "shaman" and an early cognate of the Greek and Latin words for "profane."[40] The Sanskrit term *dakshina* stands for both "right" and "south" (relating the sacred to warmth),[41] and if we associate the language with the source, "the implication is that before our ancestors divided into an Asiatic and a European branch, there were basic terms of left and right which came to designate north and south."[42] From the Sanskrit, Left and Right would endure with all their connotations of sacred and profane and good and evil into Latin and Greek, English, French, German, and a host of other European languages.

The last significant Indo-European expansion, however, occurred around 1500 BCE.[43] Prominent in this wave were the Iranian Mitanni people from the Caspian Sea. They may also have been the source of the Vedic religion,[44] and their occupation of Syria for a time brought the dualistic influence of the Vedic pantheon to the semitic Canaanites of Palestine.[45] The Caspian region was also the homeland of another Indo-Iranian steppe people called the Medes. By the second millennium BCE, the Medes managed a peaceful pastoral existence in northern Iran. But they had never known the horse and they soon found themselves helpessly facing mounted herder-warriors from further north.[46] The effects would be profound. Slaughtered, enslaved, and made to pay tribute in cattle, the foot-bound herders found little comfort in a Vedic pantheon, which seemed to celebrate the aggressor, or in its powerful god Indra, who embodied storm and war. Even Mithra, the god of contracts, provided little assurance against an enemy who respected none. The profane, once invisible and devious, was suddenly embodied in an implacable human enemy: in short, sacred and profane were politicized.

Among the beleaguered Medes, there appeared a seer who may have been a shaman. His name was Zoroaster.[47] After witnessing the carnage, he had an ecstatic vision of a new sun god called Mazda,[48] and the god told him something different: the real war was neither between tribes or territories or people, nor between sacred and profane, which were still entangled in nature and taboo. The new war was between Good and Evil. The terms were changing but the dualism remained. The Good of the shepherds was embodied in the deity Ahura Mazda, and the Evil of the raiders in the demonic Angra Mainyu. Both gods had always been, and would never die. Both represented irreconcilable principles and were locked in a battle in which the arena was no longer the steppe or a few acres of pasture but the world itself, and the stakes not a few acres of pasture, but humanity.[49] In this universalization of the steppe, heaven is promised for the good, and eternal hellfire for the evil. Joining heaven and earth and providing a perilous passage for the judged, there persisted the traditional Vedic device of the Cinvat Bridge.

It is through Zoroaster that the ancient world connects with the medieval and modern. As Mircea Eliade tells us, referring to the Zoroastrian book of *Artay Viraf*, the hero, "like Dante, visited all parts of the Mazdean paradise and Hades, witnessed the tortures of the impious, and saw the rewards of the just. From this point of view his otherworldly journey is comparable to the account of shamanic descents, some of which . . . also contain references to the punishment of sinners."[50] I.S. Wile goes further. Remarking that the image of a bridge across the valley of death is also found among the Asian Kalmucks, the North American Chippewa, in Islam, and among the Magi of Persia, he concludes that "such ideas of futurity suggest a common origin before the dispersion of languages."[51]

After the fashion of the shamanic journey, the Zoroastrian universe itself passes through a three-part journey of division, beginning in purity, passing into a present time of the coexistence of good and evil, and ending in the age of their final separation. This battle for the soul of man is foretold in a sacred book, the *Avesta* — a historical process at the end of which there is a day of judgement when the good of Ahura Mazda will triumph over the evil of Angra Mainyu, and paradise will be brought down to earth.[56] In the seventh century, the Median princes took up the cause, and Zoroastrianism, true to its shamanic origins, became a proselytizing religion in which the individual waged a universal war against Evil.[53] It became the state religion and eventually the binding belief of a Persian Empire, which would stretch from India to the shores of the Mediterranean, where it would rub shoulders with Judaism and Christianity.

It was not only through Zoroastrianism that Europe would be influenced by Vedic dualism. Around 1500 BCE, as Zoroaster preached, a second Indo-European expansion brought to eastern Europe and the lower Danube a distinctive patriarchal culture with Indo-European characteristics. Here there were also traces of shamanism with its tripartite journey through life, death, and afterlife. As the culture spread, the indigenous, mesolithic West Mediterranean peoples hadn't the structures to resist or to assimilate the new arrivals. And so the patriarchal, dualistic ways of the steppe took hold. In another few centuries, the Germanic peoples would exhibit variants of the passage through heaven, world, and hell, not to mention "antagonistic and complementary pairs of sovereign gods."[54] But the most fateful migration from the steppe homeland was the one that carried the Indo-European influence to the south and west, through the Balkans to Greece.

Popular history traces much of Western civilization to Greece, as if Greece itself had emerged *ex nihilo*. But the philosophy upon which much of modern Western thought depends arises from a dualism of which Greece was only the mediator. This last Indo-European migration of around 1500 BCE betrays itself first in the Indo-European roots of the Greek language. But in Greece too, the cosmos is a quadrapartitioned circle, and here the first compass, the *gruma*, is devised.[55] In Greece the left hand is profane, and the evening sun sets on the left as it sinks to the underworld; the sun is on the right hand when it is reborn in the East. The Elysian fields, the land of dead heroes, is always in the west.[56]

It seems, however, that the Indo-European influence held on with more intensity in the north of Greece, in Thrace. Thrace lived in primeval contrast to the playful sophistication of the south. It was more emotional, more sympathetic to the poor, and to those who got little comfort from the aristocratic gods of Olympus and their tragi-comic human frailties. Thrace cleaved privately to older, more personal religions that had come down through Asia Minor with the Indo-Europeans. The most important of these "poor man's" religions was the cult of Dionysus.

If Left and Right are the modern forms of Good and Evil, Heaven and Hell, the religious threshold to this dualism is latent in the cult of Dionysus. Dionysus, half god, half man, is himself dual. Like the shaman he is ecstatic — the god of wine, of disorder, fancy, and intoxication. The worship of Dionysus expressed itself as the reaction of a lower class against patrician Olympus and Attica. Around the ninth and eighth centuries BCE, Dionysian practice grew from a cult to a movement of complete dissolution that threatened the established order. Whether the rite came to Thrace from Asia Minor or from the Danube, both regions could be traced backward to Asia where *haoma*, the sacred drink of the Indo-European steppe, anticipates the Dionysian sacramental intoxication with wine.[57] In periodic dissolution came purification. It seems no accident that Dionysus shares something with the shaman.

The decadence of the cult produced another reaction. The Orphic cult, a moralistic reversal of Dionysian worship, was the foundation, it might be argued, of the sacred and profane in Greek philosophy. But unlike the Dionysian rite, where deliverance is found through the body and in this life, the journey of Orpheus through hell and his hypnotic singing after his decapitation suggest a salvation outside the body and beyond the world. The Orphic myth is believed to have originated north of the Black Sea, and indeed it bears the hallmarks of the steppe: in the spiritual journey from profane to sacred, in purification, and in the separation of body from spirit it is undeniably shamanistic.[58] A depiction of Orpheus carries through the theme of sacred and profane: "In his right hand is pity and benevolence, in his left, severity and punishment."[59] From beginning to end, this myth is riven with dualities.

Pythagoras, a sixth-century mathematician, was the first significant Greek philosopher to be influenced by Orphism, which was well-known to have infiltrated the Ionian island of Samos, where he was educated, and also southern Italy, where he spent most of his life.[60] In Pythagoreanism, a highly developed descendant of shamanism, the body was condemned as profane and unclean. Its Orphic exaltation of the spirit was philosophically expressed in the abstraction of mathematics. Since Orpheus was a musician, music, the only truly abstract art, was considered mystical, and the key to the scales of music was number. The elevation of the abstract mind over matter culminated in the idea that the contemplation of mathematics would purge the flesh of sin and free the spirit from entrapment in the world. Pythagoreanism envisaged a world divided by all possible dualities, beginning with body and soul, visible and invisible, beyond which were "short-cuts or short circuits between different sets of symbols in Pythagorean mystic number-lore such as the correlation of odd and even numbers with male and female; right and left."[61] Orpheus had taken his toll: "The abstract, spiritual direction of Western thought with its mistrust of the senses: and its complete faith in mechanical reasoning begins with Pythagoras."[62] The template of dualistic thinking was cut for good: from Pythagoras there would be no turning back.

With its exacting rites of purification, Pythagoreanism also bequeathed to the West the concept of an ethical elect, and carried forward from Dionysian and Orphic beliefs a tradition of protest combined with aloofness from an established social order that was associated with the material world. Aristocratic communism, as this expression of egalitarian individualism of the Indo-European is known,[63] favoured members of an elect group or tribe, and it was matched, perhaps, only by the Semites of the Arabian desert. The Indo-European and the Semitic cultures, although evolving far apart, were hardened alike in arid climates characterized by extremes, and it was their highly influential legacies that would combine in the polarities of Judeo-Christianity.

The Arabian desert, like the steppes of Central Asia, "is the least open to communication, the least affected by what goes on around it. Such a condition makes for ethnical and linguistic conservatism; it is in such a region that we must expect to find the most archaic forms."[64] The Semites were also patriarchal, nomadic and pastoral, and like the Vedic gods of the Indo-Europeans, their early pantheon leaned toward monotheism and universalism.[65] Lacking the security of cities, the Semites were clannish and warlike. As in the steppes of the north, the open desert encouraged abstract territorial distinctions between friend and foe. There are other parallels. In Semitic cultures, so-called shamans of the desert were considered to have the sacred powers of divination essential to the protection and guidance of the tribe.[66] But most haunting of all is the Semitic peoples' loading of the right and left hands with a cargo of sacred and profane similar to that of the Indo-Europeans. Likewise, the early Israelites worshipped facing the east and in ceremonies "the right hand occupies the place of superiority, strength and honour."[67] The word *yamin* is at once "right hand" and "south" in Hebrew, and "oath" in Arabic.[68] *Kadem* means both "in front" and "east," and the cardinal points — east, west, south, and north — correspond with uncanny exactness to in front, behind, right, and left.

In massive eastward migrations around 2500 BCE, the pastoral Semitic herders were absorbed by Sumer-Akkad and they even comprised the elite of the first Mesopotamian Semitic king, Sargon I of Akkad. When the Sargonic Empire began to collapse, Abraham, the first patriarch, took his tribe to new pastures in the western land of Canaan. Thus would begin a repeated search for a lost paradise that, not unlike the vision of the dreaming shaman or that of the migrant Medes, was constantly exalted in past and future in a quest that is recognizable in millennial forms of Judaism and Christianity — and the politics associated with them — even in our time. In Canaan, the Hebrews found themselves at the heart of a knot of buffer states between greedy empires and the sense of siege, the enclosure of identity in a spiritual garrison, increased when the Jews of Canaan were enslaved and deported to Egypt.

Dualism, to retain its resilience, needs the talisman of a term evoking both unity and separateness. Like the Indo-European furrow that divided inside from out, monotheism provided the Jews not only with unity but with a moral definition of the nation. Likewise, the worship of a single sun god, Aton, provided a theological-political strategy for social reform, even though it was the brainchild of the great Pharaoh Ikhnaton. Indeed, it also had enormous appeal for a displaced and disoriented desert people. At the exodus, Moses brought the Jews and the concept of a single god back to the lost land of Canaan. What was more, he bound his people to that single god with tablets of law. But in Canaan this newly conscious collection of tribes found itself once again a despised herding people, struggling from highland desert margins against the lowland, agricultural city states of Canaan. Here, as in the steppe, emerges the struggle for territory, tribe, and identity. Here once again the dual morality of the hunter-herder becomes political.

With the founding of a Hebrew nation, the one true god was exalted as the tribal, national god, and all neighbouring gods were *ipso facto* demonized. Beneath this stark duality persisted the earlier neolithic distinction between herder and gentile planter[69] suddenly underwritten by sacred and profane. In the book of Genesis, God duly prefers the superior sacrifice of the herdsman Abel to the poorer offering of the farmer Cain. When a jealous Cain kills Abel, murder deepens the dividing line between those acceptable to God and those unacceptable.[70] In this metaphysical extrapolation of a local war, "old wounds stemming from the conflict between the desert god of battles and the [agricultural] village deities of Canaan could never entirely heal"[71] — indeed, they continue to the present day.

Archaeology has yet to discover whether there was much mutual influence between the Indo-Europeans and the Jews. As we have seen, the invasion out of the steppe brought the Mitanni from the Caspian down as far as Canaan, where their dualistic Vedic pantheon may have influenced the Canaanite gods, which were in turn assimilated in different ways to the Jewish Yaweh. This spiritual genealogy may explain Yaweh's own dualism, his alternate benevolence and ferocity. But as to common origins, there are only hints: the Jewish ark of the covenant is sacred and untouchable by profane human hands; and rituals involving circulation around the ark suggest a common source for Semitic and Indo-European spatial symbolism. The Islamic circuit about the Kabasch and the Vedic Hindu Brahman movement around their altar follow precisely the same circuit of the sun, with the profane hand on the outside and the sacred hand closest to the object of devotion. But if an ultimate common source is still shadowy, the Indo-European Zoroastrians and the Jews can both trace an intermediate influence to Mesopotamia, whence each derived the myth of the creation of the world in six stages, primordial parents for mankind, and the dualistic, eschatological ideas of a primal garden of innocence, a critical god, and a punitive flood.

In modern times the outcroppings of ancient dualism reveal themselves like a chain of islands in an archipelago — their continuity submerged but implied. In 1789, the reduction of the three Estates into Right and Left presents a strange mixture of ritual tripartite belief, sacred and profane, and modern abstraction. Soon, personal life would come under the influence of a political duality that placed cool reason, Spartan manners, and casual forms of address with the Republican Left; and refined manners, passion, poetry, impulse, and elegance with the aristocratic Right.

But religion is the parent of politics, and so the foundations of political thought are no more rational than religion. Even if politics *rationalizes* society, it is not a technology; too much of it is rooted in the past. But this revolutionary leap forward in the rationalization of culture and morality would condemn freedom, poetry, aristocracy, and monarchy as if they were a single term. Likewise, the struggle for some measure of equality would be associated with envy, blasphemy, cynicism, and evil by an aristocracy all too ready to play by the new, metaphysical rules laid down by the Revolution. And the liberty and equality that had, in the neolithic world of herder and planter, been complex and interwoven in their relations but never in themselves diametrically opposed, would in the new world of Right and Left become antonyms.

3

Logos:
The Paris Quarter and the Flux of Heraclitus

W e take Left and Right for granted. They determine the language in which we speak of politics and the form in which we enact it. We forget, however, that Left and Right as a framework for a science of politics was hastily fashioned in a spontaneous response to a particular event. As 1790 dawned, so François Furet tells us, politics was an exercise invented on the spot and practised by amateurs. What was more, as the process was improvised in an emergency under threat of anarchy, it was a *techne* — a *praxis* — of organization, winnowing, and separating. The members of the Constituent Assembly had to stay ahead of the angry crowd in Paris and create the political forms that could contain or direct their violence; politics in 1789–93 was like building a millrace in the midst of a rapids. It was jury-rigged, and its haphazard result would be passed on to the world.

As a *techne*, it did provide a forum for dialogue and moral decipherability. But it was political, not social. Although the nobility was officially abolished in June of 1790, French society would remain essentially feudal — at least in temperament and habit — for years to come. And feudalism does not easily divide into two; it is far easier to cut capitalist society in two since capitalism has already done the job by creating a proletariat. Feudalism was a tangle. So historians have

51

tended to distinguish in France a "political" revolution in contrast to the social reality it attempted to marshal. A disharmony would persist between them. We must also distinguish between the early stages of the Revolution, when the split was voluntary, and the later stages, when it was forced upon the nation.

If the separation of Left and Right later provided fodder for a new science of dialectic, it was partly because attempts to mend the break were as inept as the science was new. Inexperience would produce a mistake that is repeated even today: whenever parties make radical attempts to unify a nation, they tend just as radically to divide it. When the part (or party) presents itself as the whole, it alienates the moiety that disagrees. In the summer of 1790, for example, the Left realized that the economic crisis could be solved by converting Church lands into a stable currency. The corollary was the formation of a new, landless, state clergy that swore to the Revolution rather than to Rome. But if the new Civil Constitution of the Clergy was thought to be a force of unity, it was in fact a slap at the sacred Right Hand — and would divide a "non-juring" Monarchist right-wing clergy from a left-wing nationalized clergy. And it would inevitably push socially progressive but religiously conservative people onto a political Right. (We have seen the same thing today in debates over abortion.)

In the fall of 1791, a similar mistake was made in the formulation of the new Legislative Assembly upon the king's dissolution of the old Constituent Assembly. The far Left — galvanized by Robespierre — and the monarchist far Right joined in asking the original deputies to stand down so that an entirely new, more unified assembly might be elected to better represent the nation. Here again the part — the right or the left — was masquerading as the whole. "Unity" to each meant, respectively, a "new Right-wing Monarchist Assembly" or a "new Left-wing Republican Assembly." These were of course disingenuous appeals to some alleged higher unity, which in reality would block the re-election of the old moderates. The radicals of both wings got their way and so helped engender yet another split assembly.

Meanwhile, popular expectations of the Revolution in the streets of Paris created a leftward undertow. The newly elected body, known as the Legislative Assembly, was to last barely a year. Its Left continued to draw strength from the streets while the aristocratic right-wing minority, riddled with resignations and absenteeism, fell off the end of the spectrum, making way for an assembly that for the moment supported a constitutional monarchy.

Then it was the king's turn to further polarize the nation in another attempt to unify it — a part once again posing as the whole. His stratagem was to leave the country, join up with the royalist emigrés and monarchies of Europe, and unite France by armed force. His return to Paris after his capture at Varennes alienated still more of the nation. What had once been a division between Monarchists and Constitutional Monarchists now began to appear as a contest between Constitutional Monarchists, who wanted to forgive the king, and nascent Republicans, who wanted his abdication.

The last and most authentic expression of unity was, tellingly, popular rather than strictly political: a peaceful mass protest against the king's attempted escape in the Champ de Mars. In spirit, it reconciled diverging forces of monarchy and democracy by reaffirming the monarchy with a reprimand — that it remain responsible to the people. This time it was the supposedly popular and non-partisan National Guard that split the nation further by claiming to act on its behalf. Overreacting to a provocation, it killed fifty demonstrators. This was the precise moment of the divergence of a radical, republican, potentially atheist Left from the rest of the nation: the powerful and talented minority who decided that after the Champ de Mars there was no turning back.

The massacre in the Champ de Mars penetrated to the heart of the Jacobin Club. As the authorities cracked down, the club's more conservative Constitutional Monarchists seceded rightward to meet at the convent of the *Feuillants*, while a more populist, lower-class secession formed a sort of "political centre" that met at the monastery of the *Cordeliers*. These seminal "purges" and secessions within the Jacobins were not yet the work of ideologues, however — they were provoked by poor judgement on the part of the monarchy and the National Guard. The next move toward irreparable division came again from the crown. If the king could not participate in an invasion, he would now invite one from outside the country. Leopold II of Austria and Wilhelm II of Prussia complied.

Brissot, a persuasive Jacobin deputy from the Gironde, favoured armed mobilization. Many of the *Feuillants* were opposed. Robespierre protested only because he thought it a tactical mistake; the Revolution was not ready for war. Perhaps he was also irritated because Brissot was now the leading voice of the Jacobins and his clique was favoured by a monarchy hoping to manipulate it. Robespierre was vindicated when the "Brissotin" army suffered reverses at the front. Now everything hung on military success or defeat. Opinion was pushed and pulled by the accidents, blunders, and circumstances of war. Only the most atavistic dualism turned on the issue of the monarchy. Otherwise, ideology still had much of the vagueness and looseness that it has begun to assume again today.

As the Revolution surged ahead in early 1792, politics and political parties did not yet exist. The Legislative Assembly of the previous fall had suggested, if anything, a plurality of opinion: 350 independents and moderates still sat apart from 260 royalists and 136 Jacobins.[1] A plurality of opinion resisted alignment with Left or Right, arguing less for the existence of a centre "party" than for political individualism. In its infancy, the Revolution was in fact opposed to the party system. A Jacobin would later comment, "Patriots do not form a party, that designation can only be applied to intriguers in the Convention."[2] Rather, "the movements of political fragments within the kaleidoscopic assembly only formed a pattern when reflected in the fixed mirrors of a crucial issue, or, when jolted by a great oration."[3] So casual were the alignments that loyalties were still grouped under the names of cafés, neighbourhoods, seminaries, and deputies. *Les Feuillants*, for example, was a negative formulation, representing the amorphous majority of Constitutional Monarchists who had decamped from the Jacobins after the massacre in the Champ de Mars. Within the remaining Jacobins, a few *Girondist* deputies were so designated simply because they hailed from the *Gironde* and happened, together, to be vocal and persuasive; the most eloquent of these was Brissot, whose small group of admirers were called *Brissotins*.

And so, the assemblies were more of a shifting and poorly differentiated mass, drawn mostly from the same class. And if ideology was not as formed as we might have thought, it may at least be argued that, "if the main function of a parliament is not to govern but to provide a focus for public opinion for the guidance of the governors, then the group system, since it frankly accepts existing diversity of opinion, is better than a two-party system which tries to gloss over such a diversity."[4] It followed that personalities acted as polestars for crowds and voters, and sparked furious debates. Indeed, as historian Simon Schama remarks, "Overlooking (the) personality feuds as a serious issue in revolutionary politics has been one of the most glaring omissions in modern historiography."[5] Personality, indeed, seems to have come before ideology, just as efficiency often took the lead over ideas. And so the radical journalist Hébert would in disgust coin such terms as "Brissotism," "Buzotism," or "Dantonism," suggesting that temperamental idiosyncrasies somehow found their voice in the larger population. And they probably did. It may even be argued that personality is a significant stone in the foundations of ideology.

The respective adherents of Brissot and Robespierre did to an extent follow their personality types. The "Girondins" have thus been called tender-hearted and the Jacobins tough-minded; and so they reappear, in a peculiar sense, as inspired shaman and rationalist priest. Or, in Thompson's more aphoristic formulation, "A Girondin was a Jacobin who 'had not lived': a Jacobin was a Girondin 'man of the world.'"[6] The persuasiveness of personal vision turned, of course, on its claims to reason. And behind it was a peculiarly atavistic religious power; a religious fervour that subsumed all personal problems and politicized moral and intellectual concerns: "That is why the revolutionary militants identified their private lives with their public ones and with the defence of their ideas . . . It was a formidable logic which, in a laicised form, reproduced the psychological commitment that springs from religious beliefs."[7]

If style was a determinant, corruption and personal life were an incalculable element in the mix of temperament and fashion — the same subterranean current that continues to skew the truth of Left and Right today. Voters, adherents, and ideologues had to be warned of "another world of corruption in which many of the leaders were equally involved. The alliances, secrets, opponents to be conciliated or blackmailed into silence, created a political underworld whose alignments often differed from those of public debate."[8] In 1792 self-interest consumed even the best. Whatever their political stripe, those who forged the ideology of revolution were professionals, officials, and landowners whose material interests were mostly represented in property.[9] Though their economic beliefs were *laissez faire*,[10] they had no ideological truck with business, which they considered impure and unworthy. Urban commerce and finance were not associated so much with class as with profiteering, hoarding, and piracy, its volatile interests in conflict with the immobile and virtuous wealth of property.[11]

It is something of a paradox that the urban and rural lower classes were in fact the social rivals of the egalitarian Jacobin Left, and that the economic protest of the wage-earning urban proletariat was considered by the propertied, left-wing political class to be the venal activity of men whose logical salvation ought to be self-employment. There are other inconsistencies. In the French countryside, communal ownership of land did not in fact favour the landless peasant. It tended instead to benefit the town-based proprietor who wanted the land for his herds. By contrast it was the landless peasant who stood to benefit by the private property that might arrive with the break-up of the common lands into small private plots. In this anomaly we see collectivism's affinity for hierarchy and individualism's association with egalitarianism playing itself out in the revolutionary fracas. We shall meet it again. Meanwhile, professional men of property and peasant proprietors alike were set against the large class of landless labourers. As long as the Left was defined only by anti-monarchism, its wealthy men of property accused poor farmers who grasped for land of "aristocratic" greed. In short, the wish to own property defined not only the Jacobin Left but egalitarianism itself.

The city, where modest self-employment became the revolutionary ideal, was almost as complex. The Jacobin moral optimum was embodied in the small proprietor; the manufacturer or artisan, family-loving and unambitious. This class, a minority, would be promoted and celebrated to the exclusion, indeed to the detriment, of any other; the alliances of the left-wing Jacobins with proletariat and poor, for example, would be merely tactical and ultimately exploitive.[12] Meanwhile the poor, as in feudal France, were considered everyone's enemy and were pushed to a despairing anarchism.[13] And so the collision of Left and Right in the guise of egalitarianism and hierarchy in the vipers' nest of feudalism tended to divert itself into hatreds that were feudal and archaic rather than ideological. And all of this within the supposedly revolutionary mass of the Third Estate.

In fact, the deputies in the Legislative Assembly were still more concerned with rights and regulations than with wealth, with caste rather than class; and on the powers of the king, especially, it was easier to find a consensus. The concept of a revolutionary Constitutional Monarchy was still favoured by deputies from both Right and Left who disagreed more about the speed of reform than about the sort of government. But that last unity was broken when Prussia's Duke of Brunswick declared that he would massacre Paris if Louis came to harm. The suspicion that the enemy already had a foot inside the royal court removed any hope that a Constitutional Monarchy could bridge a gap between Left and Right. With the Assembly polarizing between king and people, the role of unifier of the nation was now passing from the king to the Jacobin Club and outright Republicanism. As Paris boiled on the verge of anarchy, public order became another shibboleth of Left and Right. The municipal government — the Commune — was closest to the streets and to hunger. And yet it seemed to abdicate any political responsibility.

At the time of the Duke of Brunswick's declaration, however, the Jacobins were seen to represent the common population of Paris, the common people to represent the city, and the city to represent the Nation. That way the Nation was held to be identical with the Left. If the Nation itself was the Left, monarchical Europe was Right; and monarchical Europe had an agent in the midst of Paris — the king. On August 9, 1792, the neighbourhoods of Paris seized control of the city by replacing the inactive municipal government of the Commune with a revolutionary Commune of their own. On the following day it was Paris and its new Commune that marshalled the neighbourhood crowds and organized the bloody insurrection that forced the king from the palace of the Tuileries and made him a prisoner. For the brief moment of the Commune's rule, the Revolution was once again whole. In the euphoria, liberty and equality were not yet at loggerheads, not yet separated into opposed principles of Right and Left. A spirit of democracy ruled, and social differences seemed for the moment to dissolve.

It was, of course, as brief as it was ecstatic: the anarchic hiatus, properly neither Left nor Right, which thrives in the shadow of impending authority and fanaticism. Perhaps it was a dream-like recollection of that primeval "peasant anarchy" that had endured the collision of hunter and planter. But it had a closer root, the protean and versatile Parisian neighbourhood. It was the Parisian neighbourhood that made up that political-historical phenomenon, the "Paris Crowd." They were the *menus*, or the "small" people: artisans and tradesmen in all their variety. They were not opposed to property because most were property owners, however small. In a time before the Industrial Revolution, fewer were wage earners. Among their leaders, who represented a low level of Parisian society, there numbered several well-to-do. There was Santerre, a brewery-owner who led the attack on the Tuileries. There was also Legendre, a butcher; and another was a jeweller's assistant.

However much and for however long the Jacobins and the *menus* people were in sympathy, the politics that moved the latter came from the Jacobins' bourgeois. It was the Jacobins who tried to make of the shopkeeper a puritanical prototype of Rousseauian virtue that was contrary to his nature, his origins, and his desires. This would be the work of the Left, while the Right would content itself with his exploitation. The *menus*, like many of the propertied class who made their politics, were northern French, and in fact, that culture has been described, anthropologically, as "individualistic egalitarianism."[14] As northerners and Indo-Europeans, the primordial roots of their culture stretched back to the Eurasian forest and steppe; they had inherited the egalitarian individualism of the paleolithic nomad and the barbarian hunter-herder. Indeed, liberty and equality together, however crude and inchoate, were the abiding if unconscious values that would come to distinguish Europe.[15]

Life in the Parisian neighbourhoods was still a "whole world, multi-coloured, mixed-up, disparate, passing and circulating, swarming on badly paved streets."[16] The fluidity of the neighbourhood and the mixture of classes might even be called "pre-ideological." Classes rubbed shoulders, dividing buildings between the upper classes on the ground floor and the poor on the upper floors, rather than sifting into separate neighbourhoods as they would do a half-century later. Fed by and feeding this life was a neighbourhood institution essential to the Revolution — the independent workshop. It was here that political discussion began, here that news of Court, Assembly, and Commune was received and disseminated.[17] In the café, the political functions of the neighbourhood came together and in turn became the basis for the political club. Here was the forcing-house for a healthy politics among the people, a natural dynamic that would be rationalized, formalized, and ultimately lost in the hands of the political class.

Pure politics is essentially incompatible with ideology. In its essence, politics is pluralistic: it assumes freedom on the part of the individual; ideology, usually monistic or dualistic, assumes that all are prisoners of "their attitudes or 'false consciousness.'"[18] Ideology, of course, is no freer than those prisoners it condemns, and William Blake might well have been referring to the ideological mind when he wrote, "The man who never alters his opinion is like standing water and breeds reptiles of the mind."[19] So politics, from the French Revolution and into the twenty-first century, would come to involve the individual in so much compromise that, as Hannah Arendt observes, "to look upon politics from the perspective of truth means to take one's stand outside the political realm."[20] Long before, even Socrates had said of politics that "his position as a champion of justice would have kept him apart from it."[21]

It is hard to imagine what a pure politics would have looked like. It might have functioned in the spirit of the Parisian *sections*, whose common people knew of revolution before they knew of Left and Right. It might perhaps be a process of continuous change or the "becoming" of the pre-Socratic Greek philosopher Heraclitus, as described by Nietzsche: "affirmation of transitoriness *and destruction*, and the decisive element in a dionysian philosophy, affirmation of antithesis and war, *becoming* with a radical rejection even of the concept of 'being.'"[22] George Woodcock goes as far as to assign to Heraclitus the legacy of a political ideal: "the flux of never-ending change rather than the forward movement of the Hegelians and the Marxists; it suggests a world in which history loses its rigidity in the interflow of balancing forces; it suggests contradiction as a positive and productive element and equilibrium as a dynamic condition in a world that changes constantly and never reaches a stillness of perfection because imperfection is a cause and a consequence of its everlasting movement."[23]

As the distinction of Left and Right weakens today, the spirit of Heraclitus starts to become relevant again. We find a resonance of his thought when Greenpeace seeks models in nature and attempts a more holistic politics — and especially when it cuts across the old, industrial consensus of Left and Right.

■

It was Heraclitus' radical rejection of static, monolithic *Being*, and its forced conceptual divisions that provided metaphors for dynamic concepts of human society. Born in Ionia around 500 BCE a generation after Pythagoras, Heraclitus began by attacking his predecessors: Homer and Hesiod for their tragic view of the world; Pythagoras for his separation of body and spirit; Thales for saying the world was constituted of nothing but water; and Anaximander for *adikia*, the melancholy "injustice" by which the many separated from the sacred one, the *apeiron*. He dared instead to say the impossible — that the One *is* the Many; the Many *are* the One.

His was a conciliatory vision that affirmed the world as it appeared before him, by rejecting any high, ethereal concept of *being* in favour of *becoming* — even violent, visible changes in the weather, in the seasons, in birth and death, in creation and dissolution. In this view, duality, stretched by time-bound causality, becomes oscillation — which in turn expresses itself in history, society, and people. Ideology, by contrast, seeks to put paradox to rest and aims for victory, for fixed states. Heraclitus gave his idea form in the concept of the flux; the ever-changing entity whose essential shape remains the same; the river which is both the same and never the same. As Nietzsche would interpret it, "the struggle of plurality can yet bear within itself law and justice."[24] This is *logos*, the law behind the flux: order, ground, reason, principle, concept, limits, "deeper than logic, beyond opposites . . . the left and right of one being that is no being and neither is nor is not."[25]

In Heraclitus' thought, we recall the social, all-inclusive circle of the neolithic. It stands in contrast to the dividing line, separating and exclusive, the principle that grew out of the north. On the steppe there is order and disorder; with Heraclitus there is only order; disorder is only apparent. On the steppe, fire exists in salutary, bright opposition to cold and darkness; with Heraclitus the flux of fire is everything. He remains a brilliant aberration in an intellectual tradition that was already, with Pythagoras, on the road to a static dualism. In the West, the heritage of Heraclitus was to remain subversive.

If this was the spirit of political anarchism, it was also "a comprehensive intellectual system which could be applied to physical phenomena and to the movements of human society but which still displayed a strong tendency to think mythically rather than empirically."[26] Nonetheless, we have in *logos*, inherent in humanity and nature, "one immanent law and Reason in the universe of which human laws should be the embodiment, though at best they can be but its imperfect and relative embodiment."[27] One would be a fool to "legislate" Heraclitus, but perhaps at least his spirit can be seen in the street, in the marketplace of the French Revolution. Here, among the neither rich nor very poor lay the latent desire of the people that the new politicians were at such pains to exploit, to second-guess, or to change. Like *logos*, the Paris quarter, with its majority of *menus* artisans, was a dynamic world, nearly self-sufficient, defined by its own limits. In the late summer and early fall of 1792, however, its ethic did have a short-lived period of ascendance. For an optimum moment, after the people had moved beyond the political innocence of patriotic symbol but before their submission by the Jacobin Club, a popular politics was freely embodied in the Commune's sixty-six wards or *sections* — dozens of inchoate "utopias" where individualism and egalitarianism were sustained in precarious balance. Here, briefly, was an integration of social and political life in primitive democracy.

The point is that the *sections* worked in concert with, and not in bondage to, the political clubs. By August they were in session twenty-four hours a day. It was a time when, in all its Dionysian spirit, city and neighbourhood must nearly have been at one. And if Paris commanded France, the city was ruled by the city hall Commune, which in turn was ruled by its representative *sections* and the populace that filled them. Paris, indeed France, was ruled from below. While the *sections* constituted the spearhead of another leftward turn in the Revolution, there was nothing yet doctrinaire about them; culturally, they still represented the neighbourhoods from which they arose. Before long, however, all would harden into instruments of oppression and surveillance, as the revolution they had fomented became centralized and authoritarian.

In the brief moment when they thrived, it was for good reason that the revolutionary *sections* were described as "sixty-six little Republics," and that the members of Danton's *Cordeliers* section "already saw themselves as reincarnations of Athenian democrats: the primary cells of freedom to which, ultimately, elected representatives had to defer."[28] But it was only the lower levels of French society that seemed, however briefly, to reflect the Greek *polis* in its Heraclitean variety and dynamism. The legacy of Athenian democracy reappeared in quite a different way in the election of increasingly powerful assemblies. And in the Revolution itself, in the growing division between politicians and people in French political life, one could also trace a hidden similarity to Indo-European and Semitic dualism.

In ancient Athens, however, social organization had little of the stark dualism of the Athenians' Asian origins. In Greek society, chaos, ordered by limits, law, or Heraclitean *logos*, tended to be the rule. To the Greeks, blessed as they were with an appreciation of things in life for their own sake, excess had its consequences in the here and now, and not in any anticipated permanent states like Heaven and Hell.[29]

The confined and defensive city state, or *polis*, was (with a few exceptions, such as Sparta) a symptom of the fragmentation of the Greek mainland into mountains and valleys. The mountain top was the only sure means of defence and the extent of the city state was strictly limited to the radius of its protection, the area *visible* from the fortified summit. In such confinement, morality was inseparable from political life.

But no permanent dual division of politics could have rooted itself. There was class conflict; but a dual politics, as we shall see, is rather a function of modern masses, of an atomized population whose susceptibility to monolithic division increases the weaker its bonds. Modern political ties are ties to ideas, while ancient ties tended to be to people and to places. Contemporary Left and Right developed over a century when other bonds were decaying, and reached their height in a time of maximum social homogenization and conformity. One of the signal facts about ancient Greece was that steps were taken to *prevent* the formation of permanent blocs.

Greek society was structured on the scale of the individual. Not only did the small size and the *limits* of the city state encourage strong civic identity, local gods, and a native liturgical drama, but friendship was the primary bond and households were the essential social unit. The city state was conceived as a collection of households where political and local ties were inseparable. Friendship, sacred and strongly conditioned by obligations, cemented the links between households, which comprised family members, slaves, property, and ancestral spirits. The smallest administrative unit, combining friendship, household, and clan, was the *deme*; rather like a village or neighbourhood council. Few loyalties could function outside these units.

A public life without limits, like our own with its mass media, is bound to create inadequate, meaningless, mass identifications. But an intimate public life works against large coalescences. The *polis* was integrated first and foremost on the intimate principles of friendship and emotive connection, less on economic class, and, as we shall see, still less along political lines. It was embodied in the marketplace, or *agora*. The *agora*, too, was strictly circumscribed. Its comprehensiveness was expressed in temples to Zeus, Athena, and Apollo — each of whom functioned triply as god of city, clan, and family.

It might be argued that a dual, mass politics arises directly from the social realm — that intermediate field between public and private which began, roughly speaking, with Rome and which in our times has drained public life of its vigour and set it apart from private life.[30] This is the semi-private chattering zone where classes segregate themselves and ideas are pressed into conformity, where birds of a feather stick together and ideologues preach to the converted. Where this semi-private zone and its monolithic politics predominate, there is no truly public space in which all classes are forced out of their privacy. Privacy, after all, is the hothouse of ideology: like William Blake's standing water, it breeds reptiles of the mind. So it was to their benefit that the Greeks did not have a "social" realm but entered the public world directly from home.

Indeed, in Athens, the political expert was a veteran of public life; in France in 1789, the experts were amateurs who brought with them from the salons an introverted literary idealism.[31] That sort of very modern "atomism" or isolation of the individual was described by the Greeks quite literally as "idiocy": the state of the idiot, "private person" or amateur, who deals in theory, not in fact. Thus it is that "idiocy," or modern privacy, provides fertile ground for political ideology and its simplistic dualism. In Athens at its height, public life ensured that political life amounted to more than just utility; it fulfilled the dictum of Aristotle that "a state exists for the sake of a good life and not for the sake of life only."[32] For in Athens, "men . . . felt that their own individual actions made a difference to the survival or well-being of the community with an immediacy unobtainable by members of modern nations."[33] In the end, the *polis*, says Hannah Arendt, was a "guarantee against the futility of public life."[34]

The dynamism of Athens depended on the absence of permanent factions. The drawing of lots for many public postings prevented the occupation of any administrative body by a single interest. It was likewise for stability that the Hoplites or "unmounted knights" had transformed their ethic of mutual self-defence on the battlefield into a system of democratic rule. The experience of tyranny had taught them to fear factions. They passed their ethic on to their successors, the voting citizens or *demos*: "surprising moderation, the fruit of the oligarchic tradition of mutual forbearance, essential to the working of a democracy. Each side must be confident that the other will not push its victories too far; awareness of a common interest must be stronger than mistrust."[35] A strong sense of the *logos* of Heraclitus, even the *adikia* of Anaximander, was present. To the extent that duality existed, it was expressed in Heraclitean positive or complementary tensions; for example, in the distinction between competitiveness and cooperation; or between the relative virtues of priest and warrior[36] — the sort of tensions that might divide friends but never a society.

That is not to say there was no social animosity between rich and poor. Indeed the aristocracy despised the *demos*. But politics rarely settled into schism.[37] There were of course occasional struggles: in the mid-sixth century, economic circumstances conspired for a time to divide the country into a farmers' lobby (the hills), a faction of aristocrats (the plain), and merchants and fishermen (the shore). If the factions did not last, it was because political groups still formed on the basis of clan kinship and even more around individuals[38] and friends. As in the early days of the French Revolution, actual political parties were condemned as sources of conspiracy. Athenian society was bound by a consensus best described by Aristotle: "family connections, brotherhoods, common sacrifice, amusements which draw men together . . . created by friendship, for the will to live together is friendship. The end of the state is the good life and these are the means toward it. And the state is the union of families and villages in a perfect and self-sufficient life by which we mean a happy and honourable life."[39] Would anybody have defined the goals of Left or Right in such terms?

Just as "friendship" was the function that most distinguished the social and political life of the *polis*, it was fundamental to most societies before modern times and survived in important, though lesser forms, into the eighteenth century. By that time, however, there had begun, as Martin Buber laments, "the increasing decay of the old organic forms of the direct life of man with man." To allow relationships of friendship, we need "communities which qualitatively must not be too big to allow the men who are connected by them to be brought together ever anew and set in a direct relation with one another and which quantitatively are of such a nature that men are ever anew born into them or grow into them, who thus understand their membership not as the result of a free agreement with others but as their destiny and as a vital tradition. Such forms are the family, union in work, the community in village and town. Their increasing decay is the price that had to be paid for man's political liberation in the French Revolution and for the subsequent establishment of bourgeois society."[40]

Indeed, political liberation also meant the liberty to forge huge political monoliths. By the end of September 1792, no one in Paris could have imagined such a fate, for the vibrant neighbourhoods had only then reached their potential, while hubris still lay hidden behind success. France was a Republic, military victories had turned back the allies, and power lay in the streets and in the political clubs. The assembly itself, now a backwater in the cataract of events, was dissolved. The Revolution, for the moment, seemed once again whole and indivisible. Robespierre, clear-sighted, and with a ready answer in the fog of every crisis, proposed that Republic and Revolution be represented by the plain and beautifully simple idea of a Convention directly elected by all the people of France. Once again the dream of unity was alive. This absence of faction was what the Revolution called fraternity.

Fraternity was the only surviving equivalent to Aristotle's principle of "friendship." But like liberty and equality, it was soon to lose its meaning. On the Right, liberty would be corrupted to the pursuit of capital and the exaltation of the autonomous ("idiotic") individual;

and on the Left, equality became degraded to the enforcement of mediocrity by authority. Of the three, fraternity (as the common bond of friendship that underwrote the *polis*) was the only transcendent principle, the only one that could fit harmoniously with the others. But as equality and liberty would go to war under the banners of Left and Right, fraternity — their sole mediator and bond — would be sacrificed.

How did this happen? Of the three values, fraternity, the most difficult to define, was the most vulnerable. Richard Sennett makes the point in his commentary on the vagueness surrounding the concept of human rights: "We have two clichéd formulations of them, both originating in the eighteenth century: life, liberty and the pursuit of happiness; liberty, equality and fraternity. Among these rights it is easier to discuss life, liberty or equality than the pursuit of happiness or fraternity; they seem almost tacked on as benefits of the first set rather than equally fundamental rights."[41]

In 1792, with the pressures of war, fraternity was quickly reduced to "the discovery amidst a struggle against others that one's immediate neighbours are one's brothers — linguistically, culturally, geographically — fellow sons of a common father land."[42] It is exactly in the junction between "immediate neighbours" and "common father land" that tragedy was sewn; in which the immediacy of friendship of the Athenian *agora* or Revolutionary *section* would be reduced to, and ultimately replaced by, the vast, impersonal force of nationalism. And nationalism, a concept both symmetrical and massive, was perfectly susceptible to being co-opted by two other monolithic associations — the Left or the Right. With the bonds of community in all its plurality sold off in the great, abstract expanse of nationalism, an open field was created — we might even say as open and divisible as the steppe — and Left and Right, in the ideological split of the propertied class, were free to claim the field and go to war on behalf of liberty or equality, both claiming fraternity as weapon and trophy.

Only the ordinary people would retain a skepticism about such distinctions, joking — "le côté *droit* est toujours gauche, et *le gauche* n'est jamais droit."[43] — and so perfectly turning the anthropologically loaded double entendres to advantage: "The right is always clumsy (gauche, or 'left'), and the left is never straight ('right')." But the die had been cast; such practical thinking was doomed.

4

Polarity:

Being and Not Being a Jacobin

Upon the overthrow of the king on August 10, 1792, extremely well organized forces would proceed, effectively, to define the nation of France as "One" — as a philosophical, political, and institutional whole in which anomaly and defect would be conceived as the "Right." "Left," of course, was not an appellation the Jacobins would have taken by choice; in their best of all possible worlds, the terms "Left" and "Right" would not have existed. The image that filled the Jacobin mind had never been of a battle — but of a *fait accompli* — a vision of harmonious uniformity wrought through spontaneous transformation. Indeed, the continual divisions that developed seemed to take everyone by surprise.

In this respect, we might add, the world has changed little. Two centuries later, free marketeers hold a similar view — that the global market is a seamless whole — whether determined by nature or by man. But any conception of the world as One — philosophical or political — is innately, inevitably, dualistic. It is a paradox which, as we shall see, originally emerged as far back as ancient Greece, and re-emerged in a living model in revolutionary France.

Of course, that is not how things appeared in the fall of 1792. By late August, the Jacobins seemed to have their work cut out for them with a provisional government that had fallen into their hands by default. They were caretakers in an assembly whose centre and right were now intimidated or absent, and it all looked very Left. To the more radical Jacobins, of course, it looked like an incipient One. The Jacobin deputies also knew that the fury of the hungry Parisian mob could always be delegated the dirty work of moulding the nation into that seamless and just unity. And after imprisoned aristocrats and non-juring priests were massacred by the mob in the spontaneous bloodbath known as the "September Massacres," the silence of the future assembly would be taken as assent. The killing was, after all, the first step toward uncovering the essence of the nation.

By now, the monarchy had become less an object of debate than an impediment toward unity. The discovery of secret correspondence between Louis and the Austrian court gave France's new architects what they needed. The Paris Jacobin Club held that the king ought to be dethroned in a legal formality, and differences over this issue produced lists of "good" and "bad" deputies. The result, the summary abolition of the monarchy, also implied building the Republic on the foundation of the "good" deputies. So emerged the blueprint for the actual con-struction of the new nation, the forging of reality according to a plan. This modus operandi would become a hallmark of the Left in general. But in a world that was still uneducated, unequal, and chaotic, the enactment of such a plan could not count on simple democracy. (It might here be remarked that democracy, down to the present day, is the preserve neither of the Left nor of the Right; and that Left and Right, insofar as their visions are uncompromising and lay claim to the truth of underlying reality, are in their essence totalitarian. Each lays claim to the whole and in effect denies any real existence to the other.)

But simple democracy was not up to the task. The expression of the concept of a whole by using democracy to "uncover" the truth of the nation required the shaping and limitation of democracy itself. By supplying their club for the electoral college, the Jacobins had the "bad candidates" struck from the voters' lists, purging the Convention before it was even elected. Moreover, in the voting that followed, intimidation was often the rule, and the agenda and nominees for president were frequently set in the Jacobin Club. Democracy, at the mercy of limited choices, already had eschatological, and even totalitarian, implications. In the words of the Girondin Alexandre Lameth after the start of the new Convention, "the elections were almost always carried by the left wing, although up to that point they had been almost entirely controlled by the right."[1]

But even then, the expressed tendency was toward unity, and in the early days of the Convention the party divisions were once again invisible. In fact, in a replay of the original chaos in the *Salle des Menus Plaisirs*, "the deputies sat indiscriminately wherever they pleased."[2] The new assembly was represented almost entirely by the professional middle class, most of whom belonged to the Jacobin Club. A majority of those were still Girondins, and they formed the largest group, under the leadership of Brissot. There were divisions, but they were not yet dual: every deputy considered himself part of an orthodox core and blamed every diversion on "factionalists."

It was perhaps then that the continual secessions and subdivisions that characterize modern politics began. The new Right-Left division appeared not in the Convention but at the heart of the Jacobin Club itself. The split first became apparent when Brissot's group suggested that a new guard be set up by the Département to protect the Convention and the ministers from the Paris crowd, thus provoking outrage from the more radical Jacobins. The moment of physical separation seems to have taken place in the bosom of the club two weeks later, when Brissot and his group ceased to attend. From this moment, the history of France and of the West was set on a course of no return.

How could the Brissotins have given up an institution that was becoming central to national unity? As historian M.L. Kennedy observes, "It was clear that this was a mistake. They should have fought for control of the society. By gathering separately and in secret, they exposed themselves to charges of conspiracy . . . Their names were gradually taken from the rolls."[3] Thus were born Girondins and Jacobins. Hence, the inception of the political Right and Left occurred by default. And once again, in the Convention, "as the quarrel between Jacobins and Girondins developed, they grouped themselves to the right and left of the president's chair, whilst the extreme Jacobins found a place of vantage in the higher seats at one end of the hall . . . right and left could, indeed, have no fixed meaning. The president's chair was moved from the north to the south side of the Manège."[4]

Even then, the centre remained the biggest grouping. Although its members voted with one side or the other on different issues, it still comprised those deputies faithful to the early spirit of an undivided revolution. And the names and descriptions of the two main parties came not from within but from their enemies.[5] It is indicative of the reluctance to divide that the desire was to distinguish the other — and never oneself — as different. So "Jacobin" and "Girondin" had likely begun as terms of opprobrium directed at deputies who considered themselves merely patriots. Eventually, opposing politicians ceased to address one another and spoke only to their parties.

They might still have found some unity in the ownership of property, but some, like those Girondins who wanted a guard for the Convention, were more concerned to erect a political principle to protect their land and possessions from violence and confiscation. So property soon replaced the king as the fulcrum of division. Although it may have been a precursor of the capitalism that created modern Left and Right, property ownership in itself is *not* capitalism. Few of the Girondins were monopolists, and with the destruction of feudalism and the growth of industry, landowning would no longer husband the monopoly, power, and wealth that manufacturing would. Nevertheless, with the fury of the Paris streets, property began here and there to replace fraternity in the triumvirate with liberty and equality. Soon the Girondins were seen by their critics as protecting privilege in wealth, and, whether they liked it or not, they would succeed the aristocracy on the spectral right hand of an absent king.

"Property," however, did not provide a tidy division. Property owners were large and small, peasant and bourgeois, Left and Right. The weakness of the term is similar to the vagueness of "Business" in today's electronic age as, with the growth in the number of struggling single entrepreneurs, small capitalism becomes pitted against big capitalism. The Girondins were likewise drawn into a messy quarrel between rich and poor defined by occupation rather than wealth, every class of proprietor accusing every other of attempting to take control of the Revolution. Even in the provinces, the Jacobin clubs began to divide in two, the bourgeoisie and the artisan-farming class dividing into separate associations.

Perhaps the more profound point of division was that indefinable thing that can only be called collective personality. Originally as radical as the Jacobins, the Girondins were clumsier, more emotional. For example, they had tended even more than the Jacobins toward radical anti-clericalism and atheism,[6] but instead of stealing the thunder and initiative from the Jacobins, they merely reacted. Like the Jacobins the Girondins held property sacred, but unlike the Jacobins they proved incapable of expressing any idea that transcended it; and at heart they represented no unified body of opinion.[7] They spoke better than they thought; in all their poetry and passion, they abandoned the *realpolitik* of revolution to the Jacobins. A constitution hammered out by the Girondin philosopher Condorcet enshrining property and the individual was typically poetic and obscure. Thus, by the time the mob had pushed poverty onto the agenda, the Girondins had allowed themselves to be defined as property's party.[8] More radical even than the Jacobins in some areas, the Girondins failed to define themselves clearly on property. The effect was to leave a vacuum for Robespierre to fill with an eloquent warning of its dangers.[9]

Once property was preserved as a principle of division, there was no shortage of things to succumb to it. There was demography: the provincial Girondins resented Jacobin Parisian cosmopolitanism. There was a royalist uprising in the Vendée and a counter-revolution in the south, which served further to weaken the image of the provincial Girondins. And the corpse of the monarchy still cast a long shadow. Linked inexorably to the allies, the king was little more than a common traitor, and worse, a focus for subversion. In the Convention, democracy had become an instrument of the Jacobins' One Nation and a harbinger of dictatorship: Jacobin rhetoric made the vote on the king's death into a public declaration for patriotism or treason, Left or Right. Finally, sufficient numbers voted against their consciences to get Louis XVI publicly executed in January 1793.

The removal of the monarchy as a fulcrum of division exposed the issue of property and its corollary, poverty. The poor had borne the brunt of economic hardships caused by the war. Within weeks of the king's death emerged the *enragés*, who attacked any moderation and pressed the government for economic action. Neither the Girondins nor the Jacobins who followed, it may be said at once, had much success with poverty — no more than has any bourgeois Left or Right government today. Even so, the Jacobins' strong rhetoric, their affinity for the street, and their rhetorical exploitation of the Girondins won them the weapon of the mob.

By early May 1793, the split between Left and Right showed itself with even greater physical starkness. When the Convention moved out of the *Manège* and into the *Salle des Machines* of the Tuileries Palace, the old circular seating was abandoned for a hemispheric amphitheatre — as if to emphasize the bisection of the Revolution. In their midst, the speaker's bar faced the president's desk, which no longer sat among the people but faced them. Finally, in a geographical metaphor, Left and Right were entrenched for good: the left side of the *Salle*, where the Jacobins stacked up their radicals, became the "Mountain"; the bland Girondin right was called the "Plain"; and, as if to condemn any sort of moderation, the undecided centre were dismissed as the "*Marais*," the "Swamp."

In the primed atmosphere of 1793, the issue of treason could only turn the lowlands that defined the pliable *Marais* into an abyss. Here could be witnessed that perennial and empty tactic of Left and Right, where absolute claims to patriotism from one side impugn the other with the sale of the nation's interests. On June 2, 1793, when the Jacobins accused the Girondins of maintaining ties to the counter-revolution abroad, the Jacobin Club and the *Sections* incited the streets to action. A crowd of 80,000 surrounded the Convention and demanded that it vote for the arrest of the Girondin leaders for treason. The deputies of the *Marais*, intimidated, threw their votes in with the Left and had the Girondin leaders arrested. But the issue of impending dictatorship caused fissures of subdivision within the Jacobins as well. The more cautious, whether for legality, liberty, or public order, formed a new "Right" within the far Left as they entered a struggle for control with the fanatics. Even then, their leader, the Jacobin minister of justice Georges Danton, certainly did not see himself occupying any Right. His position, in his opinion, was revolutionary: to stabilize, centralize, and above all to legalize the Revolution with the institution of a Committee of Public Safety.

To understand how the Jacobin Club got control of a body meant as a non-partisan organ of control and moderation for the preservation of the gains of the Revolution, one must discern the difference between the club and the party. The less radical, more amorphous Jacobin *Party* worked *within* democracy in the Convention; the Jacobin *Club* worked outside. The Club was the corps of human engineers who would remake the Whole Nation as the Left. Danton was a member of the party, not the club. His own club was the populist Cordeliers, and his days were numbered.

The Jacobin Club represented the radical faction of the Jacobin Party everywhere in France. With the fall of the old regime's bureaucracy and the effective abolition of the provincial adminstration, the Club quickly seized the local administrations by attracting the regional élites to its outlying branches, all of them tightly controlled by the mother society in Paris. By the time of the Terror, the mother society sent out *représentants en mission* to oversee purges of the provincial societies. Needless to say, the Jacobin Club did not have to justify itself before the Party, much less to the Committee of Public Safety; rather, it was the Committee of Public Safety that had to justify itself before the Club. If Club, committees, and party could be tailored until all were identical, a single *ecclesia* of believers could presumably mould the Convention and finally the nation in the Jacobins' own image. By such means did the Jacobin Club get moral control of the institutions of the Revolution. And moral control was actual control: a few weeks after the arrest of the Girondins, the Jacobins, with undisputed power in the Convention and a majority on Public Safety, had them executed.

It is perhaps late to ask: how did the Jacobins manage the religious-intellectual feat of conceiving the nation — with its myriad feudal irregularities and conflicts — to be One and Whole? Robespierre's invocation of Rousseau's doctrine of the General Will seems to have helped. An exercise in the coldest reasoning, the General Will was an optimum extracted from the wills of all individuals, in contrast to the Will of All, which was a mere aggregate. The General Will treats people as atoms. For political revolution, which had to simplify society and individual into manageable concepts, the General Will was a perfect, rational synthesis of the "One" of the state, and the "Many" of its citizens. An abstraction, it is more easily understood by philosophy than by politics.

The whole inevitably implies individuals, and that very duality involves abstractions: the whole relies on the use of concepts; the individuals or parts apply to the multiplicity of the physical world. Western philosophy has tended to favour one side of the duality — the conceptual and the whole — as reality: Being, pure and simple.

■

The exaltation of the One over the Many began with a group of philosophers known as the Eleatics. Elea, a Greek colony on the southwest coast of Italy, was, together with Sicily, part of Magna Graecia. Here, as opposed to Greece, a more "Asiatic" Dionysian-Orphic tradition tended to Asian polarities and absolutes, swinging wildly back and forth between oligarchy and aristocracy, rejecting the moderation of democracy. The all-powerful state, a weak idea of the citizen, and terrible wars between local city states conspired to encourage refuge in religion. Moreover, the native Italians had preserved, via the Balkans, something of a spirit-bound Indo-European, Asiatic culture.[10] So thought was volatile; it was here, after all, in the Sicilian city of Kroton, that Pythagoras provoked a violent duality of spirit and matter, and a rationalistic exaltation of number to the point of fetish. The Pythagorean tendency, of course, was to divide, conceptually and mathematically.

The elitist Eleatic and Pythagorean mysticism of classical reason would persist into Christianity, and both would carry forward in disguised forms into Jacobinism. The political clubs of 1789 were full of Pythagorean mysticism and ritual. After all, they had evolved from philosophical societies, and of those the most influential had begun as Freemasons' clubs.[11] It is no coincidence that the Jacobin preoccupation with building a new and perfect society, *tabula rasa*, shares with Freemasonry the symbols of architecture and measurement, especially the set square, the divider, and the Masonic-Pythagorean symbol of the triangle. The mason's level was preserved as a symbol of Jacobin equality, which in turn implied wholeness.

And it was in Elea that the One as an *abstraction* first became significant. Xenophanes of Colophon, in the sixth century BCE, inaugurated this departure into abstraction by condemning all the Homeric gods as anthropomorphic fantasies, naming the unity of all of existence the "One," and naming that One "God." This was an early step in the objectification and breaking up of existence by language. The One of Xenophanes was further elaborated and rationalized by his student,

Parmenides of Elea, and it was in reaction to Heraclitean dynamic pluralism that he developed even further the static idea of the One. This *entity* is founded on the idea that *"Being"* (the Greek *on*) or "is-ness" is all there is. The fateful, cataclysmic moment came, it is said, when Parmenides had a vision: an "ice-cold abstraction-horror caught him, and the simplest proposition treating of 'Being' and 'not being' was advanced by him."[12]

Since "not-being" is a contradiction in terms, there can only be Being. If there is only Being, there can be no empty space. Without empty space there can be no individual parts and no movement, and without movement there cannot be change. Abstract Being was real — the visible world of individual things in motion was false. Henceforward, existence could be broken down into separable concepts. After "being" and "non-being," the third way is the Way of Becoming, the human compromise between Being and Not Being. This is the route of motion, change, and plurality. In the Way of Becoming, opposites are the source of all the world's sensual falsity and illusion. Nevertheless, Parmenides goes on to make his own contributions to the ancient dualities of active and passive, hot and cold, masculine and feminine, dry and wet, not to mention the One and the Many, and right hand and left hand. After all, duality, for Parmenides as for any dictatorial political ideologist, would violate his One. By denying duality, he enshrines it in the very act of defining it and setting it apart. In short "Being" is the whole; and "Non-Being," together with the illusory "Becoming," represents the parts. The Whole and the Parts would come to dominate the conceptual thinking of the West.

The ethereal and absolute nature of this itinerary toward the Whole or the "One" brings us not to Ionia or Attica but inexorably backward into the Central Asian steppe. Parmenides' guide to the worlds of the Sun and Light of Being and the Darkness of Non-Being was a horse-drawn chariot. The horse, in Indo-European imagery, is the engine of the divine; the abiding images of sun and fire are the discovery of truth and falsehood by means of a celestial journey along a specified path; the duality of upper worlds of light and truth and lower worlds of darkness and deception are all distinctly the terms and environment of the shaman.[13] All Parmenides' successor, Eucleides, had to do was say that the *entity* was "Good," and as exalted Whole, Reason, or *logos*, it would become a pole of moral perfection that the illusory parts of existence could never match. It is not far from there to Rousseau's General Will.

After Parmenides and Eucleides, there would arise the opposition between those who supported the Whole in mental constructs and concepts and those who saw material reality first in all its parts. The way of the Whole establishes forever "gradations between Parmenidean poles of light and darkness, of above and below . . . and forms an integral part of early Christianity at the time of St. Paul." The very existence of such polarities, adds Jung, "is incontrovertible proof of the split that had occurred in the original unity of man as a being entirely in the grip of his emotions . . . The ingrained dichotomy of the Greek mind had now become acute, with the result that the accent shifted significantly to the psychic and spiritual which was unavoidably split off from the [material] realm of the body. All the highest and ultimate goals lay in man's moral destination, in a spiritual supramundane end-state, and the separation . . . broadened into a cleavage between world and spirit.[14]

The Jacobin vision of the One Republic is essentially a "moral destination," a matter of spirit, an abstraction that indeed resembles the monistic doctrine of Parmenides — the elimination of difference and plurality in the name of truth.[15] Its architects would constitute the Left; the remainder, the great dross of disordered, unreformed society — the parts — would by default form the Right. Truth and untruth would conform to Left and Right. This was a *monistic* philosophy, which, by exalting a single principle above all others, not only framed falsity as an active opposite but provoked opposition and, in so doing, incarnated the duality it both imagined and tried to abolish.

The Girondins, like Parmenides' "parts," were reduced not only to an opposite force but to a privation, freeing Jacobin rhetoric to bully them into appearing as whatever Falsity it chose. Although they were no wealthier than the Jacobins, their opponents made them out to be the party of greed. With nothing else to defend, their sentiment and ideals were reduced in the public eye to mere survival and materialism. Since the Girondins had less in common among themselves than the Jacobins, the duality was as asymmetrical as the One and the Many of Parmenides. In this sense, the Revolution divided over the Jacobin success in institutionalizing it and the Girondin failure to do so.

But to some minds Left and Right have been not only inevitable but logical — the outcome of a rational, historical process of developmental change known as dialectic. Dialectic, in a sense, is a forward-moving drama in which a virtuous present fights the forces of an evil past and in so doing transforms itself into something new; and then the process starts again. We hear Marxists use dialectic as the axiom that proves their entire argument. In contrast to the coeternal, parallel dualism of mutual exclusion in Zoroastrianism, the dualism of Parmenides has indeed been called dialectical because it develops through rational argument between naturally opposed principles like the One and the Many.[16]

The inventor of dialectic was Parmenides' own student, Zeno of Elea. Zeno was in a sense a founder of the logical process that would come to justify Left and Right. He set out to prove by a rational theory of infinite divisibility an argument which for Parmenides had begun in poetic inspiration. He also came from the Italian colonies. (Where else but in a region intoxicated with religion and experiment could a philosopher argue into existence a theory that already existed?) Dialectical reasoning is thought in motion, and it has become more important for what it is than for where it leads. Even before Parmenides, "it was supposed, on the basis of mathematics, that thought is superior to sense, intuition to observation . . . In various ways, methods of approaching nearer to the mathematician's ideal were sought, and the resulting suggestions were the source of much that was mistaken in metaphysics and the theory of knowledge. This form of philosophy began with Pythagoras."[17] And it passed onward through Parmenides to Zeno.

Dialectic (as it came to be used in ideology) is always founded on some unquestioned axiom and is limited, as Plato himself says, to the intellectual understanding of things and concepts without empirical observation.[18] Its weakness lies in its inability to account for the arrival of new facts.[19] As a science of change, which tames and rationalizes away the unexpected, dialectic has provided immense comfort in charting the chaos of history and society. That is because it deals only with the self-development of single concepts and can only move forward on its own, narrow track — as its etymology suggests: *dia-lect* ("through" speech), literally "the assertion and response of conversation." After all, any conclusion one hopes for can be reached from any point of departure, whether or not the observable facts agree —

precisely because dialectic argues that invisible ideas are at work behind an illusory, visible world. In this it is rather like *eristic*, the art of argument for victory rather than truth. Indeed, "in scope and method, dialectic and eristic are the same."[20]

We complain of the superficiality of *eristic* when we discover issues that don't fall neatly into Left and Right. Dialectical movement between Left and Right and between good and evil must in principle show that every attitude, position, or citizen moving away from its own position will, through inexorable linkage, contaminate its neighbours from good to evil — from the left side to the right side of the old riding school in the Tuileries. Along the same one-dimensional line, capitalism is necessarily connected with racism and fascism, socialism with communism, virtue with the oppressed; even in the face of the fact that there are non-racist capitalists, anti-communist socialists, racist socialists, and the unvirtuous among the oppressed. Like Zeno's matter and space, Left and Right, Whole and Parts, or freedom and authority are treated as horizontal and opposed concepts. This is the heritage of the sacred and profane, the good and evil of the Shaman and the Asian steppe.

It was precisely a penchant for moral abstraction that held the Jacobin Club together. Its members displayed enormous talent within a wide spectrum of classes who had no common material interest. Their power was marked not by economic ideology but by abstract thought and abstract organization, with a bent for the forms of Christian eschatology. Though the members were represented by the "classes who stood for the smaller property owners against the rich and the propertyless, the bond that united them was not class but faith."[21] And that faith was already informed by the Zoroastrian scales of judgement that open the way for Judeo-Christianity.

A sacred history, committed to constant improvement, must separate the future from the past in the same way that it separates good from evil. By 1794 no Jacobin could admit that the Revolution had been started by aristocrats; that the Republic had evolved in a continuum; that the constitutional monarchy of Mirabeau had been necessary, to give form to the first explosions of revolt; that it had been the supposedly conservative Girondins who had the thankless task of ferrying the nation from Monarchy to Republic. But in the "church" of the Jacobins, time itself was a Zoroastrian progression; like the cosmos, like the

nation, it was cut in two: the past was always evil, the future embla-
zoned with the Good, and the present contested. The persistence of
such duality in the face of plurality, humanity, and time itself would
only go to show that *"sociological and economic class oppositions
cannot provide a general explication for dualism. All dualities are necessarily relevant to religious dualism."*22

What exalted the rising present over the fallen past was precisely
action; and, as François Furet writes, in their "laicised version of revolutionary ideology," action "totally encompassed the world of values
and this became the very meaning of life. Not only was man conscious
of the history he was making but he also knew that he was saved or
condemned by that history. That *lay eschatology*, which was destined
to so great a future, was the most powerful driving force of the French
Revolution."23 Whatever it was, it gave the Jacobins unprecedented
power to separate good from evil, the saved from the damned. Spirit
indeed forced itself on matter: "[As] the new electoral alignments
broke the traditional networks within communities . . . only the philosophical societies were in a position to provide the voters with ideas
[and] leadership . . . Ideology was the only principle on which to base
the selection of the 'pure,' that is, the members of a philosophical
society or a manipulating group. It thus functioned as a substitute for
collective experience and for non-existent competition, causing the
assemblies to coalesce around a set of values that integrated only by
means of exclusion. In order to ensure the election of the 'good' it was
necessary to detect the 'wicked' in the light of accepted principles; and
that is why from the very beginning of the Revolution the struggles for
power were characterised by ideological exclusion."24

The religious character maintained by Left and Right even today —
the way they attack, impugn, condemn, excommunicate, and declare
heresies — has its political ancestor in the Jacobins. The Club, its premises, its rituals, its rules, and its political liturgy all copied Christian
forms.25 But not until François Furet wrote these words in the 1970s
was the Jacobins' tissue of religious organization and fervour so clearly
discerned. Like the eschatology of religion, Furet points out, ideology
must trade in simple dualities: "Ideology, in order to move from the
fictitious society of abstract individuals — as embodied in the philosophical society — to real society, had to compose a new society by

excisions and exclusions. It had to designate and personalise the powers of evil . . . Individuals still had to be placed into categories. This was a practical task for which principles were no help at all, since the facts often did not square with them. After all, there were nobles who were patriots and artisans who were not . . . Ideology endows all aspects of society and all institutions, powers and classes with either favourable or nefarious significance, using them as reference points for the militant action that must combat and exclude the wicked in order to recreate in real society the philosophical society's consensus."[26]

After the elimination of the Girondin right, the Jacobins installed their dictatorship. But with the nation theoretically One, a new problem arose. Dualism itself was subject to the infinite divisibility of Zeno, and new gradations appeared within the Left. This time the split was along the fault line of economics; and it was not altogether different from the tension between modern government intervention against inflation from the Right and against unemployment from the Left. In early 1794, to maintain control of the streets and draw power from them, the Jacobins adopted the quasi-socialistic policy of price controls. This provoked a "rightist" reaction within the Jacobin Left of the shopkeepers. From the Right also, and in the name of peace and stability, Danton favoured the relaxing of the Terror and some sort of accommodation with the allied monarchies. The Committee of Public Safety called it treachery. And even Robespierre, to mollify a Right of artisans and small industrialists, sponsored wage controls. This prompted reaction from a Left of wage earners. Lead by the caustic and radical proselytizer and journalist Hébert, they demanded bread. To define his Left boundary, Robespierre had the *Hébertistes* arrested, tried, and executed.

What was the axis of Left-Right division within the Jacobins now? When Robespierre urged the burying of differences in *"une volonté, une,"* it was not just a temporary appeal to some vague chimera of the General Will. The General Will, as One and Reason, had a perfect, fictitious life in the minds of an inner group on the Committee. It was, as we shall see, the abstraction of some narrow optimum of virtue embodied no longer in any particular issue but in some incorporeal idea of the perfect citizen embalmed in the mind of the Committee of Public Safety. Not throne, not property, but an abstract idea of the perfect citizen had become the arbiter of Left and Right.

Lest the infinite divisibility of Zeno go too far and eat into his phantasm of the virtuous citizen from the right, Robespierre had now to define his "right" boundary against Danton. Danton, for all his ethical failings and the corruption of his cohorts, was the last to straddle the chasm between Left and Right. But all his efforts to maintain representation from both Left and Right on the Committee of Public Safety failed. With his departure from the Committee in July 1793, and the exodus of the last moderates from the *Marais* to the safer, if more extreme, confines of the Jacobins, all he had left was his charisma. In March 1794, his efforts at reconciliation with Robespierre were rebuffed; with his execution in April ended any hope of revolutionary unity in the world to come. Danton, in his physical way, might have said with Buddha and Nietzsche, "'Not by enmity is enmity ended, by Friendship is enmity ended' . . . it is *not* morality that speaks thus, it is physiology that speaks thus."[27]

But physiology, the body and matter of the parts of existence, had crumbled before the juggernaut of Robespierre's Jacobin Whole of mind and morality. By May, the split had penetrated inexorably, like an arrow, into the very mind of Jacobin policy: the Committee of Public Safety. Within its inner sanctum there now reappeared a ghost of the "Girondin-Jacobin" personality distinction. The notorious "twelve" were now divided "broadly speaking between the ecstatically devout and the less exacting, more worldly men of affairs,"[28] that is, the Shaman and the Priest.

In 1794, Left and Right were finally formed, not so much by natural bifurcation as by the Left's "militant inclusiveness [which] by definition required outsiders in order to define its limits and to give insiders a sense of their own bonds."[29] In turn, by forging the nation on the model of an exclusive club, "society recomposed itself through ideology . . . recognising only faithful followers or adversaries."[30] Robespierre, loath to acknowledge finer differences to the Left or the Right, would tar all divergences, Left as well as Right, with the single brush of vice, evil, and aristocratic reaction.

One can't help but wonder if Robespierre had tried to *think* the new France into existence. But he could no more abolish the chaotic plurality of post-feudal France than Parmenides could abolish change and motion in that featureless plenum he called the *Entity* or the One.

In Danton and Robespierre reappear the Shaman and the Priest, except that now, the once-dualizing shaman senses danger in a duality too radically rationalized by the priest. Danton, like today's Libertarian right, had accepted the "assemblage" or aggregate that was France and rejected Robespierre's conforming *entity* of the One Republic. But by July 28, 1794, Robespierre's name had become inseparable from the Terror; and so insistent was his idea, that even though the Revolution had factionalized around it, he announced that the cowed Convention, the ever-purged Jacobin Party within it, and the feuding Committees of General Security and Public Safety were still One. In fact, he went as far as to declare some imaginary majority in the silent Convention to be that One — shortly before the Convention turned on him. Zeno's infinite indivisibility had subdivided the Left from both sides, down to the solitary figure of Robespierre himself and the tragic enigma he then represented for France.

After he made a general threat against Left, centre, and Right — the only threat that could be made by a "one" identifying himself with an unworldly Parmenidean One — all factions both in the Convention and in the streets rose against him. As the state, he had separated himself from the people by trying too hard to identify himself with them. Far from blending state and people into a single entity, the Jacobins had formed a religio-political class, preserving doctrine as studiously as any ancient city-state priesthood. Indeed, an otherwise sympathetic witness remarked, "They are just like the old court and aristocracy. They seem to think the people have quite different souls from themselves and are incapable of reasoning as they do."[31] Thus the new duality would fall into the ancient one: the Left would come to be associated with priestly government and the Right with the people.

The fall of Robespierre was the climax of a struggle between opposed concepts: society as it was imagined and society as it really was. The imagined society was conceived as a single entity, conforming to political virtue. The real society was the great, variegated remains of feudal France, which embodied not simply injustice and inequality but also difference and heterogeneity. Two centuries later, the protection of difference from authority would be associated with the Left instead of the Right, one of a succession of developments that would throw the whole duality into question.

5

Symmetry:
The Republic of Terror and Plato's Republic

For all the feeling of crisis, the parting of Left and Right in the *Salle des Menus Plaisirs* did not come into being *ex nihilo*. As simple social protest, the Left had had vague and fragmented forebears since the Middle Ages, but the French Revolutionary Left was the short-lived child of a long history of abstract ideas, while Communism, which expired in 1989 with the last breath of Stalinism, was its final and extreme exemplar. For the origin of the rationalism from which this Left evolved, we have already gone back to the time of Parmenides and his great egalitarian plenum of the *Entity*. Around the same time, it happens, the *Entity* had an actual, concrete forebear: the puritanical and militaristic city state of Sparta.

Sparta provided a peculiar precedent to the powerful philosophy of the *Entity*. *Being*, whole and indivisible, could serve as a metaphor if not as the logical vindication of an idea of the perfect, rationally conceived state. Eucleides, after all, had called *Being* good. Whatever the Spartans actually thought, history's first biographer, Plutarch, later saw in Sparta the political embodiment of rational, political *Virtue*; a civic idea of which his *Life of Lycurgus* would become the source. The *Life of Lycurgus* is in many respects a modern work, for "after the Renaissance political freedom became an issue and the ready source was Plutarch. He influenced French and English liberals of the Enlightenment."[1]

Athens and Sparta were repeatedly evoked in revolutionary speeches; and when Robespierre was asked to describe the kind of constitution he wanted, he replied, bluntly, "That of Lycurgus."[2] Referring to Rousseau's *Social Contract*, he recalled: "The State, in regard to its members, is master of all their goods. The sovereign — that is to say the people — may legitimately take away the goods of everyone, as was done at Sparta in the time of Lycurgus."[3] Altogether, it was a wishful projection of a utopian past on a fallen present, "the core of the illusion" being "the idea of a 'virtuous state' . . . patterned on a school-book model of antiquity that disregarded and went far beyond the objective facts of a civil society."[4] With the aid of the Spartan model, the Left would define itself according to a single theoretical Good — embodied in Plutarch's Sparta — the Right, in terms of a chaotic and less rational congeries of "goods" contained in tradition, custom, superstition, and hierarchy.

The constitution of Sparta, according to Plutarch's myth, was founded by Lycurgus, a noble of the Peloponnesian land of Lacedaemon in southern Greece. Discouraged by the decadence in his own society, Lycurgus brought forth a pure intellectual construct to reform it, and overthrew the established order. First, so Plutarch tells us, Lycurgus created a senate, conceived as a compromise between democracy and monarchy. But still, the people were burdened by "extreme inequality . . . and their state was overloaded with a multitude of necessitous persons, while its wealth had centred upon a very few. To the end, therefore, that he might expel from them that arrogance and envy, luxury and crime and these yet more inveterate diseases of want and superfluity, he obtained of them to renounce their properties and to consent to a new division of the land and that they should live all together on an equal footing; merit to be their only road to eminence, and the disgrace of evil and credit of worthy acts their one measure of difference between man and man."[5] Lycurgus proceeded with a program of land redistribution, outlawed all "needless and superfluous acts," decreed education by the state, and condemned innovation and business. Indeed, the goal of all Spartans was "to make themselves one with the public good, and, clustering like bees around their commander, be, by their zeal and public spirit carried all but out of themselves and devoted wholly to their country."[6]

An irony that will pursue our story down to its very end is that Lycurgus' system is essentially *conservative*. Uncompromising visions, after all, once they are brought off, evolve no further. Like much revolutionary dialectic, they begin with what ought to be rather than what is; and as Camus reminds us, "logic founded on passions reverses the traditional sequence of reasoning and places the conclusions before the premises."[7] In a sense, a utopia is concluded, conserved, before it is even begun. And as with the myth of Lycurgus, its precedents are almost always drawn out of the past. We see it today: wherever the Left has been triumphant, whether briefly in Nicaragua, or for the better part of a century in the Soviet Union, it has grown from visionary historical models and remains as conservative and rigid as any on the Right; and soon, it develops an opposition that can make new claims toward liberty and even equality. It follows that Sparta would become a model not just of the radical Left, but also of the totalitarian Right. It might even be looked upon as a point of departure for both.

The myth does not diverge as sharply from reality as one might think. The lands of the Peloponnesus were settled by Indo-European, Dorian invaders during the "dark age" around the eleventh century BCE, and so the Spartans' Asiatic roots were more recent than those of the indigenous people. Furthermore, the breadth of the Peloponnesian mainland made it more like pastoral Asia — as amenable to invasion as it was to agriculture. The sea-bound peninsula of Athens, on the other hand, prospered by commerce and overseas colonization.

The land-based system that developed out of old Lacedaemon became relatively uniform and it expanded to conquer neighbours such as the Messenians. At some point Sparta put down a Messenian revolt and after a second uprising she became a security state. The Messenians were enserfed, organized into a lower "Helot" class, and bound to the tillage of the land. In this new system, developed to exploit the Helots and keep them in place, we have the prototype of the nation as "Gulag." A controlling upper class was formed by a military caste called the *Spartiates*, while the *Perioeci* came to comprise a middle class of artisans. The *Spartiates*, within their own class, held to a rigorously enforced egalitarianism — the first of its kind. This silent system of control could not have been in greater contrast to the garrulous, chaotic democracy of Athens and its associated freedoms.

By 404 BCE, after Sparta finally crushed the Athenians and imposed a brief oligarchy, a new species of wandering teacher, the Sophists, had appeared in the fallen capital. The sordid Peloponnesian war had depopulated Greece, Athens had passed the peak of her civic glory, and the old, dreaming, naturalistic Milesian philosophies had fallen into disfavour. The Sophist, indeed, was subversive. Neither a pioneer like Thales nor a revolutionary like Parmenides, the Sophist took a practical and critical stance: it was not enough for philosophy to speculate on the cosmos; it had to touch on human behaviour. The most important Sophist was Socrates and, as he wandered in the ruins of human folly, his chief concern was to define, if not to standardize, "excellences of character."

So far, any modern social democrat would agree. But Socrates also introduced the use of definitions — the idea that each thing or value has an ultimate, unchanging form, an ideal to be aspired to. And he made a crucial assumption: that "Virtue," be it only a definition, was immutable and still "out there" somewhere, waiting to be found. There is no evidence that Socrates had any special love for Sparta, but one of his greatest achievements, the attempt to define human virtue, would be used to vindicate the Spartan model. Nor did this pioneering humanist reject abstraction. Plato says that Socrates in his youth met the aged Parmenides when the latter visited Athens, and indeed there is more than a hint of Parmenides in the thought of Socrates. Though far from dogmatic, Socrates attended as much to the rigorous reasoning of the Eleatics, with their enshrinement of the Good in perfect Being, as he did to the day-to-day need to define human virtue.

Within his democratic skepticism, there is a latent moral absolutism. It is, in short, religious. His intuition of immutable Virtue bears a tell-tale trace of the Eleatic axiom that the Good already exists in perfect Being. From there he is bound to share in its dualism; for absolute Virtue, once discovered, must, like Being, have its own negation. In the dualism of salvation and damnation, it turns out, Socrates and the Eleatics share a common source in the ancient Orphic religion of Thrace. Indeed, in his moralism, Socrates has been described as "the perfect Orphic Saint."[8] Like the Orphics, Socrates and the Sophists found themselves in opposition to the official non-moral religion of Olympus. Like the Orphics, Socrates was more interested in perfect, moral solutions than he was in conciliatory methods such as democracy that "muddled through," or in religions that explained rather than instructed. His affinity for absolutes suggested, in turn, an affinity for an absolute society such as Sparta; it was an Athenian democracy, after all, that was to try him for "impiety" and put him to death.

The suspicion that behind our most liberal assumptions there lies an intolerance goes back to a suspicion about Socrates. Nietzsche pulled no punches in mocking the subjectivism that lay behind the Socratic mask of objectivity: "This was the *falseness* of that great ironic, so rich in secrets; he got his conscience to be satisfied with a kind of self-trickery: at bottom, he had seen through the irrational element in moral judgements."[9] No matter what, the definition of the perfect Good was bound to be somebody's particular idea.

Today, whenever Left or Right exalts its particular Good as the unifying term of the nation, it becomes the term that splits the nation. In February 1794, Robespierre desperately imposed a simple standard of classical Virtue that appeared to be neither his own nor even the Jacobins' creation but to stand by itself as a marvel of nature. It wasn't just for moral focus; Virtue was the ballast to fix once and for all a central course between backsliding to the Right and the excesses of the Left. But just as Parmenides, in trying to transcend earthly opposites with his Entity, would provoke a duality between matter and spirit, so Robespierre's sword of virtue reinforced the spectrum of Left and Right that surrounded him, eventually causing it to close on him like a vice.

For Robespierre, the philosophy had come from Rousseau, the myth from Plutarch, the model from Sparta, and the founding concept of Virtue from Socrates. But it was Socrates' great student who would be held responsible for using the Spartan model to make a prototype for its realization in worldly reality. For "Sparta became the chief historical source of the ascetic and authoritarian ideals which are at work in Plato's Republic and its philosophical followers."[10] Perhaps it was in a moment of Enlightenment idealism that, despite his cautious pluralism, Montesquieu wrote, "I am not one of those who regard Plato's Republic as wholly ideal and imaginary, something impossible to create in practice."[11]

Whenever we have a dark intuition that somehow our politics, moderate or radical, is a dreary dead-ended compromise, it is almost as if that impatient desire for the absolute were something atavistic from the ancient steppe. The enduring power of the Indo-European–Asiatic-Eleatic strain is haunting, all the more so when we consider that its purveyors in Western philosophy were mostly unaware that they continued to be its carrier.

For all Plato's sophistication, the Indo-European strain is betrayed most explicitly in his *Phaedrus*, the parable of the Black and White Horses. The steeds that draw the chariot of the Gods are white pure-breds; the horses of the lower, material world are black — of mixed blood, stunted and inferior. The mind of man, Plato tells us, is a chariot discordantly drawn by a white horse of the Gods and a black horse from the world below. In Indo-European Vedic eschatology, no less, we discover the pure-bred white stallion of good and the misshapen black stallion of evil. The white stallion Trishtrya causes the clouds to take up water from the steppe and return it in salutary rainfall; and Apaosha, the hideous black stallion, will fight Trishtrya to inflict drought if man does not reform himself.[12]

And so it was in vain that Plato tried to get away from Parmenides. Impressed as he was by the Entity, he may not have been able to digest its complete denial of apparent reality. But where else could he go? Here, amid the moral and social decay of Athens, was the voice of one dead master, Parmenides, saying there was great Good but no material reality; and an even more dead and older master, Heraclitus, describing a vivid material reality, yet unable to hold up any single Good. But then his teacher Socrates provided him with a theory of Good founded on human rather than on natural or metaphysical ideas and which, moreover, seemed to reconcile the Mind of Parmenides with the Matter of Heraclitus. But not for long.

Despite his brilliance, the author of the *Republic* ended up following his master in the search, not for the truth wherever it lay, but for a redeeming moral absolute — while Reason, as always, provided a cover of dispassionate enquiry. In his quest to transfigure and freeze perfect definitions, Plato developed from Socrates the assertion that "thought . . . responds not to things but to what things have in common, that which is always there, unchanging," whereas what is different decays. The things held in common are shared qualities or "The Ideas." Here, in the hard nugget of the Perfect Ideas, is the point where the shaman, the Indo-European axiom, raises its head. With an eerie insistence, Asiatic thought, absolute and abstract — underground with the Orphics, marginal with the Eleatics and discreet, indeed dormant as a virus, in Socrates — fully enters the mainstream of Western philosophy with Plato's doctrine of the Ideas.

Plato was careful of course not to deny motion, change, and matter, as did Parmenides. Rather, sensible reality became a *weak shadow* or *derivation* from the brilliant *Being* of the world of the Ideas. Correct behaviour, no less than reality itself, was *deduced* from the Ideas rather than *induced* from our experience. Now he had to distinguish between those to whom these Ideas were more accessible — and the ignorant. And there arose a corresponding tripartite class system of "Knowers," "Believers," and "Ignorant" (not unlike the three ways of Parmenides), concealing a discrete duality between the top one and the bottom two: rulers and ruled — squarely in the tradition of the tripartite class division of the Indo-European steppe.

The wise who ruled would maintain that qualities, like the ideas, were held not individually but in common, making the community superior to its parts: "We may therefore find justice on a larger scale in the larger entity and so easier to recognize. I accordingly propose that we start our inquiry with the community, and then proceed to the individual and see if we can find in the conformation of the smaller entity anything similar to what we have found in the larger."[13] It is only a short conceptual step from there to the assertion that the perfect Idea of Justice is to be found in the state rather than in the individual. Already we have a foreshadowing of Rousseau's General Will.

And from the past there is an echo of Parmenides, the more so when Plato tells us that "when the institutions of society make it most utterly one, that is a criterion of their excellence than which no truer or better will ever be found."

Athenian: "One of these portions of the universe is thine own, unhappy man, which, however little, contributes to the whole; and you do not seem to be aware that this and every other creation is for the sake of the whole, and in order that the life of the whole may be blessed; and that you are created for the sake of the whole and not for the sake of you. For every physician and every skilled artist does all things for the sake of the whole, directing his effort toward the common good, executing the part for the sake of the whole, and not the whole for the sake of the part."[14]

Plato's ideal republic is to be ruled by Virtue, that elixir of the Good extracted from the Many; and the rulers are that gifted few with access to knowledge of that Good from the Ideas in perfect Being. This is the Guardian class. Moreover, the Guardians must abjure private property and live an austere, egalitarian, communal existence with mental and physical training to perfect themselves in the art of governing. Protecting the Guardians and the Republic are those skilled in the art of war: the Warrior class. And all are to be fed by a lower class of Producers. The state, guarantor of this order under the guidance of the Guardians, must be the object of everyone's first loyalty, before family or friendship; and prior to conscience or independent thought.[15]

Every ideology implies a model citizen, from the patriotic working man to the politically correct activist. In Plato's model, proper citizens are obtained through selective breeding. Failure to breed the right populace will allow lower values of "Iron and Bronze" to pull toward corrupting private property and away from higher Gold and Silver and the true knowledge of the good. And there will be civil war.[16] Here is a crude prototype of modern Left and Right — and of the civil war that threatened Robespierre if his ideal of Virtue were not upheld.

If Parmenides had implied dualism in the rejection or acceptance of his One, Plato had brought it down to earth — projecting an intellectual duality onto the world — although he would likely have denied that his system was dualistic. But his own pupil, Aristotle, saw this radicalizing dualism as a departure from Socrates. The Socrates who gave us inductive argument and universal definitions, after all, "did not make the universals or the definitions exist apart; his successors, however, gave them separate existence, and this was the kind of thing they called Ideas."[17]

Plato's dualism has endured, and, though it was too late, he himself began to question it in his later works. In *The Parmenides* he has his eponymous forebear say: "The significance of things in our world is not with reference to that other world, nor have those their significance with reference to us, but as I say, the things in that world are what they are with reference to one another; and so, likewise are the things in our world."[18] In trying to frame a more radical dualism between words and things, he was, in effect, trying to release the world from it. In Bertrand Russell's formulation, "words . . . apply only to the form, not to the matter of propositions. Here again, we find that logic and mathematics are peculiar. Plato, under the influence of the Pythagoreans, assimilated other knowledge too much to mathematics."[19]

But after Plato had given Virtue or the Ideas a social meaning, there was no going back. In true, shamanic, Indo-European tradition, there persists in Virtue and the Ideas the axiom whence the reasoning began: he has Socrates say in *The Meno*, "Virtue is neither natural nor acquired, but an instinct given by God to the virtuous."[20] From there all the consequences descend. We have only to think of the Christian Right in America and its Platonic axioms in scripture; the Politically Correct and their conversion of eternal subjectivity into the starting point of an elite doctrine of the New Left; and, of course, of Robespierre's attempt to find an optimum moral authority in the cult of the Supreme Being. Plato's mandatory conformity of public worship and condemnation of private worship as *impiety* lies at the root.

In every case ideas rule; it is the logical consequence of a system that, from the Orphics, exalted the mind and condemned the body until in Plato it held the body to be the actual pollutant of the mind.[21] It is the intolerance of the all-powerful concept that makes it both metaphysically and socially dualistic. Wherever it goes, it creates its own unified opposition. So it was that in Plato, "the original suave wisdom expressed in the Pythagorean pairs of opposites became a passionate moral conflict."[22]

This contempt for real life in the shadow of the intellect lies at the heart of the *Republic*. And the discordance between the idea of society and real society would endure in Western thought. Two millennia later, the Terror of the French Revolution would disclose itself not only as the sacrifice of mere society to the idea of a republic, but as "the state conceiving itself as its own end because it had no roots in society; it was the state alienated from society by ideology."[23] If the excision of the real from the ideal followed Plato almost exactly, the knife that performed it was Virtue.

Virtue cannot compromise. During the Terror, Jacobin puritanism penetrated everywhere: in cafés, in newspapers, in republicanized rituals of birth, death, and marriage, in games, in clothing, in design as much as in personal habit and social intimacy. This impossible formula of aesthetics, morality, and legalism — the attempt, through the impregnation of matter with mind, to hold the course between an even more fanatical Left and an indulgent Right — became impossible to enforce.

While it lasted, however, it was a remarkable achievement. At enormous cost, the shadow of a just Republic — "the economic ideal of Robespierre and his fellows . . . a sort of greengrocer's paradise where no one would be very rich and no one very poor,"[24] appeared perhaps for a few weeks. Under the dispassionate gaze of its ruler, the French Republic finally had its Guardian class in the Committee of Public Safety; its Warrior class in the Commune and National Guard; its Producers in the *Sans Culotte*. For a moment, perhaps, even the "false factionalism" of Left and Right was relegated to the illusory opposites of Parmenidean "non-being." It began with the mind and ended with action; and mind, as the first Greek philosophers have shown us, is not far from mysticism.

It has been said in the twentieth century that everything begins in mysticism and ends in politics. Virtue was finally and most nakedly revealed as an instrument rather than a substantial goal — as emissary rather than political exemplar — when, after dividing France, it divided the last and highest authority itself, Public Safety, between radical shamans and more cautious priests. Not only did the Terror provoke secessions from Left and Right, leaving Robespierre alone in the middle, but it finally shifted the duality to an entirely different axis, between Robespierre and the people: "The French people was nothing like Robespierre imagined. It was not all compact of goodness; it was not peculiarly governable by reason; it was not even a unitary thing at all."[25] The truth of the Terror lay precisely in the fact that Virtue turned out to be an instrument of division rather than consensus. No more real or practical than the optimum of Socrates or the Ideal of Plato, it remained without content, narrow, indeed sharp as a blade. Robespierre's ideologue St. Just said as much when he declared: "What constitutes the Republic is the destruction of everything opposed to it."[26] How much closer could you get to the Parmenidean *entity* of intellectual being that denied everything that it itself was not?

In June 1794 the Laws, or *Prairial*, made all offenses that came before the Revolutionary Tribunal punishable by death. In the last weeks before Robespierre's fall, about fifteen hundred lost their heads at the guillotine, a number that does not include the masses that perished by execution in the provinces. Like a sword that cuts — rather than the abode that might encompass — Virtue would divide right from left, people from politicians, society from ideology. The Terror was Plato's *Republic* in action.

It is perhaps needless to mention that in the *Republic* the death sentence makes its first appearance as a political corrective. As the Enlightened Guardians rule, they discover that the rest, poorly equipped with reason, will continue to do wrong even as they are taught; the only remedy for the truly incorrigible is their elimination, and punishment in the next life becomes the *Republic*'s final goad. It is not just through the duality of mind and matter in the *Republic* that we are haunted by the Asiatic steppe. It is also through the *Republic* that the old, Vedic sanctions of Heaven and Hell — as reward or punishment for embracing mind or matter — would enter Western civilization, its politics as well as its religion, with protean and enduring force. "In Plato," Hannah Arendt remarks, "we find for the first time not merely a concept of final judgement about eternal life or eternal death, about rewards and punishments, but the geographical separation of Hell, Purgatory and Paradise as well as the horribly concrete notions of graduated bodily punishment."[27]

If Plato thought he had devised a clever fiction to shore up the Republic and the observation of its laws, he had only brought to the surface the ancient, subterranean stream of Orphism. The Orphic rite seems to have retained an unconscious presence in the Greek mind and it was, as we know, Asiatic and likely Vedic. Asia, indeed, seems to be the crux. For it is in an Eastern offshoot of the Vedic religion, the religion of Zoroaster, that Mithra stands athwart the bridge over the valley of death and judges the dead, allowing the select few to pass onward and throwing the unredeemable majority to their perdition. A version of the same eschatology descends from Asia into Pythagoras, a contemporary of Parmenides. And now, in Plato, "there were, close to each other, two gaping chasms in the earth, and opposite and above them two gaping chasms in the sky. Between the chasms sat Judges, who having delivered judgement, ordered the just to take the right-hand road that led up through the sky, and fastened the evidence for judgement in front of them, while they ordered the unjust, who also carried the evidence of all they had done behind them, to take the left-hand road that led downwards."[28]

And so it is that Hannah Arendt cautions: "In view of the enormous influence these tales have exerted upon the images of hell in religious thought, it is of some importance to note that they were originally designed for purely political purposes."[29] In France, and in all revolutions that followed, the political Right would become "hell"; or, if the Right prevailed, the chasm of the damned would lie on the Left. These are the respective abodes of the enemies and avatars of the Republic. From the Left, all resistance was explained by the single aristocratic plot, which "appealed . . . to a religiously oriented moral sensibility that had always seen evil as the work of hidden forces."[30] On the margins of the new Republic, evil lurked, no more frank about itself or visible than the spirits that gibbered in the twilight world of the shaman. The Terror, once again, "was the product not of real struggle but of the Manichaean ideology that would separate the good from the wicked."[31]

This, lest we forget, was not ultimately Platonic but "Parmenidean thinking," which, says Karl Jaspers, "became the resting place of an attitude of thought rooted in faith. The thinkers of this type supposed that in cogent thought they possessed the bodily presence of being and in a valid idea the absolute truth. They concluded that this gave them the right to repress by violence any other thinking that might lay claim to the truth."[32] Since then, as Heidegger observed, "the differentiation of *essentia* (essentiality) and *existentia* (actuality) completely dominates the destiny of Western History determined by Europe."[33] Modern politics, would, as Plato had done, sacrifice any real meaning in the sensible world to the absolute ends of the world of Ideas. It emerges that the very system of Left and Right is atavistic, itself a system of belief.

How far this world is from the old Chinese way. At the very time of Parmenides, noble-born Chinese bureaucrats were compelled to rule under the worldly constraints that inspired Confucius. It was a society not greatly happy or prosperous, but at least it was stable and not at metaphysical war with itself; it was a society where "the harmonious cooperation of all beings arose, not from the orders of a superior authority external to themselves, but from the fact that they were all parts of a hierarchy of wholes forming a cosmic pattern, and what they obeyed were the integral dictates of their own natures."[34]

The greatest tragedy, perhaps, is that in the West since 1789, the external and superior authority idealized by the Left and the inferior, unenlightened masses that it names Right have been, like Plato's ideas and shadow world, not at all the same kinds of thing. And so it was that in the earliest stages of the Revolution, Left and Right were at their most real as "political" and "non-political," or "left" and "not left." After all, the royalist counter-revolution did not embrace all of those whom St. Just would have eliminated as "not the Republic." Rather, the "right" was that great human mass which, like the sensory world of Parmenides, could not quite correspond to Virtue, much less comprehend it. And Virtue, being an instrument rather than a model of substance, was not something that they could conceptually oppose. But the very rationalistic symmetry of Plato would, in Virtue and in the modern world, elevate Left and Right into opposing camps.

6

Singularity:

Bonaparte, Aeneas, and the Power of the Past

In revolutions, new rights and freedoms have tended to be more enduring than economic changes. As the Right has come to absorb the protection of freedoms, economic equality has come to distinguish the continuing struggle of the Left. With the cutbacks of the 1990s, we have seen how the rights-based legislation of rightish Liberal Democrats has lasted longer than left-wing economic regimes. Indeed, historically, socialist policy arrives as a fully fledged plan and is usually displaced as a whole. It is much slower than rights and freedoms to become part of culture or habit.

With the French Revolution, likewise, an old Left of liberty and rights would become the Right, outliving a Left of economic equality. With the fall of Robespierre, that Left of economic restraint, which had arrived as a rational unit, was almost as neatly and summarily removed. But the society that its removal exposed was *not* an opposing Right. It was the half-standing ruin of France minus a monarchy, while somewhere in the chaos lay the seeds of a new, economic duality. What germinated spontaneously from that rubble was the combined impulse of the wage-earning *enragés* and the dandified bourgeois of the *jeunesse dorée*, who briefly joined forces in street battles against Jacobin holdouts. This was a wild duality of nature, not of reason or of religion — though reason and religion would return to haunt it and name it once again: a "Right" associated with money and a "Leftish" class of wage earners.

Still, Jacobinism was not communism, and the extravagant reaction of high style and sexual license against its puritanism was not capitalist decadence; it was, rather, a diametrical reaction against Jacobinism. The concepts "capitalist" and "communist" were not yet in people's minds. Still, there was a new industry: the revolutionary wars. Military contractors led the new business class, and the stock market exploded onto the scene as a source of capital. As ostentation blossomed, deepening poverty was the more painfully felt. Speculation, seen as a moral failing in the party of Danton, had now become a social problem.

The caretaker government that oversaw this transition was the Directory, which consisted of five adept administrators. Canny rather than visionary, the Directors pursued a golden mean between the fury of the surviving Jacobins and the simmering of recessive Royalists; to do so, the five leaned both Right and Left. Economically *laissez faire*, they allowed the quiet prevalence of money. The result was a bourgeois republic that provided stability on the surface while sustaining extremes of Left and Right, inherited and resurgent, in dangerous discontent.

At the fulcrum where the throne had been, the Directory had placed gold. Nothing, it turned out, could better disinter a religious instinct to divide, to polarize, to hate. If the Right of money did not quite yet have the name "Capitalist," it was certainly implied when, in the spring of 1795, a mass delegation of the poor, organized by Jacobins and demanding bread at the doors of the Convention, was repelled with military force. Those poor still had no representation. The inheritors of the Convention that overthrew Robespierre resembled their executive in the Directory; they were a lukewarm stew of middle-of-the-road Left and Right, but above all, men of means. Anxious to perpetuate themselves, they had made a law that most of the members of the two new legislative councils (the "Ancients" and "the Five Hundred") slated to replace the Convention would be drawn from among their own numbers. In the fall, the old *sections* rose up in a desperate hybrid conspiracy of hungry Left and disenfranchised Royalist Right — united by an absence of democracy. On the steps of the church of Saint-Roche they were repelled — this time by cannon-shot, point blank.

From the moment of that cannonade, Left and Right would be put into hibernation for twenty years by the return of an older and larger duality: authority and freedom. For Right and Left, as we will discover, are secondary, modern distinctions that always blend into one when primordial authority returns either to unite them, drug them, or alienate them — and freedom once again becomes their common dream. If anarchy — at the disintegration of the Estates General and again at Thermidor — is their place of gestation, authority is their perennial dissolution. Anarchy, if only a moment or a mental state, is always a place of hope, innocent of dualism. That is why Left and Right were blissfully absent upon the promise of a new society on the eve of the fall of the Soviet Union and returned with demented fury as a radical free market forced the hand of politics. The former Soviet Union is indeed living through the Left and Right of its "Directory." And many Russians are hoping to find their "Napoleon" in Vladimir Putin.

The officer who ordered the cannonade at the behest of the Directory was of course Napoleon himself, an unknown gunnery commander then known only as Bonaparte. And with republican authority a new element in the field of Left and Right arrived — individualism — the cult of the leader, unqualified by class, blood, or political party. In short, the naked, individual will. (English individualism, as we shall see, is a very different matter.) Though a moderate Jacobin, Bonaparte would oppose individual authority to the collective One of the Jacobin Republic.

The Enlightenment was not just a rational, democratic revolution; it had at the same time a romantic, non-rational aspect that hurled forward the individual. The first modern philosopher of the solitary will was Johann Fichte, a product of that broad force, which embraced the German Romantics, the romantic poets, and also Rousseau. To Fichte, reality begins with the ego, which is itself everything.[1] Pure reason, and with it all reality, can come only from the perceiving individual, who becomes, *ipso facto*, the sole point of reference and therefore the supreme authority. The individual, no longer objectified in a social class or metaphysical order, is an independent agent of change, willing and free — self-created. With Fichte, Kant's injunction to moral responsibility, "Do what you will," is transformed into, "Become the person that you are."[2] As the heroic *ego* made its way into political consciousness, Left and Right would come to seem like rather static, almost theological distinctions, which paled beside the individual's historical memory and emotion long nourished by the eighteenth-century cult of Sensibility. And it was memory and emotion that France craved in the hangover of Revolution.

The Corsican was just what the Directors needed to bolster their popularity. In sending General Bonaparte to liberate Italy from the Austrian monarchy, the Directory played into a grand complex of heroic, historical metaphors that inspired revolutionary France with ancient republican Rome. It also represented a shift from Greek delicacy and democratic practice to Roman simplicity and muscle. The subsequent victories in northern Italy could now be seen as a metaphorical restoration of the free, ancient Roman Republic. In the future, however, this heroic liberation would be accompanied by ideological ambivalence — for Left and Right, never quite destroyed by authority, would be half-reconciled by it and then frozen.

In looking back at the Roman Republic, we are venturing into the dawn of an authoritarian tradition that was properly neither Left nor Right but would come to influence both. Rome's farthest-reaching, darkest legacy will be fascism, which, as we shall see, is likewise more about pure power than it is about economics, individualism, or collectivism. The tradition of authoritarianism — a modifier of both Left and Right and sometimes a synthesis transcending the two — has felt the heavy presence of the Caesars even down to the ethnic fascism of the end of the recent century. So, for the sake of simplicity, let us look at the legacy of Rome as the legacy of a "third force," neither Left nor Right. This "third force" in its less malignant form embodies a tradition in which empires, including even the American economic "empire" of today, gain wealth or territory by synthesis and assimilation rather than by military occupation. Its justification, "for the benefit of all," even underwrites the modern free market.

The Romans intruded upon and assimilated the older Mediterranean Etruscan world much as the Dorian Spartans had overrun the old Achaean-Ionian civilization.[3] The resulting fusion featured indigenous and feminine Etruscan extravagance in rites of sex and death, gladiatorial games, literacy, sophistication, and an organized priesthood; and on the other hand, self-reliant Latin hardiness, "manly" virtues, military endurance, and peasant simplicity;[4] primordially and crudely, they are, respectively, "Left" and "Right." The latter force was the active force and it was Indo-European.

This archaeology of ideology brings us face to face with the germination of an empire that H.G. Wells described as an "expanded Aryan republic;"[5] for Roman rites, symbols, and beliefs — and, not least of all, migrations — do take us repeatedly back to northern Asia.[6] Further, "the roots from which all [the] features common to the Greek and Roman assemblies originated, can be traced more exactly in observing the same characteristics in another environment, where the archaic culture of the old Indo-European stock-breeder societies . . . was preserved almost intact until the 18th century, isolated from the southern world of culture: [for example] the mounted shepherds of northern Asia."[7] And the Aryan strain was borne forever in the symbol of the oak tree, sacred both to the people of the steppe and the emperors of Rome. Vesta, the Aryan goddess of the tribal hearth, became the goddess of the Roman hearth, and oak was the fuel for her ceremony.

The Indo-European ancestors of the Latins migrated from Asia into the Danube basin in the early second millennium BCE and proceeded, as the pastoral, Aryan Terramaricoli, to settle among the indigenous people of Latium around 1000 BCE.[8] Another wave of pastoralists joined the native peoples and the Aryan settlers, and they were followed by a growing coalescence of outcasts, exiles, and refugees from surrounding tribes. The receptiveness of the founding Aryan-neolithic culture to these arrivals seems to lie at the root of the Romans' talent for synthesis of dualities, and later, universalism. That is, rather than distinguish itself from others, Rome will *lay claim* to other peoples.

If we think of the Left as planners and the Right as individual agents of chance, the founding sagas of Sparta and Rome fit the pattern. Lycurgus' simple, rational formation of Sparta, as given by Plutarch, contrasts starkly with Virgil's *Aeneid*, the great mythological synthesis that reveals much of Rome's ideology. In this departure from the Greek *logos*, Virgil's adventuring hero Aeneas, resorting to a destiny of the Fates that is more personal, non-rational, and Olympian than that of

Plutarch's hero, begins to resemble a modern protagonist of individualism. As a patriot of sacked and pillaged Troy in Asia Minor, he is led westward by the winds and spirits of Fortune to found a new "Troy" in Latium. While in Plutarch's *Lycurgus* the state is conceived as a radical plan, the *Aeneid* is conservative in the sense of being a story not just of fate but of nostalgic recovery. By the authority of antiquity, Romans as "primordial Trojans" could lay claim both to the Latin peasants and to the sophisticated Etruscans who had brought Greek culture to Italy. After all, that which lay eastward, as past and point of origin, was regarded as sacred, superior.

A strong topological feature re-emerges here. In the development of Western civilization, the Greek mainland forms an axis, a centre. Everything to the east is older — its points of origin in Troy, in Asia Minor, and Mesopotamia. All to the west is newer and wilder. According to the old Indo-European schema, Aeneas heads for the west, the land of the setting sun, the abode of the dead in the Elysian fields. It will be recalled that the destination of death (and hence rebirth) inclines toward the left, western, profane hand; home, the point of departure in the east of the rising sun, on the sacred right hand. Moving from Troy to Latium, from known to unknown, from sacred into profane, from right to left, Aeneas in effect moves westward to sanctify the profane and barbaric with civilization.

Upon his arrival at Cumae in Italy, an oracle commands Aeneas to descend into Hell — to the Elysian fields and the land of death — to get a certain golden bough that secures him passage across the Styx and finally into Hades. Emerging from Hades, he confronts Juno, Latium's protective feminine deity. His own protector is Jupiter — the Aryan version of the patriarchal sky-God. Aeneas triumphs, and the king of Latium is killed. The Golden Bough is effectively the symbol of heroic, *de facto* usurpation and possession — but also assimilation.

In the *Aeneid*, duality is stacked upon duality: sacred and profane, masculine and feminine on top of east and west. In victory, however, Rome does not annihilate or replace; it synthesizes this stack of dualities, term by term. Moreover, in its duality we may detect ancestors, however ghostly, of both a spirit-driven, non-rational, shamanic and individualistic "Right" and a rational, priestly, bureaucratic "Left." In every case, the former will absorb the latter. Obviously, the *Aeneid* is

101

propaganda: a dogged and linear quest with a single hero-protagonist to whom the author is partial in a way Homer never was to his own heroes. With Aeneas, all is individual, all sacrificed toward duty, egoistic ambition — hell-bent subject driven toward object.

A crucial function of the new synthesis is violence; and Rome's enduring paradox will be an oscillation between justice and brute force.[9] True to the type of Aeneas, usurpers would always arrive as individuals, as outcast adventurers — indeed, as murderous *arrivistes*.[10] Here is the "putschist" Right, the tough Right. Nowhere is killing as a political act legitimized as it is in Roman myth. We need only look at Virgil's account of Romulus and Remus, the twin heirs to Aeneas' Latium. The wall they build is circular; it still encloses, does not yet divide. But when they fight over whose augury indicates he should be king, Romulus kills Remus and takes the crown. At the foot of a sacred oak containing the spirit of Jupiter, Romulus marks off a squared space or "sacellum": inside it is the site of the sacred, consecrated to the temple to Jupiter. Outside lurks the profane.

Romulus' demarcation of the *sacellum* or sacred space for an altar at the foot of the oak recalls the Vedic Aryan symbolism of the boundary delineated on holy ground by a single furrow ploughed around an altar — distinguishing sacred from profane. Likewise, in the Indo-European Latin of early Rome there persists the sacral-linguistic connotations that we have already seen in Left and Right; the profane, as with the Aryans, drifted on the left — *sinistra*, from which we derive "sinister"; *dexter*, from which come many Latin derivatives for "straight" and "law," stood for the right hand. The difference in Rome is that the enclosing furrow of the *sacellum* (as opposed to the straight line) will transfer a lateral duality of Right and Left to a duality of within and without. That all inside this furrow was sacred and everything outside it profane anticipates another furrow ploughed by Romulus to mark off Rome itself.

And yet the boundary serves as a symbol for synthesis as well as for separation; and the Aryan line of separation is transformed to express the idea of a "contract" — which is itself the perfect compromise between union and separation, the whole and its parts. Among the Romans, contract was indeed the essence of the institution of citizenship. In one of the primal myths of citizenship, for example, Romulus' attempt to seize the Sabine women is turned (once again) to synthesis when he accepts their offer of peace and union. In theory, these were symbols of free confederation; tragically, their very wisdom and ingenuity built a legacy of pure power that would be exploited down to the twenty-first century. For, as we will later see, the legacy of the Caesars and the Empire would initiate a tradition for totalitarian assimilation both on the Left and on the Right. And it is indeed fitting that to give despotic force to Left or to Right, a primordial powerhouse that was neither would be required.

It seems evident by now that in Rome the Sacred was territorial and, instead of dividing, it would lie at the domineering heart of centripetal assimilation. Meanwhile, its emanation in citizenship would help expand the Republic into an Empire. This claim to universality is distinguished precisely by the *lack* of metaphysical dual separation in Roman thought — whether of mind and matter, being and non-being, the whole and the parts — or, most important, of Rome and not-Rome. Further, the distinction of insider and outsider was dissolved not only in citizenship but in myth. Spiritually, the Republic was held together by the mortar of the *numina*, the household gods of the Aryans of Latium, which haunted thresholds, wells, and other features of domesticity, not to mention the sacred oak.[11] In wedding these *numina* of intimate daily life with Aryan divine forces and Greek Olympian personalities, the Romans took what was immediate and practical, and made it universal.[12]

With time and space secured in the intimacy of the Roman hearth, it was as if the microcosm of the Roman household and family expanded to contain the macrocosm of the universe. This is the utter contrary of the Parmenidean abstract One and illusory Many. The legacy of the *numina* would be the very hard, real world of the many individual households making up the Good, the One, the Empire. It follows that an equal legacy of omens, evil *numina*, cannot lie *outside* a principle that lays claim to the cosmos. Rather than being a separate kingdom of darkness as in Zoroastrianism, or a Hell of *non-being* or ignorant lower classes as in Platonism, in Rome evil spirits are mundane and omnipresent. Evil takes on the ancient, paleolithic character of a defect, or infection, *within* a body or within a universal polity. Left moves from frontal opposition to internal defect.

Universalism, therefore, implies a duality without boundary or moiety: precisely the *annihilation* of the other by assimilation.[13] The ultimate legacy of such universalism, passing forward into Christianity and modern Europe, suggests not conquest and subjugation but rather the inward aggression of extermination — that is, the extermination of what would not assimilate.[14]

Lest we forget, a more primal, but antiquated dualism of Rome was the dualism that opposed Republic to Monarchy. The founding act had been Rome's forcible ejection of Etruscan Tarquins. And so, we must not forget that underlying the Imperial, concentric duality of Rome and citizen was a primordial opposition of republic to kings and people to tyrants.

The sacred, monarchist Right of Revolutionary France was slower to fade than was its Roman precursor — even with its absorption and synthesis under Napoleon. The Royalists put up a lengthy last-ditch stand alongside the new Right of money. As the century closed, a general monarchist resurrection produced a conservative majority in the Convention. By means of "an excellently organised clerical-royalist political machine . . . the conservatives were at last learning the ways of practical politics."[15] Monarchists, too, could appeal to democracy. As the Directors scrambled to please Left and Right only to please neither, the instability encouraged another Royalist plot. A failing economy conspired with military reversals to produce a Jacobin resurgence as well. The executive coup that shifted the collection of five faces a little away from the Right was probably intended to placate the Left. But by now, "coups d'état had come to be the accepted means of achieving political change, of redressing a balance bent too heavily to the Right or Left."[16] Oscillation was the harbinger of synthesis.

The Directory's new, moderate-left appointee for the crisis was the enigmatic veteran revolutionary, the Abbé Sièyes. He sought to broker a balance, but a past of Royalist plots, Jacobin tyranny, poverty, and bourgeois corruption haunted his every move. There now appeared, perhaps for the first time in our chronicle of Left and Right, a feeling well known to today's expedient politics of sound-bites, fast issues, and vague discontent: a general repudiation of Left and Right alike. The

French public, still dogged by the ghost of Robespierre, reviled both Directory and legislature for their leftward shift. Politics was breaking down; if neither Left nor Right nor even Sièyes's rather sly, esoteric Centre was working, what remained?

As France watched Napoleon strike victory after victory among the palms at the Pyramids, at Alexandria, over the turbaned Mamelukes at Aboukir, the atavistic emotional power of the individual and of history on the grand scale of civilization took hold. It touched Napoleon himself. In Egypt he felt the hand of his conquering predecessors Alexander the Great and Caesar, while a French public sick to death of politicians longed for the same touch. More than ever, Left and Right would pale into mere technical terms, as they still can today — before the temptations of glory.

In the fourth century BCE, that same disillusionment, which thirsts for great deeds rather than great ideas, was brewing in the eastern Mediterranean. While the Roman Republic was still young, the war between Athens and Sparta had precipitated the decline of the city state, and with this decline the field of great classical concepts became barren. Now, practical, conservative, individualistic philosophies grew in reaction to the perceived follies of the collective state and its Platonic conformity of duty and belief. In the wake of Plato, Antisthenes, the founder of the Cynics, eschewed abstraction, wholes, and collectivities in favour of a wholesale endorsement of the "things" of existence, right down to the state and society itself. A rejection of the two sharply separated concepts of matter and mind was implicit.

In the work of Aristotle this sort of synthetic thinking reached its peak. His thought was conciliatory in conception, comprehensive and universal in intent. He resolved Plato's dualism into a single, contiguous, material hierarchy that arranged all of existence in a single structure from low and primary to great and complex. There was less of the Parmenidean division that we find in Plato between the whole in mind and the parts in matter. The material world, once the means to the end of the Ideas, now became the end for which the Ideas were the *means*. In attacking the infinite perfection of ideas and absolutes in Plato, Aristotle salvaged *limit* — a crucial element of pre-Socratic genius.

In Aristotle, the precise limits of form describe the perfection of the organism. So if the Good was the *limited*, evil lay in the *unlimited*. No great unified concept would ever again arise with the facility that it had with Plato.

Moreover, Aryan tribal individualism was to re-enter history. Philip of Macedon had built an empire on powerful tribal values, although the influence of his sophisticated son Alexander was more cosmopolitan and synthetic. Alexander, after all, was a pupil of Aristotle, and his own reign coincided with a rejection of extremes in classical thought (foreshadowing a similar conciliation of Left and Right under Napoleon). With the individualism of the north-Asian tribalism of Macedon, Alexander brought *action* and *purpose* in contrast to static Platonic *Being*. As Northrop Frye so expressively describes it, the philosopher "worked out the organon of a deductive logic based on a theory of multiple causation, and provided a technique for arranging words to make a conquering march across reality, subjects pursuing objects through all obstacles of predicates, as Macedonian phalanxes of his pupil Alexander marched across Asia."[17]

Alexander stood at the summit of a new world in which Aristotle's natural hierarchies and inequalities were transferred into political inequalities, the culmination of which "was the magnificent great-souled man who lived on a grand scale and devoted himself to the pursuit of noble glory . . . the fullest example of a humanistic *arete* [which] represented the ideal of aristocratic individualism."[18] Alexander was in essence a cultural synthesis, itinerant and cumulative. In Greece he combined Indo-European tribal individualism with the cosmopolitanism of the Athenian *polis*; in his Middle Eastern and Asian Empire he initiated a synthesis of Hellenism and Eastern bureaucratic authoritarianism, a sort of enlightened despotism. By his death, his empire stretched from Macedon to Egypt, from the Indus River frontier of India, and into Central Asia. Grandiose and autocratic it may have been, but in conception the Alexandrian Empire emphasized synthesis and limit over philosophical or religious absolutes.

In our own time, we have seen the idea of *limit* and synthesis return in the moderate, centre-liberal reaction to the Left. It is in this sense that true conservatism is never radically conservative. In the twilight of the city state, the West's first properly individualistic, conservative reaction was precisely a function of *limits* as conceived in nature, rather than of "reactionary" absolutes as conceived in philosophical abstraction. That is, the true conservative response is synthetic rather than diametrical. In this new way of thinking, the individual discovered limits in nature and in the cosmos: a personal relationship with the cosmos that bypassed worldly institutions. This "short cut" was systematized in Stoicism, the first truly individualistic philosophy. Its counsel was to live within the limits of the laws of nature, with resignation and self-reliance — two virtues central to all conservatism to come. However, just as we have seen Idealism abused by the Left, Stoicism can equally be abused by the Right; this happens, as we shall later see, when Idealism and Stoicism are taken as absolutes rather than as guides, as ends rather than means.

But at its best, Stoicism had the virtue of being practical rather than abstract. After all, Rome, in its bloody rise from warring tribes, seems to have been as tough a place to live as the Hellenic world in its decline. Both cultures were possessed of the same protective conservatism; of practical rather than idealistic values. In Latium, since tribal values had no hope of binding the sturdy local peasants with the outcasts and fugitives who joined them, it was only those *practical values* of the hearth embodied in the *numina*, in destiny and in Aryan patriarchy, that could hold them together. In that sense alone, Rome was already "stoic" before the Stoics.

And it worked. As long as populations were moderate, distances reasonable, and conquest restrained by natural barriers, Rome was the epitome of the fulfillment of the Aristotelian limit. No one was very rich or very poor: landowning patricians and the *plebs* who were their tenants were still more or less submerged in a universal identity of republican virtue. It was only in the second century BCE that Panaetius of Rhodes introduced formal Greek Stoicism to Rome. But Roman Stoicism had already evolved. Not only did it emphasize the simple primacy of home and family and their exclusivity from the realm of the state, but it also counselled a psychological detachment from the rewards and losses of public affairs and politics. This aloofness from the public realm prefigures the modern, individualistic political Right and, especially in Anglo-American conservatism, its elevation of privacy to seclusion and exclusiveness.

To the conservative Stoic, the state was unnatural and politics a necessary evil; they were not the pursuit of the highest good as they had been with the Athenian *polis*. Ancient or modern, the Stoic upholds the model of nature in its ruthless dissolution of waste and excess in contrast to the hubristic blundering of the state. For the Stoic, the course of nature was an ethical course in which fate maintained a balance between catastrophe and good fortune. It was fortune, after all, that guided Aeneas from doomed Troy to its rebirth in Rome. For the modern Right, luck and fate are still part of the game, to be accepted as if they were law; while for the Left they are to be minimized. The Stoic way is essentially the ethic of the contemporary free market. Ancient or modern, it is the philosophy of the patrician — the "wise man" who can afford the blows of nature. But what the radical capitalist still seems to understand no better than did the aristocratic Roman Stoic is that the law of nature is a just law only in a contained, circumscribed world. Only as long as the state was small and coherent could Stoicism help "to maintain a sense of moral obligation and contribute eventually to the growth of a less exploitive form of government."[19]

It was the uncontrolled expansion of Rome that undermined the Stoic's law of nature. Having triumphed in the Punic wars, she stretched her limits to the breaking point through relentless imperial expansion and through the consumption of the irresistible luxuries provided by tribute and a vast workforce of slaves. Stoicism, which had drawn its virtue from individual survival, could no longer survive without the conditions that made it necessary. Nor could an empire be ruled with the same intimate and efficient values as a republic. It is ironic, of course, that an idealized Stoicism was formally embraced only during the decline of the stoic virtues. In their death, indeed, lies authoritarianism. A weak and decadent conservatism, we will see, is also the seedbed of modern Fascism.

The authoritarian Right, however, is romantic rather than stoical; its realm is instinct and drama. In the bloody birth of the Empire, two spectres re-emerged from the mists of its mythical foundation: the rite of ascent to power by ritual murder hallowed in Alba Longa; and the shade of Aeneas as the individual adventurer. As victorious generals paid their troops in plunder, soldiers were loyal to their leaders rather than to the state, and senate and assembly soon became the instruments, rather than the masters, of their generals. Before long, a legally appointed consul was able to use the army to extend the term of his mandate. On the pretext of emergency, tyranny was born. Although it was illegal for a general to bring his army back from the provinces onto Italian soil, Caesar crossed the Rubicon with his troops and became an outlaw. Transgression of law will be the trademark of a radical Left and a radical Right underwritten by military authority. Lawlessness will maintain them in their extremes, down to the twentieth century.

An "adventuring lawlessness" asserted itself in the closing chapter of the French Revolution. In the fall of 1799, Napoleon Bonaparte, on campaign in Egypt, was in a situation much like Caesar's in Gaul. In both cases a general had returned from campaign illegally (though only Caesar had been victorious). It is less of a coincidence when one considers that both France and ancient Rome were in that state of relapse that occurs when the triumphs of war follow upon national exhaustion, and when disputes about legitimacy haunt republics. It is less surprising still when one considers that French republicans like Bonaparte tended to model themselves on the heroes of the Roman Republic. Ancient or modern, here appeared the "third force," authority.

Like Aeneas, Napoleon arrived alone with a band of adventuring comrades out of the ancient East to recover his destiny in an adopted homeland in the West. Like Alexander he would stand above factions by containing them, much as he would claim to conserve and contain the Revolution — both its Left and its Right. Like Alexander, Napoleon would ride a wave of recrudescent individualism in a society exhausted by philosophy and revolutionary metaphysics. In true Stoic tradition, his role was not to theorize or to map out an ideology in the manner of Lycurgus, but merely to *arrive* at the right time, according to the order of luck and nature; like Aeneas, his role was to accept and capitalize on the given situation.

If static architecture may be taken as the symbolic art of the Left, and drama the art of the Right, it would seem fitting that Napoleon's favourite art was not architecture but living drama: a theatre buff, he understood the value of timed entrances and dramatic gestures. But Napoleon used this romantic, non-rational theatrical instinct as a means to ends neither Left nor Right. And the set upon which he made his entrance was a France tired of political ideologies. He had timed his entrance perfectly: he was a hero before he arrived.

The Directory was in the hands of a tottering, ragged political centre and the two legislative councils in the hands of the Jacobin Left. After ten years of insurrections, the power of the street crowd was spent into weariness and both Left and Right were utterly exhausted. From the doldrums, a pale shadow of the Parmenidean One rose again — this time in the dry, brilliant director Sièyes. The same man who had first conceived the Third Estate as the One of the nation now sought ways to install and maintain a transcendent Left-Right polity by force.

Neither Sièyes nor Napoleon cared for extremes; both did care for power. In different ways they both wanted the same thing: absolute control of a non-ideological monolith. Sièyes, like Lycurgus, the conceiver of systems, and Napoleon, like Aeneas, the agent of force, would contrive to use one another. Napoleon needed a political sponsor; Sièyes needed a general. Both, however, must be credited with one thing: they correctly intuited that France wanted neither monarchy nor Jacobinism nor bourgeois business. Neither Left, Centre nor Right, the popular pulse suggested transcendence. And here we must understand that Left and Right — and the Centre that lies between them — together constitute a *type* of politics, a contingency that can, at times, disappear.

The General dispensed with Sièyes and disguised his intentions to the Ancients and the Council of Five Hundred before taking power by force. In his proclamation to the French people, he revealed his strategy: "Every party came to me, confided to me their designs, imparted their secrets, and requested my support; but I refused to be seen as the man of any party." And he concluded: "Conservative, protective, liberal ideas have resumed their sway."[20]

The oxymoron of what later became Conservative and Liberal might be taken as the key to his reign. We sense the legacy of Rome and Alexander renascent in the consulship and empire of Napoleon, who "no longer wanted Jacobins, moderates or royalists, but simply Frenchmen." Defining his own role, he insisted: "To govern on behalf of a party . . . is to put oneself sooner or later under its domination. I shall not be drawn into that. I am a *national*."[21] His policy re-embodied the Roman Republican tradition of balance exemplified by the two-headed

God Janus, who looked to past and future, to ritual tradition and to future expansion, to authority and to people, to home and to empire. The Napoleonic way was, in sum, a Roman synthesis of opposites that would "combine the revolution with the counter-revolution."[22] In all the governing bodies of the Consulate and Empire, he combined Jacobins, Royalists, and moderates — Left, Right, and Centre — in an autocratic conciliation that rejected their extremes. This was Roman assimilation.

It might now be useful to reflect that the extremes, whether of Left, of Right, or of a transcendent authoritarian Centre, all trace their ancestry to North Asian, Indo-European roots. Originally, the three great further regions — Mesopotamia, Greece, and Italy — all had moderate matriarchal civilizations. All three began to be radicalized around 1500 BCE by the great three-pronged southward and westward sweep of the northern Asian Indo-European migrations. And it is their culturally and religiously dualistic influences that are primarily responsible not only for the prototypical extremes of both Left and Right but also for their authoritarian synthesis.

Neither the Left nor the Right is enormously indebted to Napoleon, but each owes him something. For the Left, he preserved the most important, if moderate, gains of the Revolution. He treated the vast peasant majority with equanimity, protecting their new rights as small proprietors, which were given to them by the Revolution. The principle of equality was somewhat vindicated by the Napoleonic code's entrenchment of the equality of all individuals in law. Napoleon firmly established the idea that power and position be earned by merit and not by birth. Moreover, as he imposed "citizen republics" in the Roman fashion upon conquered territories, the horrified feudal monarchies still called him "the Jacobin."

The Right has Napoleon to thank for the amnesty that returned to France forty thousand royalist emigré families. His insistence upon splendour, ceremony, and absolute authority was monarchical in all but name. To the bourgeoisie he offered economic and political stability. Although his disdain for commerce and his pursuit of war, with all its economic destabilization, stymied the development of manufacturing, his code laid the legal foundations for capitalism's later success on the continent. Meanwhile, he banned organized labour and did nothing to recognize the rights of the working man.[23] Perhaps women fared the poorest under Napoleon. The legal code, for all its celebration of the equality of all before the law, was largely predicated on the idea that "all people" were men. To the lower classes he offered the opiate of identity, nation, and glory — the dangerous and transcendent wild card that would trump Left and Right down to the horrors of our own century.

If any dialectical process was alive under Napoleon it was not the dialectic of Left and Right but the older one of Liberty and Authority. It was the person of Madame de Staël who exemplified the love-hate feelings of the romantic liberal for the romantic authoritarian. Lover of liberty, upholder of equality in principle, and a sentimentalist about monarchy, she was the prototypical *ancien régime* Liberal — "neither Left nor Right." For this she admired Napoleon; but Napoleon was an authoritarian and for that she despised him. If de Staël embodied liberty, other figures, who were compelled to oscillate before Napoleonic power, embodied authority. Fouché and Talleyrand, respectively ministers of police and foreign affairs, both had a deep authoritarian streak that weakened their respective adherence to the Jacobin Left and Monarchical Right, which their emperor had been so successful in assimilating. Indeed, assimilation rather than cultural domination would characterize Napoleon's occupation of Europe — combining recognition of peoples with universal rights. Even today, the European Union is no more "Left" (as some might complain) — than was the synthetic universalism of Alexander — or, for that matter, Roman and Napoleonic assimilation.

But in the end, France got more glory than general welfare, and "upon the altar of his lust for power, Napoleon sacrificed the synthesis of revolution and counter-revolution that he might have effected for France."[24] Nor can the Revolution and the Enlightenment themselves entirely escape blame. They counted, as we have said, on eighteenth-century abstractions — a Right that had begun to submit morality to nature, in the manner of the Romans, or a Left that held up pure reason, in the manner of the classical Greeks — as models for humanity. When taken as absolutes, after all, nature and reason both express themselves, inevitably, in tyranny. In synthesis, under the absolute authority of Napoleon, they expressed, if nothing else, an extraordinary ideal only half realized.

7

Asymmetry:
Labour, Slaves, and Paupers in England and Rome

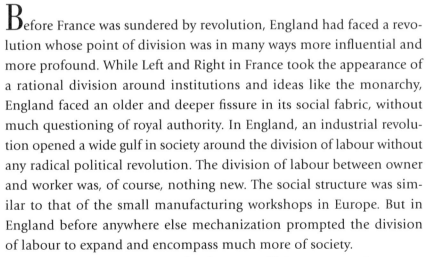

Before France was sundered by revolution, England had faced a revolution whose point of division was in many ways more influential and more profound. While Left and Right in France took the appearance of a rational division around institutions and ideas like the monarchy, England faced an older and deeper fissure in its social fabric, without much questioning of royal authority. In England, an industrial revolution opened a wide gulf in society around the division of labour without any radical political revolution. The division of labour between owner and worker was, of course, nothing new. The social structure was similar to that of the small manufacturing workshops in Europe. But in England before anywhere else mechanization prompted the division of labour to expand and encompass much more of society.

By the twentieth century the division of labour was to become a phenomenon of large-scale industry — the industry of factory floors and assembly lines — and it had a big part in defining Right and Left as Owners and Workers. Nowadays, by contrast, automation, the "outsourcing" shop, and the rise of the small-scale information age entrepreneur have led to a decline in the very forces that came to define

Left and Right. In some senses we are returning to the world from which they departed.

In most of Europe before 1800, manufacturing had been carried out through cottage industry or the "putting-out" system by which early industrialists sent raw materials to the homes of self-employed workers who laboured in family units. The cottage workers' livelihood was meagre, but it allowed them to eke out a subsistence. Even during the early stages of technological advance, the newly expanded industrialist's workshop provided a coherent way of life. Employer and employee remained a social and cultural unit as well as an economic one. With the expansion of trade consequent upon the growth of the British Empire, the wildly mercurial supply of raw materials began to determine the amount of production and hence the amount of work. During low periods, working cottage families thrown out of employment went into debt to their employers, lost everything, and had to give themselves up to their employers as propertyless employees. Even when workers did find employment, they remained entirely unprotected from the whims of the market and the new protean phenomenon of capital that could pull up stakes and move away at any moment or abruptly cease production and throw its workers onto the street. The effect was to tear the employees from their organic social world and to quantify and objectify them as a low-paid proletariat within a new social structure — the enlarged workshop or factory.

Relations between employer and employee had since the Middle Ages been communal and bound in a common cause against suppliers and princes, and were expressed in guilds, mutual obligation, ethics, religion, and custom. Now, quite suddenly, they were reduced to a reified and formalized relationship of wages and hours.[1] Workers' contact with their employers was limited to connection with an intermediary — the plant manager. The factory owner withdrew socially into a world away from the shop floor, a world of private country homes and pretensions that imitated the aristocracy. The workers withdrew into their own world of neighbourhood, pub, and religion. The division of labour divided not just the huge numbers of people engaged in industry; it divided culture — life itself — into two. It was, indeed, a social duality sharper in form and more sudden in time than any other in history, and it had no ready context to explain it.

The only paradigms available to contain and explain such an extraordinary and apparently spontaneous phenomenon were indeed religious. Religious dualism, as we have said, precedes all other dualistic thinking: to the poor, religious paradigms explained evil, greed, loss, and poverty; to the rich they justified a new state of affairs only dimly recognized as free market capitalism.

Religious ideas not only instigated and explained but they justified. A clever belief called *Deism* gave divine purpose to otherwise bewildering social processes already under way. God, after all, was a great clockmaker, and his universe a self-propelled mechanism whose mainspring produced all natural and social change in a preordained manner. Having set his creation in motion, he no longer intervened; therefore, whatever transpired, whatever *was*, was good — it was part of God's plan.[2] If it echoed the old rightish Roman submission to nature and the fates, it was still a vision of progress in its acceptance of happenstance as positive and divine.

Another force that helped to give Left and Right a concrete and social character that was nowhere yet to be seen, not even in France, was the philosophy of Empiricism. Rejecting the great continental metaphysical systems and their abstraction and idealism, David Hume turned Plato on his head by pronouncing the Ideas mere pale reflections of direct sense impressions. It was a pioneering philosophy, which set thought and morality firmly in the world of hard material phenomena, and it was perfect for the Industrial Revolution.

Adam Smith, the founder of the science of economics, was a student of Hume. Smith took the great accident of industrial change and recast it to look as if it had been divinely planned. Time and history, after all, were the divine mainspring in Smith's own Deism: thus the Industrial Revolution, with its accumulations of wealth and poverty, was all part of God's mechanical plan. In the end, Smith's support of unfettered market forces in his seminal work, *The Wealth of Nations*, led to the demise of European mercantilism — the control of the economy by the state. The new world was a world of free capital, magnificent and dangerous but divinely ordained. If workers and labourers had been torn from their old society, they were at least reintegrated as mechanical parts of God's great machine. This was done through the reifying of social relations as economic relations; in short, by the division of labour. As in Deism, one could claim that one cog in the timepiece was not "better" than the other, but that owner and worker were equally necessary to God's plan. Still, it was a mechanical hierarchy, easy to divide into Left and Right.

Deism aside, it must be understood that the capitalist fact or "event" has in itself no moral content. Rather, as it arrives, whether in rural England or colonial Africa, it demolishes existing moral systems and imposes a state of anarchy in which customary religious good and evil become confused.[3] Culture, history — even atavistic impulse — reconstruct within the chaos of the new capitalistic situation, new moralities such as "private vice and public virtue," "dialectical materialism," Deism itself, the concept of reward and punishment inherent in Protestantism . . . or even Left and Right.

From within Protestantism emerged a rationalized ethics by which discipline, self-denial, and hard work in the pursuit of profit would be seen to reveal a state of grace and virtue.[4] Scottish Calvinism, for example, held that wealth was the reward of virtuous hard work in the world and that indigent poverty was the punishment for vice,[5] both being outward signs of the state of one's soul. The Methodism of John Wesley promoted a Christian perfectibilism that provided moral justification to both upper and working classes. In transferring the Catholic idea of unlimited spiritual perfection to the prospect of the unlimited improvement of this world, the industrialist could derive his moral standing from the perfection of his enterprise.[6] In the Old Testament the worker and the Utopian socialist could find hope in millenarian perfectibilist metaphors of reward and punishment, wealth and poverty. Primal analogies to the Industrial Revolution were indeed to be found in the Bible, analogies that survive from the actual history of the ancient Middle East.

■

As in early nineteenth-century England, the sudden creation, in the eighth century BCE, of vast mercantile fortunes from Assyria to Egypt to the Phoenician trading ports produced a social revolution. A new class of rich merchants lent money to small yeoman farmers, who eventually defaulted, lost their land, and placed themselves in hock as a new class of slaves. As it happened a dualistic explanation lay ready and waiting. Formed as they were by the Arabian desert, the ancient Semites, like the Indo-Europeans, carried with them a predisposition to demarcation and dualism from the adversity of a harsh, open world without natural frontiers. The Semitic development of Israel might duly be described as the transfer of that sharp, territorial-political duality to a universal social-moral duality. This required a conception of "the world of the spirit as something distinct from and critical of the political and temporal world."[7] Such a duality, powerful in its simplicity, would make their faith "the formal religion of our western world."[8]

Jewish monotheism, like the empty throne that presided over the French Revolution, distinguished heathen and faithful on the Left and Right hands of Yaweh. But the division *on either side of* Yaweh was also a division *within* Yaweh, for the Jews still included within their God the old neolithic duality of order and chaos: the seminal Hebrew-Mesopotamian ideas of the fall from grace, the disaster of the flood, the vegetal cults of life and death, *Tsedec*, which is the grace of order, and *sheol*, the place of dreamless death, were all combined in one being, as were good and evil. Of course, they were increasingly difficult to contain.[9]

It followed that though the turbulent Canaanite thunder God Baal had been assimilated to Yaweh along with chaos, Yaweh's more destructive aspects would remain associated with the earlier Canaanite God. To Jewish purists it was the wealthy who were most indulgent in the worship of Baal, and Baal would become the prototype of the Jewish Satan. It is almost as if evil, once assimilated to Yaweh, were again separated the moment it found a social focus, but separated not yet as an enemy, rather, as a dissonant partner or adjunct to God — a servant or advisor who vetoes God's plans. Indeed, "satan" derives from *stn*, meaning obstacle thrown across a pathway, analogous to the Greek *diabolos* — "one who obstructs the way or route" — literally, a "devil's advocate" or prosecutor.[10]

Satan's role was socialized around 1000 BCE, when King David decreed a census for the purpose of taxation. The scripture held that Satan had inspired the project, for the gathering of wealth by taxation was considered an infliction on the poor if not a cause of poverty. In Psalms, we find the Sacred embodied in the poor themselves: "For he shall stand at the right hand of the poor, to save *him* from those that condemn his soul."[11] In other contexts, the poor, as we shall see, would stand at the Right hand of Yaweh, while the rich stood at his Left. Their transposition would occur with the French Revolution when the poor, no longer recognizing the divinely appointed king as their protector, were now untroubled by taking their stand on his Left hand. Thus the concept of the sacred as a point of division endures today, even if the terms are reversed.

In the eighth century BCE, not long after the reign of Solomon, the mercantile revolution arose with the wholesale pauperization of the small-holding farmers. While the rich still tended toward a hedonistic polytheism, the poor depended increasingly on the moral focus of a single God. So was born the priestly "Yaweh-alone" movement. Its prophets, having appealed in vain to the rich, had to resort to the poor for support in their drive for a lone God and moral guide. The search for a moral compass in ancient Israel was a little like the aftermath of Marxism today. We now find a Left in disarray looking for rescue in a single moral criterion — in a revival of universality or in multiculturalism. It has not yet been as lucky as ancient Israel, where monotheism — like Protestantism in the catastrophic wilderness of the Industrial Revolution — began to provide moral intelligibility. Simple in concept and light of panoply, a single god could be carried around in the heart like the ark of the covenant of the wandering tribes; for Yaweh had no image, only a voice — indeed a divine *logos*. As long as authority was one, and only one, a clear, dual morality could be preserved.

Still, decadence and destitution persisted, and the character of prophecy changed. Wandering bands of traditional, "professional" prophets were replaced by lone individuals inspired (again, in anticipation of Protestantism) by a personal calling taking the form of a direct command from God. Like the Asian shaman in whose tradition they seem to follow, they would become the agents who reconnoitre the supernatural to split good from evil all over again.

For the prophet Amos, an obscure shepherd and dresser of fruit trees, the people of Israel were God's elect and therefore were subject to God's higher moral standards: as Yaweh could not forgive the luxury and decadence of the surrounding nations, even less could he forgive the rich of Israel for selling "the righteous for silver and the poor for a pair of shoes." Not twenty years later, in 722 BCE, Israel fell to the

Assyrians, and the prophecy of Amos seemed to be fulfilled. In 538 BCE the pattern was repeated. This time the southern kingdom of Judea was attacked by the Babylonians and its population carried off into exile in Babylon, the very maw of hedonistic opulence. Domineering wealth and captive poverty were embodied inside Babylon itself, "the great harlot, whose charms bewitch all the nations of the earth; the world market whose trade enriches the merchants and shipowners."[12]

When Cyrus the Great returned the Jews to their homeland and recognized it by folding the Jewish priestly caste into the administration of a Jewish state under the auspices of the Persian Empire, Zoroastrian ideas penetrated Judaism. Moreover, Jews in the service of Zoroastrian families engaged in theological discussions with their Zoroastrian employers. So it comes as little surprise that, according to the prophet Isaiah, Cyrus was the Messiah and that the Messiah itself was a Persian idea.

Although it is difficult to know whether there was any Persian influence on the book of Job, it seems that "the figure of Satan probably developed under the influence of Iranian dualism."[13] A Satan still linked to Yaweh was finally distanced through the polarizing influence of Satan's Zoroastrian counterpart, Angra Mainyu; and it is in Isaiah 14 that we are first introduced to a heavenly courtier called Lucifer, who is thrown out of Heaven and cast down to Hell for competing with Yaweh. Even though Satan still appears in God's family as the *intimate enemy* — to use the phrase of Elaine Pagels — he was at that time considered treacherous, having *split away* as a renegade leader. The influence of Persian polarity would only strengthen Satan's association with luxury and Yaweh's status as protector of the poor.

Zoroastrian reinforcement of Jewish dualism only increased with the fall of Persia to Alexander the Great; for now the two peoples became allies in opposition to the Hellenistic Seleucids. In 164 BCE, in a fevered time of crisis and oppression, the book of Daniel was written, recalling the old Babylonian exile in the heated, nationalistic and apocalyptic terms of the age. It was specifically in opposition to the Seleucids that the Hasidim — a sect of the most orthodox and anti-Hellenistic — fully adopted Zoroastrian ideas as Jewish:[14] eternal punishment, immortality of the soul, the resurrection of the body, the last judgement, and a second coming.[15] A few decades after Daniel, the apocryphal book of

Enoch finally featured Satan as the polar opponent of God, the King of Evil, and above all the Lord of this fallen, material world and its vain luxuries.[16]

By the early nineteenth century, social conditions in England were ripe for that sort of Old Testament dualism — an emotional paradigm that would fit perfectly with the rational scaffolding of classical economics. In the latter could be seen the invisible but explanatory hand of the market, which, like the Word of Yaweh, was eternally beneficent and eternally destructive. And within the "Yaweh" of capitalism, indeed within the Manchester school, Socialism, as we shall see, had its origins. Moreover, it would split away from Capitalism, taking up its position on the Left hand — as if it had been a coeternal enemy. Of course, it has taken crises of culture and of the environment to make us realize that Industrial Left and Right are in fact very much the two faces of an old Yaweh — the traditional smokestack economy.

If we understand prophets in the Jewish sense of revolutionizing simplifiers in times of crisis and confusion, Jeremy Bentham can be considered a prophet for socialism and capitalism together. Bentham's utilitarianism was a sort of "arithmetic of happiness" for everybody. It aimed to dispose of all traditional, religious non-rational considerations in economics and politics, so that a truly just society could produce "the greatest good for the greatest number." This was to be done with rational moral laws and regulation. Religion, to Bentham, was the greatest enemy of justice, and it seems that in the end, humanity's proclivity for metaphysical absurdities made him place security and equality before liberty. Otherwise, the free play of the market was part of a fairer and more efficient world. Capitalism was the means, happiness the end, the greatest number the recipients. Utilitarianism, literal-minded and mechanical, would build the "rationalized" moral grid of pleasure and pain upon which could be constructed the industrial moral and economic theories of Left or Right — at best sensible, at worst soulless. Like a Jewish prophet, Bentham provided an idea not just of justice but also of intelligibility in a time of social revolution.

Economic revolutions are almost always accompanied by catastrophe, and the catastrophe that followed Rome's own imperial and economic expansion has commonly been compared to the Industrial Revolution in England.[17] And both bear uncanny comparison to our contemporary global market with its rapid exaggeration of wealth and poverty, and its mania for mergers and the elimination of middle-management. As was the case in England, however, in Rome the small proprietor was doomed. The yeoman farmers of Rome had had a proud history. As *Plebeians* they arose in its earliest times when the larger families subdivided their lands among numerous heirs into poorer and smaller subsistence plots. As in ancient Israel this growing class of small farmers tragically fell into debt and ultimately into the service of the larger landowners.

The Aryan talent for demarcation and division institutionalized the schema in myth: Romulus, having delineated Rome with a furrow and outlined his altar with the ploughshare, ploughed yet another furrow to divide that upper landowning class of Patricians permitted to hold office from the lower class of Plebeians constrained to serve.[18] True to Romulus, public office was reserved for the larger landowners, the only public office enjoyed by the lower class being military service. Still, the Plebeians were the growers of grain, the food staple of the Republic. The first consciously "proletarian" organization was the plebeian cult of Ceres, the grain goddess. The abuses of Etruscan rule, however, had kept Plebeians and Patricians united — until the expulsion of the Tarquin kings drew aside the veil on internal class resentment.[19]

On that new schism, Rome proceeded to develop an economic class system that had more in common with our own era than with the long age of feudalism that intervened. The worker, the farmer, the homeless person, the self-made man, the speculator, the bourgeois, landed wealth, old and new money — all have their counterparts in Rome. There were, however, other units of identification that worked — much as race, ethnicity, and gender have done today — against class consciousness. As in Greece, the *gens*, or extended family clan, still claimed one's first loyalty, allocated duties, defined social function, and secured authority. The fundamental unit of power, the *gens* was a corporate entity governing so many aspects of daily life that it was effectively a self-contained political operation; clan interest transcended class interest. The old republic was also held together by a code of civic responsibility. Political duty was understood to come before wealth: the Latin *luxus* for "luxury" originally meant weeds or excess vegetation, suggesting that idle surplus was waste.[20]

The class consciousness that would help to dissolve this tight weave of myth, household, family, and duty was initiated with the census. Although its ostensible purpose was military conscription, the real intention of the census was the civil subjugation of the plebeians. They reacted, in one of the first movements to detach the lower classes as a unit of defined interests from the rest of society: they resorted en masse to a local mountain, the *mons sacer*, which thenceforward became the historical prototype of proletarian protest. Their new class leaders, the tribunes, proceeded to break out of their *gentes* to plead plebeian causes before the assembly as representatives of their class.[21] This movement can in some ways be thought of as the birth of the proletarian Left as a class concept.

Whatever cohesion remained between upper and lower classes was dissolved for good by the Punic wars. The forced neglect of the homesteads of farmer-soldiers absent on campaign and the expropriation of their land by larger landowners of the *equites* class; the replacement of the one-man crop of home-grown grain with cheaper imported grain; the takeover of the family grain farm by the estate and its mixed operation; the expropriation of local labour by an imported slave force — all served to transform the class of citizen soldier-farmers into a mob of propertyless unemployed. The *plebs* had now become the proles — the Latin for those with "children to spare" — the root for the word *proletarian*.

Struggles between rich and poor were expressed in a competition between the *equites* and the patricians to exploit proletarian discontent for political advantage. Poverty, in short, was a pork barrel. Representation of lower class discontent was further diffused in a politics run along clan lines. The political elite was made up of patricians, upstart plebeians, and ambitious *equites*. But it was all one class: and as origins became blurred by patronage and new money it became known simply as the *nobiles* — distinguished no longer by values or pedigree, but in simple contradistinction to the poor and landless. By 200 BCE, there was no longer anything resembling policy or ideology, but only complexes of cronyism. *Gentes* of the *nobiles* class were "liberal" or "conservative" only insofar as they listened to, or ignored the poor.[22] The *nobiles* were in fact not so far from the traditional duality of liberals and conservatives that makes up the political class so often excoriated in the modern West. As the old Republican moral sense evaporated and the social disparities radicalized, a casual "two-party" system came to represent, perhaps unintentionally, the deeper reality: the "Populares" claimed to lobby for the lower classes, and the "Optimates" pursued the interests of the upper class.

It was a long way from a world where small freeholders and patricians had worked together. The Republic had known a sort of rough and discontinuous democracy by which politics at least worked itself out under the eyes of citizen witnesses who came in to fill the assembly from the countryside. But the old free, citizen assembly could no longer accommodate an expanded empire, while the angry impoverished throng that flowed in from the hills became a scarcely controllable mob facing an uneasy senate. They were thus set against one another in unofficial class war, whereas, according to the values of the old republic, they had been intended to form a single unit. The logical resort was political violence, which retained a dark legitimacy from the founding myths and the early practice of ritual regicide. Taken as a first rather than a last resort, it radicalized both sides,[23] and the social chasm that had escalated with the Empire's overheated expansion caused the dissolution of the very assimilationist meaning of Rome itself. Even religion had lost its power to bind. For the yeoman, religion had been bound up with property. With the loss of his farm, he had lost his *numina*, his household gods, while the patrician retained them. Now, a homeless and godless proletariat was forced, through despair of this world, to resort to salvation in the next or in philosophy. What followed was the freezing and rationalizing of a disastrous class dualism in religious and philosophical ideas. The means, for rich and poor alike, was Stoicism.

In the Republic, Stoicism had been the practice of life in a defined and limited world. With the Empire and the collapse of social cohesion, it became a private and nostalgic philosophy for the rich and a quasi-religion for the poor. Only recently, Aristotle had helped to provide the ancient world with a cosmology in which everything would have its place. But Aristotle's integrated world picture carried through from Plato a discrete dualism which gave Stoicism an elitist aspect. His claim of founding his thought in the natural world contained a deductive flaw: perception, he held, was not a function of direct observation, but of *nous* — the spirit or wisdom of the *noetic* vision.[24] He placed wisdom over experience, divine intellect over human soul, spirit over matter; finally, as in Plato, intellectuals had superior status to the men of the world. This duality was in turn bequeathed, whether in conservative or revolutionary form, to the upper and lower classes of the medieval and modern worlds. So the Aristotelian Cosmos, the Deist clockwork universe of the free market, Benthamite utilitarianism, and Roman Stoicism all had one thing in common: by rationalizing the world as it was — both as a unity and as a duality — they helped institutionalize wealth with abstraction, and poverty with the earth, in a fatalistic world stripped of its *numina*, that is, disenchanted.

Wealthy Stoics, as we have seen, discovered in the natural cosmos a transcendent law that enabled them to rationalize their fortunes as facts of nature and detach themselves from emotional involvement in society or politics. In dissimilar fashion but with similar effects, the slave Epictetus, a founder of lower-class Stoicism, held worldly misery to be irrelevant to one's essential soul and dignity; it was to be borne without fear or resentment.

Altogether, the philosophies of the encroaching social wasteland of the late Hellenistic and Roman worlds counselled survival within the status quo and (*ipso facto*) helped to maintain it. In the sense that they counselled evasion, patience, delay, and displacement they also resemble utopians, both socialist and Marxist. Indeed, some plebeian Stoics found a sort of personal and exclusive salvation in the communal ownership of property and an idea of Heaven as a communist state.

By contrast, Jewish Stoicism did little to quieten Jewish servitude. By now, after all, new Roman masters had inherited from the Seleucids the mantle of Satan. Duly, in the last books of the Old Testament, written on the eve of the birth of Christ, the old desert-steppe dualism of the left and right hands is amplified: the left hand is still connected with wealth, the warding off of evil, temptation, the passive bow-hand of the archer. The right hand, ever superior, signifies time, life, the law, conscience, salvation, eternal pleasure, the active arrow-hand of the archer, and the hand of righteous vengeance.[25] With the Jews, the splitting off of

Israel from Rome, and the increasing and wider application of the left and right hands, goes back to a single origin: the banishment of Satan from God. This biblical alignment of the political and the religious would be projected into the history of the West.[26]

■

The Industrial Revolution, like the Middle Eastern mercantile revolution and the Roman Imperial revolution, gave birth to a mass of theories and beliefs pointing to the "salvation" of a society in crisis. Likewise, the theories and beliefs or "isms" that we take for granted in our own age — capitalism, socialism, liberalism, and the rest — were coined in a short period of upheaval between 1820 and 1850.[27] By mid-century, however, this eclectic and wide-ranging mass of "isms" had boiled down to a debate between wealth and poverty, Right and Left. Good and evil, sacred and profane, still lay near the heart of social distinctions. And yet the early industrial socialism and capitalism that still define our politics have maintained a consensus from the beginning around the value of hard work and technology, and the idea that property ought to be productive.

Our urban landscape still expresses that idea. And indeed, socialism and capitalism have a common origin. Alongside Bentham's moral utilitarianism, classical economics laid the intellectual groundwork for both.[28] The Manchester school, which gave birth to capitalism, was itself the midwife to modern socialism. One of its students was David Ricardo, a follower of Bentham and student of Smith's classical economics. Ricardo further developed the Labour Theory of Value — the idea that a commodity's value consists solely in the labour put into it, one of the founding ideas of socialism. In turn, Thomas Hodgkinson, a follower of Ricardo, condemned private property outright. Bertrand Russell dates English socialism's separation from its capitalist parent to a letter from John Stuart Mill to Ricardo in which Mill objected to Hodgkinson's ideas on property.[29]

However intense the debate between capitalism and socialism would become, it was an intramural debate. Originating in a schism within classical economics, it was conceived and developed in a small, newly educated, industrial middle class. That is why capitalism and socialism are not true enemies and thus cannot be exact opposites.[30]

The former is essentially *descriptive*; the latter *prescriptive*, both partic-
ipating in a larger, internationally capitalistic world. Whether this
industrial debate would come to be imposed upon the nation as a
whole would be determined according to whether the industrial classes
controlled parliament. Indeed, Left and Right have become essentially
parliamentary expressions, and that is of course very much a complaint
today. Like the *nobiles* of Rome, Left and Right make up a political class
that is the middle class.

In parliament, Left and Right had a common point of origin as well.
The aristocracy was the first class to control the English parliament,
and even though its own schism was not as total and millennial as the
split in France's Constituent Assembly of 1789, Whigs and the Tories
formed, very roughly, an inchoate "Left" and "Right" — the Whigs the
mercantile aristocrats, the Tories the landed gentry. The general terms,
Left and Right, of course derived from France and they would come to
stick in England as well, though more in form than in content.

As we look more closely at Left and Right, they begin to lose their
distinctions. The contemporary debate between a Libertarian "freedom
Right" and a mainstream "authority Right," for example, goes back to
Whiggish nonconformity and Tory absolutism. The "moneyed" Whig
alliance was as broad and unwieldy as the great amorphous Third Estate
of June 1789 with its liberal aristocrats and clergy. Including all sorts of
religious nonconformists and aristocrats, radical and free thinkers,
inventors, merchants, and businessmen (not all sympathetic to one
another), it seemed to embrace anything that was new. The divide fell
not between rich and poor but between tradition and change. The central issue of division was not the king but his power; for the Tory party
was distinguished by its unswerving loyalty to monarchy and the status
quo, that is, the defence of landed interests from the disruptive forces
of Whiggish industry and free thought. By the mid-nineteenth century,
as economic and social concerns moved to the forefront, parliamentary debate would really amount to a debate within the Whigs, Right
and Left. And that required a middle-class parliament.

Parliament's shift from aristocracy towards the middle class became
effective upon the admission of a middle-class electorate to parliamentary
power with the Reform Bill of 1832. It was then thought that, with the
battle won, a large part of the nation made up of rich owners and poor

workers and comprising a single industrial Left could stand in opposition to a landed aristocratic "Right" of privilege. But the link between rich industrialists and poor workers was fragile: their common opposition to the Corn Laws by which grain-growing Tory landowners kept up the price of grain, forcing workers to pay more for their bread and industrialists to raise their salaries. With the repeal of the Corn Laws, the fulcrum between Left and Right passed from industrial versus landed power to the Chartists, who espoused the issue of working-class enfranchisement.

A parliament made up of recalcitrant aristocrats and middle-class industrialists blocked all the attempts of the Chartists to enfranchise a working-class electorate. The wealthy industrialists, having attained capitalist goals, now felt the threat to their gains from their own workers. Appealing to the natural duality of parliament, they fell back into a conservative alliance with Tory privilege. The middle class now opened a new debate between liberals, who would reform industry on behalf of the working class, and conservatives, now supported by many Tories, who would fight for the freedom to pursue the expansion of industry at lower cost.

By mid-century, it appeared, capital was triumphant and occupied the entire ground of debate. What, then, was this parliamentary, industrial middle class that came to define Left and Right in England? In population, it was sizeable but constituted a minority. Politically, it upheld constitutional monarchy at home and abroad, and limited social reform. Economically, it believed in the free market and free trade. It was spiritually Protestant and its education consisted, appropriately, of biblical scripture and the classics. The new bourgeois, industrial consensus leaned sharply toward the Whiggish "freedom Right" and was supported by a relatively wide range of thought that included not just Jeremy Bentham but Edmund Burke and John Stuart Mill. Burke maintained freedom against any tendencies toward absolute monarchy on the Tory Right. Accepting of democracy, Mill was nevertheless persuasive about the tyranny and enforced mediocrity that can be wielded by majority opinion on the "Left."[31] He was effectively an elitist — believing that only an elite could truly guarantee freedom. So Bentham's "greatest good for the greatest number" was refined and qualified by Mill's "freedom to act in any way which does not harm others."

Whereas in France it seems that equality and freedom tended to seek their maximum expression, the English appeared to define them by their limits. If we look at Bentham's distaste for irrational speculation, Burke's fear of absolutism, and Mill's fear of mass conformity, there is the unmistakable shadow of a negative reaction to French Catholic absolutism and its bloody, rationalistic, revolutionary counterpart. For all their moderation, however, Bentham, Burke, and Mill upheld liberty against equality — ultimately the Freedom Right against absolutism, Right or Left. The Whigs and their Liberal descendants, it now appeared, were like the doomed Girondins in temper and taste, for Jacobinism never successfully took hold in England, and English Left and Right remained monarchist — where the French had been in 1791.

English parliamentary middle class consensus around the utilitarian ideal, liberal or conservative, may be looked upon as a single ideology. It stands in contrast, therefore, to the extra-parliamentary political marginals who hail from what we are accustomed to calling the "far Left" and the "far Right." Running from utopian socialists to dissenting Tories, they were less concerned with the socialist-capitalist debate about how to manage the Industrial Revolution, than with the destructive effects of industrialism itself. Among the marginals was Robert Owen, a highly successful "Cotton Lord." Repelled by the degradation and social disorder of the new factory civilization in which he had taken a leading part, he seems to have felt that parliamentary agitation was useless. Instead, he reinvested the profits of his textile mills in the construction of a workers' community, providing free housing, sanitation, and moral education for the families he employed. It was, of course, non-democratic, and Owen is an ancestor of "top-down" paternalistic, socialist and capitalist industrial projects. Though it was a remarkable achievement, he could not have known that this enforced community would be admired by Fascism; that its pervasive social control and instruction would foreshadow totalitarian Communism.[32]

We are now in a territory beyond Left and Right, a place which defies the terms "conservative" and "radical" since it is both. Sharing Owen's protest against the more inhuman aspects of industrialism were the Luddites. The Luddites, however, regarded mechanization itself as evil. Behind this short-lived, disorderly rebellion lay an inarticulate longing for a more humane, rural Utopia. In Owen's egalitarian, Sparta-like Utopia and in the sheer obstructionism of the Luddites there is an essential *conservatism* infused by an undeniable sense of loss. Utopian socialism and its more nihilistic and anarchic cousins were brakes on social and technological change, and attempts to restore ideas of organic community that were often medieval.

So what we call political radicalism, whether of prophets, Stoics, or Utopians, is always a projection of a more natural past into the future: an attempt, literally speaking, at *revival* rather than *conservation*. Here lies the main reason for this provisional distinction between parliamentary and marginal politics: those socialists and capitalists who accepted industrial progress and its associated urbanism formed a victorious consensus broken only by its parliamentary debate of Left and Right. It was their vision that would come to dominate and to split the world. By contrast, it was the dissent from the industrial Left-Right consensus that was most profound, if least recognized. This is why the Utopians and Luddites found cousins among certain conservative landed Tories who protested the Industrial Revolution as much as did the Utopian far Left.

The most articulate of the dissenting conservatives were the "Tory democrats," who shared with the Utopians an aesthetic and humanist disgust at the ravages of industry.[33] But in the end it is the Left that has remained in control of the political vocabulary. In the interests of left-wing purity, "Right" would become the dumping ground for a range of dissidents and misfits wider than the more doctrinaire Left — whether or not these misfits wanted to be included under the rubric "Right."

The Left, after all, remained first and foremost a vanguard. Whether in the forefront of religious nonconformity, free enterprise, social reform, labour, socialism, or communism, it always took the first leap in the dark. The Right, drawn in its wake, would contain the bellicose reactionaries but also all second thoughts, modifications, and ultimately the tragic vision of hindsight, whether in the aftermath of industry or of socialism. But, where it flows beyond parliament, the Right is not an ideology; rather it is a looser term of *default*, containing the gentle and the violent, madmen and visionaries. And it would become even more so as an inner, bourgeois paradigm of industrial Left and Right, in England and France, would be inflated, universalized, and imposed on the world.

8

Universality:
Time and Order

The latent duality unleashed by the Revolution was briefly suspended when Napoleon brought Europe under one system. It was in theory a unity of universal Liberty, Equality, and Fraternity. But any concept of the One, as I have tried to show in discussing Parmenides, leads again to duality. The other half is all that which the One excludes in practice, or all that which disagrees. Universality, one of the great nostrums of our own time, faces the same conundrum. No matter how transcendent the universality of the United Nations, human rights, general welfare, or equality before the law, it still appears as an idea, a system; and to many it seems merely a product of a tradition that is specifically Western and liberal. What is more, the very moment universality calls its opposition "Left" or "Right," it resigns that universality by designating itself Right or Left in response.

Of course, Western concepts of universal rights did arrive by force — first in the hands of Rome, and then with Napoleon. That universality, expressed in Napoleon's synthesis of Left and Right, produced not only an opposition but a precedent of universal *power* that would only reinforce and invigorate a re-emergent Left and Right in his wake. In this Napoleon was like Jeremy Bentham, a leveller and then a builder of that vast single foundation that would serve, despite him, for two new edifices. Napoleon also remains the father of the modern authoritarian state, enlightened or reactionary, Left or Right.

But Napoleon did not invent the transcendent state, he merely built upon a tradition. The universal state, like Parmenides' Entity in the hands of Zeno, was supported by another universal idea: the relentless powerhouse of progressive Time and History. The concept of spiritual-historical time as a political force culminating in and justifying the state, requires a single engine. Though inherited from Zoroastrianism, political-historical Time had its locomotive in the monotheism of the Jewish Yaweh.

Parallels between ancient Israel and the great modern states are not so far-fetched. Like Jacobinism, as we have seen, Jewish monotheism arose of necessity, as a reform. Yaweh's people had not been treating each other properly, and their consequent punishment by Yaweh as a lone, angry father explained Israel's misfortunes. This sense of internal, individual failure, with its link to national, collective disaster, gave birth to sin as a social concept — directly derived from the primordial desert-and-steppe idea of impurity, that is, the *threat from within*. Out of this would grow a more politicized sense of the Saved and the Damned.

The maintenance of polarities of sacred and profane, saved and damned in a single conflict extended into a temporal paradigm that was not as universal as it believed itself to be. After all, "the dual conception, which the Persians and Hebrews translated into terms of a moral conflict conditioning history, was expressed by the Chinese in terms of a harmonious flow of alternating opposites."[1] Fixed polarity was indeed an Asian-Mediterranean cultural contingency whose "apocalyptic vision has taught even secular-minded people to interpret the history of Western culture as a moral history in which the forces of good contend against the forces of evil in the world."[2] The vessel of the Lord on earth was the advancing body politic of the state.

By the eighteenth century, a religious tradition was no longer enough for the demands of progressive rationalism. There had to be laws at work in the procession of time. Those laws were detected by the German thinker and contemporary of Napoleon, G.W.F. Hegel. They also happened to find embodiment in Napoleon, and "in spite of the logically contradictory nature of Napoleon's conservative and liberal ideas, and of his appeal to self-interest and revolutionary idealism, the *historical* logic of his position was accurate. Napoleon had profoundly sensed the needs of his time; he seemed to embody its dialectic spirit. It was this political genius of Napoleon that led Hegel to proclaim Napoleon a world historical figure."[3]

For Hegel, the developed state was a reconciliation of the whole and the parts, "the synthesis of the unity of family and the separateness or individuality of life in civil society."[4] The end product, supposedly, was an ideal construct: the first stage was a thesis in Greek given law, the second stage an antithesis in Roman conscious morality (in contract or citizenship, for example), and the culminating synthesis the perfect *ethical* state of the German constitutional monarchy, for which the monarch was the ultimate, indispensable symbol. Hegel's state was supposed to cancel out polarities by transcending them as their higher product in a final third stage, defined in his *Philosophy of Right* as "the stage of spirit whence the prodigious unification of self-subsistent individuality with universal substantiality has been achieved." By the mid-nineteenth century Hegel's dialectical machinery would support both the German bourgeois conservative heaven for which it had been designed, and its opposite, the idea of a Marxist Utopia. Intended as a synthesis, Hegel's concept of the state turned out to be an engine both for left- and for right-wing roads to perfection.

As the Jews had needed Yaweh to lead time, Hegel needed a force to lead history. "Passions, private aims, and the satisfaction of selfish desires are . . . most effective springs of action," he wrote. "Their power lies in the fact that they respect none of the limitations which justice and morality would impose on them; and that these natural impulses have a more direct influence over man than the artificial and tedious discipline that tends to order and self-restraint, law and morality."[5] Thus, he could argue that the Real — a mess of individually driven, violent events when viewed close — was, on the larger plane, rational; and viewed historically, the rational was the Real mess of events. Why, then, did history not follow Hegel's great synthesis, but instead produce solitudes of Left and Right in the Cold War? According to Bertrand Russell, Hegel's "mistake was a failure to distinguish between a thing's *relational* properties which can infer the whole endlessly, and its *innate* qualities which cannot infer the whole."[6] Hegel was a bright, rational Monist in the tradition of Parmenides; and rationalistic Monism, like universalism, propagates rationalistic dualism. Like Napoleon, Hegel gave a weapon to both Left and Right by supplying a system that could justify each.

This unintended consequence would follow the same pattern as with all such grand, unifying concepts. When modern politicians argue over a "world order," talking favourably of an open, global free market or a socialistic multicultural planet, they are still speaking in the absolute, "perfectibilist," system-building terms inherited in Napoleon and Hegel by various routes from the Eastern Mediterranean. In fact, so deep was the rationalism of classical Greece that it survived moderation in the Hellenistic period and in Aristotle. Even science was directed, through a lens of Aristotelian structure, toward moral and metaphysical reassurance; likewise, disinterested speculation was reduced, as we have seen, to philosophies that favoured practical survival as much as philosophical certainty. It was in such an atmosphere that Aristotle conceived his *Politics*.

The social backbone of Napoleon's system and of Hegel's was much the same as that of the ideal state in Aristotle's *Politics*: the middle class. In the nineteenth century, the bourgeoisie would (much in the same manner as Napoleon, Hegel, and Universality itself) serve a moderating function, but it also tended to mask the extremes of ideology. As a political concept, the middle class made its appearance as the prototypical "middle way" in civic virtue which, according to Aristotle, is "a mean; with regard to what is best and right, an extreme."[7] Since Aristotle suspects the rich and poor of excessive self-interest, "it is manifest that the best political community is formed by the . . . middle class and that those states are likely to be well-administered in which the middle class is large and stronger if possible than both the other classes."[8]

As with Hegel and Napoleon, the state, bound by virtue and the middle class, is the fulfillment of the individual in the whole: "though it is worthwhile to attain the end for merely one man, it is finer and more Godlike to attain it for a nation, a city state."[9] Foreshadowing Hegel, Aristotle's state is organic, "a community of families and aggregations of families in well-being, for the sake of a perfect and self-sufficing

life."[10] What strikes us here is not so much Aristotle's sense of moderation, but the rationalistic and deductive nature of his concept. Although
he researched from history and experience, he extracted from them in
turn an abstract concept of Virtue and then — as Marx would do —
deduced a politics all over again from his definition of Virtue as a mean.
(It is not for nothing that he has been called the father of all closed
"perfectibilist" systems.) The existence of rationalistic political ideas as
life-rafts in a decaying world was typical of the Hellenistic Mediterranean
— and it may find a parallel as we cling to Left and Right in the chaotic
field left behind by the Cold War.

■

In attempting to understand the certainty sought in the Hellenistic
world and its influence on the spatial, dualistic thinking of Western culture, Euclidean geometry is useful. Geometry and mathematics are,
after all, universal in their application. Euclid was still the standard at
the outbreak of the First World War. Nevertheless, the limitations of
Euclidean geometry are revealed in its mundane ancestry: the rationalization of space originated in the ancient Egyptians' desperation to redraw
field boundaries every year to accommodate the flooding of the Nile. It
continued in Plato, who still had no doubt that "the part of the mind
which relies on measurement and calculation must be the best part of
us."[11] In fact, "the belief that geometry is inherent in nature, rather
than part of the framework used to describe nature, has its origin in
Greek thought . . . Its method of starting from unquestioned axioms
and deriving theorems from these by deductive reasoning became characteristic of Greek philosophical thought; geometry was therefore at
the very centre of all intellectual activities."[12]

At the time of the Enlightenment with its love of symmetries and
axioms, Euclid was still fundamental: "When the Declaration of
Independence says, 'We hold these truths to be self-evident,' it is mod-
elling itself on Euclid. The eighteenth-century doctrine of natural rights
is a search for Euclidean axioms in politics."[13] In Euclid, of course, the
Pythagorean consecration of number is implicit, and forebears of
modern revolution duly resorted to Pythagorean concepts of spatial
organization in which to symbolize the perfect society. But Euclidean
measurement and Pythagorean mysticism were not quite the same

thing. The Pythagorean projection of a perfect future was conveyed through Freemasonry, thence entering the Jacobin clubs, as we have seen. And when the Revolution was finally in power, it too "acquired spatial dimensions and was henceforth embodied not in complex republican institutions but in simple concentric circles. The borders of France were an outer, ideological moat; Paris the inner citadel; the National Assembly the 'perfect point' of authority within Paris itself. The revolutionary nation was proclaimed 'indivisible' and its borders expandable."[14] The linear two-dimensional Left-Right description of politics, like most metaphors — like France's "ideological moat," like the furrows ploughed in the Asian steppe and in early Rome — has come to affect the very thinking about the things it was meant only to symbolize.

If geometry was midwife to Greek reasoning and binary thinking, prior to geometry itself was language. Even today, the modern media have only magnified the inversion in which the accidents of language — like metaphor — produce supposedly intelligible entities (like the "New World Order" or the "Me Generation") rather than the other way around. In ancient Greece, it was somewhat more sophisticated: the ignition of Parmenides' entire philosophy by the verb "to be" and its growth into the *being* of the entity.[15] The founding philosophy was built on a grammatically vague term — neither specifically kinetic nor static, nor, as it had been intended, one and simple; it would drag "non-being" along with it, ensuring that everything would flow out of it in opposite directions of superior and inferior. The Greek language permeated all thought in the Hellenistic world, not least through Aristotle's *Metaphysics*. Aristotle had gone beyond "to be"; his hierarchy of categories now reflected the relations of subject, predicate, and object — "predicate" usually suggesting a subordinate or auxiliary relationship. So "when Aristotle drew up his table of categories, which to him represented the grammar of existence, he was really projecting the grammar of the Greek language on the cosmos."[16]

If our own propensity for polar division is Greek in its *logos*, its *mythos* lies in the founding work of the West — the Bible. Greek rationalism and abstraction made its way into Christianity — and into modernity — through the translation of the Old Testament into Greek. Greek approximations of Jewish words remained Greek ideas[17] and in

the hands of Hellenistic translators Jewish myth and Greek *logos* completed in the Old Testament a synthesis of Greek abstraction and Jewish
monotheism; and, through Greek and Jewish sources, a synthesis of
Zoroastrianism and ultimately Central-Asian dualism. And so, in the
simplification of Jewish myth by Greek logic, we arrive at the implicit
dualism of a righteous father saving his fallen children — starkly and
explicitly simplified through the crystalline prism of the *logos*.

Thus it was that Plato entered Christianity. The seminal agent was
Philo, a Hellenized Jew of Alexandria who was writing around the time
of the birth of Jesus. The Talmudic problem with which he wrestled
was how to explain the imperfect creation of a perfect creator.[18] To do
so, he took the explicitly monistic Talmud and through the agency of
Platonic philosophy made it explicitly dualistic.[19] At the same time,
Philo's own Stoicism, with its detachment from the pleasures of the
body, would exacerbate the latent mind-body dualism both in Greek
asceticism and in Jewish puritanism.

Philo's reasoned metaphysics required the conversion of Yaweh into
logos itself;[20] that is, his reduction to logic, the kind of logic that can
act as a force of division into two. For the Greek-educated Philo, the
duality of a true One and a false polytheistic Many could find support
in the true One and illusory Many of Parmenides, not to mention the
Platonic polarity between the realm of the ideas and the shadow world
of material creation. So Philo accounted for God and his inferior creation through the agency of the *logos*, which produced from the *monad*
of God the inferior *dyad* ("Parmenidean many" of illusory opposites)
in a duality of spirit and body.[21] Philo keeps his God untarnished by
his own darkening creation because, so he explains, His perfection lies
precisely in the logic or *logos* of the duality — that is, in the *understanding*, the intellectual principle. Hence, salvation must involve a
paradox: in moving closer to that God, which is intellectual perfection,
we use only our mind, leaving our body behind.

Dualism had nowhere yet been more extreme. And such a separa-
tion of body and mind would leave its mark on Western civilization.
Comparing Western thought to the successful Japanese synthesis
between Buddhist monotheism and Shintoist polytheism, Northrop
Frye remarks: "no such compromise was ever possible in Judaism,
Christianity, Islam or (*mutatis mutandis*) Marxism."[22] Nor in the ideo-

logical rigidity that characterized the twentieth century until the fall of the Berlin Wall. After Pythagoras and Parmenides, Philo was one of its most important transmitters.

The tendency toward ideology, especially dualistic ideology, is so deep that no ideology has ever been transcended, even by the concept of law. Law has, rather, been the creature of ideology itself. Even though the rule of law remains the perennial reprimand to twentieth-century autocrats of Left and Right, it tends, rather, to serve concepts of Left or Right. Indeed, its claim to universality that (like geometry) it is rooted in nature has proven generally to be instrumental rather than objective. A natural law does to an extent determine a balance between whole and parts, collective and individual."[23]

But human law codes have their roots in culture at least as much as in nature. If an Islamic leader consents to the rule of *sharia*, he is deferring to the rule of law. Judaic law, likewise, was sacred: the *yad*, a symbolic hand used to indicate the Torah during readings of the law, was a right hand.[24] And it was by means of sacred law that the duality of good and evil was imbued in the beliefs, practices, and politics of the Jews. Even up to our time, "the official sexual rules of western society . . . were derived mainly from the laws attributed to Moses, reflecting the relatively strict standards of patriarchal pastoralism and its battle with the fertility cults."[25]

Jewish law developed among a people who had been without a nation and, who, when settled, were besieged. Discipline imposed itself more urgently upon the Jews than upon any other people. By exacting order in daily political and ethical life as the price for divine protection, the law placed the survival of the chosen of Israel in their own hands. Personal failing could only be regarded as a fifth column of the enemy and there was nothing that could not be divided in two on the principle of loyalty and betrayal. It is what Joseph Campbell calls the "Levantine mandatory consensus."[26] And its preservation was the duty of an elite, a priesthood.

In fact, Biblical, social judgement would form a precedent for the modern revolutionary purge: "The feeling that a pure or homogenous group, no matter how small, is the only effective one, and in times of crisis is the one to be kept for seed, so to speak, until a new age dawns, is an integral part of the revolutionary consciousness."[27] The radically dualistic nature of a state that must protect itself from the outside and from enemies within, and at the same time reform itself, produced the dynamics of internal purification through debate that would last down to modern times. "The numerous conflicts and contradictions with the Western ethical system were all present in Judaism, and were caused by the adoption into Christianity of the entire Jewish national heritage and the assumption that every part of it was a product of divine inspiration. Thus, Christianity became a religion both of war and peace, both conservatism and radicalism. Christians could imitate the bellicose and bloodthirsty nationalism of the Mosaic tribes, the Davidian monarchy, and the book of Esther, or they could imitate the pacifism of Jeremiah or the non-resistance of the Hasidim."[28] In every case, each side could appeal to a law conceived as universal.

Surrounding this dualistic Judaic law and covering an infinitely vaster territory was Roman law. In its intent, it was no less universal. Both codes contributed to the dualism of the West; and the civilizational transition from Israel to Rome is echoed in that of Jacobin to Napoleonic rule. The Jews, as the Jacobins would do, inaugurated a political duality profound enough to outlast them carrying on, respectively, through the rational grids of Roman law and the *Code Napoléon*. Both Jewish and Roman law expressed dual relationships. In contradistinction to that of the Jews, however, the legal relation for the Romans existed not vertically between the individual and God, but laterally, between individuals. We have seen its origins in the Aryan value of *contract*. More civil, less sacred, more practical, less ritualistic, "their belief that states and individuals were bound by contractual obligations pervaded their whole view of life, and led to the practice of an elementary honesty that may be regarded as the basic Roman contribution to human development."[29]

But neither Judaic law nor Roman law enshrined equality. In Judaic law a moral elite was implicit: in Roman law a dual distinction of property. Both would carry through to the modern day. The imbalance encoded in Roman law was born of differing religious impulses aplying to the part and to the whole. As to the part, there was the sanctity of individual property originating in the *numina* under the Republic; the whole, on the other hand, was forged in the Empire by the memory of Emperors legally deified at death. Under the Republic, however,

Roman law had honoured the universality of the private realm by legally separating individual home and property from the public realm. As long as the lower class was composed of yeoman farmers, equality was implied. But after the eviction of the smallholder and the dispossession of a large part of the population, the law continued to favour the private property that accumulated in the hands of the larger proprietors who survived. Thus the old realms of private and public were reinforced in landowners and dispossessed to the benefit of the former and the detriment of the latter. In the end, although "property law created a sense of theoretic equality . . . in practice it only deepened class divisions."[30] These divisions were universalized when the emperor Justinian organized the entire corpus of laws into a single Code.

Napoleon did the same for France. Like Roman law, the *Code Napoléon* gave primacy to property, securing farmers and the middle class more rights than the growing population of renters and proletariat; and on the continent, as in England, the voting franchise was tied to property as well. In this sense alone, the Napoleonic Code laid the legal groundwork for another edifice whose apparent universality would give birth to a further principle of dualism: capitalism — for in theory the Napoleonic Code provided the same sort of rational "monistic" foundation for it that Jeremy Bentham provided in England. We have said that Monism produces Dualism. Napoleon, following the absolutist traditions laid down by Louis XIV and refined by the Jacobins, imposed his synthesis by force. Banning all public manifestation of Left and Right, he drove them underground. Since repression is the best way to restore religious force to political creeds, it is not surprising that ideology, the "modern surrogate of religion was born both as a phrase and as a force — in the political-intellectual opposition to Napoleon."[31]

His singular power was to represent a force that even his enemies couldn't agree on. Royalists at home and throughout the Empire called him a covert Jacobin, and radical republicans everywhere accused him of being a Royalist in disguise. But those from Left or Right who hated his imperialism or his republicanism generally admired his universalism and technique of power — and they adopted them. The proto-communist Gracchus Babeuf may have drifted on the extreme margins of the Revolution, but under Napoleon he became the prototype of the universal "Napoleonic" Left and a predecessor of modern

Communism. There was also Buonarotti, a young Italian aristocrat who drifted on the margins of the French Revolution before joining Napoleon's campaign in Italy in 1796; in his ensuing rebellion he produced an anti-world of diametric imitation along Napoleonic lines, before joining the conspiracy of Babeuf.[32]

On the Right, the effect was similar. The theocratic political thinker de Maistre, in exalting the Church, deployed a scope and universalism that copied that of Napoleon even to the exclusion of the secular monarchies, while his concept of dialectical change followed that of the Revolution: "De Maistre's counter-revolutionary manifesto of 1806, *Considérations en France*, betrayed a hypnotic fascination with the revolution," calling it "a direct, mysterious act of providence, a 'miracle' of evil calling for a counter-miracle: the establishment of papal theocracy."[33]

Before long, radicals from both sides shared a common territory of protest against the Empire. Taking their cue from Napoleonic logic, Jacobin Left and Royalist Right would briefly join forces in diametrical "Napoleonic" opposition to the Emperor with the result that "concepts of the Right often filtered into the programs of the Left."[34] The Philadelphians, a concoction of radical Monarchists and Jacobins, submerged their differences in a spiritual idealism:[35] a riposte to Napoleonic rationalism. This development of ideology in the grand Napoleonic style spread from France to Europe and provided the leaven for the modern phenomenon of the mass, mechanized ideology that endured until 1989. If its political agent was Napoleon himself, its philosophical purveyor was Hegel. With Hegel, the distinction of Left and Right leaves its constitutional foundation in the French Revolution and takes up a deeper foundation in metaphysics.

While Hegel had maintained both that "the real is rational" and that "the rational is real" in the participation of anarchic events in the logic of history, his students took the expressions as opposing banners and split into two groups. The former interpreted the real world with all its irrationality and plurality to be discretely rational; they anticipated the modern Right. Those anticipating the Left, including the young Karl Marx, claimed that strict, morally progressive rationality was the only reality — a realm of forms with which the world ought to be brought into conformity. In the new Hegelian duality re-emerged an opposition between the "conservative" empiricism of the pre-Socratics and the pure, "progressive" rationalism of Parmenides and Plato; an opposition between the world of chaotic natural reality and bright, shining Reason. In their passionate adoption of these tragically renewed and opposed viewpoints, the Young Hegelians became the prototypes respectively of romantic and rationalist revolutionaries.

Their effect endures. When the modern Left talks about rational planning and social programs, and the Right talks about the spontaneous play of market forces, they are perpetuating the rational–non-rational, post-Napoleonic, Hegelian duality. In turn, the decline of those same mass ideological types is starting to leave the world in an uncharted territory resembling France on the eve of Napoleon. Two centuries later, the attempt by the liberal hegemony of the free market to find a balance with the Left (in Clinton and Blair, for example) is not unlike the hedonistic moderatism of the Directory.

The combination of moderate Jacobinism and authoritarianism that came with Napoleon and would shape world politics until 1989 has been called by Alexandre Kojeve, "Robespierran Bonapartism." The term not only conceived the French Revolutionary compound of equality and liberty as a single force of progress; it suggested that its Left and Right were participants in the same, discrete process. In the words of Francis Fukuyama, "Communism did not represent a higher stage than liberal democracy; it was part of the same stage of history that would eventually universalize the spread of liberty and equality to all parts of the world. Though the Bolshevik and Chinese revolutions seemed like monumental events at the time, their only lasting effect would be to spread already established principles of liberty and equality to formerly backward and oppressed peoples — and to force those countries of the developed world already living in accordance with such principles to implement them more completely."[36]

Robespierran Bonapartism has not been the inevitable synthesis the term might suggest. When that universalist wave of European ideology crashed on the shores of Latin America, it exacerbated rather than reconciled an indigenous complex of racial, economic, and demographic conflicts. To this day, discordant elements of Latin American society have been lumped into Left and Right, an alignment that made effective revolution all but impossible in the 1980s and provides a poor road map for political and social reform today.

Robespierran Bonapartism was brought to Latin America by Simon Bolivar, the liberator of South America from the Spanish crown. Bolivar was tragic, if prophetic: he himself warned against importing abstract European ideas wholesale to the wild dissonance of South America — warned against autocracy, recommended the safety valve of a loose, regional federalism against a brittle centralism. But the great ideological blueprint of Europe was equipped constantly to reassert itself. After Bolivar set up a republican junta in Caracas in 1810, there appeared the fissure that was to spread through all of Latin America. The white Creoles tended to accept his esoteric, liberal, European constitution, while the Indian and half-caste *mestizos* found it alien and incomprehensible.

In South America, liberal and conservative forms confronted and were drawn into a much older world for which they were ill-prepared: a continent of scattered colonies grouped under administrative captaincies general, divided more by mountains, river valleys, and jungle than by frontiers. If equality to most of the inhabitants was an abstraction, perhaps it was because it was nowhere visible: to the indigenous majority, tribe, village, church, and race meant everything. Politics was personal, emotional, without ideological content, the fundamental duality a rough and ready sense of "us and them."[37] The conditions of the half-whites, or *mestizos*, did improve moderately under Bolivar's republicanism, but the white Creoles remained dominant and things changed little for the destitute Natives.

What could Left and Right, Liberal and Conservative mean in such a world? The conflict between the Natives and Europeans could find little reflection in European opposition of monarchism to republicanism and later, of capitalism to socialism — nor even of equality to hierarchy: "In post-liberation Argentina, the dilemma to be resolved was not whether the new state should avow an Atlantic or transatlantic identity but whether it should be dominated by the European civilization of the cities or the 'Asiatic' barbarism of the pampas, where wild gauchos, powerful enough to impose dictators of their choice on the country, were likened by sickened city-slickers to Tartars of the steppes."[38]

In the Creole-Indian confrontation, the great dualizing, abstracting Indo-European hunters and shamans were, in effect, meeting the monistic city-state planters again — in Caracas, in Lima, in Mexico. Even to call the age-old Indians "conservative" is to impose Hegelian ideas of history, of monarchy and reaction — and later of capitalism — on a people for whom society had been timeless.[39]

Another axis of conflict as old as the Bronze Age is city versus country. It still cuts across Right and Left in poor countries; in Latin America it separates European-educated cosmopolitans and an indigenous peasantry. It has caused city-country splits within left-wing revolutions and it has made the idea of a conservative consensus hollow. It goes back to the republican world that appeared in the wake of Bolivar. When elections were waged on a slate of Liberal and Conservative, city and country was the local topographical duality to which the governing Creole class hitched not only the jungle, mountain, tribe, river, and plantation of South America but — and with more difficulty — the theoretical duality of Left and Right. The urban liberals wanted freedom for commerce and religion, higher taxation, democracy in principle, and greater centralization. The rural aristocracy opposed free enterprise, wanted lower taxes, stood behind regional autonomy, and hoped for the restoration of Church and throne. But the Conservatives represented very little of the countryside, and together the opposing parties shared a "little Europe" that made up only a minority of the population.

In the end, Liberal and Conservative turned out to be the template upon which were aligned city versus country, Creole versus Indian. And instead of electoral positions, Left and Right became racial and tribal banners. The result was a style of rule we have until recently seen everywhere in Latin America: "Since even the liberals could not envisage universal suffrage and completely fair and open elections, both groups rallied around individual personal heroes in every country, and rule by an individual, be he benevolent patriarch or malevolent tyrant became the 19th century pattern in Latin America."[40] The upstart leader would start out in the country as a conservative, decentralizing *Federale* and, if he found himself in possession of the presidential palace, turn around and become a "liberal" centralizer acting in the name of the nation. Sometimes he was white, sometimes *mestizo* or Indian. To the masses in the hinterlands, personality counted more than ideology; in Nicaragua in the 1980s "Sandinista" and "Somocista" referred not just to Left and Right, but to the personal styles and views of Augusto Sandino or the Somozas.

In the end, Left and Right served as masks for archaic, competing authorities. Although "independence abolished the monarchy [it] retained what is natural to a monarchy — centralism, authoritarianism and aristocracy — mainly because the revolutionists were themselves reared in the Spanish tradition and knew no other."[41] And Bolivar's European, Napoleonic universalism turned out to be a weapon convenient not just to warring Liberals and Conservatives, but to white and Indian, city and country, cosmopolitans and peasants.

The lesson of Napoleon and Bolivar had already been learned and forgotten with the fall of Rome. It was Caesar Augustus, nephew of the tyrant Caesar, who rationalized by reason and by force the conflicts left unresolved in the ruins of the civil wars, and who therefore might be called the prototype of Robespierran Bonapartism. With a genius for formula and propaganda, Augustus wedded the parts to the whole, Roman tribalism to universalism, and the old household gods to Hellenic Olympians. He combined the practical with the theoretical, the human with the divine, and made the diadem of personal divinity borrowed from the Egyptian pharaohs seem natural on the head of an earthly administrator. It was Augustus who commissioned Virgil to cobble together that brilliant propaganda, the *Aeneid*, which presented Rome as the culminating synthesis of all the great dualities of the Eastern Mediterranean. Anticipating and outstripping the short work of Napoleon in time and space, his empire was the first to pound the stamp of universality on Europe with *techne* — law, merchant fleets, roads, aqueducts, and armies.

But even under Augustus, the imposition of the One forced the re-emergence of a duality. With the desanctification of the small farm and the demise of the freeholder, the universal, the theoretical, and the impersonal overshadowed and devoured the very mortar that once held the body politic together. All that was integrative, practical, and personal — the old *numina* of the household, the local myths and intimate things that had sustained the Republic — dissolved in the face of the Empire and emptied the very universalism itself of content. The Stoicism that replaced it was by comparison urban, ethereal, distended — its helpless nostalgia giving the lie to its thinness. Instead, the Western tendency toward abstraction, the same that would re-emerge in Hegelianism, carried on a persistent if spectral life.

In late Rome, "both the Platonic doctrine of the ideas and the Aristotelian doctrine of forms meant that human beings and institutions must always be copies of the same eternal models of perfection, unaffected by the movement of time."[42] The One, ever-rigid and ever-alienating, fared onward with the same overweening self-promotion that, reduced to a duality of self-and-other, nation and enemy, became the heritage of Rome's sectarian successors: dwindling medieval Byzantium; Moscow's "Third Rome" with its slavic Caesar, the "Tsar" — not to mention its terminal trivialization in "Kaiser"; and puniest, if most destructively, the parochial *Lederhosen* of a Third Reich backed by a stage set of Doric columns, crowns of oak leaves, and faked "Aryanism." What is modern Fascism but the trivialization and final perversion of Augustan universality in egoistic, sectarian, ethnic ambition — in which the whole is placed at the service of a mere part, be it nation, race, or ruling party?

In the centuries before and after the birth of Christ there did flicker the flame of a type of universalism that resisted both the monolith and its inevitable dualism. Under the hegemony of Rome, Mithraism arose in Asia Minor, a synthesis of Zoroastrianism and Greek religion. Exalting neither whole nor parts, God nor the devil, night nor day, self nor other, it referred instead to that which lay between them — *contract*, precisely the boundary itself. Its patron, Mithra, was the sun god of the Vedic steppe and, it will be recalled, the god of contract and friendship. As an Iranian solar god, Mithra had "formed a link between the Ahura Mazda and the Angra Mainyu of Zoroaster; for it is time, marked by the revolutions of the sun, which regulates the alternation between light and darkness."[43] Mithra was born from a stone, "a symbol of being, of cohesion and harmonious reconciliation with self."[44] The key is the preservation rather than the annihilation of contradiction, compromise and oscillation rather than synthesis and monolithic consensus.

By contrast, Roman universality, Christian love, Jewish law, and Napoleonic Empire, while they were expected to reconcile duality, reinforced it; in recognizing no alternative to the missionary *self*, they made an enemy of the *other* by displacing or submerging it. If modern Liberal Democracy aims also to submerge rather than to preserve, it too will produce a dual reaction — from within and without.

MIXTURE

9

Marginality:
Romanticism and Gnosticism

The cultural consensus that ruled Europe from the Enlightenment to the end of the Napoleonic era is known as Classicism. It is a paradox, however, that the classical, Mediterranean symmetry reflected in the left-right fracture of the assemblies was little more than a rationalized form of the ancient sacred and profane. But the newer rationalizing distinction would continue to penetrate even the most chaotic social change. Though the Left has always defined itself more clearly than the Right, in modern times it has expanded to include all kinds of marginal and individual protest. That "cultural Left" dates more or less to the early nineteenth century, a time when classical civilization would turn out to be a restraint on that private and difficult aspect of humanity that we call "soul" or individuality.

With the end of Napoleonic universalism in 1815, it became evident that an older political order had merely been suspended. As it returned, a kind of sleepy stasis set in — a constitutional compromise between the classical parliament and the classical monarchy. In France, with the restoration of a king in the person of Louis XVIII, protest reverted to the hands of the upper-class bourgeoisie, who demanded reforms from a mistrustful constitutional monarchy. The difference was that now everyone knew their cues: for the chronology of the Revolution and its rhetoric had been ingrained like a playscript in the mind of the nation. Thus the period was characterized by the sedimentation of political discourse into a more or less permanent Left, Centre, and Right with "the years 1815–1820 [being] the first in which 'isms' began to be generally discussed and to play a leading role in politics and culture."[1]

Still, history seemed to flow backward. In the 1820s, Charles X, having restricted the franchise to exclude most of the middle class, reverted to the primordial stance of defending aristocracy from the interests of business. With business back on a Girondin Left, the insurrection that erupted in 1830 was directed by the liberal middle class but staged by students and workers. What was new was that finance had begun to take the place of land, so that business was for the first time purely at the centre of the "Left."

By the same token, the bourgeois revolution was still hung up on the old divide of 1791: between constitutional monarchists and republicans. The compromise was effected by the ancient Marquis de Lafayette and a few bourgeois officials, supporters of Louis Philippe of the house of Orleans, a constitutional monarch with a head for business. Here was the "Limousine Liberal," the accommodating aristocratic businessman who stood almost exactly where capitalist Right meets disenfranchised Left. It was in that regime that the concept of a "ruling centre" developed, perhaps the first foreshadowing of the centrist liberal establishment that has gradually taken hold in the West since the 1960s.[2] But in 1840, with the business class occupying the Left in the assembly, Louis Philippe's happy centrist coalition comprised a very small centre indeed. The wage earners — the descendants of Hébert's disenfranchised *enragés* of 1794 — remained outside of society.

Here, once again, the Right can take the credit for the creation of a hard, monolithic Left that drew its definition more than ever from class. The July monarchy, entirely concerned with liberty and unconcerned with equality or the conditions and enfranchisement of labour, provoked the formation of an ideologically motivated working class — and a new and deeper split in society. The wild card in the game of Left and Right was held by those who were marginalized from the other classes: bohemians, artists, students, renegade aristocrats, and the poor. The anger they would lend to the support of working class revolt had, however, little to do with the material want that moved the workers. The marginalized classes rejected the very world in which the workers wanted representation. With the appearance of what might truly be called a large, alienated section of society, a "third class," our story takes a new turn. This third class, a third force in which spirit and culture take precedence over economics, foreshadows multiculturalism and the "politics of identity" of the present day. Then, as today, it would distort and complicate Left and Right.

Classicism, with all its tidy rationality, was a bourgeois-aristocratic creation. Its forms tended to conceal the great base of the social pyramid where discontent had as much to do with desire for power and recognition as with deprivation. There was little choice but to play the dualistic political game invented by the middle class. Industrial workers had not yet been gathered into the factory as they had in England, but remained, poorly paid, in artisans' shops. Their consciousness was still tied to the shop and the neighbourhood, and proletarian identity had not yet formed into a single unit as it was doing in England. When under pressure from mechanization and modernization, French workers still felt a psychological need at least as strongly as an economic one. Their rebellion arose from a fraternity of the past — that sense of emotional conviction in mutual obligation and identity once found in nationalism — which held a vision still quite beyond the economic future offered by parliamentary Left and Right. So there evolved a working class Third Way beyond Equality and Liberty: a spiritual link between the individual and the whole, transcending Left and Right. Not surprisingly, the working class discovered its longing in "Bonapartism." Most important, Bonapartism was now subversive.

The appeal to the spirit of Napoleon was part of a more widespread discontent with the return to the symmetries of Enlightenment Classicism. The movement, like its heroic progenitor, was a symptom of Romanticism. Dangerous in masses, the volatile *amour propre* of the Romantic mood remains as natural to the individual as it is beyond the classical materialist paradigm of Left and Right. This desire of the individual for recognition and self-respect — for soul, spirit, and memory — characterizes the Romantic third force. The new, romantic individual looked to the immediate past and saw, not an advancing civilization, but ruins: Greek and Roman ruins, *classical* ruins that had

culminated in the rationalist argument of the Revolution and concluded in mass slaughter.

The assault of the individual against rigid classical structures was
further directed against industrialism and the classical economics that
supported them. Capitalism, after all, had begun with no vision of how
society ought to be, but rather as an uncontrolled process of acquisi-
tion for the sole purpose of material comfort. Even in France, it was
dissolving the natural bonds of the community and replacing them
with the shop floor, the trade union, and the professional association.
These affiliations were specialized and separate, and had little to do
with where and how one lived, and so "certain qualities of individual
intercourse, the organic community taken for granted at the time, were
effaced."[3] That is why the romantic impulse looked back to a pre-clas-
sical past and to unspoiled nature; to life untrammelled by the ugliness
of an industrial "Right" or the excesses of a utopian "Left."

Even the aristocratic ethic, in its more positive, individualistic aspects,
began to look rather good. Perhaps because it was nearly out of the running, it seemed free of political posturing and conveyed a certain
authenticity. For the aristocratic principle is not only a class distinction;
it can also be a model for the dignity and freedom of the sovereign
individual. This passionate individualism where opposite extremes rub
shoulders may have been new to the modern age. But it was not new
to civilization.

The sort of malaise that appeared in the wake of the Napoleonic Wars
had earlier appeared in another age: during the decline of the Olympian
religion and the cultural exhaustion that shadowed the Augustan era of
the Roman Empire. At that time classical religion was displaced by a
type of thinking that offered rescue for the individual rather than for
the community or the empire. Its main expression was Gnosticism,
which became widespread not long before Christianity in the Eastern
Mediterranean. The Gnostic motif of escape from the world re-emerges
in extreme religious and political movements, Left or Right, wherever
they pose total renunciation of the status quo. It will appear whenever
the fringes — from radical Communists to punk rockers to Neo-Nazis
— place themselves outside any consensus.

Before the formation of actual Gnostic sects, a *Zeitgeist* had prevailed all over the Middle East that saw the struggle between good and evil as cosmic rather than earthly. Through Hinduism, its oldest influence, Gnosticism had despaired of hope and salvation in this world. From its deepest source, Persian dualism,[4] it had drawn a stark duality of heaven and earth, body and soul, that defied rational and earthly distinctions; and it placed the relationship of man to the Cosmos prior to any relationship in the world. Through Platonism, above all, it conceived a deep dualism between material and ideal worlds. For lack of a better term, this inchoate feeling might be called the *Gnostic mood*. Its legacy was extensive, to the point that "dualisms have appeared in Western religion chiefly under the impact of Gnostic influences."[5]

The early Gnostic features of a pre-Christian theological scheme, and even a Gnostic prototype saviour, were woven into the life of Christ and other local figures; for "in this patchwork the joins are everywhere clearly to be recognized . . . Thus the essential part of most of the conceptions of what we call Gnosticism was already in existence and fully developed before the rise of Christianity."[6] Even Simone Pétrement, the strongest exponent of placing Christianity prior to Gnosticism, concedes that a generally dualistic, pessimistic *Gnostic attitude* informed much of the ancient world *before* Christ[7] and that Christianity is one of its variants.

The core of Gnostic feeling is *gnosis*, the knowledge, usually occult, that one's true deepest affinity is not of this world. In its spiritualism it suited the growing poverty, transience, and uprootedness of the Hellenistic world,[8] although among its acolytes numbered educated dissenters from the traditional religions. It was probably as a result of their Greek learning that the Gnostic attitude was rationalized and ordered by the sharp dualism of Middle Platonism: that is, by the *logos* of Philo — the "blueprint" that imparts to politics the theological, dualistic forms it has retained in the modern world.

Gnosis holds that beyond all creation there is an unknown God — the All or the *pleroma* in which the prototype of primal, perfect man resides; in politics its prototype is an eternal self-image in Utopia. The projection of this prototypical ideal of the *self*, as we will see, haunts the radical politics of Left and Right in the future. Its inferior and opposite was born when a defect in the All detached itself and fell downward to form a lower God, the *Demiurge*, thus explaining evil by its origin in the divine.[9] This evil Demiurge, or *creator God*, is a lower father of creation, who created the *cosmos* and rules it through his seven deputies, the *archons* or planets. This is the primordial form of the fallen world from which, in effect, the revolutionary tries to free himself; and of society, which the idealist sees as a failed utopia.

Gnosticism stresses the vertical dimension, which divides the higher world of perfection from the present, lower world of the lie and its worldly, broken-down duality of moral opposites. Good and evil are creations of the demiurge and of humanity, but since they are only manifestations of a shattered divinity trapped in the lower world, they ought to be treated as pairs of complementary terms rather than opposites. Indeed, comparison will show that Gnosticism is a brutally extreme — almost literal — application of the doctrine of Parmenides to the declining life of the Hellenistic world.

Humanity itself has its origins (or, as we have said, its prototype) in the All (the Entity), the unknown transcendent God. Man also separated from God, but not as defect; rather, as a spark of the divine purity broken away from the All, whence comes the idea of man's original goodness. In a primal, metaphysical tragedy, the divine spark falls into the created evil world of the *Demiurge* and there becomes imprisoned in soul, body, and society successively, all three in turn incarcerated in the great prison of the Cosmos ruled by the *Demiurge* and his archons. While the lost All is real, the present world where man is imprisoned is illusory.

With *Gnosis*, however, man becomes aware of his home in the All and his separation from the Primal Man, his original prototype. In this he carries unique *knowledge* in loss and in longing for his original form. The nostalgia for the All produces a complete indifference to the world — expressed in extremes of asceticism or lawlessness. Either way, superior, "utopian" knowledge exempts the gnostic from the rules of society; it is the response of metaphysical liberty to an evil world.

If the Persian element was the strongest of those that contributed to Gnosticism, we might suppose that the hard territorial life of the steppe, a protective inclination to despair, and the discipline and denial of the mortal body in favour of an everlasting spirit produced this formative paradigm of Western thought. In the Gnostic concept of the world as metaphysical prison, there is still the murmur of the Indo-Europeans' engraving of the cardinal points, their taming of terrifying empty space with rationalizing lines, boundaries, and divisions. These formed, as we shall see, the orientation points, although artificial, of a cosmos which, if it was not loveable, was at least divisible and therefore decipherable and navigable.[10] What are Left and Right, after all, but provisional charts of political navigation in a fallen world? Primal rebellion defies rational ordering: it is both Left and Right and neither, for the Gnostic problem is authority — the Demiurge — and not ideology.

Modern gnostic feeling first found expression among artists. Drawing on the same ancient Eastern religions that had influenced Gnosticism, Arthur Schopenhauer took up the lone individual as his central concern. For Schopenhauer, the world is dual: *the world as idea* is a place of constant paradox, illusion, and deception. It is a hall of mirrors where the only stable thing the philosopher can discern is the acting individual. His or her world is the world as *will*. Schopenhauer[11] interprets the irreconcilable opposition between the *world as idea* and the insatiable *world as will* as tragic. The only redemption from this dual prison lies in art — literally in a recovery of the *self*.

When nineteenth-century bohemians, modern fringe artists, and radicals of gender or race oppose all of society in favour of their own narrowly defined identity, they are carrying on the pattern of gnostic despair revived by Schopenhauer. The impulse is to look to art or identity to retrieve something they recognize but have lost, or from which they claim to have been disenfranchised. But in the confines of classical politics they can only gravitate toward what is available: the loose and ragged ends of Left or Right. The formal ideologies, after all, are only provisional — a precarious purchase from which to attack the stagnant banality that encompasses mainstream Right and Left. At the heart of their protest is an urge to overthrow that represents nothing less than a longing to return to innocence and origins.

In the nineteenth century — as in the hippie movement — innocence and origins mean "nature," that last breath of the All, the divine, in a fallen world. For William Blake, "the most thoroughgoing Gnostic of the early Romantic movement,"[12] what is yearned for is the sublime — nature, divine and uncontainable by reason — that still speaks in thunder, in the "tyger burning bright" always hostile and incomprehensible to the designs of reasoning man. Blake's cosmic prison is a place of tragic dissolution and separation. To him, reason in the hands of the Demiurge illuminates the fragments of what ought to have been whole. But instead of reconstructing them, it aligns them into pairs of opposites or compartmentalized capacities. And so, in the immortal engraving *Urizen*, the Demiurge is seen crouching over the cosmic abyss with dividers.

> *He form'd a line and a plummet*
> *To divide the Abyss beneath*
> *He form'd a dividing rule*
> *He form'd golden compasses*
> *And began to explore the Abyss*
> *And he planted a garden of fruits.*[13]

Thus begins the tragic geometrical act of separation. But in Blake's case, opposites, precisely because complementary, must be preserved rather than reconciled (in a lawless rather than an ascetic Gnosticism):

> Without contraries is no progression. Attraction and repulsion, reason and energy, love and hate are necessary to human existence . . .
> From the contraries spring what the religious call good and evil.
> Good is the passive that obeys reason.
> Evil is the active springing from energy.[14]

It goes without saying that Blake celebrated the earlier and not the later stages of the French Revolution, before it descended into a most un-Blakean, inhuman application of Law and dualism. There is little doubt that the Jacobins and their right-wing successors together rebuilt the Blakean "dark Satanic mills," his cosmic prison. Even today, in the radical hyperbole in which the concentration camp is the metaphor for society, gnostic expression is still at work.

The image of the prison endured to express symbolic protest against the rational structures of Classicism. In the *Carceri* of the Venetian engraver Piranesi, studies of vast penitentiaries developed from Roman ruins became "hallucinatory and metaphysical,"[15] nothing less than the decaying, cosmic prison of classical civilization. The image of cosmic imprisonment rises yet again with the Marquis de Sade, the philosopher and libertine. His rebellion was directed as much against the *ancien régime* that imprisoned him as it was against the authority of the revolution that pursued him — the one through the hypocrisy of maintaining appearances, the other through revolutionary puritanism. The forms of both were thoroughly classical and in de Sade's view antinatural. The absolute victory of one side of the Revolution — Monarchist or Jacobin — was to de Sade a tragic victory for the demiurge of authority and control, whatever its face. Hence his rejection of both Left and Right, of moral legislation, of the Terror and its death penalty. The perilously moderate, eclectic stance that his philosophy and temperament forced on him was a protest against Left and Right in favour of the cosmic fulfillment and expression of the free individual.

It is something of a leap to suggest that Blake or de Sade was in sympathy with any aspect of society. But in their celebration of nature and despair of worldly forms, they were more than modern Gnostics. They were prophets of the deadening rationalization of life by the modern state, Right or Left. The nineteenth-century lower classes, having less regard for the structures of bourgeois politics, were closer to the same spirit. To coin a term that we will use again — they were the "remainder" — that vast but miscellaneous array of poor, proletarians, and artists. They included the marginalized of all classes, from disillusioned bourgeois to fallen aristocrats, for whom Left and Right, the two hands of the political demiurge, held little hope. In its alienation, the "remainder" vacillates between the extremes of Left and Right, rejecting the prevalence of either or the permanence of both.

The fact that in Goethe's *Faust* a gnostic motif, albeit in classical guise, won public acceptance shows that the gnostic spirit touched something profound, if dangerous, in the heart of Europe. Faust, after all, achieves redemption having defied worldly, Christian morality. That a humanist such as Goethe and a nihilist like de Sade could share, however remotely, the same antinomian streak suggests something deeper than a coincidence of sentiment.

In its careful husbanding of spirit — that is, identity — the gnostic attitude rejects the ordinary materialist view of politics. Repudiating the necessity to choose between leftish authoritarian control and rightish egoism in the distribution of goods is gnostic. Politically, it is Anarchism. In the words of the Russian anarchist Mikhail Bakunin: "Man is not a being whose exclusive purpose in life is eating, drinking and providing shelter for himself. As soon as his material wants are satisfied . . . needs . . . of an artistic nature will thrust themselves forward. These needs are of the greatest variety; they vary in each and every individual and the more society is civilized, the more will individuality be developed, and the more desires will be varied."[16]

Anarchism appeared in the hangover that followed the Napoleonic Wars — after politics, of which so much had been expected, had discovered the limits of Left and Right. Rejecting their debate, the anarchist as political gnostic recognizes only the conflict between the individual and the system, whether it is capitalism (on the Right) or the state (on the Left). Indeed, gnostic motifs are evident in most proponents of anarchism, not least in the first truly anarchist political theorist, Proudhon,[17] when he evokes a malevolent demiurge: "God seems to follow an inverse and retrograde path; that intelligence, liberty, personality are constituted otherwise in God than in us; and that this originality of nature . . . makes God a being who is essentially anti-civilised, antiliberal, antihuman."[18]

Implicit in Proudhon's rejection of God is a dismissal of the standard of rationality to which Left and Right both appealed. Quite beyond Right and Left, his system characteristically emphasized complementarity over polarity and was duly called "Mutualism . . . the form of socialism . . . having most in common with capitalism."[19] Proudhon's conception of property runs against both communist and capitalist ideas: in claiming that "property is theft," he really means that property must be monopolized neither by capital nor by the state (the two hands of the materialist demiurge) but should be owned by the small proprietor who promises to work it. His ideal society is made up of independent, self-governing groups of workers engaged not in a struggle to rule, but in mutual support.[20] This is no less than the principle of contract between equal parties found in Mithraism — and it places Proudhon's idea precisely (if metaphorically) in the syncretic, Gnostic tradition.

The early nineteenth-century aristocrat Saint-Simon proposed an entirely different challenge to Left and Right. Indeed it was diametrically opposed to anarchism. In the sense that "diametrical" means both opposition and similarity, his system was opposite because he embraced authority — and similar because under that authority he would equally reject the duality of capitalism and socialism by combining them instead of opposing them to one another. A humane dictatorship of business and science would manage society not as a democracy but as a vast administration of technological and human progress reconciling all opposites, from male and female to worker and owner, in a sort of mystical, androgynous authoritarianism. Saint Simonianism has had some influence on the development of modern technocracy — but it strongly foreshadows the gradual dissolution of Left, Right, and democracy all at once in a trans-national, technocratic amalgam of business, science, and state paternalism. A Saint-Simonian dissolution of Left and Right may indeed be the way of the future.

Its transcendent solution of Left and Right would arrive at the cost of freedom, whereas with anarchy freedom would, in theory, be unleashed. At their best, Saint-Simon, Proudhon, and Bakunin began with an idea of man that transcended politics. The same might be said of Karl Marx — at his best. In the period before 1850, the young Marx produced a concept of what it is to be human that was vividly gnostic and more expressive of the Romantic longing to regain the fullness of life than anything he would produce afterward. In his 1844 *Philosophical and Economic Manuscripts*, he portrays man as worker, alienated from his true essence.[21] And communism, perhaps in its earliest formulation, is described as "the return of man himself as a *social*, i.e., really human, being, a complete and conscious return . . . It is the *definitive* resolution of the antagonism between man and nature, and between man and man."[22] Man's essence as whole and part has been broken up by the subjection of his individual needs to the needs of the group; society is removed from man and becomes an entity outside him that proceeds to make demands on him. Like Blake's Urizen with his dividers, man has created his own *fallen world* through successive separations of the self. Urizen's partition is, for Marx, alienation.

Marx's early critique cannot properly be called "Left" in the monolithic, materialist sense that the Left would later connote — any more than it can be called "Right." Marx's early protest is surely in essence the same protest as found in Proudhon; the same protest against the destruction of man's essence or identity through the separation and alienation of his capacities as found in Blake; and the same abhorrence of classical modernity and bourgeois hypocrisy as found in de Sade.

The almost compulsive return of the gnostic motif in the early nine-teenth century suggests a protest not easily appeased. The search for a lost self is manifest not just in art, anarchism, and early socialism but also in nationalism. Local coalescences of history, language, and culture, in their defiance of the imperial hegemonies that still ruled Europe, can be seen as projections of the ego onto the world, projections of the unique self as a unique culture, fulfilled in a distinct frontier. Nationalism, to use a clever formulation, is "pooled self esteem."[23] In romantic fashion it emphasized what was distinct rather than what was held in common; stressing what was held in common *within* only as a *means* to that distinct entity. And so nationalism transcends material dualities, uniting whole and parts, Left and Right. The resurgence of nationalism in the post-Soviet world, for example, has likewise rele-gated the economic debate of Left and Right to the background.

In nineteenth-century nationalism we once again find loss — this time associated with landscape and folkways disappearing under the onslaught of modernity.[24] The force of nationalism was emotional and in that sense it had an ancient model: almost everyone knew the Bible — and in the Bible lay the prototype of relentless national restoration — the Old Testament account of Israel.

Because of its portrayal in scripture and its unique circumstances in history, ancient Israel remains the prototype of the nation. And the standard national myth of greatness recalled from an Eden-like idyll, to the fall into bondage and forgetfulness, and the restoration of former glory was first told in Israel's sacred history.[25] As we have seen, the journey of fall and return is a Gnostic motif. Nationalism, a non-material value like the spirit, vertically transcends lateral worldly conflicts. Indeed, nationalism and gnostic feeling both tend to arrive when a worldly classical consensus no longer holds; just as nation-alism in the former Soviet Empire arrived upon the fall of Communism, skewing economic Left and Right.

Likewise, an old consensus was collapsing in the political and reli-gious chaos of Israel in the last centuries BCE. In the midst of this collapse, the Maccabees had to shore up an ancient image of the nation, constantly lost and recovered, its temple destroyed and rebuilt, its identity carried in the heart, preserved in exile and revived even in the absence of native territory. But the Jewish identification of soul and nation with God (the All) was unique for maintaining a headstrong spirit that did not transcend Left-Right territorial rationalization. The logic of Israel's territorial claims went back to Canaan: if Israel was to claim Canaan she must repudiate the native Canaanites: to preserve a separate identity, the priestly class recalled the old distinction between what was originally Jewish and what was perpetually Canaanite. Israel was sacred, Canaan profane; Israel the right hand, Canaan the left. The repudiation of Canaan was so deep that it split Israel herself into a northern, leftish, hedonistic, Canaanite-influenced part, and a puritan, rightish nation of Judah in the desert south. In turn, successive regimes of revolutionary high priests would claim to represent the "true nation" at the *right* hand of the Lord, accusing their predecessors of backsliding, of betraying the nation to the hegemon, whether it be Persia or the Seleucids. Duly, "the nations" are aligned with Satan, the forces of chaos and all that is evil; and the chosen people of Israel with God and all that is good.[26]

The territorial dualism of ancient Israel, however, was part of its nationalism, whereas the connection of nineteenth-century nationalism with economic well-being and political freedom was innocently presumed but by no means necessary. Rather, nationalism was Left only when it subverted an international monarchical order and Right only insofar as it supported a status quo such as Republicanism. It was a protean force that could become the servant of Left or Right. Its content, after all, was never rational. The patriot and proto-socialist Buonarotti, and the Italian Carbonari movement with whom he worked, cloaked themselves in a sort of underground mysticism.[27] The same Left-Right dissonance emerged among nationalist rebels who joined forces with parochial elements, like bandits, their doctrines steeped in traditionalism.[28]

The nationalist passions in the revolutions of 1848 have often been compared to the passions of 1968 — because of their international character, their romanticism, and the youth of their actors. But their most distinguishing common feature was the disarray of a vast Left that appeared more as riotous carnival than as an organized movement.

These were movements of a Left acting precipitously in its early and formless stages; revolutions of gnostic intuition and sensuality rather than of reason. In the 1848 uprisings, everywhere in Europe, nationalism, wages, working conditions, class resentment, and the romantic urge itself began to coalesce into dozens of revolts. There was little doubt about the object of protest: international monarchy. What this vast movement stood *for*, apart from some ill-defined freedom, was amorphous.

Louis Philippe by then had lost touch with the times. His minister, Guizot, unwilling to extend the franchise, blandly suggested that everyone place their hopes on getting rich. With a depression shaking the country and the hopes of the working man still entombed with the destruction of the Hébertistes in 1794, it was an insult. In February 1848, the middle and lower classes combined to overthrow the upper bourgeoisie, and once again the old rhetoric prevailed. A republican victory over bourgeois constitutional monarchists recalled with deep solemnity the ascendancy of the Girondins in 1792. Through its insistent references to the past, the practice of revolution had itself become "conservative" (and, it could be argued, remains so to this day) demonstrating that "all men are imprisoned by history or rather by their historical imagery."[29] Left and Right were reset like railway lines.

Once again there were middle-class republican "Girondins." Once again *Orléanisme* carried through from *Egalité* through to the July Monarchy of Louis Philippe. Cabinetmakers, or *ébénistes*, led a movement that took its cues from the *Sans Culotte* Jacobins of 1793; the hosiers, or *bonnetières*, were proletarian "Bonapartists." The past was alive and well. The monarchy's almost complete indifference to labour had produced an equal and opposite authoritarian socialism in the person of labour leader Auguste Blanqui. His Jacobinism became the rallying cry for the *mécaniciens*,[30] or railway mechanics, even though they represented a new, industrialized proletariat. Spontaneous demonstrations threatened violent insurrection, and Louis Philippe abdicated.

With the monarchy overturned, an unstable coalition of nostalgic revolutionary classes elected an unstable provisional government. Its leader, the poet Lamartine, provided it with a magnificent mask of romantic liberation. But his grand phrases were vain next to the forces that still seethed beneath. Like his revolution, the poet, according to

Marx, represented "no real interest, no definite class; this was the February revolution itself, the common uprising with its illusions, its poetry, its imagined content, its phrases."[31] Behind the pretty façade lurked the descendants of ancient rivalries within the Left — now from 1794. Seven liberal republican ministers had uneasily locked arms with three socialists. Avenging the memory of the Hébertistes, the socialists heralded the arrival of the proletarian Left in mainstream politics. The working class, ignored by history, had finally made itself heard — not however, as an expression of humanity, as Proudhon would have had it, but as a political faction.

France's revolt against the July Monarchy sparked ill-organized nationalist revolts across Europe. The territorial urge, however, is a poor expression for the longing of the *pneuma*, and nationalism failed, striking the spark of its spirit on revolts that grew more individual and secessionist in their parochialism. A century and a half later, Communist Yugoslavia's seamless transformation into an authoritarian, hyper-nationalist Serbia — socialist in name only — is the continuation of a trend begun in 1848. It is the hell-bent, gnostic drive that still prevails.

Behind the drama of French national fulfillment few saw the disharmony in Lamartine's liberal-socialist coalition — until the show was disrupted by an unheard-of demand. Louis Blanc, the main socialist representative, called for a Ministry of Labour to answer the problems of industrial employment. The other ministers turned a deaf ear. Blanc's last resort was the institution of National Workshops to relieve unemployment. However compromised he may have been, he would turn out to be the father of socialism; for it was in France (and not in England) that socialism first entered government, leaving the radical Left behind it.

For now the right-wing Neo-Jacobins, the new defenders of the status quo, and they faced Auguste Blanqui's wage-earning *mécaniciens* of a radical Jacobin Left. In May, when Blanqui and Raspail were driven by unemployment to attempt an overthrow of the assembly, they were decisively quelled by the troops of the Neo-Jacobin bourgeoisie. As summer approached, political struggle turned to dualistic class war. The split that once cleaved France now cleaved Jacobinism itself. And so it was once again in France that the storm clouds first gathered, foreshadowing a rift in politics, later in society, and eventually in the world itself. The debacle was peculiarly European. Material interests, true to Western traditions going back to Parmenides, were easily separated from questions about how and why one lives. Matter, in short, was easily separated from spirit. The primary questions about humankind and happiness, which had motivated Proudhon, the anarchists, the romantics, and the young Marx, were forgotten in the practicalities of material self-interest. Tactics began to replace goals. Means became ends. Ruthless pragmatism alone was victorious.

The gnostic element that had surfaced with romanticism promised the best in imaginative anarchism; and it promised the worst in totalitarianism. As totalitarianism buried imagination in its extremes, its gnostic forms would provide the last resort of outlaw nations and individuals alienated from the materialist debate of parliamentary Right and Left. Protean, changeable, allied provisionally with the extreme Left or Right, or withdrawing from politics into the protest of art, these marginalized groups effectively constitute "the remainder," a *third force* which, as we shall see, is a historical force. And the symptom of an illness.

IO

Perfection:
Marx and Christ

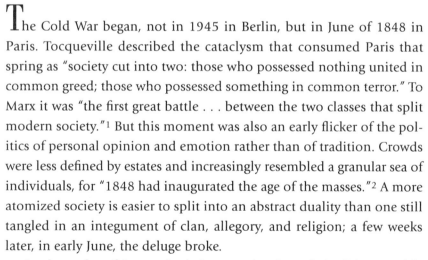

The Cold War began, not in 1945 in Berlin, but in June of 1848 in Paris. Tocqueville described the cataclysm that consumed Paris that spring as "society cut into two: those who possessed nothing united in common greed; those who possessed something in common terror." To Marx it was "the first great battle . . . between the two classes that split modern society."[1] But this moment was also an early flicker of the politics of personal opinion and emotion rather than of tradition. Crowds were less defined by estates and increasingly resembled a granular sea of individuals, for "1848 had inaugurated the age of the masses."[2] A more atomized society is easier to split into an abstract duality than one still tangled in an integument of clan, allegory, and religion; a few weeks later, in early June, the deluge broke.

In the wake of Lamartine's bourgeois triumph in February, his token socialist labour minister, Louis Blanc, looked to his immediate left and saw outside the walls of government the glowering, violent Jacobin proletarian Auguste Blanqui. On May 15, pressured by recalcitrant unemployment, Blanqui staged a mass socialist occupation of the assembly. The throngs that filled the hall took on a circus-like aspect, flying banners expressing solidarity with Polish and Italians oppressed by international monarchy. Their transnational militancy transcended republicanism and socialism, for "behind the dream, the towering image of Napoleon rose again."[3] The reborn mystical and militant moral imperialism of the Jacobins, that missionary "Bonapartism," would become a hallmark of the Left.

As a sop to the socialists, the government had allowed Blanc to set up experimental National Workshops — a giant make-work project for the unemployed. In response to proletarian unrest, the executive only fanned the flames by closing the *ateliers*. The working class was outraged into insurrection, Paris was divided, the army prevailed, and the proletariat was summarily slaughtered. Here, for the first time, in the words of Tocqueville, was an insurrection that "did not aim at changing the form of government but at altering the order of society. It was not, strictly speaking, a political struggle, in the sense which until then we have given to the word, but a combat of class against class, a sort of servile war . . . This formidable insurrection was not the enterprise of a certain number of conspirators, but the revolt of one whole section of the population against another. Women took part in it as well as men."[4]

But where in society did the split fall? The lowest on the ladder of the middle class, the *petite bourgeoisie* (the historian Georges Duveau's storekeeping *hosiers*), broke once and for all from the proletariat on the adjacent rung, adamantly calling itself bourgeois.[5] For even the poorest of those who owned property feared those who did not. Property had become the line where the Revolution divided the nation in those June days.[6] The romantic age of the high republican political rhetoric, which had ranked passions and ideas over welfare, had come to an end. The republican masses, defined by material concerns, by class and occupation, had seized the helm.

It was no accident that Karl Marx, an *émigré* social theorist who had witnessed the prelude to the crisis, claimed that circumstances in France accorded perfectly with his own science of society. And he lived in a hothouse: his fellow German exiles, cabinetmakers in the proletarian Faubourg St. Antoine, carried in their hearts not only a specifically German consciousness, but the German love-hatred of Napoleon, and global, universal Napoleonic solutions.[7] That sort of universality perfectly suited the abstract categories Marx saw everywhere around him.

Indeed, where else but in Germany, which seemed, through Leibniz, Kant, and Hegel to have swallowed Greek philosophy whole, could society be divided up conceptually?

The young Marx himself had been fully engaged in the split of the Young Hegelians in the 1830s — when a primordial Left and Right bifurcated on grounds that were baldly metaphysical. The radical "rational-is-the-real" faction, the view chosen by Marx, claimed that only pure reason had reality and that present conditions were inadequate, a mere stop on the way to the rational, just society. The mark of Platonic perfect forms and their inadequate shadows in reality would continue to inform his thinking. Ideal forms could, after all, approximate reality. Capitalism, unassisted by communism, had already built the two solitudes, whereby one class simply used the other for its own benefit. This duality was natural and true, and to get to the heart of it, Marx began with the individual. The individual, like society, had to be made whole again. To achieve fulfillment, he had to be freed from being defined only by his role in production. This was a human goal, not only a socialist goal, and it expressed the avowed terminus of Marx's communism: to be able to do "one thing today and another tomorrow, to hunt in the morning, fish in the afternoon, rear cattle in the evening, criticize after dinner . . . without ever becoming hunter, fisherman, shepherd or critic."[8] This was no grey dictatorship of the proletariat; it was, in Marx's view, the potential restoration of man's wholeness.

Marx's vision of the self was not new. Its individualism is Indo-European and Athenian; its perfectionism Platonic; its leisure and liberty aristocratic. It pictures the future in an image conjured from the distant past, a place without coercion by state or government,[9] a balance of free collectivity and individuality accidentally wrought on the Eurasian plain perhaps in late paleolithic times.[10] It was a romantic idea and not the only conservatism that Marx held in common with Western society. He shared certain premises with capitalism, if only because classical economics itself contained at its roots the very duality that produced capitalism and socialism.[11] On the one hand was the liberty required by its entrepreneurial side; and on the other the stability and justice that labour needed in order to produce, according to the theory of real value.[12]

Marx's starting point, in fact his very foundation, was the capitalist method of production.[13] Not only does capitalism lie at the heart of communism but classical economics discloses the communism that lies at the heart of capitalism; for capitalism also collectivizes the worker. Communism did not invent collectivism, but inherited it as a hand-me-down from its capitalist elder sister. Even Marx's use of history is conservative. The clockwork universe of Adam Smith's deism irresistibly suggested the no less mechanical dialectical materialism of Marx — with the difference that the latter is linear, an historical assembly line (interrupted by crises, accelerated by revolutions) producing proletarian freedom as its end product. Otherwise both were progressive perpetual motion machines.

Communism and capitalism had enough similarity that the only remaining step in Marx's theory was "the transformation of capitalised property already practically resting on socialised production, into socialised property."[14] With the full arrival of the modern era a century later, both capitalism and socialism would be implicated in the general lie that substitutes for individual welfare a fictive "general interest."[15] In the end, "Marxism and capitalism are like sisters who live in hatred and envy toward one another. Both are direct descendants of Enlightenment faith in progress. For both, industrial expansion is the guide to a happier future, the hallmark of the arrival of better times . . . The differences . . . are . . . mirror images of one another; there is a similarity precisely in the points of difference. Moreover, the remaining differences share the common denominator of the necessity of progress."[16]

By exploiting the common roots of socialism and capitalism, Marx became the agent not of newly discovered economic laws but of Western tradition. By 1848 Jacobinism itself had become a political microcosm of this same double force. And Jacobinism was especially appropriate to Marx's program; not least because concepts of messianic progress from the Old Testament endured in Jacobinism and Marxism alike.[17] Northrop Frye even goes so far as to describe Marxism as "the direct heir of the revolutionary and socially organised forms of religion derived from the Bible."[18] The son of a Jewish convert to Protestantism on a continent still steeped in Catholicism, Marx was heir to all three religious traditions and the implicit dualism of each — but especially the Jewish: "The social dualism between the elect and the reprobate, between the people of God and the Gentile world power, was a fact of bitter personal experience."[19]

The influence of European Christianity came through Marx's intellectual predecessors, the children of Royal absolutism. Robert Turgot, as controller-general of Louis XVI, moved from theology to economics, and messianic ideas slipped seamlessly into his own idea of progressive social change.[20] The Comte de Saint-Simon saw God's presence in social progress driven by an authoritarian technocracy.

The positivist Auguste Comte, a student of Saint-Simon, conceived of life as pure matter so that it was completely pliable to rational improvement — again under a technological, secular authoritarianism. But in Comte's case, it took a nervous breakdown to reveal to him the undeniable Christian messianism that lay at the heart of his atheistic, positivist mission. So it is not surprising that his contemporary, the socialist visionary Charles Fourier, expressed the secular version of an egalitarian New Jerusalem descended from Heaven to a world swept clean of civilization.

These thinkers were utopians, and Marx condemns their ideal societies if only because they are planned instead of being the natural outcome of a scientific, dialectical process. But the perfection and finality of Marx's vision is itself undeniably utopian.[21] And Marx more than anyone was to deduce from his stateless proletarian heaven the apocalyptic dualism of Christianity — in which you were one of the elect or one of the damned. Indeed, the circumstances in which Marx and Christianity appeared bear some comparison.

As prophets in times of economic and social crisis, Marx and Jesus were both able, consciously or not, to resort to firmly rooted messianic traditions. Messianism was an incentive to moral and social reform and was not confined to the prophets of Israel. Around the time that Amos decried the oppression of the poor, the Orphic Greeks reformed the decadent rites of Dionysus. A similar pattern of asceticism, restraint, and renewed moral order reappears in Marx's reform of capitalism. The concepts of the individual *self*, ancient and modern, from which these ideas are projected, also bear comparison. In both cases, the self has a better half that has been lost or alienated, and reform implies its retrieval. This sense of loss also drives contemporary Left and Right; the free marketeer longs for a stable self as defined by family, a stability left behind in the 1950s; the traditional Leftist feels the loss of a materially secure proletarian self that was abandoned in the 1970s. And without doubt loss will be a keynote of the new millennium.

Indeed nostalgia is sometimes a mask for something that is deeper. A self that is "still here" in conjunction with a "departed self" — ancient or modern — implies a self that is double. In the centuries before Christ, the gods themselves had become models for the restoration of the alienated spirit — lost innocence or lost divinity — to man. Theocrasia had produced out of polytheism dual gods integrating two specific human qualities, or two man-gods who dramatized for the individual the sense of a second, spiritual self. If the loss of one element — spirit — is associated with social or personal dislocation, morality is no longer a practical matter of maintaining order. It becomes transcendent — it chases after the spirit as if to retrieve it.

Here we recognize the old, syncretic, Gnostic distinction between this fallen world and the lost other world — between a social self and an alienated true self — which, at that time, increasingly gripped the Mediterranean. In Israel, in the middle of the second century BCE, the poor saw that the wicked were still rewarded and the humble made to suffer. The need for sanctions to protect the poor soon revived the former protective morality of the Old Testament prophetic tradition called Deutero-Isaiah, as decadence came to personify the rich and otherworldly, purity the poor. From self lost and regained developed a congruent duality of Hell and Heaven.

Gehenna, on the edge of Jerusalem, had been a constantly smouldering garbage dump, the place where deviant Jews had made burnt sacrifices of their children in heathen ritual.[22] Now, in times of moral decay and under Persian and Hasidic influence, it came to symbolize eternal fire and damnation.

But it is with the Essenes that we find the culmination and purification of all the dual influences produced in the Gnostic synthesis; reduced, in fact, to a return to the primeval code of sacred and profane in all its starkness. The Essenes' reverence for the right hand will follow into Christianity. Their rejection of the world in favour of an occulted, abstracted God indeed bears the mark of Gnosis.[23] And the influence of Persian Zurvanite (Zoroastrian) dualism upon the Essenes[24] seems indubitable. Persian-influenced late Judaism is reflected too in the eschatology of the book of Daniel, which also figures among the Dead Sea texts of the Essenes.[25]

This world — rife with confusion, uncertainty, and apocalyptic hopes and terrors — was the world into which Jesus was born. What Jesus expressed was its corollary, the Gnostic mood, if we understand Gnosticism by a *simplification*, the bypassing of worldly institutions to the direct worship of a vaster, more mysterious God of love, a more lucid duality of God and self, Good and evil; and indeed, Norman Cohn remarks that, of all the sects, the Jesus sect was most influenced by that foundation stone of Gnosticism, Zoroastrianism.[26] And so it is not surprising that the terminology associated with Jesus or attributed to him is frequently Gnostic.[27]

This simplifying Gnostic law of love, which rejects worldly dualities for the vertical duality framed as a choice between God and the world, is behind Jesus' declaration: "Do not think that I have come to bring peace on earth, no, rather division; from now on in one house there shall be five divided, three against two and two against three; they will be divided father against son and son against father, mother against daughter and daughter against mother."[28] And more starkly, "Whoever is not with me is against me and whoever does not gather with me, scatters."[29] Here was the prophet not just of salvation but of the universalizing tragedy of Western history.

That universalization began with the gradual destruction of Israel herself, whose most important holy sites, boundaries, and dualities had, until then, been internal. But, in Frye's words again, "The division of the kingdom and the conquests that followed cut the sacred space down to Judah, then to Jerusalem, then the Temple, and finally to the Holy of Holies within the Temple. With the sacrilege of Antiochus, perhaps repeated in intention by Caligula, the last vestige of the Sacred disappears. For Christianity this was an indication that a central or sacred place could no longer exist."[30] With the final rending of the curtain in the Holy of Holies upon the death of Jesus, the sacred was no longer in one place or nation, but everywhere. And with the pervasive spread of the holy into the universal and abstract, the Left and Right hands were freed to float above the ruins.

The first Christian ideologists were, in a sense, the four evangelists, if only because they saw the Jewish defeat (AD 70) as the threshold to an extended apocalypse. The life and death of Jesus became, in retrospect, the rehearsal for a cosmic drama that revived, in this case against Rome, Old Testament ideas of divine revenge upon the nations by the chosen people.[31] From here, in fact, we may date the gradual secularization of a sacred vertical duality into a horizontal secular duality through which a discrete religious polarity will endure, emerging in modern Left and Right. The depth and recalcitrance of the dualism can be traced to the Persian influence in the gnostic attitude which made its way into Revelations.[32]

In the New Testament writings of the evangelists, in fact, the symbolism of right and left reaches a density that it did not have even in the Old. Moreover, much of New Testament hand symbolism seems to have been deliberate rather than traditional. It is said to have a common source in the normative passage of Psalms 110:1,[33] which, according to Matthew, was the Old Testament verse most often quoted by Jesus: "The Lord said unto my Lord, sit thou at my right hand, until I make thine enemies a footstool."[34] In early Christian customs, orientation continued to be toward the east, where the right hand was still fixed as the south hand, the hand of light; and the left the hand of north and darkness.[35] But it was St. Paul more than anyone who would universalize that dualism. For it is he who carries the dualism in Judaism and Gnosticism into Christianity and thenceforward into the world in greater and vaster abstraction.[36] And the globalization of concepts, a hallmark of our own age, really took its first step when Pauline Christianity bypassed the Jews and moved out into the vast world of the Gentiles.

Eighteen centuries later, the Gnostic, messianic dualism in Christian doctrine, whether unconscious in Marx or conscious in Saint-Simon, was most explicit in the French proletarian revolutionaries of the Napoleonic and post-Napoleonic period. The ragged wage-earning heirs to the *Hébertistes* were the modern inheritors of the proles of Rome — those with nothing to give but children. Christian Messianism, Jacobinism, and the proletarian Left had first come together in the person of "Gracchus," François Babeuf. It was Babeuf who brought the proles into their own. Drawing on Old Testament prophecy, Spartan solidarity, and Judeo-Christian Messianism, he declared that the bourgeoisie formed a new aristocracy worse than the old; that a "war between the rich and the poor" was already in progress; and that the sheer iniquity and power of the Right made a democratic solution impossible.[37]

The conversion of Babeuf's ideas into systematic doctrine was the work of a disciple, Buonarotti. The man who put Babeuf and Buonarotti into action was the radical proletarian revolutionary and tragic hero of 1848, Auguste Blanqui. And most crucially it is to Blanqui that we owe the contribution of Jacobin authoritarianism to Marxist economic revolution, as Marx himself acknowledged: "The proletariat rallies more and more round revolutionary socialism, round communism, for which the bourgeoisie has invented the name Blanqui."[38]

The Judeo-Christian historical script transmitted from Babeuf through Blanqui to Marx was to betray itself increasingly in revolutionary practice.[39] Marx, of course, would deny it: it was history unrolling under the force of Reason that made things as they were, not religion, nor, worse, bourgeois morality or empathy. But, as Charles Taylor argues, just as the emotional content of Marx's philosophy is unacknowledged, so are its moral sources.[40] Marx, as angry and emotional as he was rational, claimed, in the paraphrase of Camus, that "work is profoundly dignified and unjustly despised. He rebelled against the degradation of work to the level of a commodity and of the worker to the level of an object."[41] Is this not the very same moral and emotional rabbinical advocacy that had been expressed on behalf of the wage earner in ancient Israel?[42] This is not historical inevitability; it is human need and human nature expressed in a reassuring religious Biblical paradigm, filled as it is with self-perpetuating metaphors and typologies.[43]

Nietzsche, who called the true moralist a "thinker who considers morality questionable . . . in short, a problem,"[44] relegated the Judeo-Christian morality that Marx took for granted to the genealogy of morals. Of course, prophets who cast themselves as revolutionaries rarely acknowledge the tradition of which they are a part.

Unable to admit intellectual forebears, Marx had to resort to an unmoved mover, and so to a form of theodicy, the intellectual superstructure that works out the justification for a god.[45] Marx's god is a *process*, dialectical materialism, the march of history toward the dictatorship of the proletariat and the destruction of class distinctions. Dialectical materialism is the arbiter of Good and Evil, the Marxist ideologist analogous to the shaman, who discerns which class is on the side of history, and which is outdated and condemned to the fires of revolution — all according to the ancient shamanism of Zoroastrian linear time, which produced "our historical time consciousness . . . in the Hebrew-Christian tradition with its rectilinear time concept."[46]

■

It is in Proudhon above all that Marx is exposed as a mechanical philosopher who merely rearranges the terms of philosophy and of society like building blocks. Marx, claiming that Proudhon simply did not understand the foundations of Hegelianism or of classical economics, was of course unwilling to question either, much less go further back. But the fact was that Proudhon was of a different family tree, that of Heraclitus, which maintained the play of opposites, while Marx descended from Parmenides and Zeno's dialectic, which worked toward their sterile elimination. But Heraclitus breathes yet. Whenever talk arises of worker-shareholders, worker participation in management, the partnership of labour and capital, this is cooperative interdependence — though imperfect — in the tradition of Proudhon and Heraclitus. Proudhon acknowledged the dialectical movement of history, but believed that the opposites of capital and labour could be mutually limiting and mutually productive if held in fertile opposition. There would be no Left or Right in a mutualist world because the interests of labour and capital would be identical.

For Marx, of course, the agenda was conquest, elimination; and since history wasn't going to do the job fast enough, he approved the Blanquiste idea of a Jacobin revolutionary vanguard. The vanguard, of course, is the new state in embryo: the Jacobin image of the state not as mediator of revolution but rather as Parmenidean plenum of perfection coterminous with society itself; a state that would attempt not to *make*, but to *be* the perfect society — so that its withering away, like the skin of a snake, would disclose a perfect, self-sustaining One. The perfect One is a mystical idea, and Marx's leap to mystical perfection is a leap into the past; for it really amounts to a modern mystery cult. His ideal of the reunion of man with his own essence as labour is but an echo of the Orphic's reunion of man as body with his purified soul as spirit. In both cases the journey, in true Indo-European fashion, is defined in pairs of opposites. Modern society's passage through a capitalist underworld to emerge in the socialist world of light is only a new form of the Orphic journey.

Could such relentless dualism originate anywhere but in the mind? Jung has remarked that the contradictions we conjure from nature are indeed in the mind.[47] As R.C. Tucker elaborates, it is "the decisive characteristic of mythic thought, that something by nature interior is apprehended as exterior, that a drama of the inner life of man is experienced and depicted as taking place in the outer world," with the result, in Marx's case, that "the dualism of conflicting forces of the alienated self was apprehended as a dualism of social forces, a class struggle in society, a warfare of labour and capital."[48] The temptation to project such cerebrally conceived dualities is still powerful. In the present world with its fragmentation, its tribalism and upsurge of new identities, permanent adherence to Left or to Right can no longer be a practical decision: the strain to preserve wholes, theories, and categories is perhaps more than ever an act of faith, of religious passion.

Is it any surprise then, that philosophy, not economics, is fundamental to Marx's work? Marx's attempt to dismantle metaphysics (with the help of Friedrich Engels) only reinforces it. Marx and Engels merely claimed that what man called spirit was his own material essence expressed in thought and action,[49] which oppression had caused him to alienate into religion.[50] All Marx had to do was to change terms of matter and spirit and move them about, thus retaining the dualism. By naming spirit thought and action, he never actually proved that spirit — and hence metaphysics — does not exist. All but hidden at the centre of the original argument is an impatient injunction to forbid that the "question" about spirit be asked; and only because it is impractical and counter-productive.[51] In fact, his efforts to reason away spirit only displace it like the proverbial attempt to push the wrinkle out of the rug. So Marx's Monism is no less vain than the Monism of

Parmenides' attempt to prove the opposite, that all is spirit and that matter and change are illusory. Part of the problem was that Marx, critical as he was of German idealistic (Hegelian) philosophy, abided by its terms, terms of a Greek provenance that he seems to have taken for granted, terms which stubbornly come in pairs and opposites no matter how they are named, no matter how they are moved about.

So radically was Marx's theory driven by the *whole*, so great was his partiality to economic and social categories, that he could not even defend the poor when the character of their work was individual — or "capitalist." But, of course, vast religio-philosophical categories allow of no such fine distinctions. Since only monopoly capital and socialized labour really counted, Proudhon's *petit bourgeois*, small proprietor, peasant, or self-employed artisan — neither owner nor proletarian, right nor left — doomed by their very ambivalence, were all lumped together as a reactionary adjunct of the bourgeoisie.[52]

Monistic concentration on massive and mobile "wholes" such as classes and economic categories leads to another problem. The assumption that stateless equality in freedom depends on economics alone entirely ignores the fact that once it is achieved, some other kind of social antagonism could then develop.[53] This indeed was Camus's observation, some thirty years before the politics of race, gender, and ethnicity began to displace the economics that had until then given the Left a single identity. Of course today's less industrialized, "electronic" small business is looking very much like a *petite bourgeoisie* — and it may very well be the small capitalist who will inherit the fight against the capitalism of big capital.

If Marx's categories were stretched to account for things that did not naturally fit, it was because, like a religious thinker who defines orthodoxy through revelation, he deduced those categories from above. Indeed, he almost admits with involuntary pride to raising his observations into Platonic ideas: "In direct contrast to German philosophy, which descends from heaven to earth, here we ascend from earth to heaven."[54] And so he ended up doing that of which he accuses others, including capitalists:[55] "First of all, an abstraction is made from a fact, then it is declared that the fact is based on abstraction."[56] His entire social theory, for example, needed for its foundation a thoroughly reactionary stunted bourgeoisie — not the energetic, protean, liberal bourgeoisie of Western Europe and America. So he chose as his straw man the immobile, stultified, German bourgeoisie.[57]

But of course he was one of them. Trapped in the terms of Hegelian idealism, Marx and Engels blindly carried moral essences forward from Feuerbach. All that remained was to link the essences and forms to social class. The answer came, ironically, from the writings of a Hegelian Prussian monarchist. Lorenz von Stein, in the service of monarchy and aristocracy, used Hegel's dual forms of *master* and *slave* to warn that in France, an ideal "master" in the capitalist class, was, by concentrating wealth, creating a dangerously embittered, ideal "slave" in the proletariat.[58] Here, surely, was a mould for Right and Left, provided by the forms of Hegelian abstraction.

In France, in the ruins of 1848, the concept of classes as ideal, scientific forms was far from most people's minds; indeed, Marx was scarcely known. Among the ruins, rich and poor were forgotten as opposing currents of authority and anarchy began to disturb the surface, breaking up proletarian Left and bourgeois Right each into opposing tendencies toward freedom and order. Under such strains, Marx's proletarian monolith had turned out to be "an indeterminate aggregate that resisted fusion because its social segments or quantities found themselves utterly incompatible under stress."[59] Perhaps indeed, Marx had "misdiagnosed the nature of the modern dilemma [in] attributing it to class struggle."[60]

The brief 1848 departmental by-election of Louis Napoleon, nephew of the one-time emperor, only goes to show the failure of the democratic, materialist Left-Right system. The sudden enthusiastic welcome of this ordinary man with an extraordinary name betrayed a feverish nostalgia for something primordial: a nostalgic rescue of self and identity — this time in authority — which, as we have said, has nothing to do with Left or Right but lies there like a sword to defy both.

II

Secession:

Anarchists and Heretics

As we have seen, it is the gnostic, vertical scheme, which opposes all authority, that confounds Left and Right. In France's spring insurrection of 1848, the marginal and bohemian element that had embraced the earlier February revolution ended up caring little for Socialists or Republicans. This odd role of poetic anti-partisan was played to perfection by the baleful figure of Charles Baudelaire. The poet mocked all "contractors for the public weal, including those whose remedy is that the poor should all accept slavery and those who preach that they are monarchs unjustly deprived of their kingdom."[1] In his rejection of worldly ideological duality, Baudelaire had adopted an attitude that can be described as politically gnostic. To avoid partisanship, a gnostic politics will resort to vacillation, satire, defiance, transcendence, withdrawal, indifference, or even nihilism. In the late 1960s it reappeared in art, sex, drugs, and rock 'n' roll.

In 1848, however, the gnostic attitude reflected a change in the legacy of revolution. As consensus stabilized again around a fixed arena of Left and Right, an anti-ideological dissonance appeared. In Europe at large, politics and anti-politics developed a new gulf: "between an extreme collectivism and an equally extreme individualism."[2] Left and Right now shared more of a consensus. "Left" no longer meant liberation or individual rights — those had been absorbed and embalmed in the Right. "Left" meant, almost exclusively, Labour. Within the confines of the nation, economics was now everything, as the romance of a heroic politics gave way to party machines and coalitions, or to benign dictatorship.

After 1850, the state was supreme, and material progress overshadowed liberty and equality. To the extent that the Right upheld the status quo, it maintained the momentum. Even in its most revolutionary initiatives, the Left, by virtue of its critical stance, was doomed to a position of constant *reaction* to the Right, which caused it to fragment according to changing cultural and economic circumstances, wealth and poverty notwithstanding.[3] That is because the Right, as the status quo, had the power to exploit changes and differences in external circumstances, while the Left tries to limit them. The same is true today as the Left, more than the Right, has had trouble agreeing on how to adapt to new technologies and the fall of communism. So the Left has never been consistent. In Teutonic Europe, trends in political authoritarianism were endorsed by the Left as well as the Right. In south-eastern France and in Spain, where rural artisanry and peasant independence dominated, the Left was anarchistic.[4] In most of Western Europe, manifestations of the Left were both democratic and anti-democratic; nationalist and internationalist; mainstream and anarchist; trade-union materialist and anti–trade-union revolutionary.

While differing circumstances split the Left, they reinforced the Right; and that meant a stable, bourgeois Europe. In that sense the situation of the mid-to-late nineteenth century resembled the situation today. England exemplified the lack of political polarity at that time.[5] An upper-class *noblesse oblige*, which leaned down and helped with its left hand while retaining power in its right, was expressed in the middle-class consensus that characterized the regime of Lord Palmerston.[6] Social tendencies were liberalized and liberal tendencies socialized.[7] Gladstone and Disraeli, as Liberal and Conservative, competed for the loyalty of the working class through education and the reform of working conditions. They differed little over the middle class. Their only real point of divergence was the aristocracy: Gladstone would curtail its privilege; Disraeli would uphold it. But Left and Right were not transcended; they were merely submerged. We have seen this submersion in our own time: in the skilfully brokered technocracies of France and South America in the 1980s and, a decade later, in the Clinton-Blair phenomenon.

At the close of the nineteenth century, a boom-and-bust economy brought back a polarization not known since the days of Chartism. The utilitarian Benthamite foundation finally reverted to its old cornerstones of Left and Right in an overt split; its conservative wing applied utilitarianism to rights and law; its Left applied Bentham to economics and social class.[8] Hard times finally brought a trade-union left into parliament with the Labour Party. At the same time, the individualism that had hovered on the outside of politics came knocking. Bread alone, it turned out, would not win dignity, and personal, non-economic issues emerged to split the economically based liberal and conservative parties, undermining the consensus they had formed around economic welfare. Female suffrage and Irish home rule began to produce a social Right and Left that often cut across the economic Right and Left of parliament. Opposition to the continued privilege of the House of Lords remained almost the only unifying force around the Left.

In France, by mid-century, Left and Right were so submerged that the terminology of dualism receded for the first time from the vocabulary of French politics.[9] Louis Napoleon's dictatorship was characterized by that petit-bourgeois neo-Jacobinism that held fast to the Left-Right technocratic paternalism of Saint-Simon and Auguste Comte, with a nod to the mutualism of Proudhon. In Germany, Bismarck suppressed Left and Right when he corralled the *Junker*, landed aristocracy into serving as an obedient managerial elite, disarmed the proletariat with a state welfare program, and assured the acquiescence of the bourgeoisie — all in the name of the Left-Right bureaucratic state.

It is somehow fitting that the sole authentic rebel of this period could only place himself beyond the whole tradition, Left, Right, or both. Friedrich Nietzsche had no use for the progressing cavalcade of Western thought. Instead, he rammed it broadside at full speed. Left and Right were both "'a distinction without a difference' since both relied on a gross materialist view of the world and both placed the same demands on the omnipotent power of the state."[10]

Nietzsche endures. His ethic is alive in American right-wing survivalists and in the left-wing relativism of the Politically Correct.

A generation younger than Marx, he was born of the same dissatisfaction with liberal, classical Europe. But if the *malaise* is the same, the terms diverge in almost every instance. Marx's interpretation is social, an array of wholes, categories, classes: it is man's essence as producer that has been lost. Nietzsche's focus is the individual: the key to remaking the world is the remaking of the individual — whose ultimate nature is not economic, but consists of a cultural and spiritual potential to be rescued from a moribund civilization. Where, Nietzsche asked, had we gone wrong? His point of recovery from the past was the intoxicated, pre-rationalist, pre-Socratic tragedian of the rites of Dionysus. That of Marx was its dialectical opposite: the rational, reforming Orphic priest who restrained the Dionysian orgiast.

Is Nietzsche Marx's opposite? Marx is now the grandfather of the Left, and Nietzsche has been popularly associated with the Right. But the Left has claimed him as well. The answer lies in a transcendent ambivalence; for the aristocracy that he exalts, as we shall see, is not the privileged group of race or class, but a hypothetical aristocracy of talent and attitude. Nietzsche's inegalitarianism may be Right; but in his spiritual — as opposed to material — liberation of the human individual, and in his attacks on capitalism, he is Left. Still, Marx was influential, long before Nietzsche.

The solution came from an odd direction. At Alexandria, Indian ideas resembling the *Upanishads* seem to have been introduced into Neoplatonism by Ammonius Saccas.[11] His colleagues, the Church fathers, Clement of Alexandria and Origen, brought a daunting rational abstraction forward into Christianity. Its harm, according to many scholars would be profound and long-lasting.[12] Appealing to the sharp, logical dualism in orientalized Neoplatonism, Origen found evil squarely in matter rather than in the human will. Without acknowledging the strong gnostic element in this sharpened Neoplatonism, Christianity exploited its powerful dualism of spirit and matter as a way of separating itself from paganism.[13] The Christian dualism that developed in the Western Mediterranean region of North Africa was different. Tertullian of Carthage eschewed Origen's mystical rationalism, consigned God to absurd mystery, and embraced the world, choosing instead the dualism of a political polemic against Imperial Rome. But either way, existence was divided: philosophically through Origen, politically through Tertullian. The process, cumbersome as it seems, was in fact the means by which Christianity cut its last ties to the pagan world.

The final, radical development of Christian dualism arrived with a thoroughly pagan Neoplatonist, the Egyptian scholar Plotinus, a student of Ammonius Saccas. In Plotinus's system, a divine Being composed of pure Parmenidean intellect emits all of creation in a vast beam of light that fades to its end in inferior matter. Alhough the Church rejected Plotinus's dogma, it was to armour itself with his God of unspeakable rational beauty and the human dependence and inferiority it defined. Here was fall and redemption, saved and damned, reinforced with the logic of an equation. Specifically, this resort to philosophy defined a single orthodoxy for a Christian Gnostic sect against the Gnostic plurality from which it has arisen: the One against the many — the perfect intellectual paradigm for politics.

■

The attitude of the early Marx was still effectively gnostic — he declared that man must aspire beyond a fallen world to a higher, reintegrated concept of self. But Marx, like the Church, would turn his gnostic heterodoxy into an orthodoxy, determining a more materialist worldly dualism by deciding what was heresy. Before he did so, the Left had been "polytheistic" — heterodox much like the post-Marxist Left of today (the Left of labour, social democracy, identity, and the environment). The last heterodox, pre-Marxist Left died with the Paris Commune of 1871.

When the conservative Third Republic of Thiers surrendered to a German army in 1870, the Parisian working class held out alone by seceding from the nation in the form of a revolutionary Commune. Of its eighty-one members, half were neo-Jacobins: small businessmen and professionals who looked back to the Jacobin Constitution of 1793. The other half was socialistic — divided almost equally between Blanquist authoritarians, Proudhonian mutualist anarchists, and Marxists.[14] Their program, moreover, was mutualist; they declared the Commune of Paris to be the first of a loose federation of Communes that would constitute all of France. After their slaughter by the army of the Third Republic, Europe had dreamed and seen, all too briefly, the government of the dispossessed, free of ideology, free of dogma; certainly not conservative but very hard to call Left or Right in any ultimate sense at all.

As if to build socialism from the ruins, Marx walked into the Congress of the International Working Men's Association of 1878, separated out Marxist socialism, and, by the logic of theology, consigned everything from old-fashioned utopianism to anarchism to all that smacked of his feared *Lumpenproletariat*, or *petite bourgeoisie*, to the Right. That is, he weeded out the "gnostics." What remained, as Roberto Calasso points out, was a pure constituency determined merely by its *organizability*, that is, the factory proletariat.[15] For the anarchist Bakunin, "Marx had repudiated revolution as a search for liberty and 'institutionalized the same "pan-Germanic" authoritarianism within the proletarian camp that Bismarck had introduced into Bourgeois political life' . . . giving rise to the taunt 'Bismarxism.'"[16]

Mechanized, expanded, and bolstered by the concept of the state, Left and Right would be carried forward by modernity itself. Armed with state, knowledge, and reason, Left and Right each disclosed itself as the force of a common, materialist modernity; of bread and circuses whether earned or distributed. Fair distribution or the right to profit became ends in themselves.

The slumber of nineteenth-century materialism may only now be wearing off as non-economic concerns try again to fit themselves into the old forms of Left and Right. But visionaries like Dostoevsky and Baudelaire had already noted that something was missing. As Nietzsche put it, "The waters of religion are ebbing and leaving swamps or stagnant pools . . . Never was the world more worldly, never poorer in goodness and love," leaving "the blurred lines and the dull colours in the picture of modern life."[17] Modernity would slowly relieve the Right — and even the Left — of variety and complexity. The German socialist Bernstein disinterred the spirit of Louis Blanc and challenged Marx by proposing socialism as a reform of capitalism, a cooperating and communicating opposite to the Right. A reaction against this rational homogenization around a narrower goal of material well-being produced what might loosely be called philosophical *vitalism*, the rescue of life from static, material reason, and a source of individual rebellion of the individual that continues today.

It was in that very spirit that the French philosopher Henri Bergson, by introducing the concept of the *élan vital*, proposed that life is a continuum and can only be understood as motion and change; the individual is not fixed by identity or interest. By the beginning of the twentieth century, his "exaltation of instinct over intelligence . . . and vital experience over social conformism had become a common ground for French thinkers of both the Left and the Right."[18] With Bergson's contemporary, Edmund Husserl, "phenomenology" posited that an individual's point of view is formed from the perception of the present moment, and not by doctrines and institutions. Choice was unleashed.

And in a sense, the philosopher of choice was Nietzsche. His observation that reason works best not as master of the passions but as their servant suggests that unquestioned allegiances to Left or Right could become an empty formality like Sunday Church for the faithless — decided *not* out of rational self-interest, but out of conformism, impulse, sentiment, hero-worship, or habit.[19] And therefore not chosen. If the private self found little real expression in politics, let alone in religion, where was it to turn? Indeed, to Left and Right, but no longer to Left and Right as the hollow forms of parties: rather, as the narrow conduits of subterranean and explosive passions. "For a century," Nietzsche wrote, "we have been ready for a world-shaking convulsion and though we have lately been trying to set the conservative strength of the so-called national state against the great modern tendency to volcanic self-destructiveness, it will only be, for a long time yet, an aggravation of the universal unrest that hangs over us."[20]

The proper and healthy release of this unrest was, of course, Anarchism. Anarchism, contrary to popular definition, is not opposition to all government. It is, rather, the attempt to find the minimum authority that can guarantee an optimum of individual liberty and equality — beyond Left or Right. So it's not the "fringe lifestyle" Left that the media describe when so-called anarchists meet in conventions today. Rather, the great Anarchists are distinguished from one another by the degree of centralization they would concede to authority. Proudhon advocated the worker's gradual rise to autonomy and the decentralization of capitalist society into a loose association of communes. The Russian aristocrat Mikhail Bakunin revered Proudhon but diverged in his belief that state and society must immediately be destroyed and then replaced with communes in a tighter association. What distinguishes the Russian philosopher Prince Pyotr Kropotkin from Proudhon and Bakunin is his proposal to replace wages with a loose, federal system of barter and distribution, based on respective needs rather than on work. None gives a significant place to the state.

Altogether, these three anarchist thinkers reveal the weakness at the heart of the distinction of Left and Right. If "Right" is defined as individual liberty and "Left" as equality guaranteed by authority — Proudhon sits firmly on the Right and Marx on the Left. If, on the contrary, "Right" is authority and "Left" is individual freedom guaranteed by loose association, then Proudhon sits at the far Left and Marx sits at the far Right next to the authoritarian capitalist state.

Max Stirner, author of *The Ego and His Own*, is the only anarchist who refuses to lean either way. *The Ego and His Own* is a manifesto of the individual triumphant, free, and unique. Justice, in the complete absence of authority, is reduced to ferocious self-assertion in a state of natural violence, in a timeless zone where Left and Right meet and become both and neither. Roberto Calasso suggests Stirner's sovereign individual was the uneasy, hidden reality that ultimately drove Nietzsche and Marx.[21] And if he were *lumpen* — unrecognized or exploited — so dangerous and uncontainable that Marx quickly drew the veil of the collective proletarian over this unbearable spectre that haunted Europe,[22] it likely caused less unease to Nietzsche, who cared less than Marx that the common man unbound did not mean an obedient, socialized worker, of Left or Right.

Stirner's book sold far better in the 1890s than it had upon its publication in mid-century — perhaps because it reflected the growing gulf between the outer world and the private self. Bureaucracy had moved seamlessly from servant to master: if on the Left it would reach further into the private realm, on the Right it encouraged the subordination of politics to the market.[23] In either case, authority became management, or, in Hannah Arendt's term, "rule by nobody."[24] Democracy was much the same. Left or Right, elected governments had been selected from socio-political elites with pre-formed sets of ideas and only a limited relation to the individuals who voted for them.[25]

Even the concept of society was fast losing its old sense of moral leadership by an elite authorized by religion, history, and allegory. As an object of dissent, society provided a less focused target — having expanded to contain so much of the population that the marginal areas for revolutionary activity diminished. Society expanded became "the crowd," typified in the anarchic human river of all classes on the Nevsky Prospekt, on the Champs Elysées, the Strand, on Broadway — indefinable, mute, and intimidating. Political choices became as faceless as the amorphous collectivity they tried to represent, Left or Right. "The crowd is the lie,"[26] said Søren Kierkegaard. A mere agglomeration of individuals, a crowd cannot be responsible, cannot have a voice, cannot think. As society expanded it lost meaning; as Left and Right became coterminous with society, so did they.

The amorphousness of Left and Right lies heavy on our time. But the reaction against society-as-crowd began a century ago when gnostic thinking made a reappearance among the marginalized, sharper and darker than any emotional stirrings during the Romantic period. In a new cosmos rendered meaningless by the opacity of the masses and by the infinity discovered by science, there was the echo of an ancient malaise.[27] For ancient and modern Gnostics alike, all dualities evaporate save for the individual and an unresponsive world; or the individual and a silent God.[28] In the first existentialists, Stirner, Nietzsche, Baudelaire, and Kierkegaard, we have the modern age's final rebellion against Parmenides; as Parmenides inverted, it is the *whole* as crowd, the *idea* of society, that is the illusion, the individual that becomes the sovereign fact.

This is existentialism; it will qualify and even dissolve political Left and Right. For Kierkegaard, true faith is the frightened striving toward the God that does not disclose itself in reason: he is the *anti-Plotinus* par excellence. With Kierkegaard, the evaporation of rational dualism in religion, involvement in any rational social duality disappears as well. Rejecting the liberal-rational attempt to understand the world — typified by Benthamite reason — Kierkegaard anticipates what John Carroll calls the anarcho-psychological critique.[29]

The anarcho-psychological critique consigns Left and Right to the tired and profane realm of Enlightenment Reason. Behind it looms a larger, gnostic dialectic between self and rational world — between the non-ideological and the ideological. For Nietzsche it is sheer talent ranged against the reasoned consensus of the herd. For Dostoevsky the duality is strung between Jesus, who dares man to seize his freedom and choose Good, come what may, and the Grand Inquisitor as earthly authority in the guise of Western Reason, Left or Right. In the modern gnostic duality, the healthy take joy in the tragic tension between the finite and the infinite; while the sickly — socialism, capitalism, and European Christianity — languish in a rational pursuit of justice conceived solely as material comfort.

On behalf of the latter, Marx still stands with Plato between Parmenides and Heraclitus, using classes as essential wholes and history as a process of *becoming*. In contrast, the anarcho-psychological approach amounts to an absolute rejection of Western metaphysics. Hans Jonas points us again to the Gnostic, Hellenistic antecedent, which began to disdain the rationalism of the whole and the parts.[30] Duly, Kierkegaard rejects the reduction of man to "races" and "species,"[31] seeing him only as a striving *possibility*. And Nietzsche, at one blow, smashes the duality of being and becoming when he pulls *being* down from heaven, enthroning it as the supreme value here on earth — *life as it is*.[32]

This is why Nietzsche judges thinkers only as *personalities*, dismissing radical Rousseau as reckless and superficial, and conservative Goethe as too cautious and ruminative: he transcends the two as his "left" and "right" with Schopenhauer, who stares wryly and frankly at the problem of the insatiable individual will.[33]

So it is Nietzsche as a *personality* who disdains the capitalism that starves the individual of nourishment by the community, and deprives the community of any common project.[34] He turns equally against socialism as a "collectivist messianism" that can only end in mediocrity, and meanwhile calls[35] for a Roman Caesar with the soul of Christ. To his mind this was to say yes to both slave and master.[36] Like a true Athenian he would even combine aristocracy and democracy. After all, "the greatest evil belongs with the greatest good. This, however is the creative good."[37] Dostoevsky defends the personality of Russia against faceless socialism and capitalism. Baudelaire declares "commerce is, in its very essence, Satanic"[38] and remains "a revolutionary who despised the masses and an aristocrat who loathed the ruling class."[39] Indeed, "the notion of ambivalence frames the entire anarcho-psychological perspective," writes John Carroll.[40] Baudelaire at the same time praises abstract socialism against the chaos of capitalism[41] and aristocracy against the socialist mediocrity. Left and Right, like worldly good and

187

evil, are fragments, bits and pieces of a shattered truth (God), in the final ruin after the fall.

By the late nineteenth century, the artist's relationship to the world was no longer rational; it was once again a posture of gnostic detachment. Never before had Europe's greatest talents so little participated in politics or served the state. In painting and literature we find the move toward private, unacknowledged truth, a tendency not toward *essences* but toward nominal fact, mundane and painful — in Flaubert, in Ibsen, in Strindberg. But it is still Baudelaire who is the master at putting irony before partisanship: attacking the bourgeois idolatry of life and nature, he delights in the cold and artificial.[42] His insurrectional type is the *dandy*, the high fop; his rebellion is blatant aristocratic artifice,[43] a protest against the dreary rationalism of Left and Right. As gnostic puppeteer, he refuses to take sides, instead regarding all oppositions as *dramatis personae* in his own comedy of existence. For the divine spark does not come from any spirit above the stage, but from Baudelaire himself, the artist as demiurge. Thus reality belongs to man and not to God or to reason: this is gnostic freedom of the libertine (not the ascetic) type.[44]

The problem in the late nineteenth century was that society had conceived of freedom without making a world for it. Aware of his freedom among rigid forms, man was cut adrift in his mind. This disparity was most acutely felt by the low clerical workers, the self-employed, the *petite bourgeoisie*. Their only hope was the very over-education that flaunted a world they could not enter. The *petit bourgeois* answer was defiance. Rejecting the autocratic Right, the Left, the bourgeois Liberal, and their rational, scientific self-interest were Marx's most loathed and "reactionary" *Lumpen* as well as Dostoevsky's *underground man*.[45] The first to be atomized by social change, this class forms a periphery, the *déclassés*, "no longer inside but opposite society."[46]

The unwanted children of capitalism and socialism are the *lumpen petits bourgeois* as *Gnostics*. But gone is any form onto which their dreams can be projected. As Robert Calasso interprets it, gone are the limits of myth, of allegory, the constraints of Apollonian, classical structure.[47] All that remain are husks, the forms of Left and Right, empty even of sacred and profane. Only time and place will determine whether their limitless, cosmic projection fills the form of Left as Communism or of Right as Fascism, with the masses as their raw material.

The *déclassés* were not without antecedents. In the third century, the Cynics, despising civilization and culture in favour of unadorned nature, were nearly cast into its deserts. Not unlike the underclass of the *petite bourgeoisie*, they were marginalized by a declining patrician class that would no longer pay them as tutors; and so they resorted to desert monasteries where, from their Cynicism, they developed heresies, among which was Gnosticism.[48]

Gnosticism, modern and ancient, betrays roots in the most ancient dualism of all: it is in the old Asia of the sacred and the profane that the Shaman undergoes a spiritual death before wakening to discover the true scheme of things. The first Shaman discovers sacred and profane. The second, discovering that it has been systematized as good and evil (or Left and Right) goes beyond it. For Nietzsche, Zoroaster was the first; and Nietzsche's own prototype, Zarathustra, was the second: Zoroaster reborn as an ironist. The first was neolithic, the second gnostic.

Gnosticism is really a default, a foundation from which humanity departs when it believes it has found a new worldly order in Good and Evil or Left and Right, and to which it returns when that morality begins to break down. But when the Church departed from Gnosticism, it retained the philosophical dualism in Gnosticism as a way of fighting gnostic and pagan heresy. That way it could align the Platonic whole: God and Church on one side against heretical Gnostic individualism, pagan polytheism, the Roman state and society on the other.[49] Indeed, in Christopher Dawson's analysis: "This social dualism is one of the most striking characteristics of early Christianity."[50]

But this dualism, this theological schism, still separates two worlds, above and below. In another century, as the Church finally absorbs the state and claims it as part of the kingdom of God against the heathen and the kingdom of Satan, the axis of conflict will fall ninety degrees toward an earthly, secular plane, anticipating the horizontal conflict of Left and Right. The Gnostic battle, which had been cosmic and vertical, becomes horizontal and divides the real world. These haunted, gnostic origins with their cosmic claims will reappear in communism and fascism. Left and Right, no longer eternal forms, will become their tools. But the sword that cleaved extreme Left from Right would still, like Robespierre's Virtue, have more *edge*, more power to cut, than it would have breadth or substance.

12

Totality:

Lenin and Augustine

As an instrument of dualism, the blade of Virtue was, as we have said, a Jacobin invention. In carving away a perfect social Whole from a fragmentary and unredeemable world, its legacy has come down to modern radicalism and revolution. At the time that radical Jacobinism made its last stand in the Paris Commune, Russia was suffering a social duality of rich and poor more extreme than any in Europe. The problem among the budding revolutionary groups was: Would a gradual social revolution really prepare the way for the necessary political upheaval? Or would the political upheaval first have to clear the field for building the social revolution?

The latter suited the student Peter Zaichnevsky's model for summary destruction — the Jacobin revolutionary élite: "We have not studied stern European History for nothing . . . We will henceforth not be the pitiful revolutionaries of 1848, but rather the great terrorists of 1792 . . . Elections for a national assembly must take place under the surveillance of the [revolutionary] government which will at once make sure that no partisans of the old order . . . make up the composition of this new assembly."[1] Zaichnevsky's writings influenced another Russian, Peter Tkachev. After Tkachev had joined a Blanquiste Communard circle in Geneva in 1875, he was imbued with Jacobin revolutionary

technique and the legacy of Robespierre.[2] Jacobin ideas were disseminated in Tkachev's journal, the *Tocsin* — which was to have a profound
influence on Vladimir Ilich Lenin.

▨

Jacobinism has often been described as "Manichaean" in the Left-Right
sense of seeing the world in "black and white." But the application of
"Manichaeism" to Jacobinism is more than a metaphor: their dualism
is linked, quite literally, through Christianity. In the middle of the third
century the first Manichaean, a Persian prophet called Mani, outdid even
Persian state Zoroastrianism in the polarity of his thinking. Mani conceived of two forces, Light and Darkness, as coeternal; that is, as having
different origins and thus being utterly alien[3] and irreconcilable. The
moral miasma that had begun to develop in the wake of Rome's rapid
expansion seemed to invite a more rational account of the coexistence
of Good and Evil. Mani's idea was attractive: the entire physical world,
down to and including the human body, is deep in the kingdom of darkness, while the human souls trapped within it are shattered bits of the
kingdom of light awaiting redemption.[4] The liberation of the Light from
Darkness would, centuries to come, provide an analogue to Revolution.

By the fourth century, Manichaeism had spread through North
Africa. There, it shared with Christianity and Neoplatonism a common
foundation in a gnostic, dualistic understanding of the cosmos. In St.
Augustine of Hippo we find the actual confluence of these three dualistic streams of thought. Born a pagan, Augustine embraced the perfect,
abstract Neoplatonic God of Plotinus, which had already split the universe between soul and body, mind and world;[5] while his youthful
Manichaeism would later cause him to stress St. Paul's gnostic rejection
of the material world. Even if evil was latent in the human *will*, that will
itself was understood by Augustine as an almost alien force that encloses
us and sins within us.[6] Society is part of that darkness, and cannot be
saved. And so, like the trapped Light in Manichaeism, our souls are in
need of superior intervention by the grace of God through the Church
and the sacraments. But only a few are foreordained to be saved. Not
only is there a strong streak of Gnostic pessimism here but we can discern a foreshadowing of the modern fringe radical who behaves as one
of the all-knowing elect.

Time, with its past and future, provided Augustine with yet another polarity. To explain the Church's difficulty in saving the world from paganism, he took from the Jewish Christian diaspora of the Western Mediterranean the old Hebrew moral-historical concept in which damned and saved were slowly brought to their judgement. This temporary coexistence of good and evil was worked out in *The City of God*, which distinguished "those who wish to live after the flesh, and those who wish to live after the spirit."[8] The City of God, represented by the Church, can advise the City of Man, or secular government, but cannot save it — a scheme in which the superior and inferior worlds of Plato are all too evident.[9]

Augustine is seminal in the roots of Left and Right. His doctrine of the predestination of saved and damned would boldly resurface in Protestant capitalism and in Jacobin and Marxist millenarianism alike. More conservative is his conviction that piracy and theft are man's natural tendency. Common ownership, impossible given man's evil, can only be realized in the City of God, that is, in Paradise.[9] More influential on the Left is his very idea that natural piracy includes the notion that all earthly power, indeed whole kingdoms, are seized in acts of theft. But perhaps most importantly, Augustine's philosophy implies altogether that the whole, the community, is emphasized over the individual.[10] Moreover, in time, "the modern linkage of destructive, coercive, terroristic revolution and the promise of utopia at the end is but a secularization (or rhetorical modification) of a cognate linkage to be seen throughout the Middle Ages and the Reformation, a link that goes directly back to Augustine's *The City of God*."[11] In the end, the irreconcilable dualism of what is and what ought to be — in the cities of Man and God — would produce a protracted conflict between Church and State.

The situation was quite different in the eastern realm of the Empire, in Constantinople. There, the Byzantine Church became a subordinate arm of the state, a ministry rather than a critic. This was partly the effect of a cultural duality between "collectivist" East and "individualist" West. In the ancient East, the mystery cults had stressed abstract wholes, concepts of purity, virtue, and salvation. In the West, the older gods of Rome still backed up the more worldly, individualist, and aristocratic, if fractious, Republic.

Security matters reinforced the same duality. Rome maintained a frontier that was manageable. In the east, the frontier was under constant attack, and the taxation needed for an expanding army produced the collective, bureaucratized polity that would become renowned as Byzantium. Law, trade syndicate, *polis*, and even citizenship began to lose their significance for the individual in favour of their importance for the welfare and defence of the whole. And the whole, of course, was seen to be identical with the despot, who reinforced his rule by emulating the divine right that the Zoroastrian Sassanids across the Bosphorus derived from Ahura Mazda.[12] Since absolute authority also required the exclusion of the aristocracy from the military, the empire in the East became at once more egalitarian and more authoritarian than in the West.[13] In the same way, the identity of the Emperor with the state made him custodian of public places, food subsidies, and public entertainments[14] — a sort of primitive "state welfare."

In the East, as well, the Church anticipated, copied, and then shared this authority. It had, during its time underground, formed a "shadow government" that already resembled a centralized state. As Christians grew in numbers, it became wiser for Emperor Constantine to draw strength from the Church by absorbing it than to place further stresses on the state by opposing it. Soon the Church was custodian of the poor and the sick; a welfare state within a state financed by donations from the god-fearing rich.[15]

In the Eastern Church, we see a primitive Left. Following St. Paul, it remained closer to its Gnostic roots;[16] it was simpler, its God more occulted, its focus more mystical, its theology more dogmatic. Its monistic sense of the One, from Origen through Neoplatonism, inclined it to join with the state, in contrast to the dualistic, critical stance taken by the Western, Augustinian tradition. That is why Eusebius, the court ideologist of Constantine, declared that the Byzantine state would *embody* rather than *indicate* the route to salvation.[17] This was a utopianism in which the loss of freedom was compensated for by social stability (a dilemma that hounds Russians to the present day). At its worst, it would produce form without content — like the "entity" of Parmenides. By contrast, the modern Western tradition of adversarial, democratic debate, which harks back to Augustine, carries with it a dark history of internal, Manichaean conflict. If division would be internal in the West, in the East the state as a unity would oppose itself as a unity to the West and to the world.

At this point it might be fair to ask if the Russian-Byzantine tradition truly forms part of the heritage of the Left, since many on the Left consider the Soviet model to be a betrayal. But it seems that indeed there is a line of descent, however broken. The Left's political evolution in Europe notwithstanding, it was through the Bosphorus and the Black Sea that the Gnostic and Early Christian monolith of Byzantium made its way north.

There, in the great barbarian bushlands near ninth-century Kiev and Muscovy, there had not been any durable concept of social organization beyond the tribe. Following the expansion of trade, Byzantine concepts of rule and kingship entered the hinterlands; and finally Orthodox Christianity. The tendency, however, was to transplant rather than to adapt. Orthodoxy is only one example; Gnosticism is another. In subsequent history, poverty would be the dominant social fact, and the nihilistic rejection of the present world in favour of a personal connection with a remote idea (the All) made the Gnosticism of the great dissenting heretic Marcion influential. From Marcion's cruel *Demiurge* (the Yaweh of the Old Testament) it is only a short step to atheism.[18] It was that gnostic distancing from a good god that freed man as Czar, or revolutionary state, to use unlimited power to save or to control the masses.[19] By the second half of the nineteenth century, the same gnostic nihilism would cause radical Rightists in the monarchy to prefer divine authority to worldly democratic ideas. And a similar gnostic mistrust of the world caused young Russian nihilists to embrace revolutionary authoritarianism instead of democracy.

This Russian equivalent to the marginalized, revolutionary European *petite bourgeoisie* was the intelligentsia, and it came from two sources. One part was plebeian, the other part aristocratic. The plebeian marginals, the *Raznochintsy*, were the offspring of the lower Orthodox clergy, the bureaucracy, and the army — the *apparat* of the Russian state. They used European ideas, unmodified, for "militant atheism, nihilism, anarchism — all amounting to an inverted Orthodoxy."[20] It is no surprise that many of the most radical among them arose from the seminaries,[21] nor that the "aristocrats," like Herzen and Bakunin, were more imaginative. But the *Raznochintsy*, of course, would prevail.

Despite them, the native semi-autonomous peasant cooperative, the *mir*, was seen as a model for positive change. Herzen, especially, saw the *mir* as the incarnation of the peasant's natural affinity for a primitive communism that mixed "rightish" liberties with the "leftish" cooperative. But it was not to be. With the liberation of the serfs in 1861, the Czar introduced a system of private property by which the peasants would purchase their land from the gentry through the gradual repayment of massive loans. The result was effective debt slavery and the perpetuation of the *mir* as an unfulfilled dream. And so in Russia, as in the seventh-century Middle East, as in the expansion of Rome, the impoverishment of the smallholder by debt would provoke equal and opposite dreams of utopia in this world or beyond.

The Russian peasant, after all, understood little of the Western, Roman conception of private property (approved and sanctified by Augustine).[22] Indeed, he understood even less of Right and Left. The peasant saw things "up and down" between God and Man, not laterally opposed between Czar and People, or even less between the alien forms of capitalism and socialism. And so, when the *Narodniks*, the *Raznochintsy* of the populist "young Left," set out to politicize the Russian peasant, they were wasting their energies on a mass that was innately neither Left nor Right, which still celebrated the rightish Czar as saviour and potential patron of their leftish primitive communism.

Land and Liberty, the first revolutionary movement, was no more coherent. Founded by westernizer Alexander Herzen, it contained upper and lower class, urban and rural, democratic and authoritarian revolutionary factions. From its Left, Herzen's "liberal" way fell victim to "The People's Will," a Raznochintsy terrorist outfit in southern Russia that operated without any concept of organization or discipline until a *Raznochinets* called Romanenko imported the solution of Jacobinism. It was around then that Peter Tkachev brought Jacobinism to the most influential of the Nihilists, Sergei Nechaev, in the urban cells of Moscow and St. Petersburg. In the Jacobinism of Nechaev we have, finally, a rational *technique* whose pure abstraction enables one moiety of society to displace or annihilate the other, all in the hands of a small number of technicians.

In their gnostic preoccupation with absolute power, the more despairing of these Slavic Jacobins even resorted to the authority of the

Czar as the means toward peasant communism. In their darkest hour, Russian Left and Right were never far apart. What counted was what both exalted — an authority seen to be more or less divine. For that sombre region where Jacobinism, Orthodoxy, Gnosticism, and primitive Christianity meet in Russian society, we need only look to Dostoevsky.

Like the Russian peasant, Dostoevsky was concerned with neither capitalism nor socialism; both were foreign and decadent. His concern was more elemental, that is, gnostic — founded in the vertical dialectic of freedom and authority. His heroes (Jesus, Shatov, Alyosha, and Prince Myshkin) seek goodness without resort to coercion or to the social rationalism of Left or Right. Their faith bypasses Church and State, combining simple nationalism, socialism, and Christian benevolence in a synthesis that defies both Left and Right. Freedom can count on faith, whereas authority is constrained to use the inferior and more damaging instrument of reason, that is, the way of the westernizing intelligentsia. Capitalism, scientific revolutionary utopianism, and Stirner's wilful egoist were personified in Dostoevsky's villains like Raskolnikov, Stavrogin, and Peter Verkhovensky. All of this, Left or Right, Dostoevsky embodied in the oppressive demiurge of Western Reason.

If Dostoevsky is any indication, it is not surprising that by 1900 Russia still had no common social culture of Left and Right. For the uneducated majority, socialism and capitalism were equally Western: alien and radical. And so, when Marxism was formally introduced by Georgi Plekhanov, it had no natural seedbed in society, and could only take root in the Russian technical schools, chiefly the Petersburg Institute of Engineering, which was a closed, self-sustaining hothouse. It is from this beginning, perhaps, that we get the association of communism with social engineering — a wholesale grafting, much like the transplanting of Orthodoxy into the Slavic bush. Like Orthodoxy, like the Czar, Marxism would loom as a uniquely Russian saviour, quite above any squabble between Left and Right.

Predictably, however, a Left and Right grew up within Marxism itself. The rural Social Revolutionaries who recruited among the peasants were condemned for their democratic tendencies as "Left deviationists" by the authoritarian Jacobins or "Social Democrats" who focused on the urban proletariat. Among the latter, the urban, rationalizing, and technical environment of St. Petersburg produced Vladimir Ilich Lenin. Not long out of law school, Lenin came into contact with the cell group of Zaichnevsky. He got his second dose of Jacobinism in Geneva through the works of Tkachev and especially Tkachev's journal, the *Tocsin*.[23] Plekhanov noted that "from the beginning, Lenin was more of a Blanquiste than a Marxist."[24] And Lenin himself admitted to being in awe of the organizational genius of the demented, quasi-Jacobin Nechaev.[25]

In due course, means began to overshadow ends. After Lenin, the revolutionary Left would forever be associated with the idea that *the seizure of power must come first, even to the extent that the very technique of overthrow would condition the ultimate goal.* But that technique only concealed a deep philosophical influence, which once again contained an archaic glimmer of Parmenides. Lenin writes repeatedly in terms of an opposition between the Whole and the Parts; he identifies the proletariat with the Whole. Individuals and classes are the Parts, a mere illusion imposed by capitalism to maintain power. The Platonic-Manichaean dualism between the way of truth and the way of illusion is implicit: "The only choice," he wrote, "is either bourgeois, or socialist ideology. There is no middle course."[26]

The Russian affinity for Parmenidean thinking is well summed up by Nicholas Berdyaev: "The Russian spirit craves for wholeness . . . It yearns for the Absolute and desires to subordinate everything to the Absolute, and this is a religious trait in it. But it easily leads to confusion, takes the relative for the Absolute, the partial for the universal, and then falls into idolatry."[27] Lenin mistook the proletariat for the Whole much as Parmenides made Mind into the entire Entity. The means, after Blanqui, would be the seizure of the bourgeois state as proxy for the Whole; and after Marx, the elimination of the parts through the destruction of trade unions and the indeterminate classes like the *petite bourgeoisie.*

The Parmenidean Whole had (through Neoplatonism) been further developed in St. Augustine, and finally in Marxism, which "has a number of basic characteristics in common with the Christian system in its Augustinian and later medieval expression. One of these is the aspiration to totality of scope."[28] Lenin also inherited from Christianity a sort of millenarianism, in which the bourgeoisie crumbles like decadent

Rome to be replaced by the New Jerusalem of the proletariat. And, like Augustine's souls entrapped in evil, the proletariat needed the Church of the Party to rescue them. The difference was that Lenin's elect could theoretically achieve their perfection in this world. In his certainty about the perfectibility of man, Lenin had a fifth-century predecessor — Pelagius.

Pelagius, a British monk, defied Augustine by preaching that humanity could perfect itself of its own free will — without the intervention of the Church. His gnostic confidence in a direct connection between the soul (*pneuma*) and the divine caused him to be better received in the Byzantine world,[29] where the church was more mystical and less interventionist, and where the soul's ultimate custodian was the earthly state. This divergence between Augustine and Pelagius has been cited explicitly by Leo Moulin as a key source in the origins of a modern political Right, cautious about man's moral improvement, and a Left, optimistic in man's perfectibilism.[30] This is certainly true in cases where the Left rejects tradition and official interpretation. When the "Deconstructionist" Left, for example, bypasses the "sacred canon" of Western literature in search of supra-textual, supra-cultural meaning, its attitude is Pelagian. Both the modern Left and Pelagianism hark back to the superior and exclusive claims of the gnostic attitude.

As it was completely detached from the state, the Augustinian Church could more easily be inclusive than exclusive: it embraced baptized Christians everywhere. By contrast, the Donatist heresy insisted that only Christians untouched by persecution, or strong enough to resist, were worthy as the elect of God. In short, for Pelagians and Donatists alike the Church comprised the chosen few — a garrison; the Augustinian Church wanted to give everyone a chance. The contrast between elitism and democracy is implicit.

This debate between exclusiveness and inclusiveness, between elitist and democrat, would resurface in almost precisely the same outlines in Russia a millennium and a half later. At the conference of the Social Democrats in 1903, a Menshevik majority maintained an inclusive,

"Augustinian" democratic approach, while the authoritarian elitism of the dominant Bolsheviks recalled the more severe exclusivist doctrine of the Donatists and the Pelagians.

Russian attitudes on the Right as well had a way of simplifying complex situations. In 1905, deepening poverty brought an upsurge of revolution. The truly "gnostic" elimination of any hope that parliament could act as a third, mediating force came not from the revolutionaries, but from above, from Nicholas II. Henceforward, at each attempt to introduce a horizontal, European, and secular Left and Right, Left and Right would be set on end and transformed into the old Gnostic, Byzantine Russian, vertical duality. The heaven-and-earth New Jerusalem populism of the Byzantine Emperor had already re-emerged in Czarist attempts at reform from above, and now, finally and most vividly, in the extraordinary figure of the monk and advisor to Nicholas II, Grigori Rasputin.

Rasputin, popularly maligned as a satanic villain, was in fact a tragic carrier of that "alien" inner Russia of the *mir* that was both Left and Right and neither. Moreover, he had imbibed the backwaters of sectarian gnostic belief in the Russian hinterland.[31] Rasputin was primordial, deeper even than the Russian soil. As a *starets*, or wandering holy man, he was a continuation of the Asian shaman in Christian tradition. As a shaman, he reconnoitred the furthest reaches of sacred and profane for the monarchy. Suspecting the nobility, the bourgeoisie, and the Bolsheviks alike of betraying his own people, the Russian peasantry, he found good and evil beyond secular Left and Right. From the "Right" he urged the Czar to avert revolution by supporting the peasantry "from the Left." His recommendations meant massive social reform, improvement of food distribution, refusal to waste peasant lives by entering the Great War, and the dismissal of nobility and bourgeoisie alike as social forces. How different was this from radical Jacobinism, indeed from Leninism?

This was monolithic Russia, the same Russia in which, by 1917, Left and Right still had little meaning for the majority: life and politics were immediate and practical. The uprising, brought on by hunger, began haphazardly, involving all sectors of society. Behind, moved the Bolsheviks. The Duma had been resuscitated, but the debate between authoritarian Left and parliamentarian Right was really not a debate; it was a cultural confrontation between East and West. If things were confused, the Bolsheviks would use Jacobin French history for clarification.

Lenin, wise to Russia's emergency, saw no reason to rush perfect equality. Instead he wrote the slogan: "Peace, Bread and Land." A Czar as brilliant would have kept his throne. Prophetically, a contemporary of Dostoevsky named Lyonteyev had mused long before: "Sometimes I dream that a Russian Czar may put himself at the head of the socialist movement and organize it, as Constantine organized Christianity."[32] Authority was the key. Lenin's immediate obstacle was the very un-Russian anomaly of Alexander Kerensky's moderate-left provisional government. Kerensky's ideology lay along bourgeois, European lines of individualism and liberty and had no social roots in Russia's conception of masses organized vertically and maintained under strict authority. Individualism, where it existed, lay diffused among better-off peasants, anarchists, and a tiny bourgeoisie. So Kerensky's tragedy lay in his attempt to impose a western Right and Left — as individualism and cooperation — on a culture that had no individualist social tradition.

Another obstacle to Lenin's perfect, conceptual Whole was the phenomenon of the factory-based worker's cooperative, the Soviet. It was too autonomous, too "Left-Right" mutualist (like the *mir*) for his liking, and so he moved quickly to absorb its representation into larger, more centralized bodies. But the next step, the distribution of land, was done ham-handedly and destructively, and starvation reared its head. The Bolsheviks' "New Economic Policy" re-established just enough of a market economy among the peasants to generate the capital to end the famine and smooth the transition to communism. This would be one of many increasing instances where socialism and capitalism would prove interdependent: as they have since their Siamese birth from the womb of classical economics. Today, China's resort to capitalism to sustain the one-party state is only a version of Lenin's New Economic Policy on a grander scale.

Of course, the injection of capitalism into Bolshevik Communism resulted in new adaptations of the tricky Marxist lexicon of Left and Right: those who objected to the authoritarian "capitalist" New Economic Policy as treachery and wanted more democracy were labelled "Left Deviationists," and those who felt the policy hadn't gone far enough were called "Right Deviationists." Trotsky is a case in point. As brilliant commander-in-chief of the Red Army he was a Bolshevik authoritarian. But his inclination to democratize and his eloquent attack on the elitism and privilege of the Leninist bureaucracy made him a "Left Deviationist" on the road back to capitalism.

All the foggy terminology hid a salient fact: Bolshevik modernization meant inextricable entanglement in the methods and ideas of the West. So the litmus test was no longer "for or against socialism," or "for or against the authority," or even "for or against the Czar." Left or Right was reduced to nothing more than *for or against present Bolshevik policy*. There were so many different means to so many deviant versions of communism and so many different roads back to capitalism, that Left and Right deviation could only have a narrow, gnostic meaning: toward too much democracy or too much authority, respectively. The result was that, while Bolshevism claimed to be "Left," it plotted so rigid a course as to be opposed by the widest spectrum of resistances — including separatists, local lobbies, anarchists, dissident socialists, and capitalistic Kulaks.

But of course the sides in the civil war were aligned between Czarist "Whites" and Bolshevik "Reds." "Whites" as "Right" cruelly disguised a tradition of Russian dissidence and individualism, however diffuse, which included peasants who feared their old landlords as much as they feared Bolshevik confiscation. By the sword of dualism, the small entities of the Bolshevik elite and the remains of the Czarist army were each inflated to become quite imaginary "Left" and "Right" hemispheres of a society most of which had little in common with either. And in that sense, the widespread discontent that feeds totalitarian revolution turns out to be quite distinct from the totalitarian revolutionaries who actually conduct it.

13

Barbarism:
Totalitarian,
Millenarian

A totalitarian mood latent among the population of Europe in the closing decades of the nineteenth century was born with the First World War, when the ordinary populace on both sides of the conflict lost faith in what they saw as an international establishment of monarchs and moneyed interests waging a private war. For the first time there was a separation between rulers and ruled that was psychological and cultural rather than merely economic, cutting across traditional Left and Right and isolating the elites of both from the masses. Ominously, it would also confirm the restive alienation of that uprooted nineteenth-century urban mass that I have called "gnostic" and which Hannah Arendt calls "the mob."[1]

It began with the "War Economy." A war economy entails the centralization not just of capital but of the means of production — in capitalist nations a suspension of the traditional rivalry between business and government — indeed, a sort of quasi-socialism. Business takes on roles in government, and government moves into business.[2] In some senses, Left and Right tend to dissolve in government itself. The consequence in this case was an accelerated industrialization and civilian mobilization that provoked the anger and anomie of a new type of individual who, although gradually emancipated, became rootless within the new community of the nation.

But by 1919, at war's end, this early military-industrial complex, an extraordinary machine made for an empty purpose, now lay idle and ready to hand. In the vacuum left by the recession of neighbourhood, throne, and altar, mass popular belief would seize hold. And in the wake of the devastation there also lay a moral pessimism that recalled an earlier cataclysm, in which "Augustine . . . was led by the Fall of Rome sharply to separate men's hopes for salvation from their hopes for social progress."[3] Likewise, hopes for immediate change would be displaced into utopian ideologies, which seemed, like machines of war, to be built for confrontation by polar opposites.

But ideologies are not always symmetrically organized around polarities or even single ideas,[4] and, "it may well be that one of the functions of many ideologies is to disguise the inconsistencies among a set of ideas to promote political consensus."[5] So these aggregate or asymmetrical ideologies tend to be more coherent in outer form than in content. The most significant of these is Fascism, and for this reason alone Fascism cannot form a tidy opposite to a more consistent ideology like Communism. After all, the roots of Fascism were, like those of Communism, anti-capitalist.

In Austria and Germany, as early as the 1860s and 1870s, the economic recession that had shaken the continent was laid at the door of the capitalist liberal establishment and its policies of industrialization and urbanization.[6] There followed a reaction — the fetishization of countryside and village — only to be followed by the Nietzschean assault on an enfeebling, Socratic, bourgeois, Christian civilization. In fact, Germany, which had been recipient rather than master of the influences that dominated Europe, was stranded in the heart of a continent still culturally defined by the French, and a commercial, colonial world dominated by Britain. In short, before the First World War, all the preconditions for a sense of cosmic imprisonment and the rhythmically recurring gnostic motif were present.

By the 1920s the aftermath of the war and the exactions of the treaty of Versailles had driven Germany into destitution and starvation. After repeated humiliation, it is typical that the self, like the *pneuma* of the

Gnostic, seeks salvation in grandiose abstractions, polarities, historical justification, and above all in *praxis*, which disregards the authority of law or consensus — the direct translation of fantasy into action. As the underlying justification of universal law, Reason is only the demiurge that the gnostic ignores altogether or subordinates as servant to a higher, cosmic idea.

So, Germany no longer posed simply a problem of economics or of ideological debate after the end of the First World War; it posed — still — a problem of *identity*. And Nazi ideology, when it came to power, was perfectly suited for this problem. Above all practical, Nazism would not reject but rather *cannibalize* other ideologies. Socialism, capitalism, ecology, gangsterism, environmentalism, holism, existentialism — and vegetarianism — were all at one time or another conceived as essential to a reborn Germany. (Milosevich has done much the same for Serbia.) As a composite, Nazism had none of the uniformity that could make it the "opposite" of another ideology.

Nazism's only real defining mark was its anti-Semitism. So the schema of conflict, far from being rational or lateral, was one of *defilement*; of impurity within purity, of black within white. As in the Roman Empire, it was circular, concentric; once again, inside versus outside. Such a scheme runs contrary to a linear concept such as Left and Right, which, by its very nature, is defined almost entirely by gradations of grey between two extremes. The motif endures in our own time, in the "politics of identity" not *because of* Nazism, but despite it. Though they bear no moral comparison, Nazism and "Identity Politics" both elevate the question of identity over Left-Right questions of class and universality.

Nazi ideologists, grasping for an identity, found a precedent in barbarian defiance of Rome in the last survivals of Teutonic mythology. But even Teutonic myth, like Roman myth, cleaved to some universal ideas like the cardinal points and a primitive sacred and profane with their inchoate right and left hands. The difference was that for the Teutons those dualities were still unconditioned by *moral opposites*.[7] So Teutonic belief was the Aryan religion *before* Zoroaster — an ethic of practical survival and tribal combat that seems to have come westward in the earliest migrations, before the Iranians discovered Good and Evil. The Nazi-liberal dialectic, then, is a conflict between morally primitive and morally advanced Aryan cultures. Perhaps the greatest difference between them had to do with law. The Aryan tripartite class structure of priest, warrior, and producer was reflected in Woden, Thor, and the Vanir. But the lawmaker in Teutonic mythology is recessive — since Tiw, the god of law, is partnered with Woden, the priest-shaman. In the myth of the law, a monstrous daemon-wolf, to ensure fair play in a tug-of-war with the Gods, had the sacred right hand of Tiw placed in his jaws as security. The Gods broke the rules, the wolf bit, and Tiw's hand was sacrificed.[8] Through the loss of the right hand, the law was assimilated to the powers of the priest-shaman Woden. So here was a culture with a profane left hand, but no sacred right; magic and force, but no law. Of course the Germanic tribes did have laws, but they were local and tribal. What the myth explains is the absence of any inviolable, sacred universal Law.

So modern Germany did not have to go far to find a systematic, mythological, and native opposition to liberal, Christian, universal morality. Moreover, Germany could claim a single line of descent from the free Barbarians who had resisted Rome to the Holy Roman Emperors who resisted the Papacy. How is it, then, that the lawless "rightish" barbarian was naturally democratic, the tribal leader ruling only by consent of the governed; and that a lawgiving "leftish" Church was in fact rigidly top-down authoritarian? (Henceforward I make descriptive use of the modifiers Left and Right to show how certain forms in the past appear in our eyes. They are not to be taken literally.) The answer seems to be that democracy is itself neither Left nor Right. Rather, it is only a *means* to ends that are "Left" or "Right." This way, "Left" is seen to be rooted not in democracy or even collectivity but in morality, acting as a restraint on the Right, which is pure liberty and power. We will find that this minimum definition of "Left" in its restraining role as "most recent moral critic" will actually stand the test of time.

In the "Dark Ages," the centralizing Christian Church, with its inherited Roman Law, would stand on the "Left," trying its best to reign in the centrifugal, secular kingdoms, which were newly converted but still defending traditional tribal power and independence on the "Right." By the eleventh century, the struggle finally resolved itself into the great contest between Church and State. In 1074, the dualism was sharpened when Pope Gregory VII eschewed canon law as a basis for the claims of the Church. He chose instead simply to align the secular state, Holy Roman Emperor Henry IV, and the whole pagan world with the forces of Satan, and the Church with Heaven and the saved.[9]

Here, the vertical distinction of sacred and profane resumes its long fall to the horizontal — the political and secular. The trend would increase through the twelfth century, when Holy Roman Emperor Frederick Barbarossa invaded Italy, intent on creating his own papacy and prefiguring two ominous forces: a German claim to Europe and the challenge of rightish Barbarian power to leftish Roman universal morality. That Barbarossa became a touchstone for the Nazis is of no small significance.[12]

Despite the territorial weakness of the Church, Pope Innocent III, with brilliant diplomacy, brought Rome to moral supremacy at the beginning of the thirteenth century. And he did so with the help of a system of theology and philosophy that worked, for all practical purposes, like an ideology. Scholasticism, the highest and most arcane development of Plato and Aristotle, was actually a halfway mark on a road that had begun with Parmenides and would end with the revolutionary ideologies of the nineteenth century.

Beginning in the schools founded by Charlemagne, scholasticism was, in effect, a dialectical debate between the Whole and the Parts, as *Realism* and *Nominalism*. Realism tended toward the "Whole," nominalism toward the "Parts." Realism held that the Ideas, or the "ideal forms" that united things through qualities held in common, were themselves real — even more real than the things they represented. The nominalists held that the Ideas were merely names, that *difference* was at the heart of truth and that only the individual things of this world had reality. Realism tended to support the Church, while nominalism came to imply dissidence and subversion. But after intellectual warfare gave way to philosophy, nominalism would appear as subjectivism, and realism as universal morality. And they would correspond roughly to the intellectual predispositions found, respectively, in Right and Left.

In the hands of St. Thomas Aquinas, a thirteenth-century Aristotelian symbiosis of nominalism and realism arose, which has since been called *conceptualism* — an attempt to affirm faith with reason, a realist God with nominalist nature. And indeed it is for his conceptualist reconciliation of (leftish) Church Law and (rightish) State power that Aquinas has also been called the founder of political science.[11] In modern terms, Aquinas was something of a social democrat; and in fact he began a tradition of applying scholasticism to economic justice, in which "the last of the schoolmen was Karl Marx."[12]

From Aquinas's natural law we derive the concept of limits on profit and the theory that a commodity's value is determined by the labour that went into it.[13] The Church of the High Middle Ages indeed worked a little like "big government" and, as regulator of the economy, it was, for our purposes, Left. Even its enormous centralization of capital through taxation and endowments and its supply of permanent employment through the working of Church lands, monastic expansion, and the erection of cathedrals, encouraged public over private enterprise.

My point here is that the Left did not begin with socialism; rather, its ethic is rooted in forms that are deeply conservative. The most pervasive of those forms, the moral accord known to history as the *Pax Dei*, was due at least in part to the Church and it was certainly the triumph of a moral ideology. In this it bears a resemblance to the aims of our own New World Order: from the Left, NATO as Rome provides moral authority and the G-8 nations, like Christian princes, back it up with might — while those more to the Right do so more or less reluctantly.

With the stresses of an early economic revolution in the twelfth century, however, came a resurgence of skepticism and heresy. To resist it, the Church leaned toward totalitarianism, imposing by force a middle way between libertine-ascetic Gnostic heresies of world and spirit, that is, between radical extremes of nominalism and realism. An orthodoxy was enforced by means of intellectual acrobatics similar to those used by Marx, Kautsky, and the Bolsheviks.[14] And so, an equivalent to "Left deviationists," for example, were the extreme puritanical Catharist Gnostics, known as the Albigensians, who were exterminated in a crusade mounted by Innocent III.

Another Christian persecution, that of the Jews, was to endure politically in various forms through to the Holocaust. The medieval idea that the Jews were parasites on Christian society and a fifth column of Satan perfectly fit the old concentric dialectic of outer and inner, perfection and defilement that the Church had inherited from Rome. So claimants to the mastery of Christian Europe through Roman tradition — like Barbarossa — provided the Nazis with perfect precedents. Anti-Semitism, in short, is a function of any totalitarianism, Left, Right, Roman, Christian, or Nazi. Heedless of Left-Right distinctions, it is at its roots gnostic, since the barbarians and Nazis alike practised the gnostic rejection of mediation by any transcendent moral Law, not least that which the Jews themselves had received as "agents of Yaweh, the Demiurge." That is, it partakes in an older, vertical duality rather than in the lateral worldly one. The gnostic roots of anti-Semitism also explain why it was, until the rise of Hitler, more prevalent in the Eastern Church than in the West, and the same Gnostic provenance helps to explain the future influence of Eastern cultural variations. Byzantine feudalism was maintained by absolutism and local might, not by law, canon or secular; class gradations were fewer, the serfs were poorer and bound more closely to the land, and the feudal terrains were larger. This deeper homogeneity with fewer classes and less regard for Roman Law would indeed provide fertile soil for Communism.

The political affinity of Orthodox absolutism for the absolute collectivism of Mongol rule after the fall of Kiev to the Mongols circa 1240[15] leaves little doubt about the creation of a proto-communist culture. The Mongol way was a work of utter genius born of necessity: the modernization and regimentation of fratricidal tribes by Genghis Khan around 1200 had proved the only alternative to extinction through starvation on the frozen plains. Its extraordinary efficiency reduced Russia to being an oppressed, if stable, tributary. In another six centuries, the Stalinist idea of a powerhouse national state built on a similar regimented collectivism was to provide the Left, for a generation at least, with its global definition.

Stalinism, like Mongol rule, used collectivism as an absolute value. Thinking in absolutes was something Russia also had in common with Germany. By the 1930s, both countries were given to gnostic extremes, in other words, to metaphysical, rather than worldly claims. We need only refer, for example, to Russia's affinity for German *praxis*, the search for absolute solutions and their literal application unmediated by law or by service to any principle outside themselves. Between the wars, the

Russian-German phenomenon was manifested in a shared resentment of triumphant Western Europe, an animus which seemed to transcend ideology and which Lenin even termed "reactionary-revolutionary."[16] Moreover, this desperate spiritual alliance disclosed Stalin's need for Bolshevism to have a name and an identity for the divine spark of its soul, a name posed (like the Nazism to come) against the liberal West. That name was Russia, and Russian nationalism became identical with Communist survival.

The quick assertion of Communist Russia against the West meant material competition, which in turn meant the rapid collectivization of the myriad small farms constituting the last vestiges of private enterprise. But communism, as we have seen, shares something basic with capitalism. Early communist labour conditions were decidedly Dickensian;[17] and collectivization had some resemblance to the long process of expropriation brought about by the enclosures in England.[18] But it also meant the punishment of Russia's more productive farmers. And so, while the Kulaks, the better-off peasants, could have helped communism, Stalinist egalitarian absolutism could not countenance paradox. And just as the Roman Church had aligned heresy, paganism, and secularism with the kingdom of Satan, Stalin aligned the Kulaks with the West and a demonized Right.

Scholastic reasoning helped. If Realism is a world of Ideas where all is known and Nominalism is a realm of indeterminacy in the actual world, then the Bolshevik prosecutor of the dissident Bukharin "takes his stand in a world of objects where nothing is indeterminate. He would like to erase the region of indeterminism, Bukharin's conscience, where there exist *things not yet known*, empty zones; he would like to leave only *things he has made or had made*."[19] The parallel held true not just in essences but in time. The Right, like paganism, was associated with a historical past; Communism, like the Church, with the future and salvation.[20] And without much difficulty, one can see in the Moscow of the 1930s the long heritage of Zoroastrianism and Orphism condensed in caricature.

How and when had this ancient eschatology become secular? We have seen the beginnings of this development with the politicization of the

Jesus sect upon the fall of Jerusalem, with the Christianization of the Empire under Constantine, and then with the struggle between Church and State. But religious thinking really began to infiltrate politics just as the Roman Church reached its zenith around 1300; that is, at the very beginning of its decline. What was seen by many as the final achievement of a balance between the sacred and the secular was, in fact, a transition from the former to the latter. Whether synthesis or transition, this pivotal moment found its fullest and most hopeful expression in Dante Alighieri's *Divine Comedy*.[21]

While Dante's redemptive plot is ancient, Orphic, and sacred, its references and illustrations are overwhelmingly worldly and secular; in the *Inferno*, sins are expressed in political terms. At the *Vestibule* before the gate of hell and the first circle of the damned are the doubters, who in life have not taken a side. The last circle of hell, Cocytus, is reserved for those who have *changed* sides — the traitors. From the Vestibule to Cocytus, Hell must swallow up all those who protest a divided cosmos. Instead of exalting a synthesis, Dante has really transferred the Manichaeism of Augustinian Christianity to the secular world.

Dante's synthesis finds more prosaic expression in his political essay *De Monarchia*. By proposing that the monarch be removed from the authority of the Pope and raised to the same level, Dante suggests that both obtain their divine right equally from God. This is a significant step in the shift from a vertical to a horizontal political duality. Resurrecting the memory of Rome, Dante then exalts church and state together as a new, all-encompassing organic whole.[22] And from another theorist of the period, Marsiglio of Padua, we hear unlimited, absolutist claims for democracy and mob self-rule, which seem gnostic. As Leo Moulin has observed, "This affirmation, clearly Pelagian, does nothing to stand in the way of a 'totalitarian conception of the state' . . . Jacobinism *avant la lettre*."[23]

But the balance could not last. The eventual collapse of Aquinas's conceptualist synthesis opened the way for a polarization between a leftish Christian asceticism and a rightish blend of pagan myth and the romance of courtly love with Christian ideas. The scheme could not become fully horizontal until the sacred had weakened further; and indeed, as pagan passions re-emerged, scholasticism unravelled. Early in the fourteenth century, the arguments of Realism had begun to take the form of a rearguard action, intellectual coherence having deserted the Church under the strain of its battle with a proliferation of heresies. If, for a moment, we see the theological challenges to Rome now coming from the "Left" in its role as "most recent moral critic," everything that is subversive — from nominalism to John Wycliffe's unmediated recourse to scripture, to Protestantism, and to capitalism — will successively take up the banner of dissent. The metaphysical scheme even as it falls horizontally toward the world (though perhaps not the faith) is once again gnostic.

Within this new landscape, which was now essentially nominalist, a fresh conflict was developing. The great enclosures consequent upon the economic expansion of the twelfth century had already displaced part of the labour force from the land, and the mantle of protest began to pass from the nobility to the merchants and common people. In France, the conversion of an advisory council, the Estates General, into an organ of tax protest against Philip IV gives us the early fourteenth century as a rough date of "conception" (though not of birth) for an institutional, political Right and Left founded on new opposition between King and parliament.

With the Hundred Years' War, which straddled the fourteenth and fifteenth centuries, the split was socialized. Like the cataclysmic First World War, it was a watershed for the masses. Both wars were essentially dynastic, and meaningless to the majority that fought them. In both cases an old order was discredited and whatever masses were not sacrificed were polarized in opposition to traditional wealth and authority. Spontaneous French and English peasant rebellions with apocalyptic, religious overtones foreshadowed the Bolshevik revolution and the European Leftist insurrections of 1919–1920.

From as early as 1100, in fact, revolts against the unemployment and displacement wrought by the spread of textile manufacturing had taken on the form of the same resurgent cosmic, indeed gnostic, impulse that would produce a resounding echo in the twentieth-century totalitarianism of Left and Right.[24] After all, the medieval, millenarian insurgents who launched bitter class wars constituted a displaced urban horde without class affiliation. They were the direct forebears of the same type of "gnostic" mob displaced by modernization that later threw its weight behind the Bolsheviks and behind Hitler.

■

If the movements of the Middle Ages were gnostic in form, Norman Cohn has described the most famous of them, the Beghards, or the Brethren of the Free Spirit, as genuinely gnostic in descent and in content. Their tenet was that "whatever existed was bound to yearn for its Divine Origin and to strive to find its way back to that Origin; and at the end of time everything would in fact be reabsorbed into God."[25] Freed by consciousness of their divine identification from the "lower sanctions" of the law, the Brethren delivered themselves up to sexual abandon and lawlessness in principle,[26] and adopted an anti-papism and anti-Semitism that would anticipate much modern paranoid radicalism, Left and Right. And, although they still used old messianic paradigms, their rebellion amounted to a barbarian rejection of European civilization to the extent that Norman Cohn has counted them as predecessors of Bakunin and Nietzsche.[27] It should come as little surprise that ideologues of Nazism turned to the Free Spirit movement as one of its precedents. Indeed, fascism and its Nazi variant might be looked upon as descendants of post-feudal corporatism; like bands of brigands and millenarians, they provided identity and meaning where liberal or Christian Europe had left it lacking.

When industrial revolution and social dislocation recurred in the nineteenth century, its ad hoc form was anarcho-syndicalism, a political faith that "appealed to the small group, to local loyalties."[28] By the 1890s, anarcho-syndicalism had conceived of the trade union as the fundamental unit of society and as a revolutionary force. Its ethnic focus and tribalism resembled the multifarious political fringe groups of today — the ill-disciplined peacetime military units, the chat rooms and Web-sites — sub-political units that proliferate in times of political disenchantment or indifference. Neither "Right" nor "Left," they form a sort of "individual collectivism"; that is, collective forms with strongly individual identities. Anarcho-syndicalism was an anti-capitalist mixture of factory socialism and archaic, collective, and emotional irrationalism. Sorel, its leading thinker in early twentieth-century France, kept it explicitly violent and anti-intellectual: the middle class was not to be won over but rather destroyed.

With the ebbing of religion — indeed of myth — society had begun to feel what Max Weber has called "disenchantment." Anarcho-syndicalism filled the void for the working class with a revolutionary myth: socialism driven by passion and archaism rather than reason; and that became one of the roots of fascism. Like fascism, anarcho-syndicalism was really a symptom of the failure of liberal Left and Right to diagnose the modern world and respond to its needs. In fact, communism and fascism, and their common forebear in anarcho-syndicalism, were all collective and proletarian in spirit and indeed all three had more in common with one another than with the liberal democratic capitalism they attacked. Like the Millenarians, they were anti-aristocratic, anti-clerical, anti-capitalistic. That is, each recognized no principle higher than itself; in that sense alone, they were "gnostic."

In the aftermath of the First World War, the Italian Fascists, decrying the atomization of Italian society by liberal capitalism, would integrate, by force and subordination if necessary, a disintegrating society.[29] They mobilized with the ferocity of medieval millenarians. Progressive in form only, Fascism claimed to transcend Left and Right by combining the best of both in a structure of corporate bodies[30] based on the models of the factory floor and the military barracks. But with the Soviet Comintern calling the shots, Italian society saw the fight between Capitalism and Socialism to be more important than the danger of Fascism, so overwhelmingly had the political dualism of Left and Right penetrated Europe. No one anticipated that the King of Italy would recognize the organizational power of the Fascists and ask Mussolini to form the government.

To the north as well, the perennially weak axis of Europe continued to throw up compensatory dreams and nightmares of domination. As Germany's imaginative, social-democratic Weimar government put forward progressive policies in line with the allies who had brokered it, archaic emotions festered all the more, and the National Socialists, a party of national regeneration, took root. A lower and middle class battered by war reparations and world-wide depression gravitated toward the opiates of Nazism, now termed the "far Right," and Communism on the far Left. As in Italy, a European Left-Right dualism of "dogmatic sectarians"[31] split any potential opposition to Nazism, while Hitler drew a wide spectrum behind him by advertising a fear of Communism.

But naming the Nazis "Right" is a matter of convenience, not of precision. Hitler's hatred of Communism does not mean he was its direct opposite. In fact, for Hitler, communism and capitalism as economic systems were not important. At heart Nazism was the receptacle of an otherness that grew out of the German past: the refuge of a barbarian Germany marginalized by classical Europe, the rallying place for historical revenge. (The Nazis' justification was epitomized in *The Myth of the Twentieth Century* by the party ideologist Alfred Rosenberg; it was a bestseller, second only to *Mein Kampf*.[32])

It follows that the polar enemy of Nazism could not be capital, or socialism, but rather law and morality. Hitler's ethic, after all, was Teutonic and gnostic, striking not just at the Christian consensus and universal law, but at its roots in Judaism. By 1919, according to George Steiner, the ancient threat of Jewish moral superiority, of the primordial law of Yaweh-as-Demiurge, had become intolerable to a Germany in defeat.[33] So the Jews would have to be sacrificed. Meanwhile the Nazi, as modern political gnostic, desired not only to destroy the Demiurge but to supplant it with his own image,[34] "issuing from the subjective, but always broadening out and as it were laying hold of the Cosmos,"[35] to use Thomas Mann's perfect phrase. The Christian cosmos was indeed Hitler's plaything, as it had been for some gnostics: "If today Satan would come along and offer to be my ally against France, I would give him my hand, and I would march with him."[36] And man, in a super-Pelagian sense was his own master — indeed, his own deity: "You shall be Gods," said Hitler, exalting each *pneuma* in the German people and indeed Rosenberg's *Myth of the Twentieth Century* made explicit an admiring reference to the "Beghards," the Brethren of the Free Spirit.[37]

Some might call the Nazi belief in might and liberty over legality right-wing, but the complete absence of individualism in Nazi notions of freedom, and its reservation of freedom mostly for the state and for corporate bodies, keeps it a long distance even from the modern libertarian right. Rather, Nazi freedom is archaic. It recalls the withering away of Tiw, the barbarian God of Law, and his supplanting by Woden as priest God.

If Nazism was so archaic, how, then, did it win popular acceptance in a modern world defined by Right and Left? It did so by selling itself as all things to all people — a "holistic nationalism" with a "'Third Way,' neither Left nor Right" seeking "to achieve individual prosperity but linked to communal goals."[38] Hitler himself "argued that the right lacked a social sense, whereas the left failed to see the importance of the national community."[39] But that did not stop him from using everyone's talents, learning "from the Austrian and German Marxists . . . the need to go to the people" from which he "built up for the first time a mass following."[40] And with the Left as well he shared hatred of the bourgeois, the carrier of European and "Jewish" cosmopolitanism. Goebbels rivalled Marx in his class hatred and his obsessive denunciation of bourgeois capitalism, even to the point of entertaining a sort of "National Bolshevism" which "not only sought domestic links with communists but also a closer understanding with the Soviet Union."[41] Hitler even entertained a "genuine admiration for the Bolshevik regime in Russia (and the Communist Party in Germany)."[42]

On the Right, Hitler expressed support for private property, but limiting it as he did to the small proprietor's right to "socialism without expropriation,"[43] it was clear that private property did not lie at the heart of his convictions. Otherwise, Nazism had no interest in free enterprise except insofar as it could be pressed into the service of Nazism itself, the leadership agreeing to "stress national goals and long-run stability more than individual profit or short-run gain."[44] In the end, "all the essential characteristics of private property had been destroyed by the Nazis."[45] So it is obvious that Hitler's loathing for Bolshevism was not due to its collectivism, but almost solely to his conviction that it was Jewish.[46] That, in large part, is where the Nazi designation as "Right" comes from.

It is perhaps true that Hitler attracted enough conservatives. But there were also many conservatives who hated him for his contempt for their classical traditions. And J.M. Roberts has made the important point that conservatives in general (such as the strongmen of Latin America) are subjects of history, while Nazis and Fascists tend to be its masters, manipulating the past for their own ends.[47] In fact they exploited everything to the purposes of race and Germanness: from conservative tradition to socialism and capitalism. They also exploited existentialism.

Existentialism is really a modern form of gnosticism; like gnosticism it is neither Left nor Right; like gnosticism, it can seize hold of, and exploit, either to its own ends. A modern source of existentialism is Martin Heidegger. Heidegger built a system that, if it was brilliant on its own terms, happened also to be convenient to the Nazis. In the tradition of a radical nominalism, Heidegger explicitly attacks Aquinas: humanity is not to aspire to Reason, to God, or to any other scholastic, timeless moral essence, but only to itself.[48] He then pleads for a more down-to-earth concept of Being — something he calls *Dasein*. In doing so, he is rejecting Roman Christian humanism and opening the way for a nordic, open-ended, Germanic nominalism; eternal Truth and its Left and Right must give way to Nietzsche's revaluation of all values. Man takes the place of Being. And so the earthly immediacy of *Dasein* was amenable to the Nazis' elevation of earthly, tribal "blood and soil" into an absolute. The gnostic implications are self-evident; and indeed the existentialism of Sartre would do the same for Marxism.

Nazism and Communism are both totalitarian descendants of medieval, gnostic, and apocalyptic attitudes.[49] What then, we might ask, is the real difference between them? Arendt distinguishes Communist salvation aboard the "ship of history" from a Nazi promised land within the law of nature.[50] For Emmanuel Todd the key divergence is anthropological.[51] Todd discovers "authoritarian" family types in Germany, for example, and "egalitarian" family types in Italy and Russia. But these are differences in kind rather than moral opposites.

If Nazism and Communism came to be framed as categorical opposites in Right and Left, it was because of a lazy tendency to use one's stance toward Communism — and that alone — to determine Left and Right, and the Nazis' use of the Jews to do the same thing. It's not much more clarifying than dividing all flowers between those that are roses and those that are not. The horrors of the camps sealed the distinction by reintroducing a medieval eschatology into the twentieth century. As George Steiner puts it, "In our current barbarism an extinct theology is at work, a body of transcendent reference whose slow, incomplete death has produced surrogate, parodistic forms" of Heaven and Hell and "of the two, Hell proved the easier to re-create."[52]

To the radical socialist Left, the rhetorical advantage of aligning the hellish criminality of the Holocaust with capitalism — despite the fact that the Nazis had made as much if not more use of socialism — was irresistible. The Left is always the first to frame the discourse, and it worked. It followed that some members of the Frankfurt school portrayed capitalism not as an instrument of Nazism, but Nazism as an instrument of capitalism, seen as the true global Satan. And so the gentlest conservatism came to be aligned with Nazism, while the mildest social democracy was seen as the first step toward Stalinism. It is a gnostic type of thinking in which everything in the world around us refers not to the world itself but outward to a primordial, dualistic Cosmos.

14

Liberty:
Capitalism and the
Rise of the Prince

With the Russian occupation of East Berlin in 1945, perfect equality set itself up in the graveyard of a radical hierarchy. By then, sacred dreams of freedom, both on the Left and on what has come to be called the Right, had instead produced shackles. An ideology centred on freedom had only one successful political expression, and that was Liberal Democracy, the system — in theory neither Left nor Right because it contains both — that ruled the Western allies at the end of the war. But even Western European liberal democracies continued to bear seeds of intolerance in their Left and Right. Having marginalized anarchism, Europe had never really found an ideology that began and ended in liberty. For that, one had to look across the Atlantic.

America's republican break from the British monarchy in 1776 was the closest any revolution has ever come to asserting freedom for its own sake. In a fight against monarchy and privilege waged mostly by small farmers and merchants, there was an assumption that liberty would mean equality as well. In a state of perfect liberty, the whole and parts would be identical — neither symmetrical entity nor asymmetrical struggle — and Liberty itself might make a third ideology.

Liberty and its expression in the natural equality of rights was taken by the Americans as a Euclidean axiom ("We deem these truths to be self-evident . . ."), making it more of an absolute end in itself than a relative means. And that, perhaps, is where the trouble began. Even so, there was, for a point of departure, an egalitarian spirit and a relative material equality in the population. But where freedom might have been a *means* to some higher vision, it remained an end in itself. As an end in itself it produced an equality of manners, "a democratic spirit." But with the rapid development of material inequality and then America's inevitable if unwilling involvement with the old world — the birthplace of the sacred and the profane — Right and Left, liberty and equality would seem an innocent memory.

An ideology of freedom is of course an oxymoron, as is anything that attempts to give freedom a definition. This is because Liberal Democracy ought not to be an end in itself, but a *means* to contained and realistic ends. In the formulation of Benjamin Barber it is "a 'thin' theory of democracy, one whose democratic values are prudential and thus provisional, optional and conditional — means to exclusively individualistic and private ends."[1] As an ideal, however, Liberal Democracy fails to transcend the vices of either Left or Right precisely because they have come to be its content and its expression, and, for the most part, its only choices.

In Liberal Democracy, in North America and Europe, the forms of Left and Right are elevated into endless, repetitive opposition by a condition that we call *Modernity*. Modernity is the state of society after which the means toward ends that have been lost to view (or that were never articulated) have *become* ends in themselves, as have Left and Right. Left and Right, in short, are the unintended consequence of the material progress that in turn maintains them instead of resolving them.

The first glimmer of modernity appears in the Middle Ages when the Sacred begins to go into decline. But modernity only fully arrives with the First World War when the old monarchies, discredited, breathe the last breath of the Sacred itself. But the Sacred has an afterglow in the Right and Left of Liberal Democracy — precisely because, like sacred and profane, these are eschatological in origin and depend, not on secular, democratic feeling, but on faith in the authority of some boundless idea of man reflected on the cosmos in a place once occupied by God. What the late Middle Ages witnessed was the sudden rise of a secular material world, the decline of its sacred moral critic, and the displacement of that sacred moral critic into the secular realm — *but without losing its sense of the sacred and its sacred forms*. This pattern was entirely peculiar to Europe and it was crucial because Europe would impose its political forms on the rest of the globe.[2]

In the fifteenth century, the domains of the biggest feudal lords began to coalesce into middle-sized national monarchies at the expense of Papal empire and feudal locality. Slowly acquiescing, the Church began to lose the sacred power of moral criticism. Rome, finally closing ranks with the new feudal-national order, would become "Right"; and the city states and the merchants would become revolutionary. While the "old Left" of the sacred had discovered morality in order, a new moral critic, a secular Left, would use secular humanism to express a spirit of liberty. But this transition from sacred to secular, from order to freedom, is *not* transitional for the Left — it is *cumulative*, because the Left will carry forward both freedom and its old, sacred order in an internal conflict.

Humanism, the means by which the Left, as most recent moral critic, passed over into the secular world, would end in the mild and cheerful spirit of Liberal Democracy. The birthdate that history gives to humanism comes a generation after Dante with the fourteenth-century poet Petrarch, perhaps the first scholar to treat the classics of the ancient world as ends in themselves and not merely as a support for the church. Ends in themselves they have been, but ends imply limits. And this is why the values of humanism, which really ought to be means or processes — such as nature, freedom, equality, fraternity, and love — when treated as ends in themselves, lose sight of the ideal to which they are meant to contribute. The sacred, which had sought ends that could not be described by single values, has instead made ends out of values which ought only to be means. And so, it is in that degraded form that the sacred has been unconsciously brought by humanism into the secular world. These means, freed from the stewardship of the sacred and mistaken for ends, are destined to run up against the wall of their own limits: politicization, excess, anomie, and dead-end materialism — the ills of the present age.

In the fifteenth century, nature-as-means was science. In its infancy, science was what, in its maturity, it still pretends not to be — a pathway to absolutes. Even the practice of the scientific experiment, introduced in the Renaissance, was thought to lead to the discovery of some Platonic perfection.[3] It was not the disinterested pursuit of knowledge as *means* to contained and realistic ends; it was an attempt to conquer the cosmic, and pioneering experiments were done purely in a gnostic spirit — to discover a link between one's *pneuma* and some perfect truth in the cosmos. This very immodesty began to make science an end, a value in itself. Capitalism, no less than science, alchemy, and gnosticism, also had a man-god Promethean element that was, finally, to become part of the religious cargo of humanism.

So humanism carried not only the old "Left" of sacred order but also the old "Right" of secular freedom forward into the material world, and the antinomies would in turn be carried forward into a secular compromise, Liberal Democracy. On the surface mild and banal, Liberal Democracy was anticipated by humanists like Thomas More and Erasmus, whose ethic would draw the contempt of minds like Nietzsche's. But humanism and Liberal Democracy still conceal religious and illiberal forms within; a Left and a Right, totalitarian and authoritarian. Moreover, Left and Right would be armed with a science of power, which slips into politics with Machiavelli's *The Prince*. With Machiavelli, the state no longer cloaks its ruthless *realpolitik* in the sacred robes of the church, but studies them as a technology of coercion and control, learning the barbarian-classical conduct of force without reference to the Law, sacred or secular.

The humane uses of reason, on the other hand, were turned to the "Left" with Thomas More, a lawyer and counsellor to England's Henry VIII. As enclosures by the English aristocracy evicted more peasants from the land and suppliers of wool put weavers out of work, More drew on the old scholastic doctrines about just price, usury, and exploitation. To the extent that he tried to preserve an existing order of land tenure by the sacred morality of Aquinas, he was a "conservative." In today's terms, he is, of course, "Left" — a roundabout way of saying that the Left is still actually drawing upon very old, sacred forms. But as a layman and an erudite humanist, More might in some sense be called the father of the secular Left, since he embodies the moment at which the Left moves from sacred into secular, carrying with it sacred

Christian premises of equality and brotherly love. The Left continues today to count on axioms that are Christian in form if no longer in name and to deduce itself from theory.

In the opposite sense, we can, for convenience, call Machiavelli "Right." It is easier to detect the origins of the modern right in a conception of secular power heedless of the sacred, than it is to find them in early capitalism. Capitalism, after all, did not begin as a political or moral strategy but rather appeared accidentally in the midst of feudal Christendom. Nevertheless, there was a sense of danger and the profane in its origins, since commerce and trade had grown out of the river piracy of the Vikings,[4] passing on to the bourgeoisie a sense of barbarian resistance to civilized control.[5] Indeed, commerce prospered wherever Church and State — as the sacred — were weak.

The gradual loosening of the Church's grip on the sacred had begun early. It was the need to finance the Crusades that had caused the Holy See to close ranks with Italian financiers and middle-eastern money-lenders.[6] In the mid-fourteenth century, after continental Europe's collapse from recession and plague, the Mediterranean merchants had moved into the vacuum,[7] making Venice the crossroads of trade and the birthplace of modern capitalism.[8] In need of huge loans, the Church quietly acquiesced as financiers and wool merchants broke the moral rules of scholastic economics. Soon, private wealth, far from being sinful, was deemed beneficial for the family and for the improvement of Christendom.[9] And so for a time the secular world as a whole was without an institutional Left, without a strong moral critic. (And thus began that age most highly praised by Nietzsche.)

Parliaments, the only moral platform apart from the Church, had tended to evolve only where mercantile activity was strong. And even then they were only the forum of the bourgeoisie against nobility and the crown. The nobility and the clergy, on the one hand, and the merchants on the other made up its respective Right and Left — until June of 1789. The bourgeois parliament suggested egalitarianism in nothing but rights; and it was not yet armed with the sacred. It would take a protest driven by poverty — less legal, more violent and more gnostic — to signal the first *radical* shift of the Sacred Left into the secular world. It is not through the vehicle of letters or law, but rather through prophets and religious visionaries, that we will see the displacement of a Sacred Left as a real *political* (and not just a legal or an intellectual) force from inside the Church out to the secular world. Moral censure — indeed outrage — on behalf of faith and the poor came from religious, not secular sources — from the fringes of the Church with Florence's Girolamo Savonarola, or from solitary, reforming renegades like John Hus of Bohemia.

There were, however, a few peaceful examples of popular democracy where an egalitarianism in spirit overcame inequalities in fact. One was Florence. A charmed political and diplomatic situation afforded the city state both independence and wealth, and there flourished within its walls a patriotism that was for a short time so solid and so free of treachery as to form a sort of internal commonwealth and a democracy that extended to the common people and the artisans. But as always the search for legitimacy hardened this harmonious felicity, and the Florentine patriciate, conscious of its freedom and inspired by the individualism of revived classical heroes, began to draw a spiritual justification from Plato.

And in fact, murmurs of a secular, philosophical "Left," anxious to shake off the shackles of tradition, do arise in Neoplatonism. Here we must recall that Platonism with its unworldly Ideas, was one of the foundations of the gnostic attitude. And so, for the moment we will call the current Aristotelian establishment "Right," if only in its emphasis upon the individual things of the world and its ideals expressed as earthly *forms* rather than heavenly *Ideas*.

Moreover, the Platonic idea of direct inspiration encouraged the imagining, through the picturing of ideals and ideal forms, of perfect city states and perfect societies — such as that already implied by Florence. If the force behind such imaging was contemplation, and the heroic classical revival had come to celebrate action, humanism celebrated a synthesis of both. But the two soon again separated: into action for the political Right and Platonic contemplation in the long lineage on the Left, from Aquinas through Marx.

Plato, of course, was an inspiration for Thomas More's *Utopia*, which the Italian city state had made relevant if not vaguely plausible. While *Utopia* prohibits wealth, it recognizes, true to its humanism, the bodily pleasures. However its rule by hierarchy and strict laws, as well as its simplistic absence of individual ambition, betrays its origin in pure contemplation; at once recalling Plutarch's rationalistic myth of Sparta and foreshadowing the totalitarian vision.

Neoplatonism is one of the more peaceful vessels through which the sacred Left is ferried out of Christianity to be landed in the secular world. But there was, in the static perfection of the Neoplatonic vision and its arming of every individual (in theory) with the power to apprehend that vision, a contradiction between collective and individual ideas of perfection. The latter was expressed in *virtú*, the individual's development to the maximum of all of his or her capacities. And it seemed that *virtú*, however Platonic, expressed itself most quickly and easily in commerce.

■

A Platonism of the individual implies liberty as an absolute ideal. And only in a newly independent United States of America, which had never known anything but bourgeois individualism, could the values of *virtú* be seized as a common, founding right — as they were in the New England intellectual trend called transcendentalism. Here, in the oldest part of the land of liberty, the classical source once again is Plato — at least insofar as *virtú* seeks an absolute for the individual rather than for the state. In Ralph Waldo Emerson, who drew on Plato, and in Henry David Thoreau, we find a Platonic ideal described as self-sufficiency, individual conscience, and mistrust of the state. The focus, as in the Italian Renaissance, and as in America today, is a gnostic ideal image of the self as self-fulfillment to be aspired to and grasped without intermediaries. At its best this is north-European egalitarian individualism; at its worst it contains the seeds of a gnostic Right.

Emerson and Thoreau were followed at the end of the nineteenth century by the movement of pragmatism. As the "exaltation of life and action over thought"[10] and a modern, less organic form of *virtú*, pragmatism also embraces the Platonic absolute in the sense that it regards even a life of practical decisions as unfinished and perpetually open-ended, as if to embrace *possibility* as well as finished work. This sort of egalitarian individualism conceives the nation not as a mass or as classes but as an agglomeration of small universes, each freed to discover its own maximum, free to create and recreate itself.

Although the American ideology was more resistant to schism, a split between Left and Right did develop, just as it had on the floor of the *Salle des Menus Plaisirs*. But the issue, of course, was liberty alone: a Federalist commercial North wanted a central government strong enough to protect commerce — while a countryside of independent farmers sought protection from central authority in principle. At first a "Left" of Democrats, the party of the small farmer, prevailed in the hands of the adventuring Andrew Jackson. As defenders of the egalitarian small proprietor from the interests of commerce and centralism, the Jacksonian Democrats were perhaps the closest thing to a Jacobin Left that America would ever know. Jacksonian democracy does have a sacred place in American history, and indeed an egalitarianism of the small entrepreneur could even return in the information age.

After the Federal Party shrank to a regional, Northern lobby, the party system lost its distinct duality. When polarity returned in 1860, it is no surprise that liberty once again provided the axis. The ostensible issue, of course, was slavery — a much easier subject for Americans to disagree on than money. By a paradox, the Southern slave system supported a liberty-loving Jacksonian democracy of individual planters; while the liberty-loving, centralizing, capitalist North sought (in the view of the South) to force its policy of anti-slavery on all the states. The duality, again, was non-economic, sharply defined around liberty, and difficult to fit into modern Left and Right. In the Civil War, the Americans were in a sense fighting an older, pre-republican style of conflict between bourgeois capitalism and landed aristocracy, a war over rights rather than over material goods — which is still the opening gambit before most revolutions formalize their Left and Right.

As the issue of liberty stabilized in the post–Civil War period, the Republicans and Democrats became so nearly indistinguishable that difference seemed to revolve around scandal and incompetence rather than reform. One wonders if perhaps the only real duality at the time was between degrees of Liberty, while an unacknowledged economic duality broke each party up vertically into its own plutocrats and populists.

The paradox of the classless but nevertheless stratified society is best described by Tocqueville. It was not so much capitalism, he says, but the specialization required for mechanized manufacturing that left the worker trapped in a nominally free society.[11] Meanwhile, as the educated owner became more versatile, he undertook less responsibility

225

for his workers and engaged less sociably with them; nor did he have time for responsibility or sociability with members of his own class.[12] With little of the sense of internal obligation that endured in Europe, it made for a lonely, less neighbourly society where advantage and strength came more from within the individual and less from the community. Dynamic rather than static in its middle and upper ranges, the American class system defied ideology and fixed destinies; even the worker adhered to the idea of mobility, though often an illusion, as if it were his birthright.

Labour, as a major political entity, was inevitably weak. After all, in a nation where community bonds were loose and one could always head for the frontier rather than improve the present situation, liberty was the first resort. To the extent that labour was organized, its structures were imported through immigrants who brought the anarchist traditions of southern Europe — fissile, perhaps, and self-defeating, but suitable, ironically, to a mobile society.

It is not that there is no Left and Right in America. It is that Left and Right in America, in theory, ought not to exist. Just as it took slavery to determine a Left and a Right around liberty, it took the luxury of an economic boom and an experiment such as Prohibition to create a moral, rather than an economic, divide in the 1920s. A rural Protestant south and west, for example, stood behind prohibition and religious morality; and a cosmopolitan urban north and east was inclined to be liberal. Indeed, the abiding political fulcrum in America may yet turn out to be morality itself, its liberty or restraint, as the storm over the president's sexual conduct in the White House of the late 1990s would suggest.

In a society that would never be proletarian, the liberty and democracy of the small producer would remain the practical bellwether; and so there is little doubt that the great capitalist boom after the First World War was ideologically un-American — it went directly against the interests of liberty itself. Large financial interests extended credit so liberally that the small proprietor could not make repayments, and overproduced to the extent that retailers could not make a living from selling and were eventually too poor even to buy. If the crash of 1929 had reinforced the predictions of Marx, American patriots might at least have reassured themselves that there was still good capitalism and bad capitalism: capitalism that would preserve liberty and capitalism that would strangle it; capitalism that might one day dissolve Right and Left and capitalism that would aggravate them. But, as the continued abuses in the stock and bond markets of the 1980s have suggested, bad capitalism still threatens to become an American ideology.

Franklin Roosevelt ought to be associated with good capitalism but even today he is still associated with the Left. His solution to the Depression, the National Recovery Act, was wisely even-handed, suspending anti-trust laws to resuscitate business while instituting relief and public works for the working class. National and nation-wide programs of electrification and soil conservation can be called neither Left nor Right but universal. His policies seem yet another demonstration that social policy and state intervention are themselves integral to the survival of capitalism.[13]

But if there were some on the far Right who also admired Roosevelt, it is because the expanded state is not merely a left-wing phenomenon. It is a phenomenon of modernity, which we have defined as the decline of sacred ends since the Middle Ages and the rise of practical means which have become ends in themselves,[14] a phenomenon in which Left and Right both take part. Capital's critique of welfare and socialism's critique of profit together become a self-perpetuating debate between different means to ends now lost to view. It is a solipsism in which ultimate values disappear because they are no longer required for the maintenance of a system made entirely of means. Ends are lost to sight, and without ends there are no limits and the system becomes an endless proliferation of means.[15] The complex of state and capital not only expands without reason but it expands blindly in the form of bureaucracy, which is itself neither Left nor Right but both.[16]

In bureaucracy, management becomes more important than imagination. It replaces politics.[17] In business, profitable innovation and ingenuity are mistaken for vision. The conglomerate of Right as corporate capital and Left as the state, where skills are in more demand than vision or values, has become what Max Weber called the Iron Cage — a solipsistic trap of means-as-ends where Left and Right are in collusion. Culture — the life of talk, memory, entertainment, and intimacy that once embraced the world — is gently pushed to the margins. The new duality that begins dimly to rise in the early twentieth century is not a duality of Left and Right, but a duality of power: of a citizen culture in opposition to the modern state.

It is of course one of Liberal Democracy's least admirable accomplishments that, in all its sheepish reasonableness, it has perfectly adapted its resident ideologies to the Iron Cage — indeed has become its manager and its collaborator. It is here, in the Iron Cage, that Left and Right are clearly disclosed not as ends — but only as means toward something still not articulated. This is why the call for a new politics beyond Left and Right is as urgent as it is — still — inarticulate.

The seeds of large-scale rationality and control can be found in the fifteenth century, when *virtú* would pass from ends to means — the turning of individual talent to the blind ends of the state. Self-mastery for Machiavelli's Prince was inseparable from the ability to form the "landed aristocracy and urban bourgeoisie into an effective territorial-political community, held together partly by a professional bureaucracy"[18] or "a compulsory association which organizes domination."[19] Confronted with the Sacred Left of the Papacy (at the beginning of its decline), the state, as the crown, would still be on the Right — as it would be in times of revolution. But it is in the Renaissance that the Sacred begins to shift from the Left, away from the Church and into the enemy camp as feudal domains expanded into nations and "secular rulers brought ecclesiastical administration within their scope."[20] This was a process, as Weber says, in which "the *jus modernus* of the late medieval . . . jurists and canonists was blended with theories of natural law which were born from juristic and Christian thought and which were later secularized."[21] Thus the rightish state absorbed and disarmed the leftish moral critic.

As a vast and impersonal force built by an individual, as opposed to the instrument of a class, the state of the fifteenth century had its paragon in Russia. The system inherited by Ivan III, Ivan the Great, from the Mongols and their Russian governors was patrimonial rather than feudal. Ivan ruled not by treaty but by ownership — body and soul — of the serfs in his domain and of the Boyar nobles, who effectively sold their freedom for sinecures in a crown bureaucracy.

Just as sacred and secular lost their distinctiveness upon the expansion of the nation state, the determinants of Left and Right weakened, with the combination of state and expanding corporatism. Indeed, some would say that Left and Right, even in Liberal Democracy, do not represent the poor or even the people, but only large interests and a political elite. In this respect the problem of poverty remains little different than it was in the waning Middle Ages. Perhaps until the thirteenth century the guild had been a source of democracy where masters and artisans, rich and poor, mounted a common defence against the supplier.[22] But now, in the fifteenth century, the guild itself would divide, as artisans, increasingly urbanized and with livings expressed in wages, had begun to appear as masses rather than as members of villages or parishes. Soon merchants maintained artisans at mere subsistence wages — and if there was no work there was no bread on the table. As the new poor, the artisans saw the guildmasters "as enemies, no longer as protectors but as exploiters, as Dives, the rich man consigned to hellfire, as wolves, and themselves as lambs."[23]

It is poverty coexisting with wealth — not social class, race, or gender — that has brought the most poisonous aspects of Manichaean thinking into the secular world. And its manifestation in Bohemia at the beginning of the fifteenth century would produce the most radical yet of the millenarian movements. Around Prague, the merchant guilds had produced among the weavers a great ramshackle slum of poor, all of it presided over by a Church mired in wealth and the profits from the sale of indulgences. With the poor stranded without a sacred protector, the role of the Sacred would shift to the margins of the Church in the secular population. John Hus, the precursor of the great Protestant rebellion, preached against Church corruption on behalf of the destitute and was burned at the stake. The uprising of his followers, the Taborites,[24] was cosmic and gnostic in its ambition, totalitarian in scope, with a stark agenda of killing the rich and bringing to earth a New Jerusalem of primitive Christian communism for a thousand year reign. Prevented by their idealism from making a work economy, the throng withdrew to a stronghold and lived on outlawry. Like the modernity to follow, means became ends: warfare, secession, and isolation became the goal; like modern revolutions, the movement dissolved into anarchy and then extreme and moderate factions before it collapsed.

If Liberal Democracy proves no better than its predecessor,

Christendom, at stopping the worst cycles of poverty, can it expect a better outcome? As a Right guided and corrected by a Left, it is rational but lacks the staying power of passion. As a compromise between the spirit on the Right and the body on the Left, it lacks conviction. In T.S. Eliot's dismissive description, it is "everything which is neither, including Protestantism, 'Whiggery', liberalism and humanism . . . and consequently forms a series of queasy transitional hesitations, each worse than the one before it."[25] Or, in the words of Francis Fukuyama, liberal democracies are "hamstrung by their very democratic nature: by the plurality of the voices, the self-doubt and self-criticism that characterize democratic debate."[26] It has no exciting terminus, no vision. Even the equal recognition of passionately held identities is ultimately self-defeating to that aspect of "recognition," or *thymos*, which remains excited by true distinction.[27] Although it claims to be a compromise between Left and Right, its Left and its Right are each intolerant insofar as each suspects the other of totalitarian tendencies. In the words of Eliot again: "Fascism and Communism are the products of strong tendencies within democracy itself."[28] Liberal Democracy is, in fact, not an ideology but a form of extended emergency rule. As Keynes described the technical superficiality of the logical positivists, it is "the thin crust on the lava."[29] But this, of course, is modernity.

The critique of modernity is called Modernism, and according to Charles Taylor, Modernism "avails itself equally to Left and to Right — because it can attack a liberal democratic enterprise which constitutes itself as both."[30] Liberal Democracy, in fact, has three enemies: the far Left, the far Right, and the gnostic position, which in its purest form, rejects both. If the Gnostics had discovered the inner self in the *pneuma*, Modernism rediscovered the *pneuma* as the unconscious, and its new polarity of *conscious* and *unconscious* went deeper than Left and Right. Like far Left and far Right, progressive and conservative modernist positions overlapped in their common project of attacking the centre, Liberal Democracy.

In the wake of the First World War, Modernism, seeing nature turned to rational domination, rejected the nineteenth-century romantic's refuge in the natural world. Now the unconscious, the *pneuma* or god-self, was the last, gnostic realm of freedom. Its prophet, Baudelaire, had rejected pastoral harmony for urban chaos and decay, a paradigm for the disorder of the unconscious, the lonely self. To the gnostic individualist such as the dramatist Antonin Artaud,[31] the fact of a compromised existence under the rule of the Demiurge is more worthy of contemplation than how the Demiurge keeps us alive. "If it is important for us to eat first of all," he warned, "it is even more important for us not to waste in the sole concern for eating our simple power of being hungry."[32] This is not far from Eliot's caution: "What the natural man wants is only generic: food, houses, sexual intercourse and possessions, and a society which accepts these wants as genuine social ends becomes totalitarian."[33] Both types of modernists, the "leftish" and the "rightish" scorn the banality of a material politics. In a similar vein, James Joyce exposes the wild *pneuma* that lives on under the surface concerns of one day in the life of Bloom, the Dublin Jew. And in *A Portrait of the Artist as a Young Man*, could Joyce get any closer to describing Gnosticism by name as an existential fact: "the All in all of us: the same ubiquitous presence that in alchemical terms may be represented as the solar king in the dark depths of the sea"?[34]

The protests of Orwell and Kafka need no elaboration. Closer yet to the mainstream, the Frankfurt school of Marxism attacked not just bourgeois economic outrages, but its aesthetic and cultural emptiness. And Carl Jung demanded that the soul and its myths not be kept separate as religious phenomena but be accepted as living, material facts. All have political implications; none finds a voice on the Left or the Right of Liberal Democracy. But Thomas Mann seems to have known earlier and better than anyone that Left and Right were masks: the former for life-loving spirituality, the latter for the thrill and violence of nature.[35] They were masks because the one was unattainable, the other unthinkable; the one blandly repressive, the other frankly charming and inclined toward destructiveness. Here was a reality too harsh for Liberal Democracy to embrace, but which art, "simultaneously conservative and radical,"[36] could accommodate.

The same might be said of Eliot. It is modernity, the whole environment of Liberal Democracy, Communism, and Fascism together, that Eliot seems to summarize as form without content — a desert where culture has long strayed from its purpose of providing fundamental meaning, binding the community from birth to death. It is a dying land littered with empty shells of programs, subsidies, and national policies — precisely the marginalization and departmental-ization of culture lamented by Max Weber. Eliot's position was that we live in a decline from the Middle Ages, the decline of the Sacred. But if we take the view of Max Weber that the sacred is actually the enchanted — that it is *meaning, substance,* and *coherence* — the popular tendency to call Eliot a conservative (much less to label him "Right") is to miss Eliot's point, indeed his value. Eliot has been censured (with reason) for his anti-Semitism, which blames the Jews for the travesties of modernity. Indeed, like that of the Nazis, his attack is not political but civilizational; his historical-critical purchase for an attack on modernity is the Middle Ages. But whereas the historical prototype of the Nazi was the Barbarian, that of Eliot is the Christian. Pointing to the spiri-tual coherence of time, place, and meaning in the medieval world — in opposition to the unbounded gigantism of modernity — Eliot could only excoriate Fascism, not to mention Communism and the political Left and Right all at once. For all his high Toryism, Eliot's critique is wise enough to be critical, never silly enough to be revivalist: as Frye points out, Eliot's conception of time is cumulative not linear, and allows a recovery *into* meaning, not a regression.[37]

When the Sacred is repressed, that is, neurotically internalized, it gives religious value to non-religious things. That is why I am inclined to call Left and Right the fetishism of qualities like equality and hier-archy, collectivism and individualism. For the latter are descriptive and complementary terms and not values in themselves. For a time, the inchoate forms of American politics promised a synthesis of these forms — until a sacred and profane in Bolshevism, the Great Depression, and Fascism would help to turn Democrats and Republicans into hostile kingdoms. In the words of George Santayana: "Let us hope at least that the new morality, when it comes, may be more broadly based than the old on knowledge of the world, not so absolute, not so meticulous, and not chanted so much in the monotone of an abstracted age."[38]

15

Atomization:

Protestants
and Americans

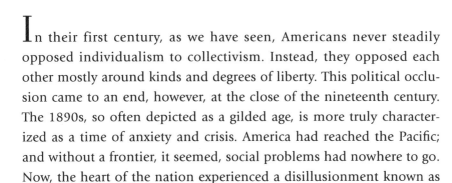

In their first century, as we have seen, Americans never steadily opposed individualism to collectivism. Instead, they opposed each other mostly around kinds and degrees of liberty. This political occlusion came to an end, however, at the close of the nineteenth century. The 1890s, so often depicted as a gilded age, is more truly characterized as a time of anxiety and crisis. America had reached the Pacific; and without a frontier, it seemed, social problems had nowhere to go. Now, the heart of the nation experienced a disillusionment known as the "great schism" — a consciousness, belated yet sudden, that the Promised Land had slipped from America's grasp.

More than ever rich and poor faced one another rather than a common horizon of freedom. Countryside was alienated from city, farmer from businessman, and even neighbour from neighbour, as communities still dissolved in the rush for wealth. And above all, a dissolute modern urban America was separated from a virtuous heartland. Now, "farmers used a higher law — the need to right insufferable wrongs, the very justification of the American revolution — to justify the use of violence in uprising after uprising."[1] Finally, Theodore

Roosevelt "warned the capitalists that a reform of abuses was the price which they would have to pay in order to save themselves from a socialist revolution."[2] "The land of the free" now had problems like those of the old world — and a politics defined more than before by socialism and capitalism.

The mass of farmers and a portion of labour, who had been living at the whims of big city control of the economy, gathered round the radical wing of the Democrats and put the loquacious populist William Jennings Bryan at the helm of the party. Bryan's politics was an amalgam of fundamentalist puritan Right and economic Left. It was, in fact, a populist puritanism that is often shared by Left and Right. In short, it was Protestantism. This is not surprising, for the common source for the modern forms of radical Left and Right was indeed the Reformation, a fact that still produces quintessentially American paradoxes. The anomaly of present-day left-wing feminists and the right-wing moral majority joining in an assault on pornography; of the radical Left and the radical Right sharing a protest against modernity — is only a bifurcation of something that was whole in Bryan, and before him, in Protestantism. Protestantism might indeed be called the third force of radical dualism after Indo-European–Semitic antiquity and Judeo-Christianity. It began as a reaction against Rome.

By the sixteenth century, the Church's scholastic defences had already crumbled before an onslaught of nominalist skepticism. As the quotidian details of the world began to attain their own integrity, God became remote, mysterious. A God occulted from the world of nature could only be reached by private, individual contemplation. Conversely, such a God relinquished to man a good part of the definition of the world. The pattern in its alienation and metaphysical polarization is gnostic; and indeed, one of its forerunners had been Pelagius. Even in the Middle Ages, an educated lay population had begun independently of the Church to embrace contemplation and good works, and, most importantly, to question the monopoly of the Roman clergy on spiritual interpretation. The Sacred Left as moral critic had already begun its shift from the Roman Church outward into the secular world.

The Dutch scholar Desiderius Erasmus tried to achieve the same thing from within the Church by recognizing as pleasing to God many of the more frivolous and worldly pursuits of an increasingly materialistic Renaissance. His work *In Praise of Folly* appealed strongly to commercial, northern Europe and was entirely in harmony with the new Christian humanism, which upheld wealth as a just reward and a means toward virtue. Indeed, *In Praise of Folly* has been regarded as perhaps the first ideological tract of the bourgeoisie[3] — even of the modern, liberal Right. But Erasmus would be bested by his enemy, Protestantism; because what capitalism really needed was a spiritual revolution — not a dispensation.

As we have seen, capitalism germinated with the Vikings, and so it long preceded Protestantism.[4] And anyway, it is evident from Protestantism's appearance all over northern Europe in all trades and in all classes that it was not (as has been thought) a cause of capitalism. But Protestantism did facilitate burgeoning capitalism by removing it from the shadow of sin. The layman's direct experience of a God who was somewhat detached from the world seemed to free the world to go its own way in economic matters, thus releasing business from the restrictions of canon law.

Such freedom to act directly in the world comes from the transmission of this recognizably gnostic feeling through an early Christianity that had neither Church nor clergy — the world of the New Testament. True to his gnostic origins, Jesus had attacked the rich and defended the poor on grounds of revelation alone, with no condemnation of commerce in itself or any demand that the law curb it. On the contrary, the problem was the Church. In sixteenth-century Europe the critics of Rome were able to find all the proof they needed in the New Testament to expose the ecclesiastical edifice as a means of hoarding secular and economic power. And Jesus' attitude provided the justification for the secular world to seize the power to govern its own economic conduct. And so religion, by way of economics, entered politics — and the Left as sacred moral critic took root in the secular world, identifying the Church and economic corruption, in effect, as a "profane" Right.

It was the dissemination of the Bible, especially the New Testament, through Gutenberg's discovery of printing in the previous century that popularized the revolt against Rome. By losing proprietorship of the

Bible to the people, the priesthood lost its ancient monopoly on propaganda by art, dogma, and canon law.[5]

In Europe, the gradual breakdown of old feudal forms had produced a wilderness within — of terrifying liberty. It was compounded by an equally daunting wilderness without: the dissolution of the Church-sanctioned Ptolemaic world through exploration and trade. From the Indian Ocean and from the Atlantic, godless hinterlands threatened to go on forever. In response to this new and disordered wilderness, inner and outer, the ideological structures of the modern age were born.

It began with the *reconquista* — Christendom's expulsion of the Muslims and the Jews from Spain at the end of the fifteenth century. With Columbus's simultaneous arrival on the shores of America, the Church's confrontation with the threat of universal disintegration would acquire an enlarged geographical dimension; the "other" now embraced indigenous peoples as well as the Christian heretics, Jews, and Muslim infidels. But instead of reunifying Christianity, the appearance of the New World exacerbated its divisions. The temptation to erect new ideological forms afresh upon virgin soil was impossible to resist. And as we shall see, the Protestants would use the Bible in North America while the Church used the ecclesiastical structures of Rome in Latin America as experiments for the renewal of what are essentially ancient ideas in the New World. Whether Catholic Spain or Protestant England, each cultural force would, by modern times, have produced its own Left and Right in the new world, all the ideologies heavily conditioned by their cultural origins.

The ideology of Rome faced even greater challenges from another wilderness closer to home — the spread of capitalism in the heart of Europe. In German mercantile towns, joint stock companies had been founded in order to finance the costly expeditions to the New World. When weaver shareholders could no longer compete with their merchants and masters, they became destitute, and the guild that had once protected both lost its function. Now they faced a world without shelter just as feudal Germany began to disintegrate. The lack of authority encouraged local princes to strip the knights below them of feudal privileges. The knights, in response, extracted what they could from a poor peasantry, reducing them to the fate of the unemployed weavers.

The hairline cracks of a religious break with Rome appeared just in time to align, and indeed to reinforce, the social protest.

In the silver mining town of Zwickau[6] a desperate industrial revolt erupted, driven by the apocalyptic Zwickau Prophets. Revelations in the New Testament and also the book of Daniel in the Old provided reassuring models of eschatological victory for a secular cause.[7] The Peasants' War (1524–1526) of which the Zwickau rebellion was a part, engulfed central Germany. What is important is that it was a *conservative* protest: a demand for the restoration of eroded feudal rights, a reaction against the modernizing princes and capitalists that had been spawned by the Renaissance. Rebellion, of course, is never, literally speaking, revolutionary. Nor is the Left — which can indeed trace its penchant for protest against loss back to the Peasants' War[8] — ever entirely new either.

But the spreading upheaval that followed, of which the Peasants' War was only an early symptom, could not have occurred without the protest of a single Augustinian monk, Martin Luther. The issue at stake was Rome's sale of indulgences — availing the rich of salvation at the expense of the poor. But Luther was not attacking medieval society — he was attacking Rome's monopoly on salvation and on the interpretation of scripture. His emphasis on salvation by faith and grace alone, not by good works, was strongly Augustinian, as was his belief that God had already determined the saved and the damned. But his attack on ritual and on canon law provoked the revival in Protestantism of the gnostic roots of primitive Christianity. All in all it was a democratic message, in the sense that it allowed each soul to reach its faith freely and internally, indeed mystically.

This simple faith laid a single spiritual foundation for two massive ideologies — capitalism and socialism. For the merchant on the Right it meant that successful business and good civic conduct were signs of the chosen, of *pneuma* — faith or the God within. For the peasants it meant that all were equally blessed by their share of *pneuma*, and that the Church and state that crushed them were, as Luther had said, the glutted forms of Babylon. Luther's Augustinian "saved and damned," predetermined on a messianic time frame, tended to reinforce a sense of the rightness in both causes. The effect has endured in capitalism and Marxism alike.

Luther was now well to the Left of Erasmus's liberal, worldly Catholicism. But he also represented a Left moving from liberator to sacred disciplinarian, potentially Puritan — a shade the Left maintains to the present day. But Luther's teaching also had a direct, practical effect. His democratic instincts, his attack on clergy, merchants, and knights altogether;[9] his nostalgia for the secure peasant of the Middle Ages[10] — all of this produced a sympathetic, though unintended upswell from the peasants.[11] Indeed, Luther provided a spiritual basis for peasant and merchant ideologies alike. In the Flemish and Northwest-German textile towns, peasant weavers formed an egalitarian republic behind the millenarian prophet Thomas Muntzer — eventually claimed as a forebear by Marxists.[12] Furthest of all to the Left were the Anabaptists, who rejected outright all the pleasures of the world. They converted the town of Munster into a walled republic, banning worldly pleasures and pooling all property in common under pain of death. The echo of Sparta and the fantasy of utopia are obvious, as is the foreshadowing in caricature of the Jacobin Republic. [13]

A generation after Luther, John Calvin unleashed a more radical form of Protestantism that opposed Catholic Europe almost on principle. Calvin's followers produced a controlled capitalism, pursuing economic freedom rather than wealth; interest rather than usury.[14] As well as being ethical, theirs was "a certain methodical, rational way of life which — given certain conditions — paved the way for the spirit of modern capitalism."[15] Equating work with virtue, Calvinism effectively outlawed unemployment. For the first time the poor became morally suspect, a prejudice rooted in St. Paul: "If a man will not work, neither shall he eat."[16] (We find the same instincts at work when modern conservatives try to outlaw panhandling.) Indeed, morality was everyone's duty: the faithful were their own priesthood and their own government; Church, state, and people were one. Calvin's theocracy, under which a rule of daily conduct and religious conformity were enforced upon penalty of death, was briefly realized when Geneva invited him to impose his rule there.

While Luther focused his work on Germany, the appeal of Calvin's *Institutes* was more international and widespread. Since Calvinism took root within alien, Catholic majorities as far afield as Poland, Hungary, Scotland, France, and England (under Mary Tudor), their situation as a

"Sacred Capitalist Left" encouraged a solidarity that was subversive, indeed revolutionary: capitalism as most recent moral critic. Unable to reform the Church, Luther had broken with it. Calvin completed the process by moving faith fully into the secular world. Thus ended the great European synthesis of sacred and secular celebrated by Dante — for whom "the coronation of the Emperor was to represent the sacred marriage of Sun and Moon, empire and papacy." For Luther, Calvin, and Thomas Muntzer, "it was too late: rebirth could be achieved only by divorce."[17] It is, of course, impossible to pinpoint the moment at which religion began to shape politics. But it seems to have begun during the first Catholic-Protestant war, which followed the Peasants' War. In this struggle for mastery among classes and towns in the political vacuum of central Europe, religious affiliations were paradoxically secular — you adopted the faith opposite to that of your secular enemy, attributing your oppression either to greedy Catholic prelates or to fat Protestant merchants.

But it was the peasant side of the Protestant revolt that would in future supply historical inspiration for a Left to stand against a capitalist Calvinist Right, its antecedents Anabaptism and Calvinism. Both showed that extreme asceticism could be enforced beyond the walls of monasteries. Although Anabaptism died out, Calvinism still represents the trunk beyond which the Left and Right branches divide for good. It was only a short step from the Calvinist public confession that bared souls and exposed lapses in community duty[18] to the left-wing Jacobin surveillance of public morals and the politicization of culture. On the Right, the legacy of the Calvinist inspection of intimacy and of sexuality, not to mention repentance by public confession, was revisited in the Republican inquisition of American President Clinton in 1998.

Indeed, Calvinist puritanism remains the rootstock of Left and Right. In Capitalism, Jacobinism, and Marxism we find the imposition of an orthodox morality upon daily life. (Indeed we can trace back to Calvinism the radical feminist belief that "the personal is political.") And we find in it the thread of millenarianism: the exaltation of an elect, a theoretically democratic egalitarianism, moral censure of dissidents, the rejection of the marginalized, and a morality considered to be universal. In Jacobinism especially, we will trace not only a Christian but a Calvinist descent — partly through Jean Jacques Rousseau's

Geneva. And its influence will be found equally in a Calvinist Scottish Right through Adam Smith — likewise driven to bind society in a universal morality of work as virtue.

But there is another common thread. All these movements were, without exception, European. The forces involved were not rational, but cultural forces conceived as rational; that is, they were only "rationalized." That is why they were transplanted to non-European cultures at such terrible cost. Even in Europe, the secularization of a religious idea had been brought about only through a bloody war. A respite finally came in 1555 with the Peace of Augsburg, which determined that each independent state could decide the faith of its subjects. Perhaps it was here that history first witnessed ideology's attempt to shape reality rather than to reflect it. Henry VIII of England did a similar thing when he made Catholicism into a state Church after failing to win papal dispensation for the annulment of a marriage. His problem with Rome had been different from Luther's, and so he condemned Luther and more especially Calvin. When he joined the continental trend of religious persecution, accordingly, he arrested and burned Catholics on his right and Calvinists on his Left. As with Robespierre and Luther, the Middle Way was simply another ideology whose course had to be stayed.

And it was stayed, perhaps only because England was an island, still relatively immune from the fray. Without the threat of domineering neighbours, she could experiment with softer secular ideologies. With legions of poor created by the new enclosures and by Henry's nationalization of Church lands, Robert Cecil, advisor to Elizabeth I, met the problem by increasing employment through the development of domestic industries for export.[19] From the standpoint of the twentieth century this move does not look much like an ideology, but it signalled the British trend toward a conservatism that was improvisational and practical, dealing with life as it is, without any specially clear vision of how it ought to be. From this period in England we can trace much of the direction the world is taking today — unless Free Market Capitalism really does harden into an inflexible ideology with utopian pretensions.

British conservatism, this least ideological of ideologies, finds much of its justification in the inductive science of Francis Bacon. And yet it is ironic that this thinker — who induced principles solely from the observation of the material world, and thus was perhaps the first systematic anti-ideologist — arguably contributed to the materialist ideology that helped engender socialism and capitalism. Indeed such a thoroughgoing materialism does have a gnostic aspect that can be traced directly to Calvinism's more occulted God and Bacon's own replacement of theological interpretation with science:[20] in Bacon's words, "a restitution and reinvigorating . . . of man to the sovereignty and power . . . which he had in his first state of creation" in the Garden of Eden.[21] If this is technology, its sovereignty amounts to an ideology, and Bacon is certainly one of its founders.

But the same conservative attention to the material world has a humane side. It seeks delight rather than dominion, life as spectacle rather than project. Patiently bemused and fascinated with folly and rarely censorious, it follows Erasmus. Its first significant appearance was in the humanist of the late French Renaissance, Michel de Montaigne. Montaigne was modern in his skepticism of systems. Perhaps in the same spirit as the souls who would vouch neither for God nor for Satan in the vestibule of Dante's Hell, he would "light one candle to Saint Michael and the other to the Dragon." Suspicious of claims to reason, he was likewise impartial in the debate between Catholic and Calvinist. Rationality was only an animal attribute, as proven by the human propensity for irrational cruelty. This humanist sort of thinking is inspired by the chaos of the individual life, more directly by the revival of Plutarch, the West's first biographer, the man to whom Europeans turned "when, after the Renaissance, men began to value their freedom."[22]

Plutarch influenced Montaigne. Plutarch and Montaigne together influenced Shakespeare. Shakespeare's own skeptical, conservative absorption with life-as-it-is came from Plutarch's *Lives* and from Holinshed's chronicles of British history. Shakespeare is descriptive rather than exemplary, and in that he was socially revolutionary: his display of life, in all its "sound and fury," smashes broadside into ancient, classical models of behaviour. Still, he is conservative because, like Montaigne, he accepts in the limits of personality the limits of life and politics, a "mode" which, according to sociologist Karl Mannheim, conveys an understanding of "time as the creator of value," and suggests that "everything that exists has a positive and nominal value merely because it has come into existence slowly and gradually."[23]

Elizabethan conservatism endures on a somewhat lower level in our own time in American entertainment and in the unabashedly commercial and journalistic novels of Tom Wolfe. This tolerant type of conservatism, as we will see, will be challenged from the Left by Calvinism — in Puritan England as well as in modern America.

Karl Mannheim has also defined conservative ideology by its tendency to launch cautious pre-emptive reforms that follow revolts by the Left.[24] That is what Rome did in its Counter-Reformation. But like any true conservative, she reformed herself and reiterated her doctrine in the same breath, calling the Council of Trent and going on with the Inquisition in Spain and in Holland. But its cruelties notwithstanding, the Counter-Reformation would eventually reveal the Catholic Church as a force of moderation. In future times the Left and Right in Roman Catholic culture would prove less extreme than the Left and Right produced by Protestantism.

To understand Protestant radicalism and the Catholic middle way it is useful to recall their philosophical foundations. Protestantism, like its gnostic forebear, has a powerful foundation in Platonism. Platonism and gnosticism alike see the single part, or individual, as an aspect of the whole. The two meet face to face, one the reflection of the other. This meeting allows radically divergent interpretations. Either you are omnipotent as an individual because you reflect the whole (the All) — as in *virtú* — or the whole is omnipotent because it contains, equally, you and all your brethren. Between these alternatives, Platonism offered no middle way, no "power-sharing." In consequence, "Platonist" Protestant peasants could take egalitarian justification from the whole; or, by the same thinking, the individual merchant could see himself as a sovereign *part* drawing his strength from the whole.

Roman Catholicism, on the other hand, having grounded itself in the Aristotelian synthesis of whole and parts and its emphasis on *limits* rather than on the infinite duality of Platonism, strongly discouraged radical expression of the individual as "whole" or as "part." And so it was the ultimate failure of the scholastic restraints on Platonism that freed the cosmic ambition of Protestant radicalism, Right and Left. Nevertheless, in a paradoxical expression of the Catholic spirit of synthesis, Rome became "more Protestant."

The means for this transition was the Society of Jesus, an order that in some ways resembled a Protestant movement — and still supplies force to the Left today. In Ignatius Loyola's mission to make Catholicism more active in the world, there is a revealing, if cautious, similarity to Calvinism. Like those of the Calvinists, the Jesuits' principles were international, their scope universal; their ambitions were political as well as religious. Like the Calvinists, they developed what amounted to a revolutionary solidarity and a strict code of behaviour linked to an international network that went underground in times of persecution. It is now well known that the Jesuit structures of secret organization were copied to build the cell structures of Leftist revolutionary organization in the eighteenth and nineteenth centuries.[25] And as the Calvinists tried to build ideal communities in Europe, the Jesuits, borrowing from More's *Utopia*, built egalitarian utopian missions among the indigenous peoples of South America.[26]

Egalitarianism, as the Jesuits demonstrated, could flourish in small spaces and under religious supervision. In other words utopianism could work provided it was not gnostic — meaning absolute and cosmic in its ambitions. But where it was ideological and unlimited it was Pelagian — and Pelagianism, as we have seen, counted on abstract goodness, upon a dismissal of experience, history, and human nature. It has become a cliché that Heaven enforced becomes hell on earth; the harsh means needed for perfection become ends in themselves.

The Europeanization of the Americas was to some extent a failed experiment in utopianism of the more ambitious, Pelagian sort. The Spanish settlement of South America produced the first disaster. Upstart ("rightish") conquistadors wanted to use the American utopia as a proving ground for their ambition — to hoard private wealth unhindered by the Crown. With this greed came the worst sort of indulgence-inspired Catholic utopianism, Columbus himself having remarked, "Gold constitutes treasure, and he who possess it has all the needs in the world, as also the means of rescuing souls from Purgatory, and restoring them to the enjoyment of paradise."[27]

Despite the extermination or enserfment of the indigenous peoples, a duality of utopia and the real world endured. The ecclesiastical decision that the indigenous peoples were actually human and must be treated according to Christian, humanist principles was accompanied by the idea that the land remained theirs, while it was only on loan to the Spanish settlers. So developed parallel worlds — the visible world of the real country with all its abuses and the ideal, invisible world of the legal country. From this double standard Carlos Fuentes traces the "constantly contradictory and dualistic nature of Latin American societies."[28] Latin America is a place where Utopia has never quite been forgotten.

Latin American authoritarianism, Right and Left, has depended upon the fictional "legal country" — on the Right for its legitimacy, on the Left for its grievances. Poverty and the culture of Catholic hierarchy have encouraged authoritarianism on both sides. But the authoritarianism has rarely been overtly racist. This restraint was due, at least in part, to the Catholic universalism of the New Testament. (The worst violence and oppression turned upon class rather than colour.) Even Latin American slavery tended to be closer to peonage, *ecomienda*, and *repartimiento*, where slavery blended with sharecropping and the slave could in theory buy his freedom.

Thus Catholic authoritarianism (though slower to change) was milder than the early authoritarianism of the Protestants. The latter's harsher attitude to race and to slavery derives largely from a partiality to the Old Testament.[29]

In the Protestant thinking of New England, the hinterlands beyond the coast were waiting to be reclaimed as the land of Canaan, and the Indians became "godless Canaanites" who needed to be expelled. Deuteronomy[30] was the model; it established the exclusive application of Mosaic law to the Chosen, and declared an internal equality while relegating resident foreigners to slave labour.[31] The consequences in racism persisted.[32] The American South, with its better soil and climate, encouraged a big plantation economy, suiting it even more to the metaphors of the ancient world and the Old Testament. The white, Anglo-Scottish population was in spirit, if not in fact, Calvinist, with an intellectual baggage that "consisted of the Protestant theology of the sixteenth century,"[33] taking from Augustine the idea that every person has his or her permanent place in God's hierarchy — a concept used to reinforce slavery, and eventually racial discrimination. Faced with a world beyond its borders that was liberalizing more rapidly, the

South was all the readier to seek its justification in the garrison-state history of Israel.[34] From the Bible Southern aristocrats imbibed the "rightish" rhetoric of the high priests; and its Christianized Africans sipped the "leftish" messianic ideology of the prophets and the Exile.

For America in general, the most ideological settlers remained the Calvinists. Long experience in Europe as a persecuted minority had encouraged them to find strength in the dispersal of government and priesthood among its people. In 1776, in America, the revolution of free Protestant merchants against British rule produced, in democracy and in an armed citizenry, something of that sense of the "priesthood of all believers." It is here that the passage of the sacred Left from the ecclesiastical over into the secular reached its peak, in the dispersal of the law among the people. Its inevitable expression was popular violence. As the priesthood had once been dispersed, so now was law enforcement. Freedom came to express itself in a common right to exercise authority or "bear arms." Citizen law enforcement became indecipherable from atrocities committed against the radical Tory Right or Indians, and from personal vendettas. Nor was the vigilantism that developed in the end democratic: it was carried out by "U.S. Senators and congressmen, governors, lawyers and capitalists."[35] "Freedom Left" had passed over into "authority Right." In the absence of a moral critic, the secular Right alone — as in the European Renaissance — defined society.

With the "great schism" of the 1890s, social protest finally appeared, directing itself inward from the frontier. Dualities began to shake themselves out, and gradually there appeared the determination of a more formal Left and Right. Even then, the Democratic Party could only form a Left that was vague and incoherent and never strictly egalitarian. Since material wealth was in theory available to all as the reward for hard work, and everyone was "guaranteed the future" there was, officially, no material debate. And so the shibboleth for this culture of Calvinist refugees from authoritarian Europe continued to be liberty. That is why the Democratic Party, the "party of liberty," became internally contradictory when the guarantee of universal prosperity evaporated in the 1890s: it tried to contain regional liberty in "rightish" votes from a Southern elite and material equalization in "leftish" votes from farmers, labour, and immigrants.

By the twentieth century, the Americas were divided into a capitalist,

Protestant, north-European culture and, to the south, a mercantilist, Indian-Catholic, and south-European culture. North America is descended from Pelagius through Calvin, and Latin America from Augustine.[36] The one dispenses with mediation between man and God; the other counts upon it. A horizontal, ascetic, puritan, frugal culture of bookkeeping and delayed gratification becomes opposed to a vertical, sacramental, ceremonial culture, ritualistic and profligate.[37]

Even then, the duality between Latin America and North America was neither simple nor symmetrical. As Latin America modernized, its Left and Right each developed Protestant aspects, stirring the pot and causing an ambiguity that further reveals the ancestry of politics in religion. Liberals, formally "Left," would draw inspiration from Protestant free enterprise, and reinforce economic privilege; conservatives who still drew support from Church and landed aristocracy would resist liberal modernization with aspects of "leftish," democratic Protestantism.[38]

Even after capitalism and its Marxist reaction had begun to take root in Latin America, both remained industrial ideologies that had grown from the Protestantism and classical economics of Northern Europe. And so it was difficult for a Catholic landowning class to become good Calvinist capitalists and just as hard for a non-proletarian peasantry to become obedient European Marxists. The revolutionary solution to extreme poverty would, in fact, never be uniformly "Left." A good example is Nicaragua. Although the name and the philosophy of the early twentieth-century revolutionary Augusto Sandino were claimed by his Sandinista Marxist-Leninist descendants in the 1980s, Sandino's ideology was a patchwork of imported ideas adapted to a Nicaraguan peasantry. It had "Right and Left" elements: anarcho-syndicalism, spiritualism, and populism, as well as a dose of Protestant Freemasonry, all mixed with a base of Marxism. And of course it had to accommodate the small-scale peasant proprietor, who, however poor, could never be a proletarian communist.

Left-Right political dualism hides these facts in much the same way that it distorts the current multicultural debate. Indigenous activists and their white lobbyists usually define themselves as Left, but the left-right form they have given the protest is European. After all, the "encounter with the other" is, at best, a meeting of "strong and weak." Otherwise it has little to do with socialism and capitalism, or with hierarchy or egalitarianism. It turns upon cultures that meet as categorical aliens, not as dialectical opposites like owner and worker. And so, there are points of opposition as well as points of incomprehension, and even of rough sympathy: for example, Christian Church hierarchies were able to absorb similar Indian religious structures, and the Jesuits would graft Indian ideas of egalitarianism onto Christian concepts.

Calvinism, having consigned the heathen to Magog, made no such effort at synthesis. The stamp it left on America was more or less unadulterated. Even if visible Calvinism has faded away, it endures in Platonic, Pelagian ideologies of inner, individual freedom and in the intense belief in liberty won through technology[39] as well as through the social sciences.[40]

In an era when independence and self-sufficiency are valued above all else and American families are disintegrating as their members disperse on inner or outer journeys of self-discovery and self-invention, the atomization of society is, in effect, a conservative, not a progressive movement. It is conservative because it maintains the direction that Protestants took long before — that one's ultimate relationship is not with the community but with God. And in modern, gnostic terms, that means the Self. The "Pro-Choice" movement is distinctly Protestant-gnostic in its exaltation of private conscience and the detachment of ethical matters from religious or social authority.

The Protestant American Right shares something else with its Left. Both are utopian. Among capitalists there has always been the belief that capitalism can, either by fulfilling itself or by taming itself, reach a happy-ever-after. The perennial dream by which the Right "eliminates" Left and Right by successfully spreading the wealth has been expressed in different ways by J.P. Morgan, John Maynard Keynes,[41] and Milton Friedman. Not only has that failed to happen but entrenched poverty and unemployment unrelated to the boom and bust of business have become a fixture in the free, global market. Capitalist utopianism may insist that it's only a matter of time. But this assertion employs the same self-affirming, elastic history as does Marxism. After all, both are Christian; both are Protestant; both explain everything in terms of tomorrow.

PART

3

SEPARATION

16

Culmination:
Cold Wars
and Witch Hunts

Whenthinking of the long genealogy that engendered Marxism and modern capitalism out of Protestantism, a lineage that can be traced back to early Christianity and Judaism, it is easy to forget that Zoroastrianism was a progenitor of all of them. But the culmination of this long history in the haunted standoff that we call the Cold War brings this primordial religion of danger surging back into view. Indeed, it all gives a sort of prophetic credence to the eschatology of Zoroaster. The world, once whole and primitive, had passed through a second stage of "mixture," when individual and collective forms coexisted; and then, by the mid-twentieth century it had undergone separation, a split between the empires of Left and Right — each good, each the other's evil — dividing not just parliaments and nations, but the earth and the soul itself.

Moreover, the West had its own long-developed culture of division. Rational, almost mathematical, categories like individualism and collectivism, the parts and the whole, as we have seen, make polarization and simplification virtually inescapable. And yet such abstractions could not adequately describe the more emotional currents that underlay the Cold War. The mind is always older than the era it lives in, and

Americans of the 1950s saw in the Soviet Union not so much a threat to individualism as the reincarnation of the sinister qualities they had once rejected in monarchy.[1] For them, the American Revolution of 1776 had been the last possible left-wing revolution for liberty and democratic equality, the last revolution at all.[2] In effect, Communism did not represent equality in the American view, but rather it evoked the absolutism of seventeenth-century Europe, which, as we shall see, arose from the anarchy of the Wars of Religion. When the United States and the Soviet Union are considered to represent theories within classical economics, however, they could be thought of as symmetrical, mutually exclusive opposites. Each power, aggrandized by the strategic advantages it had gained as a victor in the Second World War, defined its side of the globe. In doing so, as historian J.M. Roberts points out, and as this book argues, the two of them made any alternative economics (beyond Left and Right) impossible.[3]

Moreover, history and culture from Kamchatka to East Berlin made the subsequent domination of classical Soviet Communism equally unworkable. Communist Poland was never able to forgo the dream of trade-union freedom or an age-old peasant dream of private property.[4] The natural way of Tito's Yugoslavia was a balance of limited capitalist and trade-union autonomy against Communist authority.[5] In Hungary, relative autonomy under the Habsburgs promised resistance to Stalin. And Czechoslovakia, the home of John Hus and the first sustained rebellion against the absolutism of Rome, was by no means naturally submissive.

In such a heterogeneous world, neither superpower was able to reflect its ideology very clearly in its strategy. The Cold War was a ragged battle of tactical advantages rather than a contest for hearts and minds. In the United States, "there was never a master-plan; more a series of makeshift expedients, with huge holes and gaps and many contradictions."[6] There were early attempts at détente with Castro's Cuba; America here and there encouraged socialism abroad for the sake of stability. In Yugoslavia, the Soviet Union preferred to countenance Tito's local ideology rather than face intervention. In neither case could the world really be made to conform; strategy was about the furtherance of ideology through power and security, and yet was powerless to reflect the ideologies it served.

In the West, however, that *realpolitik* was pursued only to the extent that American foreign policy was conducted by Washington. The inner drive, by contrast, came from the heartland: the Manichaean anticommunism of ordinary Americans of the middle and lower middle class. So the *realpolitik* was, in the end, the compromised expression of something hell-bent and unrealistic. "Whoever interprets American foreign policy in terms of economic interest or imperial power," wrote a Swiss journalist, "does not understand that it springs from sincere convictions rooted in the Puritan inheritance . . . The idealistic approach to foreign policy of a people who are assumed to be hard-headed businessmen is one of the most important reasons for serious misunderstanding between Europe and America."[7] And so the policy of containing Soviet aggression conceived by Truman's advisor, George F. Kennan, was the mask of realism for a policy that nevertheless occasionally showed its true colours: as in the overthrow of Arbenz's democratically elected socialists in Guatemala, or in the interventions in Korea and Vietnam.

This archaism at the heart of the conflict was fully revealed in the competition for nuclear dominance. About the Bomb that impelled it all, little needs saying: it was designed not to advance front lines, but to wipe out hemispheres. The breadth of its destructiveness was Manichaean, not tactical: the most perfect, awful expression of Western dualism. In fact the idea is best characterized by its provenance: it came not from the Cold Warriors themselves, but, as Paul Johnson has pointed out, from a much more nihilistic, atavistic mind — that of Adolf Hitler.[8]

In modern times such primal and haunted distinctions are held most ardently by the marginalized. Those who supported Senator Joseph McCarthy in his crusade to cleanse America of suspected communists were not the majority and certainly not the establishment. They were the American *petite bourgeoisie*, the *déclassé* equivalent of the forgotten "gnostic masses" in Europe. These were the self-reliant, self-employed small-town descendants of the old New England Puritan classes — those who clung to anticommunist patriotism in a world in fact more threatened by larger, corporate forces. And in their extremes they characteristically met the far Left, for McCarthyism "appealed to the same groups as did 'left-wing' populism."[9] Today, its radical progeny populate the militias in the American heartland. They are the antiquated rural classes who were far more essential for the founding of the nation than they are today.[10]

But the instinctive resistance that many Americans feel toward an omnipotent state is rooted even more deeply in the past. It comes specifically from their inherited knowledge of the state that it evolved in Europe as a solution to the chaos of the sixteenth century, for it was precisely to avoid a new absolutism that many religious communities fled across the face of Europe to the shores of America.

■

It was only after Europe's Wars of Religion reignited in 1613 that the state rather than the Church started to become the vehicle of a national ideology. Protestantism and Catholicism vied again for control of Central Europe, and in the ensuing three decades the chaos engulfed Sweden, Holland, France, and Germany in opposition to the Catholic Holy Roman Empire in Austria-Hungary and Spain. Though the Empire was fatally weakened, the wars ended in an effective stalemate; the only real victor was the nation state, which arose in fear and necessity out of the ashes of religious conflict. And no sooner had the state become the determinant and protector of religion than the sacred began to pass into the secular as Jesuit schools taught "young minds . . . to see Europe as divided by religious and ideological conflicts."[11]

The Thirty Years' War also gave birth to the disciplined, hard-scrabble entity of Brandenburg–East Pomerania, wary and defensive from near disintegration. It would later materialize as Prussia, the prototype of the hell-bent nationalist state. Meanwhile, in Eastern Europe, in Poland, and among the Austrian Habsburgs, frontiers with alien Russia and Turkey encouraged the development of counter-ideologies, Christian and conservative. On the western end of the same Catholic ideological axis was Spain. In the north she exercised a religious totalitarianism in the Netherland territories of her Habsburg connection. In between, in Catholic France, the first truly secular foreign policy seems to arrive with Cardinal Richelieu, who sought alliance with the Protestant powers in order to face down his over-strong Habsburg co-religionists. It is indeed with France that ideology, without losing the force of the sacred, first seems to have set foot in the secular realm.

Louis XIV went further, identifying France not so much with a religious idea as with the personal power and splendour of the monarch. Moreover his expulsion of the Huguenots killed Protestantism as a socio-political force in France.[12] With the Sun King's territorial aggression and splendid court, the Sacred moved not only into the secular, but became fully Profane. In quite another sense, Louis XIV provided the foundation of the Left as well as of the Right in the French Revolution. His rationalization and modernization of the state set down patterns of control and consolidation for the Jacobins, while his cult of personal glory made monarchy more than ever absolute. By exalting Whole in nation and Part in monarchy in one institution, he exemplified the contradiction between them that helped to make France the ground for the split.

In Russia, likewise, monarchical absolutism laid the ground for the modern absolutism of 1917. Czar Peter the Great launched a technological and state mercantilist revolution through the wholesale enforcement of Western education and culture within his nobility. Peter's other, perhaps more significant, innovation was to convert much of Russia's free peasantry into an army of serf labour to press forward the clearing and cultivation of Russia's frontiers.[13] The inadvertent effect was to create the demographic atomization that, over two centuries, brought about the radicalization and alienation of new economic classes. When post-Soviet reformers complained in the 1990s that Communism had produced a "slave society" they needed only to look back as far as their first modernizing Czar.

The modernized state was only one factor in establishing the groundwork for modern Left and Right. Ideological differences of a secular kind started to appear in the seventeenth century as well. The issue was the extent of the absolutism of the new state: among monarchical ideologists, *de facto* divine right vied with more rational justifications of absolutism. Against the crown itself, the bourgeoisie, often puritan and parliamentarian, posed the right of resistance upon conscience alone. These were the as yet unformed modern Right and Left, which had a crude parallel in the cultural debate between the "Ancients" and "Moderns."

For the first time, *style* expressed conservative and progressive attitudes. The splendour and individual heroism extolled by the "Ancients" was disdained by the "Moderns" in favour of the practical virtues of economic pursuit, science, and technology. The "Ancients" practised the cult of the gentleman: refinement as an end in itself. The "Moderns" cultivated a diametrically opposed asceticism that held the aristocratic cult of heroism and glory in contempt. The heroic principle of the "Ancients" always supported state ideology through classical allegory, Roman law, Baroque adornment, and the tragic view of life as passing splendour. It was, indeed, the most "un-Protestant," "un-leftish" position imaginable. But after scientific utilitarianism had become ingrained in the egalitarian bourgeois Left, it too adopted Baroque pretensions of power, status, and luxury.

There is an important sense, however, in which the seventeenth-century rightish force of the state was the revolutionary force and the leftish popular protest was conservative. Russian peasant rebellions, anarchic rebellions of all classes in France (the Fronde), and uprisings of merchants and peasants in England were a *conservative* response to the erosion of feudal rights and privileges by a modernizing state. The same "conservative" Left persists today as trade unions fight to prevent the loss of their power (which some might jokingly call "feudal") to the global free market.

Another form of royal incursion upon traditional feudal freedoms and immunities was the English king's poaching of private capital through subsidies or forced loans. This method of taxation incited the English civil war, as it ran directly contrary to the spirit of English Common Law, by which the monarch was obliged to consult parliament in matters affecting its members. Accordingly when the Catholic king, Charles I, levied funds by fiat, he was accused of putting on the airs of an absolutist French Bourbon. The forces of a modernizing baroque and allegorical Catholic state now faced a severe commercial class, dressed down and defining itself with science and technology.

But this was not an egalitarian revolution against a reactionary monarchy. Barrington Moore has emphasized that the "conservative" revolutionary class in fact comprised the landowning commercial gentry.[14] As everywhere in Europe, it was protecting the past — the aristocracy's traditional fiscal immunities — and insisting on the right to proceed with the enclosures that pauperized the rural lower classes. The force that resisted the aristocratic policy of enclosures was in fact the monarchy. Here, quite suddenly, Stuart absolutism appears as a big government Left and Sacred moral critic, protecting the poor from a commercially ambitious (if politically revolutionary) aristocracy.

The Protectorate of Oliver Cromwell, having overthrown Charles I, conserved the advantages of the commercial aristocracy while maintaining a position on politics and morality that was more typically revolutionary. It even foreshadowed French Jacobinism to the extent that "the Jacobins of the 1790s [regarded] the Puritan revolutionists as their direct forebears."[15] The Puritans, like the Jacobins, pursued the new commercial asceticism, ruling with a dictatorship that almost became totalitarian.[16] But unlike the Jacobins of 1793–1794, the Protectorate was set up for the wealthy commercial gentry, not the shopkeepers and artisans. In the difference between them will lie the genesis of the economic Right and Left of the modern era.

The alliance that ensued between the aristocratic Protectorate and the millenarian rebels among the shopkeepers, artisans, and the London lower class, was uncomfortable. The millenarians — the Diggers, the Levellers, and the Fifth Monarchy Men[17] — wanted to use Cromwell's revolution to eliminate poverty, drawing their inspiration from messianic Protestantism, the book of Revelations, and the incarnation of the New Jerusalem.

When the millenarians pushed for a violent social revolution, Cromwell turned on them, inaugurating for Europe the political chasm between the commercial classes and the working class. But dialectically, it was a victory for the Puritan "centre," since the far "Right" and far "Left" of monarchy and poor were now united in opposition to landed business in a humane "leftish," if scholastic, defence of land for "use and sustenance" as opposed to speculation.[18] Cromwell's Protectorate, however shortlived, would at least leave the legacy of free enterprise that blossomed into nineteenth-century utilitarianism. Throughout, the inspiration and justification was Reason.

In Thomas Hobbes, the recourse to Reason is not surprising. His long life witnessed the brawl between Ascetic Protestantism and Baroque Catholicism played out in the sinking of the Armada, the English Civil War, and the restoration of the Stuarts. It appeared to him that conventional Reason was nothing more than opinion, violence was man's natural state, and the sole surviving moral principle was to be found in science and mathematics alone. Again, the source was

Euclid.[19] As nature needed mathematically defined ascending forms to produce order, so did man.

And so it is compassion, oddly enough, that makes Hobbes the ancestor of the rationalistic justification of the totalitarian state, Right or Left. Imagining that he is scientifically inducing the need for a strong authority from the state of nature, Hobbes's real arguments descend *downwards* from the ideal state, which he names Leviathan. *Leviathan* is in fact an idealized response to his own fears of civil war and crumbling legitimacy. In this he commits the same inversion as Marx: the sin of all systems that retain too much Platonism. The Leviathan is the determinant of religion and remains above the very law that it enforces. Fearing all liberty except economic liberty, it posits capitalism as the glue, the relation which keeps the parts together while the state keeps order.[20] On the Left Hobbes would have the state help those who cannot help themselves, but only for the sake of public safety. The modern logical conclusion of *Leviathan* would be a capitalist dictatorship run by Stalin. Or perhaps contemporary China.

Hobbes's intolerance, his belief in the state as a monolithic organism of defence, and his mistrust of human nature eerily describe both the United States and the Soviet Union after 1945. And so it is the seventeenth century more than any other epoch that resembles the Cold War, especially when we recall the witch hunts of both periods. In the wake of the Wars of Religion, the intermixture of Protestantism and Catholicism in Western Europe — each protected by national states — had the effect of secularizing religious ideology. The resulting malice and paranoia brought about the greatest incidence of witch hunts in European history, each faith detecting in the other hidden traces of paganism, if not Satanism. In charges of witchcraft, as in charges of communism by McCarthyites and of capitalism by Stalinists, the burden of proof was always on the accused.

In all cases it required technique, and the Puritans who perpetrated the witch trials in Salem, Massachusetts, were perhaps better trained for it than anyone. They had, after all, inherited four times over the injunction to ideological conformity of the garrison community: from Old Testament Israel; from the Calvinist communities of Europe; from political and religious marginalization by Anglican England; and fourthly from their isolation on the edge of a wilderness inhabited by "godless heathens."

But the Puritan Calvinism of America was not as "rightish" as Americans might assume. It contained nascent forms of modern Right and Left alike. The authoritarian-egalitarian element in what R.H. Tawney has called a "Calvinist theocracy"[21] was more similar to Jacobinism[22] than was the party of Cromwell. It was the same Calvinist just price and other early limits placed upon capitalism that made their way via Geneva and its son Jean Jacques Rousseau into Jacobinism and, *a fortiori*, into Bolshevism. It might be too much to call the fight between capitalism and communism a narcissism of small differences, but it does seem that much of the dualism that split the world in the 1950s originated with antagonistic egalitarian and individualistic elements within Calvinism itself.

Around the same time that the Puritans launched a free, sacred Self to seize the world in enterprise, France produced from philosophy an abstract, secular self that made the world its instrument in a different way. With his *cogito ergo sum*, René Descartes made the self and its perfect Creator the only two objects of certainty. Not only was this dictum more than a dose of gnostic identity with God, but it was also (in gnostic fashion) an exclusion of the material world from the world of mind and spirit. If there is any doubt, we need only observe that Descartes is an intellectual descendant of Plato, Euclid, Plotinus, and St. Augustine[23] in his use of mathematics as the projection through the self of divine, ordering reason.[24] Both the Puritan self and the Cartesian self produced a rational, instrumental approach to the world that made it easier to manage, categorize, and divide.

In Descartes' conception of the self as mind only, we find the ultimate refinement of Platonism and gnosticism which, as *logos*, separates a higher realm of abstract reason from a lower realm of matter, enabling reason to manipulate the lower realm, not just as matter but as society and finally politics — "the whole program of wilful sovereignty in the Cartesian *ergo*."[25] As the mind of Descartes entered the education of Europe, thought ruled out any ambivalence in the material world and an "*a priori* and antihistorical spirit . . . shapes the entire following century and culminates in the French Revolution."[26]

Only a generation later, we find an opposite movement in Blaise Pascal. Pascal emphasized the limitations of the very reason that Descartes had found so indubitable: "Our soul is cast into the body where it finds number, time, dimensions; it reasons about these things and calls them natural, or necessary and can believe nothing else."[27] His is a gnostic thinking more radical than that of Descartes, in which reason, especially mathematical reason, comes up short of God, leaving a cosmos absurd in its endlessness[28] beyond which God is lost to view and we ourselves abandoned.[29] More accepting of doubt, less dependent on rational authority, Pascal is closer to the spirit of Protestant anarchism. We find the same taste for ambivalence in Pascal's contemporary, Pierre Bayle. Skeptical of orthodoxy, dubious of reason's ability to determine faith, Bayle played devil's advocate on behalf of heresies and unpopular beliefs. If Cartesian reasoning would provide an instrument for ideological orthodoxy, Bayle and Pascal were the first modern skeptics who, if they could, would have chosen a third way between faith and reason. Their doubt is the precursor of modern existentialism.

■

Existentialism has been described as the final rebellion against the European rationalism of the seventeenth century. In the postwar period, the Existentialist assault on ideological dogma was taken up by Maurice Merleau-Ponty, who mounted attacks on the capitalist West and on Stalinism simultaneously. After the war had split up international pro-letarian solidarity, he said, it was "difficult to recognize the classical descriptions of 'capitalism' and 'proletariat.'"[30] The conclusion drawn by Merleau-Ponty's colleague and ally Jean-Paul Sartre was that individuals themselves and not society or thought systems bore the entire burden of political choice. Moral responsibility was as big and lonely as Pascal's universe, as bereft of divine reason as it was of Cartesian measurement.

Here begins what may have been the first great postwar adventure beyond ideology, Left and Right. But even as Sartre claims to have freed the world once and for all from the shackles of metaphysics, he reveals himself chained to the very scholastic structures he dismisses. His self is none other than the Cartesian self[31] — a bodiless, abstract rational point; and the world is nothing but its own reflection in the choices it makes. With Sartre, almost despite himself, dualism returns. There is an exalted, superior world of the self and an inferior material world relegated to being its creature; more than just a Platonic-Cartesian distinction, it is a gnostic duality reminiscent of the old Parmenidean Whole and the Parts. Resorting to "forms which are, as Plato once put it, 'laid up in heaven,'"[32] Sartre's free individual makes his moral choice on behalf of an Idea — all of humanity — every time he acts.[33] He chooses a Whole which, as in Parmenides, Plato, St. Augustine, and Kant, is morally superior because as an ideal it alone is real. In the end, any supposedly free choice is no choice at all, but only a choice on behalf of the Whole. In the words of Julian Marias, Sartre presents a "traditional Scholastic or phenomenological ontology *à rebours* [in reverse], but without transcending the basic concepts and statements of problem."[34]

If acting as one was acting for all, suggested Sartre, perhaps it was best to sidestep the messy vertigo of existential subjectivism and grasp the ready-made collectivism of Marxism ("the philosophy of our time . . . unsurpassable because the circumstances that developed it have not yet been overcome"[35]), and accept its supposed model, the Soviet Union. Perhaps indeed the fraying rope-bridge of existentialism was not yet strong enough to support a real Third Way. Instead, Sartre abandoned it, made the leap, and clung to a dogma that he somehow justified as a free, existential choice, a leap of faith rather like Pascal's wager. But predictably, he was taken to task from the Left for disdaining any social or historical sense; and for preaching a nihilistic superiority of the lone, choosing self, which felt, in fact, like a lazy bourgeois prerogative.[36]

All the while, Sartre accused his public existentialist opponent, Albert Camus, of being a bourgeois sellout. After all, Camus had broken with Marxism, in the belief that one had to be loyal to this life and to the living, and not to some utopia in the distant future. But Camus, like any truly independent thinker, always has the appearance of remaining within the safe port of the bourgeoisie, simply because there is nowhere else for him to go: there *is* no Third Party. For him, the real battle is the battle with existence; those who lose this awareness become swallowed up in dogma and to this end, he preferred the local association to the State and its ideologies. "Trade-unionism, like the commune," he wrote, "is the negation, to the benefit of reality, of bureaucratic and abstract centralism. The revolution of the twentieth century, on the contrary, claims to base itself on economics, but is primarily political and ideological."[37] It might have been the genesis of a Third Way — beyond Left and Right.[38]

In the Cartesianism that lurks in Sartre and even in structuralism, we discern the refracted rays of seventeenth-century rationalism — still using wholes and parts, self and world, inside and outside, unities and moieties — to give sense and morality to existence and politics. A generation after Descartes, it would take a more desperate, less detached mind to give to rationalism a political shape, the mind of Baruch Spinoza.

The Netherlands, the country of Spinoza, had been born in the fires of religious intolerance; Spinoza himself had been expelled from his own community of Jewish exiles, and so his rationalism had a certain urgency. Spinoza drew upon Descartes, upon scholastic wholes and parts. But his God was not separate from nature and from the self like that of Pascal and Descartes. The parts were merely aspects, manifestations of the dominant fact: a divine, all-inclusive whole. Inclined to collectivity and pantheism, Spinoza found that whatever joined men and things was good, and that what separated them led them into error. "Men can desire, I say, nothing more excellent for the preservation of their being than that all should so agree at every point that the minds and bodies of all should form, as it were, one mind and one body; that all should together endeavour as much as possible to preserve their being, and that all should together seek the common good of all."[39] In this sense Spinoza is an important forerunner of the Left — albeit that classical, scholastic Left which founds itself on the whole over the parts. On closer inspection his system has a strong resemblance to the Jacobin republic. The God of Spinoza, like the atheistic God of the Jacobins, is Reason reflected in a conception of society as a perfect, collective plenum, a seamless whole. To maintain this general good, individual freedom must be curtailed and self-interested behaviour punished.[40] In Spinoza we find perhaps the first philosophical precursor of the Jacobin dictatorship, and his materialism would pass onward into Marx.[41]

If the pantheist of Reason had upheld the whole, Gottfried Wilhelm Leibniz, Spinoza's contemporary, would see the world in terms of the parts. Although he too drew on Descartes, his cosmos is hierarchical rather than a plenum of equality; his God, far from being identical with his creation, produces it (like the God of Plotinus) through emanation. Unlike the God of Spinoza, his God has a will. And it is the *parts* that are of paramount importance. All existence is made of metaphysical points, bodies called *monads*, each of which expresses all possible aspects of the universe, each self-contained. The conservative aspect in Leibniz lies in his belief that progress is possible only for these cosmic elements, not for the world;[42] and that God has arranged that all outcomes be the best possible.[43]

Leibniz is also the model for Voltaire's stuffy conservative, Pangloss, who thought that "all is for the best in this best of all possible worlds." But I am not sure that this is fair. With Leibniz's *monads*, there is little dependency — little superiority or inferiority — precisely because their cooperation is simultaneous and harmonious, not causal or logical. Comparisons with the early Marx[44] suggest a sort of individualist egalitarianism;[45] and the spontaneous, causeless interrelationships of Leibniz's cosmos give to his system an anomalous Eastern flavour.[46] Indeed, there is some evidence that Leibniz was influenced by the Confucian Mahayana Buddhist texts that Jesuit missionaries brought back from China.[47]

The East had, of course, made itself felt before and would again, in Schopenhauer and in Nietzsche. But it is old enough, and sufficiently massive and distinct from the West, for us to conclude that the aspects we have been calling "Western" are indeed Western, and that Western dualism is contingent and unique; and finally that the Western Way ultimately turned around to influence China profoundly as an outside force. Our question here is whether China, culturally and historically, had a collectivist affinity for modern Maoism. It is true that from ancient times China had shared the quadrapartitioned cosmos of central Asia. But the bond of Confucianism and the lack of a significant messianic tradition[48] had prevented the development of any deep dualism. The Vedic ideas that had produced polarity in the West tended, after they had drifted into the Far East, to emphasize a "middle way" of oscillation and complementarity.[49]

Around the time Leibniz was born, the Manchu (1644–1911) inherited a highly centralized system that had been forged long before by the great Han dynasty (circa 200 BCE–AD 200). Moreover, it had made itself indispensable, replacing the landed nobility with a civil service of landlords and centralizing the administration, thereby virtually eliminating the inconvenience of a competing aristocracy. And so Western scholars have argued from the Right that China had a disastrous "Left" bureaucratic tendency, and from the Left that the landlord system produced a terrible "Right" tendency.[50] It seems that the society, being both, was in the end neither and that its fate was decided not by China itself but by Western ideas and interference.

So it was not internal instability that finally broke the system. Rather, it was the very lack of that internal adversarialness of self-interested classes and aristocracies that toughens most states which left China at a loss when faced with commercial disruption by Western colonialism. As we have seen, capitalism has always undermined the interdependency of traditional classes, and the sudden injections of wealth created a disruptive self-interest in Chinese society. Indeed, it is when new wealth frees the upper classes, cutting them loose from society and social obligation, that those classes are most hated. But this was not a Chinese observation. It came from the West with Marxism; moreover, Marxism in China had been preceded, as in Europe, by a Protestant rebellion.

By 1850, three centuries of penetration into China by European missionaries and merchants had earned for Protestantism a significant headway. Then a demagogue named Hung Chiu used Christian ideas of common ownership, class war, and salvation to organize the same sort of revolt as had erupted in sixteenth-century Germany. The Taiping Rebellion (1850–1864), had it not collapsed, would have been China's modernizing social revolution. And so, in the long run, communism was a European process and in fact the Taiping Rebellion has most often been compared to Europe's thirty-year Wars of Religion. Both wars began the conversion of religious and social polarities into a westernizing social polarity of Left and Right.

So, when communism arrived in China in 1923, it was not because China was naturally communistic, but because nationalist leader Sun Yat-sen, unable to secure aid from the West for his Kuomintang, turned to Stalin. Stalin sent Michael Borodin to set up a communist party on the Bolshevik model. Once communism had a foothold, there developed within the Kuomintang a clear-cut Left and Right, both with nationalist programs: the one Bolshevik, the other a weak broth of Confucianism, xenophobia, capitalism, populism, and gangsterism sadly resembling Fascism.[51] The Nationalists of Sun Yat-sen's successor Chiang Kai-shek turned upon the Communists, Stalin ordered the Communists to secede from the Kuomintang, and so began the civil war. And of course the Communists prevailed, headed by a new, charismatic personality: the young, tough, and brilliant Mao Zedong.

Throughout, two forces had remained at work: the atomization of the Chinese peasant, which increased with Western industrial disruption; and the endurance of the clan system as the focus of survival. Again we find "Left" and "Right" egalitarian and hierarchical forces at work. That we should use one to the exclusion of the other in defining Chinese society seems to be a Western prejudice. In Eastern thinking, order (Left) and progress (Right) are not seen as mutually exclusive; whereas (wrote Auguste Comte) after Oliver Cromwell's Protectorate "the requirements of order and of progress, both equally imperative, became absolutely irreconcilable. The nations of western Europe ranged themselves on one side or the other."[52] Even Mao would try to develop a concept that was supra-partisan. After all, there were deep precedents.

The Chinese ideology of "no ideology," that is, an ideology not defined in terms of the mutual exclusion of ideas, is Confucianism. Confucianism, Taoism, and Buddhism, like Gnosticism, and even like Parmenides, reject worldly polarities. But unlike Parmenides, they do not make a higher polarity between mind and matter, whole and parts. In those they discover a permanent synthesis. And so, Confucianism looks for the unchanging. Confucius himself, teaching in the wake of terrible anarchy, worked out a philosophy of daily life that emphasized social relationships; a philosophy in which *virtues were not conceived as ends in themselves, but as means to a more useful end*. And so, Confucianism "is not absolutely for or against anything in the world. It supports what is right. [It] is not 'partisan but for all'";[53] it emphasizes *Jin*, which is benevolence or humanity defined in terms not of qualities in isolation but of *relations* such as reciprocity or loyalty, and even those were conceived as an optimum, not as an absolute. Confucius' intense practicality is revealed by his main area of concern: the street, the immediate community. In this sense alone, the Confucian community is indeed like a *monad*, a self-sustaining entity that produces from *within* universal values that happen to harmonize with the outer world. Its virtues are two-fold: first, it is timeless because salvation is sought in the eternal present and not — as with the West — at the end of a messianic development; and second, it is non-dualistic.[54]

The differences between Eastern and Western thought are well known. Just as Taoist, Buddhist and Confucian thinking hold opposites to be complementary, the self does not exist in contradistinction to society (as in the West), but is integral to it. In contemporary parlance, Eastern thought is "holistic," Western thought "reductionist."[55] But "holistic" does *not* mean collective, nor that the whole is more important than the parts. Rather it holds the two in suspension and in combination as interlocking concepts, *not allowing the dominion of any single principle*. Reductionism, by contrast, does emphasize the parts over the whole and relies on distinctions, opposites, hierarchy, and mutually exclusive dualities.

The Western trend toward reductionist thinking is most commonly attributed to Isaac Newton. But by the seventeenth century it had already taken Euclid and Galileo to make the universe measurable in time and space; Descartes to describe it with analytic geometry; Spinoza to pacify it with reason; and Leibniz to parcel it out. To assemble it all into a great cosmic machine, driven by gravity, was the work of Newton. But for all his hard-headedness, he never ceased to be a Puritan, believing fervently in divine revelation, messianic history, the day of judgement, and the books of Daniel and Revelation. All his thinking was entirely compatible with the clockwork universe — salvation drawn toward its goal on a great mainspring, the world mechanically and materially evolving,[56] all regulated from above by a deity who could still separate the good from the wicked, the parliamentary from the absolutist.

In the view of Newton and other Puritans, that is precisely what happened with the expulsion of the Catholic James II by the Tory and Whig gentry. The cosmos had done its work. With Protestant Dutchman William of Orange safely on the throne, England was rid once and for all of even a whiff of Catholic absolutism. Instead, "as Newton had discovered laws which governed motion, it was possible to discover laws that should govern society, and . . . benevolent rulers could revise legal systems to conform with their principles."[57] The intellectual pioneer for such a system was John Locke. In Locke, the influence of Descartes blended with English empiricism to produce an entirely instrumental approach to the world. And while this approach helped release the creative force of capitalism by formulating a theory of government that would protect the freedom needed for capitalism to thrive, it also had the effect of exalting the individual at the expense of society. Today's ideal of the unregulated free market is really Locke's legacy.

In his assumption that nature, the very nature that supplies us with our freedom, is essentially good,[58] Locke draws upon an ancient Christian-Stoic conception of nature as an order that is reasonable and benign — an idea shared in turn by radical, global free marketeers who view crashes and economic catastrophes as growing pains in a vast, well-intentioned, Newtonian process. Accordingly, the state is only a contingency: an agreement with the people that there be a series of institutions that kick in whenever nature is a little slow. That is Locke's Social Contract. As soon as the state interferes with the God-given process of nature and its free individual, the state has broken the contract and may be pulled down. What distinguishes Locke, above all, is that *property*, as the manifestation of the freedom of the individual, becomes the motive of the entire system — and it is mostly for the protection of property that the state is instituted.[59]

If liberal democratic capitalism is founded, as Locke would argue, in the empirical facts of nature, it could not, like communism, be an ideology. But the philosopher Karl Popper tells us that anything that calls itself a theory must be deduced from a preconceived idea — even when it claims to be grounded in empirical fact; because the very minute we choose those facts, we are deducing from our choice. Locke, likewise, selected the facts for his theory. Moreover, a truly scientific theory is not constructed (as are Marxism and Judeo-Christian messianism) to evade proof through untestable premises and infinite historical elasticity. That is, scientific theories must be falsifiable.[60] For Karl Popper, the truly open (free) society must work on premises that can be exposed to the possibility of error. Locke and capitalism should be no exception: but even the capitalist George Soros has recognized in the global free-market ideology a totalitarian tendency: a belief in the natural perfection of unfettered capitalism. Like Marxism, it could cause any amount of destruction and never be proven wrong.

■

But Marxism is more truly conservative than the relatively blind adventure of capitalism. And in this sense, the infinite elasticity of Marxism, the monolithic way in which it tries to contain all of time, more resembles Eastern concepts of eternal and non-progressing stasis maintained in a tension of opposites. Mao likewise thought his brand of communism would be able to contain the whole future for China. To him, dialectic was simply a down-to-earth version of the Ying and Yang of the Tao — the interchangeable opposites in synthesis, but without much transformation;[61] a synthesis that could never be challenged because all was ordained by fate. Of course he did not see the intransigent, chaotic polarities that he had adopted along with Western thought and history.

By the late 1920s, the young Mao Zedong had taken up the Marxism of the left wing of the Kuomintang, the party of nationalist revolution, only to insist that the ideology be "rectified" — cleared of its abstraction and reinterpreted for Chinese history as a weapon against despotic wealth and foreign intervention. What he wanted at that time was something resembling the liberal democracy of America, and for a time its heroes, Washington, Jefferson, and Lincoln, were his.[62] The communist-capitalist autocracy of today is perhaps not so far from the modern power of which educated Chinese like Mao had begun to dream on the eve of the revolution.

Both Mao on the Left and his opponent Chiang Kai-shek on the Right held nationalism first and foremost. And when they turned against one another, Mao and Chiang still did not challenge one another as Left and Right. Rather, they fell into the age-old tradition of factional warlords, Mao proving the cleverer and Chiang the more corrupt and incompetent. Moreover, it was the Japanese occupation, not the revolutionaries, that annihilated the traditional ruling class. Ideology carried little weight: where the Japanese provided effective services and administration, Communist influence was minimal; where Japanese depredations unified the peasants in opposition, support for the Communists increased.[63] Mao did not even pursue land reform, since most of the land in China was already worked by its owners. After all, even "from a Marxist point of view, the China of 1949 differed from the Russia of 1917 in one vital respect: the peasants had a much clearer idea of private property than did their Russian counterparts."[64] China pined and longed for survival, and in the horrors of the civil war and occupation, the Communists proved far more effective than did the corrupt "ward-boss" system of Chiang Kai-shek. Of course, since then, Communist rule beyond emergency and anarchy has proven to be another matter.

The problem for Marxism was that the clan system, and its Confucian reinforcement of family connections among peasant, landlord, and gentry, masked or moderated class hatred. For class hatred to exist, society first must be atomized (as had happened in Russia through systematic serfdom and in Europe through industrialization). And so in China, atomization was effected by the Communists through the redistribution of land in infinitesimal plots among millions of single individuals, breaking down all links between landed property and kinship.[65] But historically, this is only the stage of breakdown after which any new system can be constructed — like dismantling bricks to make a new, and unknown building, whether capitalist or communist.

So how "communist" was China really? Indeed, how communist was Mao? Referring to earlier times, Paul Johnson remarks, "In some ways he was much more at home with the KMT, with his stress on nationalism, than in the CCP . . . He collaborated with the KMT longer than any other prominent Communist."[66] In the end, Mao was not the instrument of communism. Rather he played God, with communism his instrument in the search for a modern, dominant China. Industrializing the peasantry, inflicting a medieval tyranny on Tibet, liquidating the old bourgeoisie, he simultaneously sailed different tacks of national renewal. He could just as easily have swung China rightward toward the capitalism it now pursues. But the Chinese, in their own roughshod and costly way, may at least have tried to find a *Jin* or a *Tao* to combine rather than transform extremes. For all her tyranny, China has at least shown signs that Left and Right are the means to an end, and not ends in themselves.

17

Dissonance:
Three Worlds or a
Kantian Universe?

After the Second World War, with the rapid release of the colonies into independence, two different worlds seemed to materialize: a northern world of rich nations and a southern world of poor nations. In poor nations, old tribal or feudal structures re-emerged in conflict with the imposed colonial political structures. Pre-colonial dualities, to which most colonial peoples had long been accustomed, were not polar (like liberal and conservative) but functional; even when they were moral, they were temporary, shifting. The moral-political dualism that had received its ratification in 1789 did not hold. Nor was the world itself naturally dualistic: the three worlds of Liberal Democratic wealth, Communist state ideology, and "Third World" poverty could coexist without really changing one another, much less reducing themselves to two.

The concept of First, Second, and Third Worlds was formally recognized in 1955 at the Bandung Conference, when the poor nations declared that together they might develop a Third Way that was neither Left nor Right. They had reason to: even when the developed world, East and West, decided that it was best for everyone to assist in the development of the poor nations, practicality was sacrificed to East-West competition. From the wealthy nations came Development Theory, which claimed that poverty in underdeveloped nations was a cycle of diminishing returns: since everyone in a poor country must be poor, there could be no savings available for investment, lack of investment increased the poverty, and so on.[1] This was the "rightish" justification for foreign capital investment and the consequent supervision of poor economies. It soon began to be evident, however, that poor countries had upper as well as lower classes, with pockets of capital for local investment, and that they could independently increase their GNP by internal innovations such as the reorganization of labour.[2]

Development Theory was opposed from the Left by Dependency Theory. It suggested that poverty in the developing nations was caused solely by their exploitive *relationship* with the industrial world whereby goods were imported at high cost and exported at low cost — also producing diminishing returns.[3] But it turned out that low-priced exports could produce wealth and that higher-cost imports paid their way in quality or efficiency.[4] The two theories, Development and Dependency, bore the hallmarks of the same abstract, morally based thinking that justified the ideologies of Left and Right.

The problem had begun in innocence. By the eighteenth century the Wars of Religion had ended, colonialism was firmly established, and a single European culture had begun to acquire an identity. Despite new internal conflicts arising from commercial rivalry and the balance of power, Europe, viewed from the non-European perspective, must have looked like a single, monolithic force. But it was not yet what we can call a "right-wing" force and it was not even a capitalist force. It is true that colonialism was a product of the inquiring, aggressive, technological culture that characterized the end of the Middle Ages. But it was a function of the state, not of private wealth. The method of subsidy was mercantilism with its crown corporations and charters.

Nor is capitalism, in itself, primarily to blame for poverty in the developing world. Rather, the blame must lie in the speed and irresponsibility with which industrial development was forced on less developed cultures, whether from Left or Right. The imposition of industry wreaked social and environmental damage (as in the Soviet Union and China), increasing poverty by creating unemployment where there had been none, and destroying livelihoods through dislocation, or (as in the case of Canadian oil interests in Sudan) by funding local conflicts.

The idea that time-honoured native political systems are appropriate because they are conditioned, if not determined, by local cultures was introduced into the thinking of the Enlightenment by the Baron de Montesquieu. He relied upon experience and observation, departing from the spirit of the previous century, from the method of Hobbes and Descartes and that "unswerving deductive consistency which Frenchmen love."[5] If democracies were suited to some cultures and aristocracies to others, the common element was restraint: democracies, whether in Holland or in Florence, should not be too democratic; aristocracies not too powerful; and monarchies careful of liberties. Montesquieu's relativism contained elements of what we now recognize as Left as well as Right:[6] all systems, for example, must look after public welfare[7] and yet only their foundation on custom and the test of time can prove their suitability to their subjects.[8]

Even after the Bandung Conference (exactly two centuries after Montesquieu's death) culture still received little attention. Whether through socialism or through Christian missionary activity, Western ethics, Left or Right, were ferried into the poorer nations, concomitant with rapid industrial development. The result was maladaptation and poverty. But when broad-based nationalist liberation movements surged ahead, they showed little differentiation between Left and Right. The neo-colonial class that governed the newly independent colonies turned out to be just as exploitive as colonial rule had been; and worse, it was armed with a Western political vocabulary so vague as to suit poorly the people it was meant to serve. Nationalism, socialism, and democracy became interchangeable classroom terms for a better life: all form and little content. The only clear thing to hold on to remained nationalism — the ambiguous Left-Right force of Europe itself, or philosopher Alexandre Kojeve's "Robespierran Bonapartism," the combination of political Left and Napoleonic authoritarian centrism purveying a cocktail of socialism and capitalism.

Though nationalist neo-colonial governments continued to despoil their countries through rapid industrialization, the ideologies that took hold corresponded very little to wealth and poverty. In fact, according to Emmanuel Todd, "No theory has so far succeeded in explaining the distribution of political ideologies, systems and forces on our planet."[9] Todd's thesis is that the global diversity of family structures is the crucial element in ideological preference — an idea that might go a long way toward laying to rest the idea that economics lies at the root of Left and Right. According to Todd, ideology, broadly speaking, is determined by equal or preferential distribution of inheritance among children; paternal authority; paternal egalitarianism or preference toward sons; strength of generational ties; and complexity of marriage and inheritance rules. These considerations, for example, determine communism for Russia and China, liberty-inequality for Anglo-Americans, liberty-equality for Latin Europe, authoritarian ethnic nationalism in Japan, Germany, and Scandinavia, and a chaotic "parliamentary caste" ideology for India.[10] It is difficult to rule out other influences, but Todd is persuasive that family structure is a crucial factor.

In China the Community Family (impartial treatment of children) has indeed proven to be amenable to communism. But, as we have seen, other forces, neither "Left" nor collective, have qualified Chinese Communism. These are a particular strain of individualism, the conservative, binding forces of Confucianism, and the veneration for elders. For his efforts to suppress these forces, Mao Zedong might indeed be called a "Communist neo-colonialist." In a war against his own people, he attempted Western-style industrialization overnight, and his steam-rolling Right-Left Robespierran Bonapartism produced not only chaos but also the resistance of his middle-class bureaucracy. The means to overcoming this resistance was a "second" Chinese Revolution, the Cultural Revolution, perhaps the most literal and cataclysmic display of the contradiction at the heart of the Parmenidean conception of the whole and parts. To China's credit, she failed to reduce to Mao's atomized, homogeneous, Parmenidean plenum, which was itself an exercise of what Paul Johnson calls "mind over matter"[11] — a Parmenidean concept to begin with.

Of all the non-European cultures, Islam seems to have remained the least affected by Western ideology. As Todd puts it, Islamic "religious fundamentalism . . . does not try to apply Western terminology to ideological concepts peculiar to Islam."[12] That is because family runs far deeper than state authority.[13] The result is Arab Socialism, which is founded on a clan society that is not entirely individual or collective, a weak state, the maintenance of tradition, and a quasi-socialist economics, not entirely Left or Right.[14]

Clan power notwithstanding, the United Nations' superimposition of a twentieth-century, European-style Jewish state on a Palestinian Arab population in a region rich with oil that was eyed enviously by the West brought with it the entire cargo of Western dualism. The fact that Zionism, the founding ideology of Israel, had socialist and nonsocialist elements did not discourage pro-Arabs from branding it a right-wing outpost of American imperialism. From there the illogic flourished: support of a Jewish state could be conveniently linked, on one hand with the United States, support of capitalism, oil interests, and white racism, as well as proper recognition of the Holocaust. On the other hand, Pro-Arab opposition to a Jewish state could be linked to endorsement of the Soviet Union, Communism, Soviet Imperialism, anti-Semitism, Nazism, and even American Black Nationalism. Left and Right, once economic ideologies, had become incoherent Manichaean agglomerations tied together by little more than the terms of the Holocaust and the Cold War.

If Left and Right was a procrustean bed in the Middle East, in tribal Africa the duality was indecipherable. There, European development had compressed in less than a century what had taken five centuries in Europe; industrial urban crises like those of the Middle Ages were inflicted tenfold on African capitals. It is difficult to evaluate tribal societies from a Western point of view, but we might say, with Claude Lévi-Strauss, that they "worked," fulfilling a human function through the use of eternal structures. As we have seen, the dualism of that tribal world functioned in creative and constant flux, without fixed eschatological oppositions. While patriarchal family structures reinforced ideology in the West, in Africa, polygyny, or the taking of multiple wives by a single husband, dispersed patriarchal power horizontally among "subfamilies" headed by women. The result was a degree of social anarchy and a weak state[15] — intolerable to Western eyes, but more or less functional in pre-colonial African life.

As the chaos created by industrialization provoked a return to tribal loyalties,[16] Western-style nationalist authority weakened. Institutions like the army, and Nationalist and Socialist political parties became shells of Western ideology attempting to contain African realities. With minority groups or ethnic insurrections looking for support wherever they could find it, acquiescence to Cold War pressures followed, but it was strategic rather than ideological. Western colonial racism had often provoked African support for the Soviet Union; but racism is in fact no more endemic in capitalism than it is in socialism: it is possible in either and damaging to both. In any case, after the Cold War had plunged parts of Africa into civil war, there was little to build on. What remained — a scattering of kleptocracies, ethnic and Marxist dictatorships, and the near-anarchy of South Africa's once celebrated African National Congress — suggests that African forms are still in the process of recovery from a world for a time defined by Western ideology.

The situation in Latin America bears some comparison, but there the European influence is older and better established. As in Africa, indigenous peoples did not have a static conception of duality, or an abstract view of good and evil.[17]

The dominant Latin American family type is the *anomic* family, a compound of the Latin nuclear-egalitarian family structure with African and indigenous unstable matrimonial forms.[18] The result, according to Todd, is a culture that is at bottom anarchic.[19] But it is also an anarchy both contained and given play by Roman Catholicism: and if it some-times adopts Marxist-Leninism, it is mainly to "achieve modernist legitimation" of a culture that remains "an offshoot of deeper Latin American traditions, Thomist, Catholic, hierarchal, dogmatic, monistic, nationalistic, and anti-capitalistic."[20] Augustinian Christianity, built on forgiveness and dispensation, tolerates a little more anarchy than do stricter, more Pelagian, Protestant societies. Since Latin governments have been more concerned with public order than with private lives, this natural anarchy encouraged a tendency toward secular authoritari-anism, Left or Right.

True to form, most Latin Leftist movements have anarchist forebears. Ideas imported from other centrifugal societies such as Spain and Italy, with regional grievances and strong local and mutualist traditions, readily took root in similar conditions in Latin America.[21] Mexico's

Zapatista movement, lazily called "Left," is anarchist, since the conditions that produced it in 1912 have hardly changed. The Zapatistas, then as now, "with [their] insistence that the people must take the land themselves and govern themselves in village communities . . . resembled very closely the rural anarchism which had arisen under similar circumstances in Andalusia."[22] Argentina's Peronist ideology, a rightish form of anarchism, rejected the authority of all established structures — the Church, the army, and the landed oligarchy, not to mention the Cold War powers of East and West. Its resort to force and xenophobia on the part of the working class made it into a form of fascism of the Left.[23] And so the outer forms and language of 1789, however much they have governed the discourse, have in reality been broken at every turn.

With the Cold War, the disparity worsened. In Nicaragua and El Salvador especially, it forced groups and societies inclined to define themselves locally and culturally, to define themselves hemispherically, in the terms of two alien systems — Russian communism and American capitalism.

Because the Soviet Union preached egalitarianism and financed left-wing movements through Cuba, independent social reform in Central America was viewed (absurdly) by Washington as an open invitation to Soviet domination. The voice that warned its poor Catholic neighbours to the south that there was no middle way was of course the voice of Puritan America once again pushing back biblical frontiers against a non-Puritan heathen.[24] It seems that communism would have been impossible to maintain in Latin American society anyway, not least, perhaps, for its being socially anarchic and lacking a community family structure.[25]

In Nicaragua, a Marxist-Leninist distortion of Sandinism would have had a troubled rule even without American interference. After all, it punished peasant profits, the modest staple of Latin America's anarchistic culture. In the revolution of 1979 there had been a more representative, pluralist Sandinista Junta, but the Americans had tried to force it to accept the continued existence of the deposed dictator Somoza's hated National Guard. In so doing they strengthened the Marxist far Left,[26] which took over, appropriating the name "Sandinista." In the civil war that followed, the United States built a resistance around the old National Guard including, inevitably, many independent-minded peasants who were closer in character to the original followers of Sandino[27] than to Marx or to Washington. An indigenous break-away "Third Way" group, swearing by the original creed of Sandino, tried to exploit CIA funding to create an independent insurgency against the Marxists. Its leaders, Eden Pastora and Hugo Spadafora, tangled with both sides but were finally defeated in the vise of Cold War Left and Right.[28]

In the end, Nicaragua's anarchistic society had endured the tyranny of two political minorities, Right and Left, each resembling the other in its absolutism, its corruption, and its control by an oligarchy — to the extent that the same powerful clans appeared in both regimes.[29] With each propped up by a Cold War power, the United States and Cuba respectively, a native politics was made difficult and finally impossible.

The adaptation of a peasant ideology to the abstractions of Marxism was not unique to Nicaragua. In Peru the far-left peasant communism of *Sendero Luminoso* was developed by Abimael Guzman, a philosophy graduate of Peru's University of Ayacucho. The inspiration for his doctorate had, perhaps oddly, been Immanuel Kant's *Critique of Pure Reason*; but it is to Kant that he owed the very transcendental moral universalism that has justified the Left in the remotest corners of the earth.

There is some irony in the fact that Kant's mission to find a solid, universal ground for morality in Reason was inspired by the fear that Reason had collapsed. For indeed it had done so in hands of the eighteenth-century Scottish philosopher David Hume. Reason, according to Hume, was only a minor mechanism put into the service of the passions. The passions, in turn, were founded on nothing but knowledge composed of subjective sense impressions. Even progress was a series of accidents and accumulations, random trial and error, where (as with Montesquieu) the things that stood the test of time were judged worthy.

Hume's dismantling of Reason — not a century after Descartes — provided a philosophical basis for aristocratic, English conservatism. The key to the political element in Hume was a distinction between what actually *is* and what *ought* to be:[30] what *ought to be* was composed of vain, solipsistic mental constructions, whereas *what is* must already have good reasons for being there. Property, for example, *is* the main criterion for power. Whether or not it *ought* to be was to Hume immaterial. These were the early ghosts of political Realism (on the Right) and by inference, political Idealism (on the Left). For British Conservatism in general, Hume's assault on Reason was brilliant and convenient. For philosophy it was disastrous; and it took a powerful mind to counteract it with the reconstruction of Reason, *tabula rasa*.

Immanuel Kant, professor of philosophy at Königsberg in Enlightened Prussia, set out to save Reason by demonstrating that what we know could, at least in part, be established *a priori*, outside of experience. The categories — those vague perfect forms that Plato had placed up above — could, as time and space, actually form a mental framework upon which to make our experience decipherable. Reality did not, as Hume suggested, approach the mind from outside, as chaos. Rather, reality was *made* by the mind as a synthesis of mental categories with raw sense data. So, while the ordering process of the mind may not be divine, it was certainly not integral to the world apprehended by the senses. However rational, Kant's thought carried on a Protestant moralism that bases itself on direct inspiration from a hidden God.[31] Reason, organized "from above" by universal mental categories, provided a universal morality expressed in Kant's categorical imperative, "Act in such a way that you can will what you are doing to be a universal law of nature." Once again, we could conceive *what ought to be* over and above *what is*.

In the categorical imperative, the Sacred had reappeared in the form of Practical Reason. But if Kant, in principle, leaned neither "left" nor "right," the Left would, after the French Revolution, be his chief beneficiary. Kant had concluded, after all, that the rational person is an end in itself. If man is legitimated by Reason, then rational men could realize themselves as their own proper end, in the rational, just, and perfect State.[32] In Kant we find the phantom moral force that would vindicate universal liberty, equality, and fraternity — the very morality that makes Robespierran Bonapartism a missionary, not just a conquering, force. Kant's imperative is the means, above all, by which the Sacred, set adrift by the collapse of the authority of the Church in the Wars of Religion, would secure for good its place in a secular context from which it could resume its work as moral critic.

But Kant's universal reason carried with it the fatal Western virus: like the Gnostic God and everything that emanated from him, it kept falling into two. In Kant, justice was something that humanity *strove toward*; it required an effort, a leap of the imagination from what *is* to what *ought to be*. It advocated, in other words, a division between one's interest and one's duty — an impossible *ought to be* — the latter enshrined, after Parmenides, in abstract perfection. The same Kantian dissociation could justify destruction in the name of that higher good.[33] It was probably less of a leap for Marx, who assumed, anyway, that the abstract *ought* was already contained dialectically in the *is*,[34] "that abstract hidden truths, being latent, are just as real as truths picked up by the senses."[35]

But there was a more immediate problem. Kant had assumed that, although Reason needed power, once it reigned supreme, force would no longer be needed and the exertion of power would recede.[36] But Jacobinism and then Robespierran Bonapartism, and eventually communism, fascism, and capitalism, all having enthroned reason, would only usurp her place. It is the Kantian notion that force armed with ideology is incapable of doing wrong that has led capitalism or socialism to sacrifice the present to the future, whether in totalitarianism or in the hell-bent development of the poorer nations. It was, rather, the stable Europe of the eighteenth century, somnolent in its innocence, that made universal reason plausible. The modern forms of economic social class had not yet appeared, and a variegated chaos of local rights, privileges, feudal forms, private wealth, and increasing upward mobility prevented the coalescence of any large, intractable antagonisms.[37] But for all Europe's calm surface, the blueprint for rationalizing political antagonisms had long been present in religious and philosophical forms.

Out of Catholic monarchists and Protestant millenarians, these forms had already produced Tories and Whigs — nicknames for Catholics and Presbyterians respectively. The Whigs were the "exclusionist" party that would have excluded any Catholic relatives of Charles II from the throne of England. The "Tories" supported the Anglican or Catholic Stuarts; the Whigs comprised dissenters and nonconformists, the Tories the High Anglicans; Whigs were more worldly, mercantile, and English, whereas Tories counted more on land and were more disposed to Catholic continental ideas and royal absolutism.

In republican America however, Whigs came to define the nation, and that made the real roots of politics clearer on both sides of the Atlantic. Whig thinking, after all, came more and more to define a universal Right. In Europe, French Jacobins, for example, would turn out to share with English Tories a certain "leftish" reverence for the state as a positive force in society, while the Americans of the thirteen colonies experienced the state as an impediment to everything. In the northern colonies, meanwhile, the European way persisted, as leftish statist traditions, French and English, took effect in Quebec and in English Canada. After the fall of Quebec to the British in 1759, the maintenance of feudalism in French Canada by the Quebec Act of 1775, and a "leftish" Jacobin inspiration from the French Revolution[38] brought about a statist, "Robespierran Bonapartist" influence reflected in the use of the Napoleonic legal code.

In Upper Canada (Ontario), American Tory refugees and English Tories happened also to count on the state, in this case the Crown, producing in Ontario as well as Quebec a more "leftish" European and interventionist government than was the case south of the border.

In eighteenth-century England by contrast, the French Revolution finally made politics uniform. Tory tradition, protective of monarchy, was renewed when the French decapitated their king. Most of the Whigs, repelled by Jacobin rationalism, quickly distinguished themselves as "Romantic Whigs" and joined with the Tories in a single "Romantic" Tory party. Meanwhile the rationalist Whigs faded away — leaving England without a radical Left. Edmund Burke was the loudest and perhaps the first of the Romantic Whigs to shut England's doors to the French Revolution. While he expressed a Whiggish principle of freedom in fighting crown and oligarchy on colonial issues, he remained a diametrical antagonist to the whole ethic of Kant: like Hume, he would have rejected the justification of any good causes by Reason. In short, Burke hated French simplicity in Reason, but loved messy English comprehensiveness in tradition and aesthetics.[39] He upheld village, family, church, class, and all intermediate associations against Jacobin atomism.[40] He preferred durability to transcendental abstraction. Property was to be accumulated unequally in order to shore up the aristocratic power needed for stability whereas rational, equal distribution of property in small, defenceless plots was simple-minded: it would open all to the temptation to rob his neighbour.[41]

If England now was Tory, America was Whig, and neither of the European ideas of property, the Burkean nor the Jacobin, corresponded to the American Whig ideal. The American Revolution was in many respects a third entity, an "aristocratic-egalitarian" hybrid launched by a Whig capitalist elite — its liberty-equality paradox still expressing the principles that bind America. But even the fight for Liberty and Equality was skewed by strong, enduring elements of aristocracy and religious ethnicity which — to this day — carry through from seventeenth-century England.[42] In that sense, the American Revolution was conservative for being fought to preserve a society that had only just developed; in Burke's and Hume's sense its justification was historical. Its protest against imperial control of taxation and trade did not imply some new, rational innovation along Jacobin lines. The principles of individual rights, democracy, and economic liberty were already well established in the local administrations; a shadow nation already existed — an advanced form of the earlier landed-commercial shadow nation for which Cromwell's men had fought in the English civil war. Both revolutions were indeed *conservative* insofar as they tried to defend something that had already developed.

A further complicating factor was that the American Revolution contained from its inception egalitarian-aristocratic Left-Right elements that have endured into modern America. Its Burkean, aristocratic sense of historical rights and the individualism of its Whig-Puritan manufacturing class were "rightish." But its Lockean sense of natural rights, its Virginian, Anglican, landowning aristocracy, and its sympathy for the French Revolution were rationalist and "leftish." In this regard, I would argue, Thomas Jefferson (though skeptical of the state) leans toward that peculiar left-right hybrid tradition of the Red Tory. The same sort of liberal aristocratic tradition endures to this day somewhere near the political centre. People like Al Gore and his connection Gore Vidal are its bearers.

But if the more common "rightish" Puritans did not maintain strict control of the Revolution, its substance was theirs. Almost every clause of the Declaration of Independence could be related to a Puritan complaint against Charles I. The Puritans' deep involvement with classical economics on both sides of the Atlantic; their application of biblical, messianic progress to the American promised land; and their affinity for direct Protestant-Platonic inspiration, as in the axiom of "self-evident truths" that opens the Declaration of Independence — are all essential to America even today.

Popular loyalties in the Revolutionary War and afterward were a different matter. They were determined to a great degree by culture, religion, and ethnicity rather than by political ideology.[43] The thirteen colonies were in fact "a cultural, demographic and religious crazy-quilt."[44] On the monarchist Right, High Anglican and New York Tories stood for a "leftish" protection of minorities in the face of a "nationalist" conformity developing among the revolutionary Patriots. Such was the Crown in protecting Indian rights[45] and freed slaves from the abuses of the frontier. Loyal highland Scots supported the Tory cause in the South. Presbyterian Ulster Scots in the Appalachians, though often Whigs, were so primed by biblically inspired rancour[46] in local, sectarian vendettas that they chose whichever cause, Tory or Patriot, was opposite to that of their local enemy.[47]

In the first American administrations, the schism between Thomas Jefferson's decentralizing agrarian Republicans (later the Democrats) and Alexander Hamilton's centralizing urban Federalists (later the Republicans) came as close as possible to distinguishing a Left and a Right within an accepted ground of capitalism. Indeed, the inconsistencies in American Left and Right seem to stem from this period. After all, liberty and equality can get more equal treatment when expressed in rights, as in Jacobinism, but not when expressed in money, as in the United States. Rights stay where they are put; money is fluid and accumulates.

That is why material equality has been so difficult for Americans. Tocqueville remarked, "if the principle of equality disposes men to change, it also suggests to them certain interests and tastes that cannot be satisfied without a settled order of things. Equality urges them on, but at the same time it holds them back; it spurs them, but fastens them to earth; it kindles their desires but limits their powers."[48] That egalitarianism may be progressive, while equality, once achieved, is inherently conservative, is a paradox rarely faced by the Left. But it is fully borne out by the relative, if imperfect equality of the America of the postwar boom and the early 1960s.

In the 1960s the very conformist and complacent aspect of relative equality in America produced its diametrical opposite — an elitist countercultural Left, an aristocratic egalitarianism of liberty and individualism. On the Right, middle- and working-class America's relative progress in egalitarian reform had indeed led to a certain stasis. Advances in working-class wealth and security, civil rights, desegregation, and upward mobility suggested that America, in theory, had arrived. But it was not so in material fact; freedom had left the poor and the victims of discrimination behind. The Sacred of liberty and the Sacred of equality, inseparable in Kant's rational ideal, turned against one another in the laboratory of experience.

A head-on fight against inequality and conformity meant that the Left would have to be both egalitarian and individualist. But a good moral critic, if it respects liberty, can never be absolutely egalitarian; and the American countercultural Left had a strong liberty component. So it was that the Left was weakened by its "liberty" concern with lifestyle, contemptuous as it was of a conformist working class. To explain the American counterculture's dispersal into myriad forms of cultural elitism and esoterica, we need only look at the war in Vietnam and the great Kantian rationalist illusion that made all revolutions seem one single revolution.

In the American debate over Vietnam, an exaggerated Puritan moral absolutism, Left and Right, played to perfection the Manichaean left-right split without regard for local realities in Vietnam or anywhere else. The withdrawal from the war was perhaps the countercultural Left's one great victory, but in many respects it drew attention away from ills at home. By bringing down President Lyndon Johnson, it destroyed his war on poverty. The attempt by the Left to see the whole situation as one Kantian moral imperative had created a "baggy," incoherent ideology where some causes were bound to suffer. (And unless the forces that opposed the World Trade Organization in Seattle in 1999 develop a coherent philosophy, the same will happen to them.) The French Left wasn't much more consistent. Even Sartre went as far as to say that the ultimate cause of the student uprising in Paris in May 1968 was not Gaullism but Viet Cong success against capitalist America in the war in Vietnam. And so, of course, Sartre and the students, driven by liberation, had little use for the conservative materialism of their own French Communist working class.

If the proletarian Left in Europe and America had become alien to the student Left, how Left, then, was the student counterculture, in reality? It was shifting, after all, into that dangerous region of cultural authoritarianism shared by fascism. With a well-fed proletariat and little hope of political revolution through class warfare, it reinterpreted Marxism — with the help of the Frankfurt school — as cultural revolution through an aesthetic critique of capitalism. This way, some of the freer and more egalitarian aspects of capitalism could be dismissed as a mask concealing a deeply "fascist" structure obsessed with power and the will to exterminate the "other."[49] Was the Left not launching an equal and opposite attack against an imagined equal and opposite enemy? And does an equal and opposite attack on fascism not mire the attacker in the terms of fascism itself? Far Left and far Right, in rejecting not just a politics but an entire civilization, can only make authoritarian claims, claims on the cosmos that are gnostic in character, asserting authority over daily life and culture. This was as true of the Black Panthers as it was of the white counterculture.

That is why Philip Slater goes beyond Left and Right to speak of an Old culture and a New culture.[50] The New culture, he remarked, nostalgically revived elements of Puritan moral perfectionism from the Old. Thus, the left-wing intellectual became an Old Testament prophet, able to convert revolutionary cultural currents into dicta with the power of dividing saved from damned. Like a reformation preacher, Protestant or Catholic, philosopher Herbert Marcuse could tell his congregation that democratic forums had to be suspended because there was "no other side" in the debate with a demonic Establishment.[51] The effective annihilation of the "other" meant filling the cosmos with the All of one's own image. For the hippies, being a hippie was the only respectable reality, the only right and just way to live. In the end, Marcuse's revolutionary constituency had shades of Germany's fascist mob,[52] a gnostic mass even more marginal than that of Nazis, Bolsheviks — or unemployed medieval Flemish weavers. The Left's failure had arisen from the Kantian impression that all good causes were somehow One Cause; and from the failure of Kant's assumption that power, once enthroned by reason, would naturally recede.

It is significant that feminism, the only really successful form of liberation produced by the Left during the 1960s, grew far beyond the Left.

Perhaps it is because the more all-embracing a cause, the less likely it is to be dualistic; the more specific a cause, whether it be a social class, an ethnicity, or a language, the more easily it defines itself in a duality against everything else. And indeed, the narrow definitions of the traditional liberationist Left could not accommodate the variety of ambitions as well as grievances that feminism offered half the human population. Such a movement could never be monistic, or even dualistic; it could only be plural. After all, feminism has penetrated capitalism almost as easily as it has penetrated socialism. Moreover, women have been represented in all social classes and cultures, and every class and culture tends to produce a unique feminism. If anything, the plural universality of feminism is as natural to the world as was the matriarchal civilization that flourished (as we earlier mentioned) in the Middle East before the Indo-European invasions.

So it is no surprise that the Left, having unleashed feminism in the West, could no longer contain it. Modern feminism, after all, sprang from the narrow confines of eighteenth-century English rationalist Jacobinism and the radical Protestant tradition of England and America, whence came the strong moral and political — but short-lived — dualism of Anglo-American feminism. Even if the feminists of the sixties came to assert themselves because the Left was still run by men, they waged their fight in a tradition of polar struggle and masculine forms of identity and aggression: the rules and forms of patriarchal, Indo-European dualism. By contrast, a "third stage" feminism has fought the battle on other grounds: that men and women are different but equal. Of course, every ideology has its own biology, and "third stage" feminism seems to find support in research that shows that gender differences are most likely innate specializations of equal value. We do not need biology, however, to apply the same wisdom to collectivism and individualism, and Left and Right. And indeed, forms of feminism, like movements of cultural identity, are showing signs of a more natural fit with the developing world than could ever be imagined in the terms of Left and Right. But if the common focus of protest remains patriarchy, where, precisely, is patriarchy located? Its sovereigns are dead and it too has begun to fragment along with the rest of the world.

18

Power:

Beheading Marx,
Decapitating Louis

Two centuries after the execution of Louis XVI, the absent sovereign still throws his shadow, dividing Right from Left. Since then the sovereign has taken on many aspects, from Reason to Virtue, to Labour to Capitalism. In the 1970s it began to be said that the sovereign had turned out to be Power itself. But to question power was to question Kant's universal Reason and thereby to challenge it on the Left as well as the Right. The Left was the first to suffer when doubts about power were reinforced, indeed satisfied, by the appearance in 1974 of Alexander Solzhenitsyn's *Gulag Archipelago*. On the surface, Solzhenitsyn's portrait of the labour camps that defined the Soviet system vindicated the capitalist West; underneath, it posed questions about modern power in general.

In 1977 in France, Bernard-Henri Lévy delivered the first vocal, if indirect, assault on the idea of Left and Right itself in his despairing jeremiad *Barbarism with a Human Face*. Lévy's point was that power, the Master, the great technological-political force of the Enlightenment, not only pervaded the world but had *become* the world.[1] The Left, defined by the gulag, and the Right, by the bleakness of capitalism,

were the human face of the pervasive barbarism of power that constituted what he called the Master — what Max Weber had called the Iron
Cage. By now, as Michel Foucault observed in the 1970s, ideology was
secondary to the fact of the State itself.[2]

Indeed, Foucault's analysis of power was not ideological, but inves-
tigative, archaeological. He distinguished two forms of it in antiquity:
the Middle Eastern or pastoral, which exerted power through the individual, and the Greek, which made a single fabric of "the relation
between the one and the many in the framework of the city and its citizens":[3] respectively, power's individual and totalitarian tendencies.
Power, Left and Right, was, in effect, both; it was to be identified not as
a substance but as a web of strategic relations distributed throughout
society in social welfare, education, commerce, sexuality, and media —
anywhere that power was felt. Power was not a conspiracy — it had
coalesced though a historical process that was discontinuous.[4]

The phenomenon first took shape in the seventeenth century when the
realm of the state began to spread outward from the sovereign into a
self-sustaining, self-justifying apparatus. In the following century that
apparatus found further justification in Immanual Kant's displacement
of the Sacred from God into Reason. But it was also then that philosophy, perhaps for the first time since the Greeks, turned reason to quite
a different end: to human happiness.[5]

The pioneer in linking reason to common happiness was Voltaire,
the wit who on the eve of the Revolution wrenched Reason from the
grip of Church and throne and placed it within the reach of ordinary
humanity. For Voltaire, the English empiricism of Locke and Hume had
shown that rights were to be found in reason, and reason in nature; all
that was needed was to secure for all people the natural rights of a
common humanity that transcended class and caste. Otherwise, the more
material forms of inequality were bound to persist, since that too was in
nature, for "it is impossible for men living in society not to be divided
into classes, the one the rich who command and the other the poor who
serve."[6] Politically, his motive was to empower the bourgeoisie against
tyranny ("money is master of everything in a state[7]), and in this he was
a prophet not just of the Girondins but of the modern liberal Right.

Since, according to Voltaire, the Christian God underwrote tyranny, he ridiculed the Church, setting it firmly on what by 1789 would be the political Right, and thereby making the bourgeoisie the first class actually to be called Left. But the Reason of the *philosophes* still retained some of the forms of Christianity. Voltaire and the *Encylopédistes*, especially the Marquis de Condorcet, had inherited a conception of rational progress that was at core Protestant[8] and unconsciously millenarian. Despite them, it would carry Christian eschatology, with its severe moral judgement, into the great project of rational happiness. Its outer form was Deism, the clockwork universe with its mechanical wealth in land and labour, conveniently set in motion then abandoned by its Maker; and it would, by 1792, underwrite the Left.

The old, eschatological structure was further clothed in materialism by other thinkers of the time. On the Left Helvetius and Holbach, and on the Right the Physiocrats and Adam Smith, all provided a way in which salvation and damnation could be placed in the hands of humanity — precisely by making a material world its meaning, subject, and possession. But the march of material Reason was certainly discontinuous, serving, as it did, conflicting interests; moreover, the *Encyclopédistes* followed the paradoxes and vagaries of society as much as they led it. The rights of man that Voltaire and Tom Paine found to be rooted in the good of nature were the same Natural Rights that justified, after the fact, the pursuit of capitalism and the lottery of poverty it produced. As reason would justify capital, it would also, when torn from the hands of Voltaire by less discriminate men, build the mindless monolith of modern power and the state.[9]

What is revealing in this early development of the Janus of Power, before it shows its Left and Right faces, is the contempt in which most of the *philosophes*, especially Voltaire, held the common people. That is why Voltaire's enthusiastic endorsement of British aristocratic constitutional monarchy led to the error of entrusting the intellectual and social revolution to despots, enlightened or not. For there would also be those like Louis XV of France: lazy and dissolute with an undisciplined aristocracy — a combination that encouraged revolution from below, and caused followers of Jean Jacques Rousseau to find even the bourgeoisie of 1791 too reminiscent of the aristocracy, as they dreamt of radical equality. But Rousseau himself was far more complex; indeed, he was the greatest single source of radical forms for the Right as well as the Left.

The Left-Right dualism that informed Rousseau might be said to have germinated in his Geneva birthplace: a small Calvinist republic divided between an oligarchic "Little Council" and a lower, more popular "General Council" toward which Rousseau and his family were inclined. Here, Christian duality had passed through the conduit of an austere Protestantism into secular politics. Rousseau was proud of Genevan austerity, and contrasted the Calvinist city state's Augustinian mistrust of men and women's wilful and dark instincts to the glittering wantonness of Paris: Heaven to Hell. So he developed a secular theology, embodying Augustine's perception of *will* as evil in a rightish competitive, institutionalized society[10] (perhaps typified by Voltaire), to which he opposed a leftish natural self, innocent, ascetic, and independent.[11] The latter was Rousseau's "natural man," not so much a "noble savage," as a hypothetical optimum in human development — a self-sufficiency above brutishness but not yet competitive and materialistic.

It is not surprising that Rousseau's customized theology and anthropology falls, like so much else with a heavy Protestant influence, into an undeniably gnostic motif. For him good human nature was essentially an optimum: what is shared, not what differentiates. It was a collective idea. The All was an essential self (*pneuma*) in every human, a collective idea of something once lost and again aspired to, very much like the All — the unknown God. Fallen humanity, trapped in the Demiurge of society, contains this original and natural optimum person within, just as the Gnostic recognizes within himself the *pneuma*, the fallen spark of the All. For Rousseau the means by which humans rescue their true selves as collective beings here in this world is to recognize themselves as *citizens*.

That is what makes Rousseau the latest and greatest of the historical precedents that influenced Jacobinism and *ipso facto* the modern Left. Its Calvinist moral vigilance bears his mark.[12] The Jacobin ambivalence around property is also found in Rousseau as is the Jacobin preference for very moderate economic classes.[13] The authoritarianism comes from Rousseau as well: when Robespierre cites *The Social Contract*, it is usually to assert the authority of the majority — or of an elite that speaks for the majority — rather than on behalf of strict liberty and equality,[14] or, for that matter, democracy.[15]

But as with Marx, a host of unconscious sources make him a confluence and conduit of history at least as much as a powerful and original influence. In his main work, *The Social Contract*, we find repeated reference to the whole and the parts with a rigour that one feels could only go back to Greece — to Parmenides and Platonism,[16] the main sources of Gnosticism. The human being, says Rousseau, is at once part and whole; as a part alone he is false. Only as part of a whole can one achieve one's real integrity as an individual. The political consequences in social engineering are obvious: "He who dares to undertake the making of a people's institutions ought to feel himself capable . . . of changing human nature, of transforming each individual, who is by himself a complete and solitary whole, into part of a greater whole from which he receives his life and being."[17] This is a Platonic politics both of the Protestant rebel and of the common man, and it will come to serve not just the far Left but the far Right as well. Its source seems to lie in Rousseau's preoccupation with classical antiquity, Roman and Greek respectively, but stoical and stolid rather than aristocratic.[18] What is rightish — the civic determination of the moral citizen — hails for the most part from his admiration of Republican Rome and foreshadows totalitarian populism. So do his ideas of property (the limited and self-sufficient private plots of the Roman farmer),[19] the virtue of austerity,[20] the dignity of poverty, and the wisdom of a civic religion as guardian of the mores of the state. His selective use of law, tradition, and culture in the service of the nation has hints of Fascism.

Another Roman trait in Rousseau is his concept of a guiding elite that spoke for the majority, an authoritarian "Left" element that recalls the Roman tribunes. But this element also echoes the Spartan Ephors, and in general, the Leftism in Rousseau is more Greek than Roman. His rationalism and ascetic limitations on liberty recall Lycurgus and Sparta. His dislike of political parties[21] is Athenian and foreshadows Marx. His gnostic flavour echoes the Greek Cynics and re-emerges almost exactly in Marx's realization of man in labour.[22] Whatever the history that ran in his veins, it was all intended to make something simple and unitary. Of course it was not to be. After 1792 his influence fractured in two along the lines of the dualities in all his sources.

After the Revolution two streams of political thought emerge, both strongly influenced by Rousseau. From the British empirical tradition of Locke and Bentham, we have the "planners," who followed on from Rousseau and the Jacobins to prefigure Stalin; and the "Libertarian Anarchists,"[23] who developed Rousseau's more sentimental side into mutualist and syndicalist romanticism, and, more darkly, into nationalism and Hitler.[24] But socialism, the religion of the planners, still had trouble establishing itself as an alternative to capitalism. Tamed by Napoleon III, beaten in 1848 and 1871, and reconciled with Catholicism by Pope Leo XIII, socialism finally got grudging parliamentary acceptance through Jean Jaurès, the founder of the Socialist Party in France, and (without the Jacobinism) Keir Hardy, the Scot who founded the British Labour Party.

How, then, was the Jacobin strain reinvigorated in Bolshevism in 1917 and again with Stalin in 1945? It seems to have been the Manichaean strain that Jacobinism had inherited from Augustine, through Descartes and Rousseau, that was used by radical Jacobins to oppose revolutionary socialism so rancorously to capitalism.

By the 1970s, the problem for capitalism was not so much that socialism was evil — although it would never lose that stigma. With the recession set off by the OPEC oil cartel, socialism was revealed to be *costly* in taxes and debt — not to mention impersonal and controlling. Michel Foucault — now claimed by much of the Left — focused his microscope on the ways in which relations of power and control were distributed through social services, with an eye not to doing away with them but to humanizing them.[25] He asked if the freedom and health they promised individuals could be restored through decentralization to local levels — natural and traditional bodies such as trade unions.

But no sooner had the Left questioned power in general, than the Right questioned it in the Left. But what was the Right at this point? Neither the tax revolutionaries of California's Proposition 13 nor the free-market ideologue Ronald Reagan could claim kinship with its early Puritan tradition. Supply-side economics, which ran the market by influencing the supply of labour and goods, cutting social security benefits, and deregulating industry, was an ideology of high-speed finance capitalism. Its monetarist trickle-down theory made a tacit admission that neither the state, the rich, nor communities needed to acknowledge the poor and unemployed. Its lack of real social content, its substitution of a 1950s *Leave It to Beaver* world or a backwater fundamentalism for the original Puritan ethic suggests that it wasn't, properly speaking, an ideology. It was an economic theory.

New critics of Left-Right politics, such as American social critics Daniel Bell and Christopher Lasch remarked that the original American Calvinism had wandered from its almost Rousseauian, indeed "Jacobin," mistrust of great wealth to the unlimited hedonism that would feed on the capitalism of the 1980s. How did American culture, Left and Right, give itself over to absolutes in liberal authority and intervention on the Left or to freedom and consumption on the Right — not to mention extremes of wealth and poverty? Bell and Lasch were of course hit from both sides: from the left and the right.

The impoverishment of ideology emerged most vividly in the success of the Republicans in the 1980s. For by now the cultural impossibility of Americans embracing the Left relieved them of the need for any real ideas.[26] There was no strong Left working-class tradition, no Jacobin history, no broad Social Democratic movement. Of their old Puritan values, Americans by far preferred liberty to controls on wealth. There was in the end no ideology but the American ideology, and that is why the Democratic party, to capture the vote from the Republicans, moved Rightward toward lower taxes and economic freedom. The truth was that Left in the Land of Liberty meant not socialism but dissidence; which was why the Democrats risked incoherence to accommodate lobbies of race and gender as well as rich, unpopular labour unions. With no monolithic domestic issue to quarrel over, the Reagan Right could simply define itself against communism.

But even in Europe, labour was losing its place as the sovereign that distinguished Left from Right, and it was precisely by identifying itself with labour that the Left lost power in Britain. That was what gave Margaret Thatcher her extraordinary majority. For an expanding and diversifying middle class, the free-market dream was easier to explain, as its paragons in Reagan and Thatcher were more heroic and charismatic than a bureaucratic Left could ever hope to be.

It is, however, one of the great fallacies of our time that the fall of the Berlin Wall and the disintegration of the Soviet Union (at the height of free-market triumph) signified the victory of the right-wing principle and the abject failure of everything the Left had ever stood for.[27] That contention would imply, after all, that the Soviet Union was, by 1990, a Left-wing nation. But by the 1980s, the Soviet Union had even taken on many aspects of the *ancien régime* of eighteenth-century France. The Party had become an aristocracy with closely guarded privileges. Ghosts of the democratic forms systematically destroyed by Stalin endured in rituals, much as they had in the frustrated regional *parlements* of France. The Soviet guardians, like the French *noblesse*, had become dangerously enlightened. And indeed both the *ancien régime* and the USSR were held together by a vast system of barter, privilege, and corruption.

Mikhail Gorbachev, the revolutionizing general secretary, though more courageous, moral, and intelligent than Louis XVI, did, like Louis XVI, unleash a torrent he couldn't control. (He might better and more tragically be compared to Necker.) His Enlightenment was *Glasnost* — an honest look at the sins of the past and the institution of free speech and a free press. His *Perestroika* brought about democratic practices within the bureaucracy. His economic reforms were highlighted by the rehabilitation of Bukharin and of the spirit of compromise in Lenin's New Economic Policy.[28] Was Gorbachev moving to the Right? From the point of view of his Politburo, he was on the Right because he was going *backward* in time. By his own standard he was moving *Left* — to recover what he believed to be the original intentions of Bolshevism.[29]

Once again, Left and Right had become a hall of mirrors. The Western press, using a terminology that was political rather than economic, hailed Gorbachev as a liberal-left revolutionary. By calling him Left, they labelled those who resisted him — a conservative Politburo of self-proclaimed Marxist-Leninists — right-wing. And the murky secrets of ideology proved their point; not long before the failed coup against Gorbachev, the propaganda released by the military contained passages from *Mein Kampf*, anti-Semitic propaganda,[30] and pamphlet material from the Black Hundreds — the patriotic, reactionary party set up by the monarchy in 1906 to counteract revolutionary agitation.[31] Far Left always joins far Right in sacrificing every other value for absolute authority. Both, after all, were monolithic, Byzantine, and gnostic; radical Left and Right still claimed the universe against a hated West. It was a "third force," Boris Yeltsin's democracy, that undid him.

With the failure of Gorbachev, Russia has fallen back into a fetid history of westernizers and slavophiles, each with its futile Left and Right versions, a four-way cultural and economic fight that defies any coherent duality. Are the westernizing capitalists on the political Right? It seemed that on the eve of the liberation of Eastern Europe and of the USSR, no one had even a provisional ideology. Most leaned toward what amounted to a sterile negation: "antisocialism."[32] And that negation was not Western-style capitalism with its own controls. But rather *no controls at all*: gangsterism. But if Russia fell into piracy, the political economies of Eastern Europe have fared better, inclining Left or Right as needed, which would seem to suggest that the new determining force is not economic Left and Right, but culture. Indeed, if there is no unambiguously ascendant Right in Eastern Europe, perhaps it is because "Left and Right" is dying if not dead.

As capitalism covers the earth in all its regulated and unregulated forms, we might ask whether we can any longer call it "Right," or even an ideology. For the fall of communism has taken with it all the compass bearings, disclosing capitalism as an enormous default that preceded socialism and survives it. Moreover, it has taken the evaporation of communism to reveal something extraordinary: the degree to which the transnational free-market economy resembles communism itself.[33] This is why Lévy and Foucault disclosed capitalism and communism as the two faces of Power as an end in itself.

Power, in its modern manifestation as technology, is not, after all, a moral force. The result is that technology merely changes the form of things — in opposing directions — towards *homogenization* on the one hand and towards *amplification* on the other. Reducing many goods, evils, and differences, it accentuates many others, confusing the old bearings of Left and Right, which count on static inequalities and permanent dualities. Whatever it may be, this power has no interest in *quality*, or in *values*, Left or Right.

The largest — indeed the only — force with which the conglomerate of Power and technology has been confronted is the natural environment. Nature, after all, has sustained the most visible damage from the industrial growth not just of capitalism and communism but of the developing world as well. Like big technology, the force it opposes, the environmental position is economically neither Left nor Right, for it is too pervasive. In ecology, man is integral to a limited self-sustaining system called the *biosphere*: a planetary ecology in which cooperative, complementary roles include hierarchy, equality, and duality. It does not oppose any of them because all of them are necessary to it.

The environmental movement has been called a new Left — perhaps mostly because it has appeared as a successor to the old Left. Its opposition to the destructive aspects of technology does oppose it to capitalism and often aligns it with parliamentary socialist parties. But there is no necessary connection between environmentalism and socialism. That is because environmentalism is a moral, not an economic, ideology. Indeed it is Left only in an older, more primordial sense in which Medieval Christianity was Left. Like most religions, its precepts are conservative, preserving. But it has a new, secular form, which explains why the natural world has become the latest locus of the ever-shifting Sacred, and environmentalism the Most Recent Moral Critic.

Historian Arthur Herman divides environmentalism into moderate and radical forms: Post-Capitalism and Anti-Western. The former advocates sustainable development that can be pursued by socialistic or free-market industrial capitalism. The other branch, the radicals, see sustainable development as a contemptible confidence game where reform is reduced to ritual. The radicals have fallen into millenarian,[34] gnostic postures: Western civilization is the demiurge, inimical to a true nature, divine in its innocence.

The ambivalent social content of environmentalism prevents it from being called Left in the modern sense because it has much about it that is aristocratic. The wealthy Montana landowner and naturalist busy saving breeding marshes for ducks, for example, is not altogether different from the landed eighteenth-century aristocrat who despises the pursuit of capital and suspects the slightest incursion of industry on his land. Moreover, the aristocrat's contempt for the common man is not wholly different from the way in which the radical environmentalist disparages the unenlightened masses. And when it is callous towards loggers who must cut trees to eat or Native fishermen and hunters who pursue ritual or livelihood, the environmental Left forms an elitist "Postmodern" Sacred Left against a modern economic and multicultural Left.

Extreme environmentalism, in fact, *requires* elitism; it cannot throw life-or-death matters of hard-won scientific knowledge open to the vote. Like all extreme politics, it must sacrifice many goods to a single, exalted Good. In this alone it has fascist antecedents. Like socialism and capitalism as hard ideologies, it is an absolute that ignores the need for an internal balance of freedom (Right) and order (Left).[35] At worst, it threatens a return to radical dualism, if only because it takes nature not as a means to more creative ends, but, in the old Western way, as an absolute value, an end in itself.

Beyond environmentalism and industrialism there is a third power: the revolution in "clean" computer and electronic communications technologies. In one sort of thinking they are mistaken for a uniformly positive and collective ideological force, an idea whose pioneer was Marshall McLuhan. The rapid spread of television inspired McLuhan to declare a civilizational revolution analogous to the "Gutenberg" revolution of the printing press, a prophecy that shows few signs of fulfillment in anything as revolutionary as Protestantism. But riding the wave of the '60s, McLuhan declared that electronic media were a levelling, iconoclastic force that brought back "Homeric mimesis," a romantic, electronic primitivism — a Lévi-Straussian technological "participation mystique"[36] — which has not come to be.

McLuhan's electronic One World may have produced revolution in poor, undemocratic countries, but those revolutions have not been particularly Left or Right. They have been the consumer revolutions of a new acquisitive class that have led to populist, demagogic governments representing forces latent in their societies. Otherwise, it is hard to see clearly where or how McLuhan's prophecies have come true. Like the heavier technologies, electronic media increase existing goods and evils, exacerbate conflicts — accelerate the delivery of good and bad news, truth and lies, multiply and deliver trivia with as much rapidity as they help in important decisions. At best they have brought the horrors of poorer countries to a wealthy West, which has nevertheless failed to agree on how to respond. Nor are electronic media bringing together a "global village." In Rwanda, in the Balkans, and in the ruins of the Soviet Empire, they exacerbate differences by spreading propaganda, with the effect of accelerating a fragmentation brought about by pre-existing circumstances. In the end, McLuhan's analysis was no more "Left" than were capitalism or advertising, perhaps because he was symptom as well as analyst of both.

So it is not communications but rather the global complex of economic and state power that is the force behind transformation — a homogenization that produces centres of power characterized by knowledge and reach, of which wealth, increasingly, is only an attribute. This is the Power to which Foucault said ideology was secondary.

Indeed, nations without an adversarial Left-Right tradition are in some ways better suited to the new transnational economy. The tradition that produced fascism in Japan[37] has today produced its categorical opposite: a successful, non-fascist Left-Right politics. Japan's Tokugawa Shogunate, like Louis XIV and like the Manchu, was a great seventeenth-century modernizer. Unlike the West, however, its two-and-a-half-century dynasty modernized without destroying feudalism; began a national economy without decimating the peasantry; used the family structure instead of destroying it; put its people to work in their homes instead of displacing them; built a national economy on stable villages rather than on unstable cities; and allowed an obsolete Samurai warrior class to turn its talents to mercantile enterprise.[38] After the Tokugawa Shogunate decayed, the nineteenth-century Meiji restoration modernized yet again, transferring family and clan bonds and a religion that was social rather than dualistic and transcendental[39] into a modern capitalist economy. But at the cost, admittedly, of fascism.

Where economic Left and Right are not already in synthesis, they are weakening almost everywhere; in the West, massive deficits, accumulated in part from social spending, have spelled the end for socialism as a single, ideological force. Everyone is in some measure a capitalist — even those on the Left who have shifted their activism to non-economic issues. But in the wake of economic Left and Right, a new debate is opening up within capitalism itself. Free-market advocates claim that everyone will benefit from the unhindered accumulation of wealth by the few; but transnational financier George Soros has repudiated this claim. He has declared that only regulation and social policy can deter capitalism from its headlong course of bondage and destruction.[40] His point is that free-market fundamentalism has developed all the characteristics of a totalitarian ideology. Like Marxism, it lays claim to ultimate truth.[41] Like Marxism, it is founded on axioms — in this case, that supply and demand form an equilibrium, that a free market supplies perfect knowledge for making decisions, that market participants are in principle equal. All of these axioms have been proven false.

With the pre-eminence of capital in the wake of ideology, the world is where France was two centuries ago under the Directory in 1794–1799, a place where Left and Right had lost their political and moral force. (Even Americans must recognize that it is not their revolution but the French Revolution that has thrown its political shadow forward over two centuries.) That "Directory" in which we now live is what Daniel Bell calls "post-industrial society," and it is neither Right nor Left, because it "does not 'succeed' capitalism or socialism but, like bureaucratization, cuts across both."[42] The duality, rather, is rough and massive: those who have the power of decision and those who do not,[43] or, as Bell has said, Shareholders versus Stakeholders.[44]

Each is a miasma rather than a class. The upper miasma is hard to call right-wing or conservative in the old sense. Its capitalist elite is less stable, its taste is popular, its CEOs less permanent, their backgrounds more varied.[45] Moreover, the centre of power shows signs of passing from capital to a knowledge elite: a technocracy.[46] The lower miasma has no single consciousness, being composed of a once-bourgeois middle class diluted by computerization and downsizing;[47] a one-time industrial proletariat reduced by computerization, free trade, and outsourcing to a defensive and wary corps of specialized technicians; and a massive, low-paid, and amorphous service sector.

In many respects the world is also returning to the social-industrial problems of 1820.[48] In North America and everywhere else, factory and service workers kept poor by free-market competition worry more about what they have to lose than about any possibility of gain in wages. The preservation of language, culture, tradition, and a healthy environment and workplace have replaced class war — precisely because of the threat of homogenization by the same forces that give it employment.

Class war is also obsolete because classes have been replaced by agglomerations, and non-political pseudo-democratic forms have made for the comfortable "tutelary despotism" of which Tocqueville warned.[49] Poverty has lost its politics[50] to race, housing, culture, and immigration. The recognition and absorption of gay culture, black culture, feminism, and multiculturalism by the cultural elite have helped to substitute recognition itself for voting and citizenship. The intermixture of high and low cultures in a generic "good taste, no-brow" culture has drained the old politics of Left and Right of its cultural content; every class is now middle class and "no class." If it all seems relatively painless, it is because individual autonomy and community have been lost not to a tyrant, but to that amorphous power and child of the Enlightenment which Lévy calls the Master. It distributes thin forms of freedom, individualism, autonomy, and ideas of community by manufacturing, marketing, and selling them. It amounts, in short, to ownership of the means of revolution. "Learning skills" and "parenting skills," "retraining," and educational TV give an illusion of independence.[51] Choice, the emblem of contemporary freedom, is an array of manufacturers' logos. Even the state controls the means of political organization.[52]

Discontent has, in a sense, been bought off with an array of illusions, which provide not promise (as in the past) but rather instant gratification and a play-acting subversiveness. In all the confusion, the old dualism has been displaced into the individual. The Master, having managed the trick of being the revolution and the counter-revolution, has already absorbed the protestor into the thing he or she is protesting against. Half consumer, half rebel, we end up protesting against ourselves. And if everything is political, politics itself has all but lost its meaning.[53] The trick has been to admit protest and to absorb it, but without ever satisfying it. And so rebellion retreats into subculture and random violence — or the occulted "cultural transgression" of the University. But those too are becoming public commodities. In the United States, the only group not absorbed by the Master is the mass of the middle-American heartland whose armed militias appeal to what they see as the last realm of freedom — the past. Ironically, the only truly subversive anti-bourgeois politics may be Nazism — and even systematic evil — since the great, empty power of the Enlightenment has claimed and diffused the Good.

Nevertheless, Left and Right insist that power, somehow, is still located in one place. As Foucault observed, politics "has never ceased to be obsessed with the person of the sovereign . . . What we need, however, is a political philosophy that isn't erected around the problem of sovereignty, nor therefore around the problems of law and prohibition. We need to cut off the King's head: in political theory that still has to be done."[54]

19

Fragmentation:
The Deconstruction
of Hiram

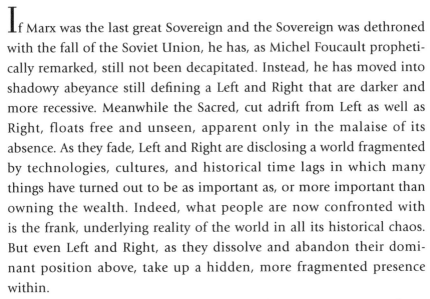

If Marx was the last great Sovereign and the Sovereign was dethroned
with the fall of the Soviet Union, he has, as Michel Foucault prophetically remarked, still not been decapitated. Instead, he has moved into
shadowy abeyance still defining a Left and Right that are darker and
more recessive. Meanwhile the Sacred, cut adrift from Left as well as
Right, floats free and unseen, apparent only in the malaise of its
absence. As they fade, Left and Right are disclosing a world fragmented
by technologies, cultures, and historical time lags in which many
things have turned out to be as important as, or more important than
owning the wealth. Indeed, what people are now confronted with
is the frank, underlying reality of the world in all its historical chaos.
But even Left and Right, as they dissolve and abandon their dominant position above, take up a hidden, more fragmented presence
within.

Fragmentation is the natural fate of artificial structures. Capitalism,
posing as a whole, was individualistic; Marxism, claiming to define
a plural reality, was monistic. The internal contradiction caused communism to fragment. The inconsistency in capitalism is causing it to

shed its old Puritan ideological content, revealing it to be little more than a naked economic force. As the ideological trappings of both have fallen away, little remains but the exercise of power in a fragmenting world.

Power, though apparent everywhere, is fragmented too. Its currency, capital, has once again become mobile. As in the early days of the nineteenth century, it has no loyalty but profit, creating migrant workforces and leaving communities behind, as Canadian philosopher George Grant might have said, like fish on the shores of a dying lake. This phenomenon, it must be emphasized, is not the ideology grasped by the free world after the Second World War. It is *fragmentation*, nothing more and nothing less. It has little to do with liberty and even less to do with happiness. For happiness is not its intention. It is a phenomenon with *no* intention.[1]

The growing fragmentation of geo-political entities is more consciously ideological but the cause is more or less the same. Separatist feelings stay dormant only when intermediate groupings like nation states are strong. And what strong nation states sustained was a class politics of Left and Right. But the old Cold War blocs and some weaker nations have turned out to be as artificial as the ideologies that tried to define them, and now people, in those places especially, seek solutions for their disenfranchisement not by demanding a part in some larger union or ideology but by looking inward to some earlier identity. Indeed, the older the polity, the more likely it is to fall apart. The old Russian-Soviet Empire has left different states to resume their histories at different points in the past, reviving baronial, warlord, and pasha- or mullah-led polities. Even China has a disparity between its wealthy cosmopolitan coastal area and its poor interior regions that is bound to express its alienation not just in local warlord economies, but in newly emergent ethnicities.[2]

Technology has been the cause of much of this. It amplifies tendencies toward difference as well as homogeneity. It makes disparities in space and in time more threatening at every level: between local and global, local and national, and national and global levels.[3] Nations and regions are less protected by blocs and thrown more into individual competition. One consequence is that nations and regions rely less on old ideas, knowing full well that capitalist economics offered no morality while Marxism offered a false one. While extreme poverty remains the most urgent problem, inequalities in wealth have proven less important to most people than those of language, culture, race, gender, and smaller collectivities. Each priority claims the loyalty of most economic classes, cutting across old industrial Left and Right. Figuratively, a vertical fragmentation of identity slices up and down across a shadowy background divided horizontally between owner and worker. With identity cutting across wealth, interests appear as isolated squares — for example, setting apart white, middle-class educated women from white lower-class women.

This post-ideological world is what has been called the Postmodern condition. Where the Modern abandoned the past, the Postmodern views time as a damming up, an accumulation of the past. It emphasizes change and variety, while Left and Right assumed simplicity and permanence. While the Modern is dual and Manichaean and rejects adornment, Postmodernism is both severe and baroque, "Left" and "Right." Boris Kapustin's description of Russia's postmodern Communist Party is apt: a "pastiche of Leninism, Russian Orthodox piety, liberal parliamentarianism and visionary 'post-industrialism.'"[4] The Modern/Postmodern dichotomy might even be called Christian-monotheistic/Pagan-polytheistic.

The prophet of neo-pagan plurality was of course Nietzsche. His assault on the dualizing force of Christian morality was, as we have seen, picked up by Heidegger. From there it has been carried on in the anti-philosophical literary criticism known as "deconstruction." Deconstruction, perhaps alone, has had the tools to tear Left and Right down to their foundations. The French deconstructionist thinkers Jean-François Lyotard and Jacques Derrida began by attacking what they called the "legitimations" of the Enlightenment: axioms such as progress, universality, emancipation, liberty, and equality; the very legitimations that we have seen undergirding both Left and Right. These legitimations served to justify European domination and exploitation of the non-European world and they were written right into the grammar of the imperial languages. The spoken *logos*, Derrida declared, was no longer sacred, but as conniving as the written word with all its binary relations of subject and object. As deconstruction did its work, it would seem that Left and Right ought to collapse after the legitimations that made them eternal were pulled out from under them.

The offensive has been bold and original and has some truth to it. Derrida took to the precipice a process begun by Heidegger and Sartre, each one successively outdoing the other.[5] In the end, Europe's most cherished intellectual instruments — progress, humanity, *man*, and even the self — were exposed as Western, subjective, and finally, political.[6] The strategy has been the ideological, "semiotic" deconstruction of literary texts to expose the way in which all language is inevitably political and invasive, reader and text engaged in a perpetual struggle for domination, so that no meaning is ever stable. The concept of any metaphysical world of ideas, it seemed, would be torn down, and with it the legacy of Parmenides. If anything could decapitate the Sovereign and his Left and Right, it would be deconstruction.

Derrida himself explicitly stated that the old legitimations were those upon which Left and Right depended: "the common ground of Christian or atheist existentialisms, of the philosophy of values . . . of personalisms of the right or the left, of Marxism in the classical style . . . or Christian-Democratic discourse."[7] Lyotard seemed to attack Parmenides at the roots, dismissing "the nostalgia of the whole and the one, for the reconciliation of the concept and the sensible."[8] He wisely held that to launch an assault diametrically, dualistically through "moves and countermoves" would only play into the old game.[9] Derrida likewise eschewed fixed battlefronts, advising that even to fight using the paradigm of (European) centre and (Non-European) periphery was likewise to reinforce the old dialectic.[10] Foucault said much the same thing in advocating "micro-strategies" of resistance.

But deconstruction involved not so much the abolition of a metaphysical duality as its reversal. It was a move from the ancient foundation of a real, immaterial Whole and illusory concrete things to a world consisting only of social realities — culture, gender, identity, for example — the Whole (all the legitimations) having been proven illusory. All that happened was that the Sacred, without quite saying so, took up lodgings under a new and more marginal *Left*. Western metaphysics was alive and well.

Like the dualities of deconstruction — self/other, centre/periphery, masculine/feminine — dualities maintained in static opposition do not produce anything transcendent.[11] Not only has deconstruction arranged its dualisms ideologically against classical thought but it has not (to my knowledge) attacked perhaps the largest structure of legitimations — the dualism of Left and Right. Perhaps that is because the proponents of deconstruction feel they must cling, however tentatively, to the moral reassurance of a fading political Left. And indeed, Derrida's most recent works admit to a nostalgia for a vague Marxist messianism — at best without Marx or God.[12] Through the exposure of linguistic games of control and the reduction of words to nominal instruments, he has, like a blind man trying to leave home, tapped his way along the reassuring footpath of medieval nominalism back to his own front door. Finally — and most recently — in discovering "justice" to be the single transcendent good, he has reverted to a sort of mystical Platonism. Critic Mark Lilla has even guessed that Derrida is throwing a lifebuoy to the Left. To follow deconstruction to its logical conclusion in the abolition of Right and Left would (some fear) open the way to complete relativism and finally to fascism.

Derrida helped pave the way not just for a New Left but for a pseudo-Left that uses deconstruction as a strategy for the most radical forms of what is called the politics of identity. Since deconstruction held that European ideas are all grammatically constructed, it could also be demonstrated that the peoples whom Europe failed to recognize could construct or reconstruct their own identities. The assumption that all identities were constructed, that even the *self* could be freely invented, put all identities on a level playing field. At best, a world of separate identities conceived as equal and distinct does transcend Left and Right as a compromise between aristocratic individualism[13] and an egalitarian collectivism.

But the politics of identity fall back into the dualism they would conceptually overcome. Identities, after all, are usually cobbled together *against* what they conceive as their opposites, "their language stamped with that of domination."[14] One can't help but suspect that these are the old Indo-European contraries, deeply embedded in Indo-European language. Feminist ideals, for example, are all too often constructed *against* masculinity. Masculinity, if we follow Susan Faludi, is being constructed *against* fear of feminization and male working-class obsolescence. Black nationalism is often an artificial counter-reflection of white supremacy. Mere opposition, after all, does not make for talent, much less for an ideology, any more than an agglomeration of all that is "not Communist"[15] or "male" constitutes a culture.

An alternative strategy is infinite relativism: but this defence against the standards of the oppressor likewise evaporates when the oppressor has gone. In freedom and equality, standards reassert themselves. Relativism is indeed the child of oppression. Taste and critical acclaim are freedom's by-product and mustn't be confused with rightish economic hierarchies that oppress for economic gain. Nor is culture, as Marx thought, a product of economic relations and social class.[16] The bourgeoisie is only the carrier of a changing and volatile culture, the same bourgeoisie from which have emerged socialism and the politics of identity that attack the bourgeoisie itself.

In universities, the aggressive relativism that says there is no good or bad but only *difference* has fallen further back into the Western political tradition by forming a sort of "difference" authoritarianism, repeating an old Platonism in which single values such as colour or physical disability are raised to absolutes. It argues in the form of messianic eschatologies, saved and damned, and New Jerusalems in which "allegory and poetry . . . take precedence over the record of events,"[17] and shows a blindness "to revolutionary despotism" coming "ultimately from its need to find new sources of structure and authority."[18] Reigniting the Left-Right Manichaeism that it showed hopes of extinguishing, it finally recalls the Jacobins of 1793–1794. And yet it is "Left" only insofar as the Right, suspicious "of the politicization of learning" has made it so[19] — and far too Ivy League to be called egalitarian. In fact, it is neither Left nor Right,[20] while at the same time it perpetuates their Manichaeism. Indeed, the politics of identity reflects Western dualism at its origins. It is, in short, gnostic: it refers to some original happiness — carried deep within a corrupt body in a fallen world. From terrorist Timothy McVeigh to activist rapper Sister Soulah, each claims a private identity in a relation to something beyond Left and Right, beyond a fallen world.

Internationally, it takes the form of religious and cultural sectarianism, where the only duality is the touted "Jihad vs McWorld" in which the most recent universal force, consumerism, with democracy and human rights in its baggage train, confronts regional resistance in ethnicity and religion. And yet, within this cultural-political bazaar, the forms of Left and Right, once official and monolithic, persist in weak and bastardized ways. Dual terms re-emerge; with "self and other," "familiar and exotic," the line between a European centre and a non-European periphery is reinforced instead of erased.

Even the most progressive nationalist liberation is fuelled by the self-conscious rescue of tradition. And tradition, as Said has rightly pointed out, is a European construction because it can only be defined in terms of progress and the destruction of the past. *Essentialism*, tradition's political promotion, has worked as a tool of colonial domination through the stereotyping of the "other" as well as for native prototypes in Third World liberation, Left and Right.[21]

But even as they persist, Left and Right, once utopian ends, are now relegated to service as the weapons of ethnic politics in a fragmenting world. Separatist, tribal southern Sudan, with its Marxist guerrilla army, makes common cause with a neo-liberal United States to resist slavery and rule from the Islamic north. Here is a perfect example of a case in which old Left and Right, in their subordination to cultural survival and geopolitics, can become secular, anti-fundamentalist partners. Nor does Militant Islam itself have a consistent political economy. Sudan and Libya call themselves socialist; Pakistan has embraced the free market; all are Islamic states. Wherever a secular ideology has attempted to impose uniformity, it has failed — most spectacularly in the Marxist-capitalist Pan-Arabism of the Ba'ath Party. In Egypt, Left or Right, under Nasser or Mubarak, poverty and rootlessness persist because it is modernization itself that has destroyed the stability of the old latifundian plantation system.

The gap, of course, is being filled by a third force, the fundamentalist Muslim Brotherhood.[22] Where the secular ideology has veered from Left to Right, the fundamentalism that provides neighbourhood social services is neither.[23] Its representative class is the *bazaaris*, small merchants less inclined to become monopolistic because of their mistrust of technology and Western business practice. Likewise, Iran has proven most resistant to a free market or socialist future. Its theocracy contains, hides, and neutralizes potential Left and Right tendencies, having liquidated the Left-wing secular Mujahedeen while damning Western-style capitalism. There too, the *bazaari* defines the nation, although in conjunction with the clergy. So even if the secular opposition triumphs, it seems unlikely that Iran will produce Western-style capitalism.

Indeed, capitalism is no longer an ideology. It is, rather, approaches to capitalism, cultural or technological, that will constitute new forms of economic belief. That is why affirmative action has replaced equality of income as the radical politics of the day. It is classed as Left only because it is directed, in theory, at the disenfranchised. But in fact, it is both Left and Right, since it favours group rights over individual rights and at the same time identity over economic class.

The deconstruction of identity has turned out to be no less dualistic than Enlightenment universalism. The universal claims of each make a separate camp out of all who disagree. And it is precisely universalist claims that are at the centre of Western dualism, whether the intolerant One of Parmenides, the All of the Gnostics, or the Many in the deconstruction of identity. However honourable and humanitarian the universalism of the Enlightenment, its discrete dualities were already well established in Kant and Rousseau. By finding the categories of perception rooted in the mind, Kant still placed essence before existence, the idea of culture before its real incarnation in the world.[24] In Rousseau's General Will we have the arrogance of a bourgeois emancipatory concept of "the people" attempting to liberate the real "peoples" of primitive lands, destroying them in the process.[25] In both Kant and Rousseau the attempt to reconcile the part with the whole by containing the former in the latter fails because the Ideal and the Real remain polarized in real life politics. And so Left and Right have both been able to turn Kant and Rousseau to their service. Thus Rousseau's universal but "inner" moral sense could equally seize passion over reason and subject over object, presenting the part as the whole in fascism[26] or in the politics of identity.[27]

But the Western tradition, in whose terms both Identity and Enlightenment argue, is not as universal in its origins as it claims to be. Indeed, it has its own anthropology. It is the anthropology not just of Western philosophy but of Left and Right, and the place where that anthropology passed over into politics is none other than Freemasonry, the forge in which myth and legend were reduced to the blank symmetry upon which Left and Right were drafted and distributed to the world.

As a philosophical society, Freemasonry was formally founded in 1717 in England. Its immediate mission was in effect Parmenideant: to reconcile the individual wills of its members with the collective good.[28] The imprint of the West is contained in the symbolism of every charter — an Indo-European scheme of opposites — the invariable, abstract presence of the compass and its cardinal points;[29] left and right hands; shamanic mystical death and rebirth;[30] and the mystical power of the artisan as manager of the divine force of fire. In its central legend, it claims ancestry in the rites of Dionysus. Its most prominent rite, the Hiramic Ritual, follows an Orphic Cycle through death and rebirth.[31] Its discovery of a higher morality through geometry[32] comes from Pythagoras and Euclid, from the universal abstraction behind the mason's compass, dividers, and set square, and the secrets of geometry supposedly imparted by Euclid to the Egyptians and the Israelites. Above all, Freemasonry has absorbed Gnostic concepts,[33] which it turns to the purposes of secular universalism by establishing Reason as the spark of the divine All in the darkness of the world.

But in the Hiramic legend[34] itself we find, in coded form, the myth of the West. It is built upon the Old Testament passage[35] in which the Tyrean artisan Hiram is retained by Solomon to complete the temple.

In the masonic rite Hiram's secret is the Promethean recovery of the Word, or *logos* — a gnostic idea[36] of the primal equality from which humanity has fallen and to which it must return. But he is also the human *demiurgos*: the secret bearer of a metaphysical technology.[37] Unaware of his secret (the Word), Hiram is murdered by jealous craftsmen for refusing to divulge what he can't express — a murder ordered by the demiurge to destroy the *logos*, the secret of the return to the wholeness of the All.[38] That way, that man may stay under his control. They bury Hiram on the west side of the temple, the direction of evening, death,[39] and the Left hand in Greek and Indo-European tradition. But, ever intent on finding the Word inside Hiram, they disinter the body, dismember and re-bury it. In remorse, they dig it up and reassemble it because of a single revelation: the word was never found because Hiram himself *was* the Word.[40] The craftsmen disperse to take the message to the world. Their descendants are Freemasons.

The murder of the truth and its burial on the Left effectively meant that the Sacred, in the terms of Freemasonry, had moved from the Right to the Left — long before the Jacobins made the Left into the moral high ground. The Left signifies, in short, that the truth as Sacred lies buried and is yet to be recovered. Motifs of gnostic dualism and Christian martyrdom are implicit. The reduction and reification of the Word to object and instrument of dismemberment recalls Robespierre's use of Virtue as a blade of excision rather than a principle of inclusion. The dismemberment of Hiram in search of a truth located within him rather than embodied in the man himself suggests the postmodern fragmentation after ideology's murderous search for the Word. If we understand Hiram to be the Word and the Word to be the truth of Man (in the sense of what it is to be human) this is the Man that Derrida, Foucault, and others decided had been abolished — that is, dismembered.

In historical fact it was the Crusaders who, like Hiram's builders, disseminated the Word by bringing the crafts' secrets and the Hiramic legend from Tyre into Europe along with elements of Middle Eastern Ophite Gnosticism. In France, in the eighteenth century, the philosophical universality of the English guilds was imported into local guilds, which then became a force of the Enlightenment. In Bavaria, however, it was the radical egalitarian brotherhood of the Illuminati[41] that brought Manichaean-Zoroastrian ideas of light and darkness[42] to the French guilds; and if indeed there is a ritual moment when the Sacred passed from Right to Left, it was "when some European aristocrats transferred their lighted candles from Christian altars to masonic lodges."[43] Thenceforward, abstract values determined membership. After all, as François Furet tells us, "to insure the election of the 'good' it was necessary to detect the 'wicked' in the light of accepted principles; and that is why from the very beginning of the revolution the struggles for power were characterized by ideological exclusion."[44] After 1789 the Freemasons' lodges were used and then assimilated by the Jacobins,[45] retaining their Masonic names right into the Revolution. Thus heaven and hell were tipped from their vertical arrangement back to the primordial, horizontal plane of sacred and profane, Right and Left.

Built on the universal absolute of the whole, Freemasonry carried forward its own Parmenidean negation in the parts. In proselytizing the egalitarian doctrines of Rousseau it transmitted Rousseau's innate gnostic duality of individual freedom and indissoluble bondage in the whole.

It seems reasonable, then, that in ages of dissolution, postmodern or post-feudal, architecture becomes a symbol.[46] Whether society is being deconstructed or reconstructed, dual symmetries in architecture imply a Left and a Right. Today, in effect, the arch they support is crumbling. Since the 1960s the Left has begun to embrace a mosaic politics of identity and ecology, none of which bears any imprimatur in Marx or Engels.[47] The Right, meanwhile, is stretched between fundamentalism, nationalism, and free-market libertarianism.

Even as Left and Right still oppose one another, nothing is hated quite so much as Liberal Democracy, the international system that protects them. It is hated for much the same reasons that Freemasonry was hated: the universality implied by all forms of globalism from General Motors to the United Nations to the European Economic Union is seen by many people as a hegemony, a force of oppression: the Free Market and the United Nations the Right and Left sides of the same coin, which dominates from somewhere near the political centre. This realignment of the extremes against the centre is a hallmark of postmodernity and it has been made possible by atomization.

The atomization of a population, as we have seen, was the first step in the destruction of the ideological status quo in medieval Europe, in France in 1789, and in China in 1949. And it is demographic fragmentation by technological forces, especially today in the United States, that is dissolving old Left and old Right into new groupings. The propaganda power of the marketplace and the increase of personal autonomy are shifting the individual's primary allegiance away from relationships with other individuals in home and community, where the bonds of ideology had been formed, to an apolitical popular culture.[48] This close identification with mass culture is what historian Christopher Lasch calls narcissism.[49] Its weak Left and Right versions are respectively holistic and egoistic, but the choices of each are increasingly made for the individual rather than by the individual. Both, according to Lasch, are versions of the same problem, a strong sense of collective culture and a lesser sense of self.[50]

The result is a psychological dissolution of Left and Right into entities

that Lasch suggests are a party of the "Super-ego," which draws on traditional non-political modes such as religion and traditional culture, a
party of the liberal-individualist self-helping "Ego," and a politics of total
liberation that challenges the first two.[51] If there is a duality to be found,
the first constitutes the Believers, the second two the Ironists. All have
strong membership in a single ruling New Class of right-wing neo-con-
servative business interests and a leftish agglomeration of Hollywood,
news media, and academia.[52] The considerable power that they wield
disguises a much more important duality: between power itself —
commercial, technological, or political — and the isolated individual.

Those who do not accept any of this status quo, Right or Left, have
almost nowhere to turn. Generally they are concentrated in the small-
town and rural South- and Mid-West, a rump of Protestant America,
nondescript and transparent to the rest of the country — the middle-
people unmentioned at Washington inaugural events.[53] Like the *petite
bourgeoisie* of late-nineteenth-century Europe, they find it hard to
define themselves as Left or Right ("We don't want to hear about left
and right, conservative and liberal, all these bullshit labels. Let's get
back to the idea of good guys and bad guys.")[54] And in some sense
they always did. Their predecessors, while culturally Right, were often
economically "welfare state" and "union" Left, like the "Country and
Western Marxism" of the far-right Southerner George Wallace.[55]

Fifteen years ago, these forgotten supported their government against
communism. When the Soviet Union collapsed, they turned against their
next biggest enemy — a government that had outlived its usefulness.
Indeed, Washington itself, Left or Right, is the new "communism." The
angry constituents of the heartland have nothing in the present to draw
on, everything in the past. Their only unifying principle is liberty. Many
have organized themselves into armed militias, patriotic or neo-Nazi
or Christian. Their suspicions are almost identical to those once directed
at Freemasonry: authoritarian, egalitarian world government. They are,
above all, where Left and Right meet,[56] in the badlands of a far-leftish
protest against technology, a far-rightish protest against big government, and a joint protest against an entertainment and commercial
establishment which, they believe, behaves as if they didn't exist. That
is why Timothy McVeigh bombed the US Government building in
Oklahoma City and why he and the leftish eco-terrorist Ted Kaczynsky

have been able to chat in prison. ("In my opinion the problem's with the government, in Ted's it's technology.")[57] However demented they may be, one has to consider that they might only be the most radical expression of a much vaster, invisible society of broken identity and discontent; dreaming "against the modern Prince, against politics as it exists concretely, and therefore against materialism and materialism alone."[58] Could there be a re-emergence of gnostic extremes?

If everything's quiet on the surface it's because the celebrated Left-Right compromise of the Clinton-Blair ethic has been about as smart an economic and political compromise as can be brokered to preside over such a society, in America or in Britain. Though it does concede that socialistic measures are a complement to capitalism,[59] the new ethic is at best a friendly broker with no new ideas — and it works in a system that still speaks and votes in the old language of Right and Left.

After all, when battlefronts are occluded, people hang on to old standards, instruments of navigation in a fragmenting world. Indeed, politics cleaves to Left and Right precisely *because*, as former Ontario premier Bob Rae reminds us, capitalism is proving "neither a demon nor a god."[60] Still, those who hold by Left and Right will one day appear a breed apart. Having agreed, or at least acquiesced, on the free market and so much else, they now fight louder battles over smaller issues.

Political philosopher Norberto Bobbio, in his reflective book *Left and Right: The Significance of a Political Distinction*, has argued in defence of Left and Right. Like the ancient Greeks or the Freemasons, he justifies their universality from geometry, saying it is symmetrical, abstract, and "accidental." But, as we have seen, the distinction is neither simple, abstract, nor accidental; Left and Right are contingent, heavily loaded with culture and anthropology.[61] And he adds that to distinguish a middle does not detract from the polarity of the wings.[62] But he does not consider the possibility that a middle may rise to over-whelm the wings as a third force, or that a group may remain in the middle because it has nowhere else to go in a linear debate — like a cultural platform in the midst of a left-right debate about economics, which it repudiates. He also compares Left and Right to the invariable duality of battle,[63] where there can be no third or neutral party. But he concentrates on tactics and excludes strategy, confining his argument to the arena and its pitched battle, and forgetting the larger field, where a third force can wait to upset the terms and goals of the conflict.

Nostalgia for tradition, Bobbio suggests, invariably lands you on the Right,[64] while the strong emotions of glory and despair place you on the extremes of Left and Right. But the entire history of the Left is permeated with a sense of loss. In its earliest stages in the late medieval period, liberty and equality on the ancestral Left were appealed to as lost traditions to be regained. Survivors of the old Left today mourn a Marxist tradition; many more miss the tradition of the welfare state. And centrists, above all, are not immune from a certain glory — from Napoleon to Trudeau in Canada to Torillos in Panama — or from cynical despair, as in the case of Noriega. He remarks as well that the Left always leads the way, moving from bourgeois freedom of capital through to working-class socialism, while the Right always follows, opposing it at every stage. But has not the Left now been reduced to reacting to the advance of the free-market Right?

In the end, Bobbio holds that Equality is the final shibboleth that defines the Left beyond doubt[65] (and therefore the Right). And yet, "equality of what? How? and of whom?"[66] In fascism and communism it is equality as conformity; in multiculturalism it is equality of recognition; in socialism, of material welfare; in liberalism, of opportunity; in libertarianism, of freedoms; in feminism, of gender. Ideologies that need freedom to assert equality develop classes; those that need authority for equality develop administrative hierarchies. An unqualified equality does not exist.

Old Left and old Right are in fact different formulas of freedom and authority — probably as required in France and England in about 1820. The terms are still defined by inhumane industry, contemptuous aristocracy, and a dangerous and hungry working class. But if Left and Right are losing their content, what remains? The technical philosophies, with their scholastic definitions of justice, have not found their way into mainstream politics, let alone the public mind. Indeed, the only hint of some sort of inclusive principle might be a nagging sense of the Sacred. Detached from Right and Left as the Sovereign recedes, the Sacred is implied by two strong forces, loss and desire. Neither individual nor collective, it is like Hiram. Like the Word, it is exemplar and not emissary. Inclusive, rather than exclusive, it is the small, natural community.

20

Community:
The City Block
and the Cosmos

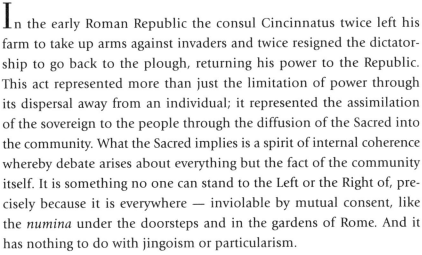

In the early Roman Republic the consul Cincinnatus twice left his farm to take up arms against invaders and twice resigned the dictatorship to go back to the plough, returning his power to the Republic. This act represented more than just the limitation of power through its dispersal away from an individual; it represented the assimilation of the sovereign to the people through the diffusion of the Sacred into the community. What the Sacred implies is a spirit of internal coherence whereby debate arises about everything but the fact of the community itself. It is something no one can stand to the Left or the Right of, precisely because it is everywhere — inviolable by mutual consent, like the *numina* under the doorsteps and in the gardens of Rome. And it has nothing to do with jingoism or particularism.

And yet the Sacred risks negative connotation through its association with the terms "community" and "conservative." Because it carries the danger of violent exclusiveness together with rooted friendship, "community" has been condemned always to arrive disguised as a symbol, in heroes and messiahs, in elusive truths necessarily reduced to empty phrases and half lies. In its true form, it arrives not as an absolute brought by an emissary but as something exemplary, as a livable and *limited* fact, just as it is represented, for example, in the craftsman Hiram, who steps onto the building site and is cut in two by dual absolutes. Of course, the very fact that the community Hiram had arrived to build is commonly defined and talked about by communitarians and populists is proof that it does not really exist anywhere.

The force that keeps destroying it is universalizing abstraction — the search for a simple foundation in love, or in rights, in freedom, and citizenship, concepts that can turn all too quickly into their own opposites, into hatred, restriction, bondage, atomism. Only a symbol such as Hiram, by virtue of being a body and therefore neither whole nor part nor value, cannot be turned into any opposite, but rather arrives, as we have suggested, in the guise of what is lacking: desire and loss.

This concept of the sacred is fragile; it flickers like a flame in a draughty room (not "religious," but simply, like religious things, elusive). Charles Taylor almost captures this sense of the sacred when he refers to *authenticity* — a sense of connectedness to others that includes loyalty to one's self. As Taylor cautions us, authenticity is not *monological* in race, ethnicity, or in gender; it is, rather, *dialogical*, the knowledge of one's self through constant dialogue with others.[1] And indeed, Taylor's authenticity is torn asunder between "boosters" and "knockers," from the Left and the Right respectively. Much as Hiram was torn apart by the two groups of artisans,[2] the knockers would force a universal legitimation upon the self, and the boosters would further dismember the self into identities.[3] The elite that comprises Left and Right expresses both as forces of destruction, and so keeps community and authenticity divided and suppressed.[4] And yet, an apparent majority of ordinary people clearly wants to find some sort of synthesis of Left and Right, for example, a combination of feminism with traditional family and the work ethic.[5]

The authentic local community, if realized, would also contain poverty by including rather than excluding the poor, the oldest and most volatile fuel for a sterile division of Left and Right — as if the world could be cut in two as a means to poverty's summary abolition. What, after all, has the progress of the Left and the Right done for the poor? Each falters at the very moment it attempts to reduce poverty. The Left stigmatizes and perpetuates it in welfare; the Right urges "sacrifices" as unending as the "difficult stages" urged by Stalin. It has been the illusion of progress that Nicholas Campion describes as "no new dawns, but periods of adjustment in which political institutions that have lost touch with social and economic pressures are replaced by those that are more appropriate to current circumstances."[6]

The illusion of progress is maintained by what Hannah Arendt called "the pathos of the new": the idea that whatever is new is somehow for the best, to be accepted as a matter of course even if it annihilates what is eternal. That is why in the last decades of the twentieth century there arose a sense, not of historical nostalgia but of *loss* — the desire for "the recovery of meaning and value of human life outside of its subjection and service to progress."[7] But the protest, still inarticulate, is not so much against improvement as against *providentialism*, the assumption of some sort of *arrival*, a *climax* or *end* requiring sacrifice, such that the "myth of progress dominates modern political discourse, whether left, right, or centre."[8] Providentialism is armed with abstractions like rights and freedom and equality without regard for their inevitable conflict. The only forgotten one is "fraternity," whose proper meaning still comes closest to Charles Taylor's "dialogical authenticity" — or perhaps, plain friendship. Since friendship is lateral, not forward-driven, it might, if it can be recovered in some common object, release us from the bonds of Providence.

Providence, with Christianity, was conceived for improving selves in isolation. Treating each self as a work in progress (Foucault's uneasy idea), its exemplar is not the community with all its relations but the *polytechnique*, so high, so professionalized (as John Ralston Saul has told us) as to be safely detached from the people whom it is meant to serve. Once invisible, Providence now has a visible end in those few *polytechnicals* who have arrived: solitude, exemplified by the walled estates of *parvenus*, the gated community, the emptiness and silence of middle-class streets that confuse solitude with safety. Surely such *rights* are the death knell of what Hannah Arendt called a truly common world, where "reality is not guaranteed primarily by the 'common nature' of all men who constitute it, but rather by the fact that, differences of position and the resulting variety of perspectives notwithstanding, everybody is always concerned with the same object. If the sameness of the object can no longer be discerned, no common nature of men, least of all the unnatural conformism of a mass society, can prevent the destruction of the common world, which is usually preceded by the destruction of the many aspects in which it presents itself to human plurality."[9] Or, as Christopher Lasch puts it, our situation is that "we conduct ourselves politically as if we had nothing in common."[10]

Providentialism's drive to perfection incurs a big cost in human association. After all, "people, like all other organisms, are not evolved to maximize health, wealth, happiness, or any other trait — but to have descendants [for] the continuation of life. Since there can be no perfect health, wealth, happiness or any other trait . . . accepting this . . . may turn out to be a 'truly conservative act.'"[11] This is conservatism not in the ideological sense but rather in the biological sense of decentralization to natural, interrelated, self-sufficient communities that exchange the pressure to perfect for coherence. But is this conservatism a move from Left to Right? Or is it a leftward move to local democracy? If it is indeed "conservative," how does one detach from the word all its alien accretions of jingoism, egoism, greed, cruelty, and self-interest?

The other worn-out word, "community," no longer connotes the affective bonds of locality but associations of commerce, special interest, and expertise. These are the communities that chain stores are proud to serve, the communities of false political and media consensus, of police protection, of the elite and their semi-annual public lectures. And then the greatest distortion of all — the exclusive community of nation and race as exalted by Hitler.[12] The coherent, limited community remains by far the best defence against fascism, if only because fascism is born of the promises of intimacy and community that mass society and its Left and Right have failed to provide.[13] Felipe Fernandez-Armesto even goes as far as to warn that "Western liberalism, enfeebled by its inconsistencies seems bound to be wishy-washed away."[14]

This is why there has been a search for new models of community that balance association and prosperity. One model is biology. Jane Jacobs, in *The Nature of Economies*, observes in successful, self-contained economic spheres the same laws that govern successful ecosystems; human organization is not an analogy to biology but part of the same process. Another model is religion. Francis Fukuyama sees in the return of popular religiosity new senses of local community that bind ordinary moral values in simple faith.[15] But real community is not in itself religious. Religion is merely one of the few surviving bonds of community, and by itself it is inadequate. If local economies do have a counterpart in ecosystems, they will be further bound together not by religion but rather by the Sacred, defined as whatever spirit lies behind their internal coherence.

Religion may promote values but it cannot fill that barren space between the population and power. Contemporary political philosophy, on the other hand, seems to have become an alchemical semantics of justice worked out in balances and trade-offs between individuals with concepts such as "flat," "narrow," "baggy," "substantial," "thick," or "thin" — a sort of paint-by-number giving colour to something colourless and ahistorical. A good example is John Rawls, who writes about justice from a liberal-democratic perspective and is duly criticized for treating individuals as atoms of self-interest devoid of affect. His politics is abstract, suggesting experimentation by means of what he calls a "veil of ignorance," a generic background against which citizens describe the kind of community they would like to have without regard to their real situations in life. He paints a world determined almost entirely by calculation.[16] Then there is Anthony Giddens, who hitches the Left to a philosophical conservatism that he distinguishes sharply from neo-liberalism, "whose links with conservatism are at best tenuous."[17] He expresses the hope that, since the Left has lost the spirit of collective welfare, distributive values might be restored without the industrial millenarian "productivism" of the old industrial Left.[18] But what can be made of a general trend in philosophy that takes no account of the past or feelings or culture?

For all the flatness and tentativeness of contemporary thought, a new dialectic does appear whose best feature is that it works poorly as a dialectic. It might crudely be visualized as a flattened oval with traditional forms of collectivist Left and individualistic Right holding on at the ends; and a new conglomeration of non-dualistic politics clustered around a centre, which bulges upward and downward in a vertical tension between the authority of Communitarianism and the liberty of Libertarianism. Communitarianism can incline to the Left or to the Right as can Libertarianism — thereby providing a scale of two dimensions instead of one.

Communitarianism (in America) hopes to combine a libertarian respect for identity with a community moral order. It maintains that human nature is neither evil (from the Right) nor Good (from the Left) but that values are internal rather than imposed.[19] It supports family values in combination with the equality of women, emphasizing the authority of parents rather than patriarchy. Its critics fear at worst a certain "Mom and Pop" left-right authoritarianism, recalling Calvin's Geneva — an apt comparison, considering that Calvin's closed community of the virtuous is Left and Right's most distinct and radical common ancestor. Nevertheless, the fact that a potential, if not actual majority of citizens has moved beyond the left-right choices for which they are still constrained to vote, suggests that society may have been living longer than generally acknowledged in the silent abstention of the Vestibule of Hell.

Variants of Communitarianism emphasize different combinations of the rightish market and the leftish state or the rejection of both — chiefly to limit the powers of either.[20] Christopher Lasch's "Populism" emphasizes a stoical respect, smallness of scale, and reduction of extremes of wealth and poverty against the lachrymose compassion and vague limits of Communitarianism.[21] For all their differences, both "reject . . . the market and the welfare state in pursuit of a third way . . . and for that very reason they seem to many people to hold out the best hope of breaking the deadlock of current debate, which has been institutionalized in the two major parties and their divided control of the federal government."[22]

Powerful, smaller communities are in fact re-emerging outside the United States in new municipal trends. In developing nations there are now what A.L. Chickering calls "conservative idealisms," upsurges of local capitalism and self-help that bring free enterprise from the Right and a protest against the ravages of big capitalism from the Left.[23] In spirit perhaps, a pale resemblance to the Mutualism of Proudhon. In Latin America, for example, a solidarity of community and small business is doing moderately what militant Marxism failed to do radically. Even before Bolivar, the tradition of the *cabildo*, the local provincial governments of monarchical Spain, had become part of a "deep well" of anti-statism.[24] With Napoleon's deposition of the Spanish king, local government became a theoretical political vacuum, ensuring "that in the absence of the king, popular sovereignty rests in the local communities"[25] — an almost literal dispersal of the sacred. Today, the *cabildo* is seen as the forebear of the new municipal democratic movements that are being revived to replace the mass politics of the Left.[26] That is because the traditional Right has focused too narrowly on democracy, civil liberties, law, and elections, while the Left has confined itself to economic democracy.[27] The result is a tendency to vote Left on the municipal level and Right federally. Sometimes it even produces a coincidence, if not an alliance of small business and left-wing or even Marxist local administrations.[28] The trend toward small business, where local firms crop up in defiance of the regulations of planned and inefficient national economies, may well be the only force in the developing world that can succeed where big capitalism, socialism, and international aid have failed.[29]

Indeed, as Benjamin Barber has remarked, "Capitalists and their socialist critics . . . share one deterministic and antidemocratic assumption: namely that communities are incapable of making their own histories through common talk and action."[30] And it was precisely the decline of the small, internally coherent community that had encouraged the formation of mass society and its products, Left and Right, and the nation state.

If the prototype of that small community was the Greek *polis*, an understanding of the reasons for its dissolution is crucial to any critique of mass society and mass ideology. It is the expropriation of private property, in the strict sense of the property of households — from the expansion of Rome to the collectivism of Stalin — that has led to a mass society. The private household had been the place dedicated to the necessities of food, clothing, shelter, and child-rearing. By contrast, the public realm, the *agora*, or *forum*, was the place of collective action and the context of another realm — politics. In the *polis*, one passed *through* realms that were distinct, from the household, across the commercial and convivial activity of the public realm, and into the world of public action in politics. And so intimacy was achieved not by homogenization, but by a separation of realms of activity. In a world without media, passive participation was impossible; one *had* to pass, physically, from one realm into the other to know what was going on, so that people were brought into contact. But now, of course, the ancient identification of property as the private realm of the household has been lost to the modern association of property with wealth and exclusiveness.[31]

Hannah Arendt tells us that what diluted this organic unity was a new phenomenon — the social — the leeching of the public and political realms into the private, and the private into the public.[32] The phenomenon of the social began with Rome; and its modern extreme has been the expansion of the household into the public realm, a Marxist or capitalist "national household" in which the necessities of life are regulated by commerce and the state,[33] Left or Right. Architecturally speaking, the contrast between *polis* and nation is symbolized by the forum with its porches, colonnades, *palaestra*, and *agora* on the one hand, and on the other, the giant open-air stadium with huge tele-screens broadcasting the single message of a single ideology. "What makes mass society so difficult to bear," writes Arendt, "is not the number of people involved, at least not primarily, but the fact that the world between them has lost its power to gather them together, to relate and to separate them."[34] In other words, there is no longer any-where specific to be a citizen.

If the world of Left and Right is the world of the massive and the undifferentiated, the small community is the unit to which human beings are rationally and biologically best suited. A hundred and fifty, the optimal group size in paleolithic times,[35] remains the maximum number of relationships that the speech and cognitive capacities of the human brain can accommodate.[36] Moreover, on that scale individu-alism and egalitarianism were so balanced that our ancestors did not even separate them as concepts.[37] This same sense of limit, in defining the extent of the Greek *polis* according to the needs of defence, pro-vided a natural and practical source of ethics. In Ming Confucianism, the confines of a "street philosophy" promoted a strong degree of local responsibility within a federated empire.[38] Montesquieu, too, found that the city state was the most appropriate context for democracy,[39] a point on which Rousseau was adamant.[40] The more personal acquain-tance there is, the better democracy is likely to work. This is why the actual physical extent of the democratic unit is important. Aristotle judged it to be the area visible to the eye from the acropolis, or the distance across which a man could walk in a day to attend the assembly. But today, such communities are almost absent, and "the difficulty of assembling a close-knit social network . . . may be the most pressing social problem of the new millennium."[41]

By contrast, it is the modern and social force of Christianity that has provided the model for an atomized mass society; for the perspective of the Christian was pastoral: not outward to public life but rather inward to the soul and beyond to the supernatural.[42] Richard Sennett shows with elegance how Christianity transferred the wall from being a defining circumference outside the community to being a symbol of division within urban areas, where it separated as sacred and profane inner from outer experience. "The shadows cast by that wall," he says, "continue to darken our society."[43]

But integration and coherence also require long acquaintance, and the community without permanence is no community at all. While the breakdown of the family is generally blamed on a decline in authority, it is more precisely transience (which has almost turned from a freedom into a social evil) that has brought about the absence of real social authority in the affective bonds of peers and friends, when they are local. Community, it seems, needs at least a generation to fulfil its essence,[44] and that sort of coherence, as Charles Taylor suggests, is also essential to individual identity. The community has neglected not only time but space. And a world of visible households is the only place where moral rules are taught by example[45] and can re-emerge, since the ideology of the market has none to give us.[46]

Benjamin Barber suggests that what has prevented the emergence of coherent communities is the foundation of politics upon economics; and that even when philosophers search for a foundation in the "pre-political" they still fall into deductive abstractions. Natural rights, for example, he says, "is at best a fiction . . . Fictitious legal persons, though secure in their rights, reside in no particular neighbourhood, belong to no particular neighbourhood, belong to no particular clubs, identify with no particular clan or tribe or nation, and are part of no particular community. Therein lies their personhood . . . Universality is an abstraction of little particular value to particular men."[47] And legal rights, absolute in their claims, tend not toward cooperation, but toward atomism.[48]

But even a pure political foundation presupposes a pre-ideological economics; that is, economics prior to its politicization by socialism and capitalism. And Barber even goes as far as to say, "Neither capitalism nor socialism has much to do with the economic realities of the modern world."[49] A pre-ideological economics does seem to emerge in Jane Jacobs's concept of the self-sufficient import-replacing city region,[50] where sheer innovation can break down big industries into versatile and profitable small ones.[51] If we think of such regions and communities as a political economy in the old sense of a "public household," cooperation is a complement to competition as well as a rejection of both the moral determinism of Marxism and the utilitarian determinism of capitalism.[52] The city region is also a far more comprehensive unit than the nation state, which, with all its regional inequalities, is a hothouse for competing ideologies of rich and poor. The city region is, finally, the best alternative to staking the life of the community and specialized regions on the hazards of the global market — and indeed the only natural defence against those hazards.

In a coherent community, business, instead of being an adjunct, is part of the community and shares a common fate.[53] A shadow of the idea has appeared in joint management between owners and workers and in profit-sharing, both of which offer a more efficient alternative to the welfare state. Effectively, ownership of the means of production is shared instead of polarized between capital and labour.[54]

If the dark side of the small community is seen to be parochialism, electronic communications, far from being forces of atomization, give people less reason to move away; more reason to stay in a place that is at once comprehensible in extent, and cosmopolitan.

But of course that begs the question of how such a place would be governed. How can a cosmopolitan community make a politics of local and cosmopolitan relevance? It would mean dismantling the shibboleth of democracy and putting it together again. Stripped to the bone, democracy then should mean freedom from politics. That is, the assimilation of politics to life by freeing people from infinite, unappeasable abstractions such as freedom and equality, held as absolutes. So we are talking not about mass, representative democracy — the very force that maintains ideological abstractions by putting forward candidates in their name — but about the *polis*.

By the *polis* I mean a fundamental unit that lends itself to visual definition: something no larger than a few city blocks, where power devolves to "the lowest, most local level at which decisions can reasonably be made, with the function of the larger unit being to support and assist the local body in carrying out its tasks."[55] So the neighbourhood becomes the primary site of democracy, a place where vote tallies cannot produce permanent majoritarian factions because votes will divide according to issues, not according to ideology, for it is the means and not the end of the community itself that is in question.[56] This is the ideal of self-government "by amateurs, where every man is compelled to encounter every other man without the intermediary of expertise,"[57] the kind of democracy advocated by Rousseau.[58]

But the culture in which people are willing to participate more than they have done in the past — to work for freedom from politics — is another matter. One needs a *place* to make the work natural, that is, a place to be a citizen. Citizens were conceived in assemblies, in *fora*, and among *gentes*. If they flourished in coffee houses and workshops, what are they to do when there are no longer workshops, coffee houses, wards, or sectional assemblies to give them a context?[59] As Charles Taylor has remarked: "Once participation declines and once the lateral associations that were its vehicle wither away, the individual citizen is left alone and feels, correctly, powerless."[60] The best and most protective politics — the kind found in revolutions — has always been conducted in an atmosphere of celebration and turbulence. That is why solitude and privacy are not civilization, but barbarism behind a mask of soft despotism. The neighbourhood, or the natural unit of politics, is not only its own politics but the centre, not the periphery, of pleasure and ideas. As Rousseau still reminds us, "In a well-ordered city every man flies to the assemblies: under a bad government no one cares to stir a step to get to them."[61]

But the language in which communities and their larger context are being discussed is still tentative and occulted. Charles Taylor talks about "nested spheres," communities of interest embedded within larger, more public communities in a sort of concentric democratic interplay.[62] Jürgen Habermas advocates "Communicative Action" in the space between a "life-world" of vital community and the "reified" world of government and bureaucracy.[63] Bob Rae is at least succinct:

"Devolve as much power as possible to local governments but insist on coordination."[64]

But Habermas is right about one thing. He appeals to a rescue of the Enlightenment in order to give universal values local force — and perhaps, more importantly, I would argue, to give local values the force not of abstraction but of universal human desires. Now, I have criticized universalism in the Enlightenment, Jacobinism, Freemasonry, and above all in Gnosticism, as the main source of dual division, of Left and Right. But in each of those universalisms there has always been buried promise: though each was an agent of dualism, none had ever intended to be. Each, tragically, had carried a conviction of unity, of common humanity. Jacobinism combined universality with the intimacy of the street in a furiously vital local politics. Freemasonry remains the model of intense discussion among citizens — exactly because they were taken out of their professional milieu and connected through nothing but local interests and love of ideas. And so, "the fusion" of the Jacobin cult of the nation with the sociability of Freemasonry must be an example for us. "The perfect opposite of Jacobinism's vision — namely our own inactive allegiance to socially inert and pluralistic democracy — is no more than a tired and fatalistic response to the (temporary) failure of their larger and more noble world view."[65]

Like any grand failure, gnostic thinking — the most magnificent failure of all — remains both the problem and the solution. If Left and Right are ever forgotten, it will come about through the lesson of Gnosticism. At its very origin, Gnosticism proposed the duality of world and God only as an *explanation*, a theogony of evil and a good God, not as a paradigm for living. Gnostic thinking discloses that Left and Right picture the same world in the *pneuma* and the All, but have been turned against one another by the Demiurge, who split the human race with debased Reason and exalted Parmenides, while forgetting Heraclitus and the Milesians and the real *logos*. For it is still Parmenides and the Eleatics who taught us to mistake means for ends — who split the whole and parts as separate values, one sacred, the other profane, so that two moieties of a crowd would one day split apart on the floor of the *Salle des Menus Plaisirs*.

Notes

PART ONE   UNITY

Chapter 1   Oneness: Enlightened and Ancient

1 Samuel Brittan notes that at this time the right hand was considered superior both in society and in the bible; thus, "it was more than mere chance that the place of honour in the French assembly of 1789 was on the king's right." Samuel Brittan, *Left or Right, the Bogus Dilemma* (London: Seeker and Warburg, 1968), 30.

2 Philippe-Joseph Buchez and Prosper Charles Roux, *Histoire Parlementaire de la Constituante de la Révolution Française*, Aug. 28, 1789. (Paris: Librairie Paulin,1834), 349. We also have from Bastid's biography of Sièyes: "La discussion durait depuis le 29 Août partisans et adversaires du véto s'étaient définitivement séparés en côté gauche et côté droit de l'assemblée." Paul Bastid, *Sièyes et Sa Pensée* (Paris: Hachette, 1970).

3 Ibid., 361. (Author's emphasis.)

4 Alexis de Tocqueville, *The Old Regime and the French Revolution* (New York: Doubleday, 1955), 81.

5 François Furet, *Interpreting the French Revolution* (Cambridge: Cambridge University Press, 1981), 174.

6 Joseph Campbell, *The Masks of God: Primitive Mythology* (New York: Viking Press, 1959), 367–71.

7 J.M. Roberts, *The Penguin History of the World* (London: Penguin, 1995), 35.

8 Ibid., 396.

9 Ibid., 402.

10 James Frazer, *The Golden Bough* (New York: Macmillan, 1951), 393.

11 Joseph Campbell, *The Masks of God: Occidental Mythology* (New York: Penguin, 1976), 13.

12 Campbell, *Primitive Mythology*, 137.

13 Frazer, *The Golden Bough*, 378.

14 This particular meaning of sacrifice is discussed at length by Roberto Calasso in his *The Ruin of Kasch* (Harvard: Belknap Press, 1994). He treats of humanity's gradual loss of moral connection with the cosmos and, although the book is not specifically a source for the present work, it has had considerable influence on the author and is highly recommended.

15 Campbell, *Primitive Mythology*, 351.

16 Wendy Doniger, in the foreword to Claude Lévi-Strauss, *Myth and Meaning* (New York: Schoecken Press, 1995), viii–ix.

17 Claude Lévi-Strauss, *Structural Anthropology* (New York: Basic Books, 1963), 161.

18 Willis, in Parkin, *Anthropology of Evil*, 211.

19 William H. McNeill, *The Rise of the West* (New York: Mentor, 1965), 34.

20 Carl Jung, *Psychological Types*, Bollingen Series XX (Princeton, NJ: Princeton University Press, 1977), 140.

21 Samuel Kramer, *The Sumerians* (Chicago: University of Chicago Press, 1963), 115.

22 Ibid., 123.

23 Kramer, *The Sumerians*, 124.

24 Norman Cohn, *Cosmos, Chaos and the World to Come* (New Haven: Yale University Press, 1993), 27.

25 Hannah Arendt, *Between Past and Future* (Harmondsworth: Penguin, 1980), 51.

26 See Roberto Calasso, *The Marriage of Cadmus and Harmony*, for an account of Greek myths built around the transgressions of Olympus on the world of men.

27 Alkis Kontos, "The World Disenchanted," in Asher Horowitz and Terry Maley, eds., *The Barbarism of Reason: Max Weber and the Twilight of Enlightenment* (Toronto: University of Toronto Press, 1994), 227.

28 Fritjof Capra, *The Tao of Physics* (London: Fontana, 1984), 285.

29 See the section on Anaximander in Kathleen Freeman, *Ancilla to the Presocratic Philosophers, a Complete Translation of the Fragments in Diels* (Oxford: Basil Blackwell, 1952).

30 According to Laponce's remarks on the French Revolution, it was during this period in the last week of June that the terms Left and Right first took hold; but since, at that early point, Left and Right were still determined by the seating of nobility and clergy, 27 August remains the date for their modern determination. See J.A. Laponce, *Left and Right: The Topography of Political Perceptions* (Toronto: University of Toronto Press), 1981.

31 Thomas Carlyle, *The French Revolution* (New York: Random House, 1837), 226.

32 Ibid., 236.

33 Le Marquis de Ferrières, *Mémoires du Marquis de Ferrières*, vol. III (Paris: Librairie Firmin Didot, 1880). Printed in Volume I of the series *Mémoires sur les Assemblées Parlementaires de la Révolution* (Paris: Picard, 1894), 138.

34 Adrien Duquesnoy, "Entry for 23 August, 1789," *Journal sur L'Assemblée Constituante* (Paris: Picard, 1894), 311–12.

35 James H. Billington, *Fire in the Minds of Men* (New York: Basic Books, 1980), 27.

Chapter 2 Division: The King's Right Hand, the Hunter's Left

1 Most of the descriptions of the *Manège* and environs come from J.M. Thompson, *The French Revolution* (Oxford: Basil Blackwell, 1966), 103–4.

2 François Furet, *Interpreting the French Revolution* (Cambridge: Cambridge University Press, 1981), 157.

3 Neil Hertz, "The Pre-eminence of the Right Hand: A Study in Religious Polarity," in Rodney Needham, *Right and Left, Essays in Dual Symbolic Classification* (Chicago: University of Chicago Press), 3.

4 Ibid., 80.

5 Ira Solomon Wile, *Handedness, and Left and Right* (Boston: Lothrop, Lee, and Shepard, 1934), 301.

6 Ibid., 302.

7 Morris Berman, *Coming to Our Senses* (New York: Simon and Schuster, 1989), 71.

8 Ibid., 72.

9 Ibid., 71.

10 William McNeill, *The Rise of the West* (Chicago: Mentor, 1965), 145.

11 Berman, *Coming to Our Senses*, 69–71.

12 Mircea Eliade, *A History of Religious Ideas* (Chicago: University of Chicago Press, 1970), vol. I, 3.

13 Wile, *Handedness*, 194–95.

14 Hertz, "The Pre-eminence of the Right Hand," 21.

15 Wile, *Handedness*, 46.

16 C. Kerenyi, "Prologomena" in C.G. Jung and C. Kerenyi, *Essays on a Science of Mythology* (New York: Bollingen Series xxii, 1949), 19–20.

17 Wile, *Handedness*, 301.

18 Hertz, "The Pre-eminence of the Right Hand," 13.

19 Ibid., 11–12.

20 Berman, *Coming to Our Senses*, 77.

21 Denis Sinor, ed., *The Cambridge History of Early Inner Asia* (Cambridge: Cambridge University Press, 1990), 95.

22 Ibid., 89.

23 "Shamanism," *Encyclopedia Britannica*, 15th edition, vol. 16, 638.

24 Mircea Eliade, *Shamanism* (Princeton, NJ: Princeton University Press, 1972), 393–94.

25 Joseph Campbell, *The Masks of God: Primitive Mythology* (New York: Viking

Press, 1959), 471. These rubrics, only partially stable, are the brain-child of William James. Campbell calls the "tender-minded" progressive; Bertrand Russell gives him a descent via Rousseau to Hitler.

26 Sinor, *Early Inner Asia*, 68.

27 Olivia Vlahos, *The Battle Axe People* (New York: Viking Press, 1968), 14. See also Campbell, *Primitive Mythology*, 3.

28 For an approximation of the origins and homeland of the Indo-Europeans I have drawn on Colin McEvedy, *The Penguin Atlas of Ancient History* (London: Penguin, 1967), 20–21; E.D. Phillips, *The Royal Hordes: Nomadic People of the Steppes* (New York: McGraw Hill, 1965), 39; and Colin Renfrew, *The Puzzle of Indo-European Origins* (New York: Cambridge University Press, 1988), 97, 205.

29 Vlahos, *The Battle Axe People*, 16.

30 Eliade, *Shamanism*, 470–72; "Shamanism," *Encyclopedia Britannica*, 15th ed., vol. 16, 638.

31 Joseph Campbell, *The Masks of God: Occidental Mythology* (New York: Penguin, 1976), 26–27.

32 See Neal Ascherson, *Black Sea* (London: Jonathan Cape, 1995), 115–17.

33 Eliade, *Shamanism*, 378–79.

34 Mary Boyce, *The Zoroastrians: Their Religious Beliefs and Practices* (London: Routledge and Kegan Paul, 1979), 10.

35 Ibid., 2–3.

36 Norman Cohn, *Cosmos, Chaos and the World to Come* (New Haven: Yale University Press, 1993), 68.

37 See Boyce, *Zoroastrianism*, 8–9.

38 Ibid., 6.

39 See V.G. Childe, *The Aryans* (New York: Barnes and Noble, 1993), 3.

40 The connection between Tunguso-Manchurian *saman* and Sanskrit *sramana* would seem to lie somewhere among Tocharian, Turkic, or even Mongolian carriers of Indo-European language and practices.

41 Wile, *Handedness*, 48.

42 Ibid., 49.

43 The periods and means of Indo-European expansion are still debated. For a skeptical view, see Renfrew, *The Puzzle of Indo-European Origins*.

44 For references here to the Mitanni I rely on Vlahos, *The Battle Axe People*, 18–19.

45 Ibid., 69.

46 E.D. Phillips, *The Royal Hordes: Nomad People of the Steppes* (New York: McGraw Hill, 1965), 47.

47 The visions suggest a paleolithic Shamanic provenance. Boyce, *Zoroastrianism*, 17–18.

48 In 1700–1500 BCE, according to Boyce, *Zoroastrianism*, 2.

49 Ibid., 20.

50 Eliade, *Shamanism*, 399–400.

51 Wile, *Handedness*, 320–21.

52 See Cohn, *Cosmos, Chaos*, 222.

53 Ibid. 222.

54 McNeill, *The Rise of the West*, 171.

55 Kerenyi, "Prologomena," 20.

56 Wile, *Handedness*, 316.

57 Arthur Evans, *The God of Ecstasy* (New York: St. Martin's Press, 1988), 141.

58 Eliade, *Shamanism*, 376. See also M.E. Pelokaan-Engel, *Hesiod and Parmenides* (Amsterdam: Adolf Hakkert, 1874), 64.

59 T.J. Dunbabin, *The Western Greeks* (London: Oxford University Press, 1968), 42; for shamanism in south Italy, see W.K.C. Guthrie, *A History of Greek Philosophy*, vol. II (Cambridge: Cambridge University Press, 1965).

60 Colin McEvedy, *The Penguin Atlas of Ancient History* (New York: Penguin, 1986), 28.

61 Arthur Koestler, *The Sleepwalkers* (London: Hutchinson, 1959), 37.

62 Bertrand Russell, *History of Western Philosophy* (New York: Simon and Schuster, 1972), 34–35.

63 S. Moscati, *Ancient Semitic Civilisations* (London: Elek Books, 1957), 38.

64 Ibid., 35.

65 Sinor Dubnov, *History of the Jews* (New York: South Brunswick, 1967), 99–100.

66 John Garraty and Peter Gay, *The Columbia History of the World* (New York: Harper and Row, 1972), 142.

67 Wile, *Handedness*, 37.

68 Ibid.

69 Eliade, *A History of Religious Ideas*, vol. I, 150.

70 Ibid., 167.

71 McNeill, *The Rise of the West*, 176.

Chapter 3 Logos: The Paris Quarter and the Flux of Heraclitus

1 J.M. Thompson, *The French Revolution* (Oxford: Basil Blackwell, 1966), 228.

2 Alfred Cobban, *A History of Modern France*, vol. 1 (Harmondsworth: Penguin, 1963), 178.

3 Thompson, *The French Revolution*, 102.

4 Crane Brinton, *A Decade of Revolution* (New York: Harper and Row, 1963), 15.

5 Simon Schama, *Citizens: A Chronicle of the French Revolution* (Toronto: Vintage Books, 1989), 479.

6 Thompson, *The French Revolution*, 231.

7 François Furet, *Interpreting the French Revolution* (London: Cambridge University Press, 1981), 25–26.

8 Norman Hampson, *The Life and Opinions of Maximilien Robespierre* (London: Duckworth, 1974), 203–4.

9 Alfred Cobban, *The Social Interpretation of the French Revolution* (London: Cambridge University Press, 1964), 66–67.

10 Ibid., 65–66.

11 Ibid., 153, 172.

12 Ibid., 65–66.

13 The poor, of course, have hardly been served by Left or Right; they have fallen under the label of degeneracy under communism and fascism, of charity under capitalism, and of perpetual welfare under socialism and social democracy.

14 Emmanuel Todd, *The Explanation of Ideology* (Oxford: Basil Blackwell, 1985), 15.

15 Individualistic egalitarianism does sit in contradistinction to Middle Eastern and East Asian cultures which were — and are — collective rather than individualistic; and if they have an egalitarian aspect, that, too, is hierarchical and collective.

16 Albert Babeau, *Paris en 1789* (Paris: Editions Albin Michel, 1989), 44.

17 See Georges Rudé, *Ideology and Popular Protest* (New York: Pantheon Books, 1980), 109–10.

18 Minogue, *Alien Powers*, 167.

19 William Blake, *The Marriage of Heaven and Hell* (Plymouth: McDonald and Evans, 1970), 60ff.

20 Hannah Arendt, "Truth and Politics" in *Between Past and Future* (Harmondsworth: Penguin, 1980), 259.

21 Edvard Zeller, *A History of Greek Philosophy* (New York: Dover, 1950), 103.

22 Friedrich Nietzsche, *Ecce Homo* (Harmondsworth: Penguin, 1983), 81.

23 George Woodcock, *Anarchism* (New York: New American Library, 1962), 30.

24 Friedrich Nietzsche, "Early Greek Philosophy and Other Essays," from Geoffrey Clive, ed., *The Philosophy of Nietzsche* (New York: Mentor, 1965), 154.

25 Joseph Campbell, *The Masks of God: Creative Mythology* (New York: Penguin, 1976), 427.

26 Henry B. Parkes, *Gods and Men* (New York: Vintage, 1965), 188.

27 Frederick Copplestone, *History of Philosophy*, vol. I, Part 1 (New York: Doubleday, 1962), 59.

28 Schama, *Citizens*, 448.

29 Crane Brinton, *A History of Western Morals* (New York: Paragon House, 1990), 34.

30 About public and private in ancient Greece and in modern times, see Hannah Arendt, *The Human Condition*, Part II (Chicago: University of Chicago Press, 1958).

31 See Furet, *Interpreting the French Revolution*.

32 Aristotle, *Politics*, in Abernathy and Langford, *History of Philosophy* (Belmont, California: Dickenson, 1966), 176.

33 Nicholas R.E. Fisher, *Social Values in Classical Athens* (Toronto: Hakkert, 1976), 1.

34 Hannah Arendt, *The Human Condition*, 56.

35 John Garraty and Peter Gay, *The Columbia History of the World* (New York: Harper and Row, 1972) 160–61.

36 Brinton, *A History of Western Morals*, 76.

37 Raphael Sealey, *A History of the Greek City States* (Berkeley: University of California Press, 1976), 297–98, 303.

38 Ibid.

39 Aristotle, *Politics*, 177.

40 Martin Buber, *Between Man and Man* (Toronto: Macmillan, 1947), 157.

41 Richard Sennett, *The Fall of Public Man*, 89.

42 James H. Billington, *Fire in the Minds of Men* (New York: Basic Books, 1980), 54.

43 Ibid., 22.

Chapter 4 Polarity: Being and Not Being a Jacobin

1 Alexandre de Lameth, quoted in J. Bronowski and Bruce Mazlisch, *The Western Intellectual Tradition* (New York: Harper and Row, 1960), 405.

2 J.M. Thompson, *The French Revolution* (Oxford: Basil Blackwell, 1966), 320.

3 Michael L. Kennedy, *The Jacobins in the French Revolution* (Princeton, NJ: Princeton University Press,1988), 196.

4 Thompson, *The French Revolution*, 320.

5 Alfred Cobban, *The Social Interpretation of the French Revolution* (London: Cambridge University Press, 1964), 64.

6 See Crane Brinton, *A Decade of Revolution* (New York: Harper and Row, 1963), 111.

7 Cobban, *The Social Interpretation*, 64.

8 See Brinton, *A Decade of Revolution*, 111.

9 Maximilien Robespierre, quoted in Georges Rudé, *Robespierre: Portrait of a Revolutionary Democrat* (New York: Viking Press, 1975), 131–32.

10 Thomas Dunbabin, *The Western Greeks* (Oxford: Clarendon, 1948), 42.

11 James H. Billington, *Fire in the Minds of Men* (New York: Basic Books, 1980), 91–107.

12 Friedrich Nietzsche, "Early Greek Philosophy" in Geoffery Clive, ed., *The Philosophy of Nietzsche* (New York: Mentor, 1965), 177.

13 See William K. Guthrie, *A History of Greek Philosophy*, vol. II (Cambridge: Cambridge University Press, 1965), 11.

14 Carl Jung, "Psychological Typology," in Anthony Storr, ed., *The Essential Jung* (Princeton: Princeton University Press, 1983), 136–37.

15 See George Steiner, *Heidegger* (New York: Fontana, 1978), 53.

16 "Dualism," *The Encyclopedia Britannica*, 15th edition, vol. V. (1982), 1070.

17 Bertrand Russell, *A History of Western Philosophy* (New York: Simon and Schuster, 1972), 34–35.

18 Plato, *The Republic*, Book 7 (Harmondsworth: Penguin, 1974), 342.

19 Russell, *A History of Western Philosophy*, 92–93.

20 Henry D.P. Lee, *Zeno of Elea* (Cambridge: The University Press, 1936), 116.

21 Alfred Cobban, *A History of Modern France*, vol. 2 (Harmondsworth: Penguin, 1963), 232.

22 "Dualism," *Encyclopedia Britannica*, 1070. (author's emphasis)

23 François Furet, *Interpreting the French Revolution* (Cambridge: Cambridge University Press, 1981), 52–53.

24 Ibid., 184–85.

25 See Cobban, *Social Interpretation*, 232; and Brinton, *A Decade of Revolution*, 157.

26 Furet, *Interpreting the French Revolution*, 187–88.

27 Friedrich Nietzsche, *Ecce Homo* (Harmondsworth: Penguin, 1983), 46.

28 Brinton, *A Decade of Revolution*, 121.

29 Simon Schama, *Citizens: A Chronicle of the French Revolution* (Toronto: Vintage Books, 1989), 492.

30 Furet, *Interpreting the French Revolution*, 25–26.

31 Thompson, *The French Revolution*, 374.

Chapter 5 Symmetry: The Republic of Terror and Plato's Republic

1 Bertrand Russell, *A History of Western Philosophy* (New York: Simon and Schuster, 1945), 101.

2 Alfred Cobban, *A History of Modern France*, vol. 1 (Harmondsworth: Penguin, 1963), 179.

3 Jean Matrat, *Robespierre* (New York: Scribner's, 1971), 17.

4 François Furet, *Interpreting the French Revolution* (Cambridge: Cambridge University Press, 1981), 129.

5 Plutarch, "Life of Lycurgus" in *Lives* (New York: J.M. Dent and Sons, 1957), 66–67.

6 Ibid., 84.

7 Albert Camus, *The Rebel* (New York: Random House, 1956), 39.

8 Russell, *A History of Western Philosophy*, 91.

9 Friedrich Nietzsche, *Beyond Good and Evil* (Harmondsworth: Penguin, 1983), 104.

10 John Garraty and Peter Gay, *The Columbia History of the World* (New York: Harper and Row, 1972), 160.

11 Charles Louis, Baron de Montesquieu, *Lettres persanes*, quoted in Hampson, *Will and Circumstance*, 5.

12 Mary Boyce, *Zoroastrians, Their Religious Beliefs and Practices* (London: Routledge & Kegan Paul, 1979), 7.

13 Plato, *The Republic*, Book II, Part II, Preliminaries, Desmond Lee trans., (Harmondsworth: Penguin, 1983), 117.

14 Plato, *The Laws*, in George Abernethy and Thomas Langford, *History of Philosophy* (Belmont, California: Dickenson, 1966), 111.

15 Plato, *The Republic*, Book V, Part VI, "Women and the Family," in Abernethy and Langford, *History of Philosophy*, 237.

16 Ibid., Book VIII, 361–62.

17 Aristotle, *The Metaphysics*, in Abernethy and Langford, *History of Philosophy*, 131.

18 Plato, *The Parmenides*, in Abernethy and Langford, *History of Philosophy*, 101.

19 Russell, *A History of Western Philosophy*, 159.

20 Plato, *The Meno*, in Abernethy and Langford, *History of Philosophy*, 96.

21 Plato, *The Republic*, Book X.

22 Carl Jung, "Psychological Typology," *The Essential Jung* (Princeton, NJ: Princeton University Press, 1983), 136–37.

23 Furet, *Interpreting the French Revolution*, 129.

24 Crane Brinton, *A Decade of Revolution* (New York: Harper and Row, 1963), 136.

25 R.R. Palmer, *Twelve Who Ruled* (Princeton, NJ: Princeton University Press, 1958), 277.

26 St. Just to the Convention, 26 February 1794. St. Just, the ideologue of the Jacobins.

27 Hannah Arendt, *Between Past and Future* (New York: Viking Press, 1968), 130.

28 Plato, *The Republic*, Book X, 448.

29 Arendt, *Between Past and Future*, 111.

30 Furet, *Interpreting the French Revolution*, 53.

31 Ibid., 128.

32 Karl Jaspers, *The Great Philosophers* (New York: Harcourt, Brace and World, 1966), vol. II, 32.

33 Martin Heidegger, "Letter on Humanism," *Martin Heidegger: Basic Writings* (New York: Harper and Row, 1977), 208.

34 J. Needham, *Science and Civilization in China*, quoted in Fritjof Capra, *The Tao of Physics* (London: Fontana, 1983), 320.

Chapter 6 Singularity: Bonaparte, Aeneas, and the Power of the Past

1 Julian Marias, *History of Philosophy* (New York: Dover, 1966), 309.

2 Ibid., 308–9.

3 See A. Alfoldi, *Early Rome and the Latins* (Michigan: University of Michigan Press, 1963), 2.

4 The Ionic-Latin duality is elucidated in Christopher Dawson, *The Dynamics of World History* (New York: New American Library, 1962), 156.

5 H.G. Wells, *A Short History of the World* (Harmondsworth: Penguin, 1965), 120–21.

6 Shan M. Winn, *Heaven, Heroes and Happiness: The Indo-European Roots of Western Ideology* (Lanham, Md.: University Press of America, 1995,) 82.

7 Alfoldi, *Early Rome and the Latins*, 6.

8 These migrations to Italy are mentioned in Alfoldi, *Early Rome and the Latins*, 1–6; and in V.G. Childe, *The Aryans: A Study of Indo-European Origins* (New York: Knopf, 1926).

9 P.F.M. Fontaine, *The Light and the Dark: A Cultural History of Dualism*, vol. X, (Amsterdam: J.C. Gieben, 1986), 31.

10 See James Frazer, *The Golden Bough* (New York: Macmillan, 1951), 3.

11 Mircea Eliade, *A History of Religious Ideas*, vol. 2 (Chicago: University of Chicago Press, 1970), 110–11.

12 Ibid., 114.

13 Fontaine, *The Light and the Dark*, vol. XI, 15.

14 Ibid., 16.

15 Crane Brinton, *A Decade of Revolution* (New York: Harper and Row, 1963), 216.

16 Ibid., 244.

17 Northrop Frye, *The Great Code* (Toronto: Academic Press Canada, 1983), 9.

18 Henry Bamford Parkes, *Gods and Men* (New York: Random House, 1965), 271.

19 Parkes, *Gods and Men*, 314.

20 Napoleon, *Proclamation to the French People*, in J. Bronowski and Bruce Mazlisch, *The Western Intellectual Tradition* (New York: Harper and Row, 1960), 411.

21 Octave Aubrey, *Napoléon* (New York: Crown Publishers, 1961), 70.

22 Bronowski and Mazlisch, *The Western Intellectual Tradition*, 411.

23 R.R. Palmer and Joel Coulton, *A History of the World to 1815* (New York: McGraw Hill, 1984), 389.

24 Bronowski and Mazlisch, *The Western Intellectual Tradition*, 413.

Chapter 7 Asymmetry: Labour, Slaves, and Paupers in England and Rome

1 Bob Goudzwaard, *Capitalism and Progress* (Toronto: Wedge Publishing, 1979), 62, 64–66.

2 Ibid., 19–23.

3 Alan MacFarlane, "The Root of All Evil," in David Parkin, *The Anthropology of Evil* (New York: Basil Blackwell, 1985), 71–72.

4 Max Weber, "The Protestant Sects and the Spirit of Capitalism," in *From Max Weber, Essays in Sociology* (New York: Oxford University Press, 1946), 283.

5 Winker Setton, ed., *Great Problems in European Civilization* (Englewood Cliffs, NJ: Prentice Hall, 1966), 397.

6 See John Passmore, *The Perfectibility of Man* (London: Cox and Wyman, 1972), 169.

7 Hugh Thomas, *A History of the World* (New York: Harper and Row, 1979), 129.

8 Crane Brinton, *Ideas and Men* (Englewood Cliffs, NJ: Prentice Hall, 1963), 77.

9 See Mircea Eliade, *A History of Religious Ideas*, vol. 2 (Chicago: University of Chicago Press, 1985), 269.

10 Elaine Pagels, *The Origin of Satan* (New York: Random House, 1998), 39.

11 Psalms, 109: 31.

12 Christopher Dawson, *The Dynamics of World History* (New York: New American Library, 1962), 251.

13 Eliade, *A History of Religious Ideas*, 269.

14 Norman Cohn, *Cosmos, Chaos and the World to Come* (London: Yale University Press, 1993), 225. See also Joseph Campbell, *The Masks of God: Occidental Mythology* (New York: Penguin, 1976), 258–68.

15 See also Cohn, *Cosmos, Chaos*, 222.

16 Eliade, *A History of Religious Ideas*, 269.

17 See H.G. Wells, *A Short History of the World* (Harmondsworth: Penguin, 1967), 282.

18 Dionysius Halicarnensis, quoted in P.M.F. Fontaine, *The Light and the Dark: A Cultural History of Dualism*, vol. XI (Amsterdam: J.C. Gieben, 1986).

19 Similarly, the republican freedom secured in 1792 laid bare painful class realities previously suppressed or modified by the organic complex of rights and obligations under feudalism.

20 Pierre Grimal, *The Civilization of Rome* (New York: Simon and Schuster, 1963), 99–100.

21 Fontaine, *The Light and the Dark*, 5.

22 H.H. Scullard, *Roman Politics, 220–150 BC* (Oxford: Clarendon Press, 1951), 55.

23 On political violence in Rome, see Stringfellow Barr, *The Mask of Jove* (New York: Lippincott, 1966), 111.

24 Julian Marias, *History of Philosophy* (New York: Dover, 1966), 372–73.

25 Judges, 5: 26; Psalms, 17: 7; Psalms, 16: 11; Job, 40: 14; Jeremiah, 22: 24; Deut., 33: 2; Ezekiel, 39: 3; Proverbs, 4:16.

26 Carl Jung, *Answer to Job* (Cleveland: World Publishing, 1968), 55.

27 R.R. Palmer and Joel Coulton, *A History of the World to 1815* (New York: McGraw Hill, 1984), 435–36.

28 John Garraty and Peter Gay, *The Columbia History of the World* (New York: Harper and Row, 1972), 832, 886.

29 Bertrand Russell, *A History of Western Philosophy* (New York: Simon and Schuster, 1945), 781.

30 See Kenneth Minogue, *Alien Powers* (London: Weidenfeld and Nicholson, 1985), 218.

31 J.S. Mill, "On Liberty," in Carl Cohen, *Communism, Fascism and Democracy* (New York: Random House, 1967), 550.

32 J. Bronowski and Bruce Mazlisch, *The Western Intellectual Tradition* (New York: Harper and Row, 1960), 463.

33 See Brinton, *Ideas and Men*, 365–66.

Chapter 8   Universality: Time and Order

1 Jack Lindsay, *A Short History of Culture from Prehistory to the Renaissance* (London: Studio Books), 206.

2 Elaine Pagels, *The Origin of Satan* (New York: Random House, 1995), 181.

3 J. Bronowski and Bruce Mazlisch, *The Western Intellectual Tradition* (New York: Harper and Row, 1960), 411.

4 T.Z. Lavine, *From Plato to Sartre* (New York: Bantam, 1984), 247.

5 G.W.F. Hegel, "Philosophical History," in Saxe Commins and Robert Linscott, eds., *The World's Great Thinkers: Man and State* (New York: Random House, 1966), 418.

6 Bertrand Russell, *A History of Western Philosophy* (New York: Simon and Schuster, 1945), 746.

7 Aristotle, "The Nichomachean Ethics," in Commins and Linscott, *The World's Great Thinkers*, 34.

8 Aristotle, "Politics," in Abernethy and Langford, *History of Philosophy* (Belmont, Cal.: Dickenson, 1966), 178.

9 Aristotle, "The Nichomachean Ethics," in Commins and Linscott, *The World's Great Thinkers*, 4.

10 Aristotle, "Politics," in Abernethy and Langford, *History of Philosophy*, 177.

11 Plato, *The Republic* (Harmondsworth: Penguin, 1983), 433.

12 Fritjof Capra, *The Tao of Physics* (London: Fontana, 1983), 178.

13 Russell, *A History of Western Philosophy*, 36–37.

14 James H. Billington, *Fire in the Minds of Men* (New York: Basic Books, 1980), 58. See also for a fuller account of eighteenth-century Pythagoreanism.

15 George Steiner, *Heidegger* (London: Fontana, 1978), 53.

16 Sidney Hook quoted in Arthur Koestler, *The Roots of Coincidence* (London: Pan Books, 1974), 80.

17 See Norman Cohn, *Cosmos, Chaos and the World to Come* (New Haven: Yale University Press, 1993), 187.

18 P.F.M. Fontaine, *The Light and the Dark: A Cultural History of Dualism*, vol. VIII (Amsterdam: J.C. Gieben, 1986). See his thorough section on dualism in *Philo*, 10–20.

19 Ibid.

20 John Passmore, *The Perfectibility of Man* (London: Cox and Wyman, 1972), 62; Fontaine, *The Light and the Dark*, vol. VIII, *Philo*, 10–20.

21 Ibid.

22 Northrop Frye, *The Great Code* (New York: Harcourt Brace, 1983), 115.

23 Arthur Koestler, *The Roots of Coincidence* (New York: Vintage, 1973), 112–13.

24 Ira Solomon Wile, *Handedness, and Left and Right* (Boston: Lothrop, Lee, and Shepard, 1934), 338.

25 Henry Parkes, *Gods and Men* (New York: Vintage, 1965), 140.

26 See Joseph Campbell, *The Mask of God: Occidental Mythology* (New York: Penguin, 1976), 408–38.

27 Frye, *The Great Code*, 118 and ff.

28 Parkes, *Gods and Men*, 141.

29 Ibid., 310.

30 Lindsay, *A Short History of Culture*, 250.

31 Billington, *Fire in the Minds of Men*, 206–7.

32 See Billington for a general account of Babeuf, Buonarotti, Bonneville, and the resistance to Napoleon.

33 Billington, *Fire in the Minds of Men*, 120–21.

34 Ibid., 91.

35 Ibid., 119.

36 Francis Fukuyama, *The End of History and the Last Man* (Toronto: Macmillan, 1992), 66.

37 Frank Tannenbaum, *Ten Keys to Latin America* (New York: Random House, 1959), 136–37.

38 Fernandez-Armesto, *Millennium* (Toronto: Doubleday Canada, 1995), 337.

39 See George Pendle, *A History of Latin America* (Harmondsworth: Penguin, 1963), 213.

40 H.M. Bailey and A. Nasatir, *Latin America: Its Development and Civilisation* (Englewood Cliffs, NJ: Prentice Hall, 1960), 336.

41 Tannenbaum, *Ten Keys to Latin America*, 148.

42 Parkes, *Gods and Men*, 340.

43 *The Larousse Encyclopedia of Mythology* (London: Batchworth Press, 1959), 326.

44 Cirlot, *A Dictionary of Symbolism*, (New York: Philosophical Library, 1995), 299.

PART TWO   MIXTURE

Chapter 9   Marginality: Romanticism and Gnosticism

1 Paul Johnson, *The Birth of the Modern: World Society, 1815–1830*, 143.
2 J.A. Laponce, *Left and Right, the Topography of Political Perceptions* (Toronto: University of Toronto Press, 1981), 52
3 Martin Buber, *Between Man and Man* (Toronto: Macmillan, 1947), 157.
4 Mircea Eliade, *A History of Religious Ideas*, vol. II (Chicago: University of Chicago Press, 1970), 542–43.
5 "Gnosticism," *Encyclopedia Britannica*, 15th edition, vol. V (Cambridge: The University Press, 1982), 1068.
6 Ibid., 11th edition, vol. XI (Cambridge: The University Press, 1910), 157.
7 Pétrement cautions us here to speak of "Gnostic motifs." See Simone Pétrement, *A Separate God: The Christian Origins of Gnosticism* (New York: Harper and Row, 1990), 25.
8 On the precedence of Gnosticism see also John Passmore, *The Perfectibility of Man* (London: Cox and Wyman, 1972) 83; Mircea Eliade, *A History of Religious Ideas* (Chicago: University of Chicago Press, 1970), 566; James M. Robinson, *The Nag Hammadi Library* (New York: Harper and Row, 1978), 9–10; Hans Jonas, *The Gnostic Religion* (Boston: Beacon Press, 1963), 3.
9 This is a rough outline of the type of the Gnostic myth — of which all the sects had variants. It is drawn from Jonas, *The Gnostic Religion*.
10 See Eliade, *A History of Religious Ideas*, vol. I, 3.
11 Arthur Schopenhauer, "The World as Will and Idea," in Saxe Commins and Robert Linscott, eds., *The World's Great Thinkers: Man and Spirit* (New York: Random House, 1947), 468.
12 Stuart Holroyd, *The Elements of Gnosticism* (Longmead, Dorset: Element Books, 1994), 102.
13 William Blake, *The Book of Urizen*.
14 William Blake, *The Marriage of Heaven and Hell* (Plymouth: MacDonald and Evans, 1970) 60ff.
15 Kenneth Clarke, *The Romantic Rebellion* (Don Mills: Longman, 1973), 48.
16 Michael Bakunin, *The Conquest of Bread*, quoted in George Woodcock, *Anarchism* (New York: New American Library, 1962), 205.
17 Woodcock, *Anarchism*, 107.
18 Pierre Joseph Proudhon, *Economic Contradictions*, in Woodcock, *Anarchism*, 122.
19 David Caute, *The Left in Europe Since 1789* (London: Weidenfeld and Nicholson, 1966), 131.
20 Proudhon, *The General Idea of Revolution*, in Woodcock, *Anarchism*, 134.
21 See James H. Billington, *Fire in the Minds of Men* (New York: Basic Books, 1980), 230.

22 Karl Marx, "Economic and Philosophical Manuscripts: Third Manuscript," in T.B. Bottomore, ed. and trans., *Karl Marx, Early Writings* (New York: McGraw Hill, 1964), 155.

23 Arthur Clutton-Brock in Crane Brinton, *A History of Western Morals* (New York: Paragon House, 1990), 331.

24 Billington, *Fire in the Minds of Men*, 130 ff.

25 See Northrop Frye, *The Great Code*, Chap. 7, Myth II (Toronto: Academic Press, 1982), 169.

26 Henry B. Parkes, *Gods and Men* (New York, Vintage, 1965), 121–22.

27 Billington, *Fire in the Minds of Men*, 132ff.

28 Ibid., 144.

29 Georges Duveau, *1848: The Making of a Revolution* (New York: Random House, 1967), 86.

30 The trade distinctions of *mécanicien*, *bonnetière*, and *ébéniste* can be found in Duveau, *1848*.

31 Karl Marx, quoted in Duveau, *1848*, xix.

Chapter 10   Perfection: Marx and Christ

1 Karl Marx and Alexis de Tocqueville, quoted in Georges Rudé, *Ideology and Popular Protest* (New York: Pantheon Books, 1980), 125.

2 David Thomson, *Europe Since Napoleon* (Harmondsworth: Penguin, 1966), 234.

3 Georges Duveau, *1848: The Making of a Revolution* (New York: Random House, 1967), 120.

4 Alexis de Tocqueville, *Recollections* (London: H. Henry and Co., 1895), 187.

5 See David Caute, *The Left in Europe Since 1789* (London: Weidenfeld and Nicholson, 1966), 172.

6 See Duveau, *The Making of a Revolution*, 81–82.

7 Ibid., 176.

8 Karl Marx and Friedrich Engels, "The German Ideology," in L.S. Feuer, ed., *Marx and Engels, Basic Writings on Politics and Philosophy* (New York: Doubleday, 1959), 254.

9 John Passmore, *The Perfectibility of Man* (London: Cox and Wyman, 1972), 237.

10 Karl Marx, *The Communist Manifesto*, in L.S. Feuer, ed., *Marx and Engels, Basic Writings on Politics and Philosophy* (New York: Doubleday, 1959), 7, fn. 2.

11 See Hannah Arendt, *The Human Condition* (Chicago: University of Chicago Press, 1958), 111.

12 Gunnar Myrdal, *The Political Element in the Development of Economic Theory* (London: Routledge and Kegan Paul, 1953), 78.

13 Eric Voegelin, *From Enlightenment to Revolution* (Durham: Duke University Press, 1975), 243.

14 Marx, *Capital*, vol. I, Chap. 22, "Historical Tendency of Capitalist Accumulation," in *The Modern World* (New York: Macmillan, 1963), 14.

15 Arendt, *The Human Condition*, 44–45.

16 Bob Goudzwaard, *Capitalism and Progress* (Toronto: Wedge Publishing, 1979), 78–79.

17 See Henry Parkes, *Gods and Men* (New York: Vintage, 1965), 142.

18 Northrop Frye, *The Great Code* (Toronto: Academic Press, 1982).

19 Christopher Dawson, *The Dynamics of World History* (New York: Mentor, 1962), 349.

20 Robert Nisbet, *History of the Idea of Progress* (New York: Basic Books, 1970), 184–86.

21 Albert Camus, *The Rebel* (New York: Random House, 1956), 208 ; see also Nisbet, *History of the Idea of Progress*, 251.

22 Jeremiah 7: 31–32.

23 *The Community Rule of the Essenes*, quoted in Norman Cohn, *Cosmos, Chaos and the World to Come* (New Haven: Yale University Press, 1993), 190; also see P.M.F. Fontaine, *The Light and the Dark*, VII, (Amsterdam: J.C. Gieben, 1986), 220.

24 Cohn, *Cosmos, Chaos*, 193; and Fontaine, *The Light and the Dark*, 221–22.

25 Elaine Pagels, *The Origin of Satan* (New York: Random House, 1995), 56; and Fontaine, *The Light and the Dark*, 238.

26 Cohn, *Cosmos, Chaos*, 226.

27 Ibid., 204; Gnostic terms used in the New Testament are listed in Fontaine, *The Light and the Dark*, 177–85.

28 Luke 12: 51–55.

29 Matthew 12: 30–71.

30 Frye, *The Great Code*, 159.

31 Pagels, *The Origin of Satan*, 11–12.

32 Fontaine, despite controversy, detects the same John as the author of New Testament writings attributed to "John." I am taking Fontaine's word; see Fontaine, vol. VII, 150. See also Cohn, *Cosmos, Chaos*, 226.

33 George Arthur Buttrick, ed., *The Interpreter's Dictionary of the Bible*, article on Psalms, vol. 3, 942.

34 See Buttrick, ed., *Interpreter's Dictionary of the Bible*, for disposition of the throne of David and the cardinal points.

35 The early Christian hand symbolism is from Ira Solomon Wile, *Handedness, and Left and Right* (Boston: Lothrop, Lee, and Shepard), 315.

36 See Campbell, *Occidental Mythology*, 379; Parkes, *Gods and Men*, 407; and St. Paul, Letter to the Ephesians, 6:12; Galatians, 3.

37 James H. Billington, *Fire in the Minds of Men* (New York: Basic Books, 1980), 76.

38 Marx, *The Class Struggles in France*, in Feuer, ed., *Marx and Engels*, 317; and Billington, ibid., 283.

39 See Frye, *The Great Code*, 114.

40 Charles Taylor, *Sources of the Self* (Cambridge, Mass: Harvard University Press, 1989), 339–40.

41 Camus, *The Rebel*, 209.

42 Gabriel Sivan, *The Bible and Civilization* (New York: New York Times Books, 1973), 86–93.

43 These are the devices that make up the biblical "code" elucidated in Frye's *The Great Code*.

44 Friedrich Nietzsche, *Beyond Good and Evil* (New York: Random House, 1966), 157.

45 Crane Brinton, *A History of Western Morals* (New York: Paragon House, 1990), 61.

46 Hannah Arendt, *Between Past and Future* (Harmondsworth: Penguin, 1980), 65.

47 Carl Jung, "Problems of Alchemy," in *The Essential Jung* (Princeton, NJ: Princeton University Press), 265–69.

48 R.C. Tucker, *Philosophy and Myth in Karl Marx* (Cambridge: Cambridge University Press, 1961), 219.

49 Friedrich Engels, "The End of Classical German Philosophy," in Feuer, ed., *Marx and Engels*, 241.

50 Marx, "Toward the Critique of Hegel's Philosophy of Right" in Feuer, ed., *Marx and Engels*, 262.

51 Eric Voegelin, *Science, Politics and Gnosticism* (Chicago: Henry Regnery, 1968), 24–26.

52 Marx, "Manifesto of the Communist Party," in Feuer, ed., *Marx and Engels*, 499.

53 Camus, *The Rebel*, 202.

54 Marx and Engels, "The German Ideology," in Feuer, ed., *Marx and Engels*, 247.

55 See Marx, "Manifesto of the Communist Party," in Feuer, ed., *Marx and Engels*, 24.

56 Marx, "The Method of German Philosophy" in Feuer, ed., *Marx and Engels*, 261.

57 See Marx, *Communist Manifesto*, in Feuer, ed., *Marx and Engels*, 515.

58 Tucker, *Philosophy and Myth in Karl Marx*, 114.

59 Samuel Brittan, *Left or Right: The Bogus Dilemma* (London: Secker and Warburg, 1968), 299.

60 A.L. Chickering, *Beyond Left and Right: Breaking the Political Stalemate* (San Francisco, California: ICS Press, 1993), 37.

Chapter 11   Secession: Anarchists and Heretics

1 Charles Baudelaire, "Petits Poèmes en Prose," quoted in F.W. Hemmings, *Baudelaire the Damned* (London: Hamish Hamilton, 1982).

2 David Thomson, *Europe Since Napoleon* (Harmondsworth: Penguin, 1966), 454.

3 David Caute, *The Left in Europe* (London: World University Library, 1966), 60.

4 Ibid., 80–81.

5 See Samuel Brittan, *Left or Right: The Bogus Dilemma* (London: Secker and Warburg, 1968), 164.

6 David Thomson, *England in the Nineteenth Century* (Harmondsworth: Pelican, 1970), 121.

7 Ibid., 136.

8 Ibid., 202–3.

9 See J.A. Laponce, *Left and Right: The Topography of Political Perceptions* (Toronto: University of Toronto Press, 1981).

10 Arthur Herman, *The Idea of Decline in Western History* (New York: The Free Press, 1997), 89.

11 William McNeill, *The Rise of the West* (New York: Mentor, 1965), 416.

12 See Arthur Koestler, *The Sleepwalkers* (London: Hutchinson, 1959), 85.

13 See Carl Jung, *Psychological Types*, Bollingen Series XX (Princeton, NJ: Princeton University Press, 1977), 15.

14 For a more detailed breakdown see Georges Rudé, *Ideology and Popular Protest* (New York: Pantheon Books, 1980), 128.

15 Roberto Calasso, *The Ruin of Kasch* (Cambridge, Mass.: Belknap Press, 1994), 269.

16 James Billington, *Fire in the Minds of Men* (London: World University Library, 1966), 354.

17 Friedrich Nietzsche, "Thoughts out of Season," vol. II, in Geoffrey Clive, ed., *The Philosophy of Nietzsche* (New York: Mentor, 1965), 346–47.

18 Herman, *The Idea of Decline in Western History*, 33.

19 The adherence to ideologies for trivial reasons is an observation of the social scientist Graham Wallas (1858–1932).

20 Nietzsche, *Thoughts out of Season*, 347.

21 Calasso, *The Ruin of Kasch*, 259–60, 278.

22 Ibid., 274.

23 T.B. Strong, "Weber and the Bourgeoisie," in Asher Horowitz and Terry Maley, eds., *The Barbarism of Reason: Max Weber and the Twilight of Enlightenment* (Toronto: University of Toronto Press, 1994), 121.

24 Hannah Arendt, *The Human Condition* (Chicago: University of Chicago Press, 1958), 40.

25 Gaetano Mosca, "The Ruling Class," in Michael Curtis, *The Great Political Theories* (New York: Avon Books, 1962), vol. 2, 303. See also Curtis, *The Great Political Theories*. Other elitist thinkers excerpted are Vilfredo Pareto and Gaetano Mosca.

26 Søren Kierkegaard, *The Present Age* (New York: Harper and Row, 1962), 63.

27 Hans Jonas, *The Gnostic Religion* (Boston: Beacon Press, 1963), 325–26.

28 Ibid., 326.

29 John Carroll, *Break-out from the Crystal Palace* (London: Routledge and Kegan Paul, 1974), 14.

30 Jonas, *The Gnostic Religion*, 330.

31 Søren Kierkegaard, "That Individual," quoted in Walter Kaufman, *Existentialism from Dostoevsky to Sartre* (New York: World Publishing, 1956), 93.

32 Nietzsche, *Thoughts out of Season*, 353.

33 Ibid., 350.

34 Keith Ansell-Pearson, *An Introduction to Nietzsche as a Political Thinker* (Cambridge, England: Cambridge University Press, 1994), 87–88.

35 Much of Nietzsche's critique of capitalism and socialism is to be found in "The Wanderer," Part II of *Human, All Too Human*. See, for example, sections 22, 218, 285.

36 Albert Camus, *The Rebel* (New York: Random House, 1956), 77.

37 Friedrich Nietzsche, *Ecce Homo* (Harmondsworth: Penguin, 1983), 126.

38 Charles Baudelaire, *Intimate Journals*, vii (London: Black Spring Press, 1989), 51.

39 Christopher Isherwood, in translator's preface to Baudelaire, *Intimate Journals*.

40 Carroll, *Break-out from the Crystal Palace*, 166.

41 Alex DeJong, Baudelaire, *Prince of Clouds* (New York: Paddington Press, 1976), 91.

42 See Charles Taylor, *Sources of the Self* (Cambridge, Mass.: Harvard University Press, 1989), 438–39.

43 We find a similar but less marginal subversiveness in Oscar Wilde: Baudelaire was a literary *Lumpen* and bourgeois *déclassé*; while Wilde's frank depiction of ritual and artificiality is presented from a point of view safely within the middle class; and his homosexuality, which he attempted to deny at the last moment, cannot really be counted as part of the same act of subversion.

44 A feature in Baudelaire that Sartre fails to see, ignoring as he does the gnostic variants of Platonism; see Jean-Paul Sartre, *Baudelaire*, trans. Martin Turrell (New York: New Directions, 1950), 179–81.

45 Feodor Dostoevsky, *Notes from the Underground* (Harmondsworth: Penguin, 1986). For a crystalline portrait of the *Lumpen petit bourgeois*, rootless, humiliated, and over-educated, see the "underground man's" experience of the Nevsky Prospekt, 55.

46 Calasso, *The Ruin of Kasch*, 270.

47 I owe this idea of an absence of cosmic limits to Calasso, *The Ruin of Kasch*, 268–83. He provides the nice metaphor of a garden whose orderly statuary is overtaken by weeds — though I do not revere the statuary quite as much as he seems to: see Calasso, *The Ruin of Kasch*, 278.

48 See John Garraty and Peter Gay, *The Columbia History of the World* (New York: Harper and Row, 1972), 232.

49 See Elaine Pagels, *The Origin of Satan* (New York: Random House, 1995), 143.

50 Christopher Dawson, *The Dynamics of World History* (New York: New American Library, 1962), 292.

Chapter 12 Totality: Lenin and Augustine

1 Peter Zaichnevsky, "Young Russia," quoted in A.L. Weeks, *The First Bolshevik* (New York: New York University Press, 1968), 29–30.

2 Deborah Hardy, *Petr Tkachev: The Critic as Jacobin* (Seattle: University of Washington Press, 1977), 249; also Weeks, *The First Bolshevik*, 55.

3 "Existentially split in two." P.F.M. Fontaine, *The Light and the Dark: A Cultural History of Dualism*, vol. IX (Amsterdam: J.C. Gieben, 1986), 176.

4 One can't help but think of Baudelaire, who wanted to reunite all the best

fragments of things shattered and separated in the world as opposites, as in Left and Right, Life and Death, Good and Evil. Also, the common spine of the Gnostic myth is paraphrased in Jonas's chapter on Manichaeism in *The Gnostic Religion* (Boston: Beacon Press, 1963).

5 See Charles Taylor, *Sources of the Self* (Cambridge, Mass.: Harvard, 1989), 128–29.

6 Augustine, *The City of God*, Book XIV, in George Abernethy and Thomas Langford, *History of Philosophy* (Belmont, California: Dickinson, 1966), 255–56. Author's emphasis.

7 Ibid.

8 Christopher Dawson, *The Dynamics of World History* (New York: Mentor, 1962), 310.

9 See John Passmore, *The Perfectibility of Man* (London: Cox and Wyman, 1972), 264.

10 See Robert Nisbet, *History of the Idea of Progress* (New York: Basic Books, 1980), 59.

11 Ibid., 74.

12 See Dawson, *The Dynamics of World History*, 295; and Edward Gibbon, *The History of the Decline and Fall of the Roman Empire*, vol. II (London: John Murray, 1855), 304.

13 William McNeill, *The Rise of the West* (New York: Mentor, 1965), 446–47 fn.

14 Cyril Mango, *Byzantium, the Empire of New Rome* (London: Weidenfeld and Nicholson, 1980), 223.

15 Ibid., 38–39.

16 "Gnosticism," *Encyclopedia Britannica*, vol. V, 11th edition (Cambridge: Cambridge University Press, 1910), 157.

17 See Dawson, *The Dynamics of World History*, 294–95.

18 Nicholas Berdyaev, *The Origin of Russian Communism* (Ann Arbor: University of Michigan Press, 1960), 42.

19 Ibid., 45.

20 Herbert Muller, *The Uses of the Past* (New York: Oxford University Press, 1952), 317.

21 Berdyaev, *The Origin of Russian Communism*, 48.

22 Ibid., 60.

23 Weeks, *The First Bolshevik*, 32; and R.W. Clarke, *Lenin, The Man Behind the Mask* (London: Faber and Faber, 1988), 91.

24 Georgi Plekhanov, quoted in Dmitri Volkogonov, *Lenin* (New York: Free Press, 1984), 22. For Lenin's general debt to Blanquiste Jacobinism and to Tkachev, see Weeks, *The First Bolshevik*, 3–7; R.W. Clarke, *Lenin*, 27 and 91; and Berdyaev, *The Origin of Russian Communism*, 73.

25 Volkogonov, *Lenin*, 22.

26 Vladimir Ilich Lenin, "What is to be done?" in Carl Cohen, ed., *Communism, Fascism, and Democracy* (New York: Random House, 1962), 212.

27 Berdyaev, *The Origin of Russian Communism*, 21.

28 R.C. Tucker, *Philosophy and Myth in Karl Marx* (Cambridge: Cambridge University Press, 1961), 22, 23.

29 "Pelagianism," *Encyclopedia Britannica*, vol. XXI, 11th ed., 64.

30 Leo Moulin, *La Gauche, la Droite, et le Péché Originel* (Paris: Librairie des Méridiens, 1984).

31 René Fullop Miller, *Rasputin, the Holy Devil* (Toronto: Viking Press, 1955), 25ff. The traits of the Khlysti sect described by Muller are clearly Gnostic.

32 Quoted in Muller, *The Uses of the Past*, 306.

Chapter 13   Barbarism: Totalitarian, Millenarian

1 Hannah Arendt, *The Origins of Totalitarianism* (New York: World Publishing, 1972), 152.

2 See William McNeill, *The Rise of the West* (New York: Mentor, 1965), 809.

3 John Passmore, *The Perfectibility of Man* (London: Cox and Wyman, 1972), 264.

4 See W.D. Smith, *The Ideological Origins of Nazi Imperialism* (New York: Oxford University Press, 1986), 14.

5 Ibid.

6 See Carl E. Schorske, *Thinking with History* (Princeton, NJ: Princeton University Press, 1998), Chap. 8, 125 ff.

7 Joseph Campbell, *The Masks of God: Occidental Mythology* (New York: Penguin, 1976), 486–87.

8 See *The Larousse Encyclopedia of Mythology* (London: Batchworth Press, 1959), 268.

9 This has been described as Gregory's "political Manichaeism": K.F. Morrison, "Canossa, a Revision," in D.H. Bennett, ed., *Church and State in the Middle Ages* (New York: John Wiley, 1970), 102.

10 Norman Cohn, *The Pursuit of the Millennium* (New York: Harper and Row, 1961), 10.

11 Walter Ullman, *A History of Political Thought: The Middle Ages* (Harmondsworth: Penguin, 1965), 177.

12 R.H. Tawney, *Religion and the Rise of Capitalism* (New York: Mentor, 1963), 38–39.

13 Ibid.

14 Nicholas Berdyaev, *The Origin of Russian Communism* (Ann Arbor: University of Michigan Press, 1960), 169.

15 Lionel Kochan, *The Making of Modern Russia* (Harmondsworth: Penguin, 1970), 18.

16 Ibid., 302.

17 Ibid., 291.

18 Ibid.

19 Maurice Merleau-Ponty, *Humanism and Terror* (Boston: Beacon Press, 1969), 53–54.

20 Ibid., 28.

21 Christopher Dawson, *The Dynamics of World History* (New York: New American Library, 1962), 274.

22 Dante Alighieri, *De Monarchia*, in Michael Curtis, *The Great Political Theories* (New York: Avon Books, 1962), vol. I, 172.

23 Leo Moulin, *La Gauche, la Droite, et le Péché Originel* (Paris: Librairie des Méridiens, 1984), 27.

24 This theme is put forward chiefly by Eric Voegelin. The contribution of Leo Moulin is well founded in Pelagianism but it is cantankerous. Norman Cohn's *The Pursuit of the Millennium* (New York: Harper and Row, 1961) is the most thorough and historical on this point.

25 Cohn, *The Pursuit of the Millennium*, 180.

26 Ibid., 193; Moulin, *La Gauche, la Droite*, 24–25.

27 Cohn, *The Pursuit of the Millennium*, 150.

28 David Thomson, *Europe Since Napoleon* (Harmondsworth: Penguin, 1966), 413.

29 Alfredo Rocco, "The Political Doctrine of Fascism," in C. Cohen, *Communism, Fascism and Democracy* (New York: Random House, 1967), 338.

30 Roger Eatwell, *Fascism: A History* (Harmondsworth: Penguin, 1996), 79.

31 David Caute, *The Left in Europe Since 1789* (London: Weidenfeld and Nicholson, 1966), 69.

32 See Eatwell, *Fascism: A History*, 152.

33 George Steiner, *Bluebeard's Castle* (London: Faber and Faber, 1971), 37, 42; and Sigmund Freud, *Civilization and Its Discontents* (New York: W.W. Norton, 1961), 81.

34 Bernard-Henri Lévy, *Barbarism with a Human Face* (New York: Harper and Row, 1979), 42.

35 Thomas Mann, *Doctor Faustus* (New York: G.E. Putnam's Sons, 1995), 465. An extraordinary passage where the chromatic art of the genius, Leverkuhn (Mann's metaphor for hell-bent Germany) takes on an authentically gnostic megalomania.

36 Adolf Hitler speaking in Munich, May 23, 1928. In Cohen, *Communism, Fascism and Democracy*, 414.

37 Cohn, *The Pursuit of the Millennium*, 309.

38 Eatwell, *Fascism: A History*, 14.

39 Ibid., 117.

40 Alan Bullock, *Hitler and Stalin* (New York: W.W. Norton, 1993), 353.

41 Eatwell, *Fascism: A History*, 125–26.

42 Arendt, *The Origins of Totalitarianism*, 309.

43 Fernandez-Armesto, *Millennium* (Toronto: Doubleday, 1995), 484.

44 Eatwell, *Fascism: A History*, 155. See also the example of the entrepreneur Hjalmar Schacht, 154–55.

45 The view of Friedrich Pollock of the Frankfurt Institute, paraphrased in Martin Jay, *The Dialectical Imagination* (Toronto: Little, Brown, 1973), 154. Jay cites two others, Neumann and Gurland, who on the contrary see monopoly capitalism fully functioning under the Nazis.

46 Adolf Hitler, "Mein Kampf," in Hans Kohn, ed., *The Modern World* (New York: Macmillan, 1963), 215.

47 J.M. Roberts, *The Penguin History of the World* (London: Penguin, 1992), 878.

48 Martin Heidegger, Introduction to "Being and Time" in *Heidegger: Basic Writings* (New York: Harper and Row, 1977), 57.

49 Cohn, *The Pursuit of the Millennium*, 309.

50 Arendt, *The Origins of Totalitarianism*, 345.

51 Emmanuel Todd, *The Explanation of Ideology* (Oxford: Basil Blackwell, 1985), 59ff.

52 Steiner, *Bluebeard's Castle*, 48.

Chapter 14 Liberty: Capitalism and the Rise of the Prince

1 Benjamin R. Barber, *Strong Democracy* (Berkeley: University of California Press, 1984), 4.

2 See William McNeill, *The Rise of the West* (New York: Mentor, 1965), 514; 580–82. I compare Europe to China in chapter 16.

3 Max Weber, "Science as a Vocation," in H.H. Gerth and C. Wright Mills, trans. and eds., *From Max Weber: Essays in Sociology* (New York: Oxford University Press, 1946), 141.

4 Hugh Thomas, *A History of the World* (New York: Harper and Row, 1979); and Norman Cohn, *The Pursuit of the Millennium* (New York: Harper and Row, 1961), 26–27.

5 McNeill, *The Rise of the West*, 514–15.

6 Thomas, *A History of the World*, 186.

7 Ferdinand Braudel, *Civilization and Capitalism* (Berkeley: University of California Press, 1992), 117.

8 Ibid., 128.

9 R.R. Palmer and Joel Coulton, *A History of the World to 1815* (New York: McGraw Hill, 1984), 54.

10 George Grant, *Philosophy in the Mass Age* (Toronto: Copp Clark, 1959), 88, 91.

11 Alexis de Tocqueville, *Democracy in America* (New York: Vintage, 1954), 169.

12 Ibid., 170.

13 Bob Goudzwaard, *Capitalism and Progress* (Toronto: Wedge Publishing, 1979), 79. Goudzwaard's book provides a tidy summary of changes in nineteenth-century American capitalism.

14 See Mark Warren in Asher Horowitz and Terry Maley, eds., *The Barbarism of Reason: Max Weber and the Twilight of Enlightenment* (Toronto: University of Toronto Press, 1994), 78.

15 See Horowitz and Maley, *The Barbarism of Reason*, 15.

16 Tracey Strong, in Horowitz and Maley, *The Barbarism of Reason*, 123.

17 Germain, in Horowitz and Maley, *The Barbarism of Reason*, 261; Max Weber, "Politics as a Vocation," in H.H. Gerth and C. Wright Mills, trans. and eds., *From Max Weber* (New York: Oxford University, 1949), 94.

18 McNeill, *The Rise of the West*, 633.

19 Weber, "Politics as a Vocation," 82.

20 McNeill, *The Rise of the West*, 633.

21 Weber, "Politics as a Vocation," 94.

22 John Garraty and Peter Gay, *The Columbia History of the World* (New York: Harper and Row, 1972), 395.

23 Barbara Tuchman, *A Distant Mirror* (New York: Ballantine Books, 1978), 38.

24 My source on Bohemia and the Taborites is Cohn, *The Pursuit of the Millennium*.

25 Eliot quoted in N. Frye, *T.S. Eliot* (London: Oliver and Boyd, 1968), 8.

26 Francis Fukuyama, *The End of History and the Last Man* (Toronto: Macmillan, 1992), 9.

27 Ibid., 300ff.

28 Eliot quoted in Frye, *T.S. Eliot*, 13.

29 John Maynard Keynes, "My Early Beliefs," in Herbert Kohl, ed., *The Age of Complexity* (New York: Mentor, 1965), 67.

30 Charles Taylor, *Sources of the Self* (Cambridge, Mass.: Harvard University Press, 1989), 462.

31 Susan Sontag, "Approaching Artaud," in *Under the Sign of Saturn* (New York: Farrar, Strauss, Giroux, 1980). Sontag gives an engaging account of Artaud and Gnostic parallels. 51 ff.

32 Antonin Artaud, *The Theater and Its Double*, Mary C. Richards, trans. (New York: Grove Press, 1988), 7.

33 Eliot quoted in Frye, *T.S. Eliot*, 13.

34 James Joyce, *A Portrait of the Artist as a Young Man*, quoted in Joseph Campbell, *The Masks of God: Creative Mythology* (New York: Penguin, 1976), 274.

35 Thomas Mann, quoted in Joseph Campbell, *Creative Mythology*, 311, 637.

36 Ibid., 61.

37 Frye, *T.S. Eliot*, 7.

38 George Santayana, "Classic Liberty" in *The Norton Reader* (New York: Norton, 1965), 1199.

Chapter 15 Atomization: Protestants and Americans

1 Richard Maxwell Brown, *Strain of Violence* (New York: Oxford University Press, 1975), 33.

2 Charles A. Beard quoted in Morton White, *Social Thought in America* (Boston: Beacon Press, 1957), 45.

3 Raymond Boudin, *The Analysis of Ideology* (Cambridge: Polity Press, 1989), 121.

4 R.H. Tawney, *Religion and the Rise of Capitalism* (New York: Harcourt, Brace, 1926), 84.

5 Hugh Thomas, *A History of the World* (New York: Harper and Row, 1979), 202.

6 Richard Marius, *Martin Luther: The Christian Between God and Death* (Cambridge, Mass.: Belknap Press of Harvard University Press, 1999), 323.

7 Nicholas Campion, *The Great Year* (London, England: Penguin Arkana, 1994), 365.

8 See Karl Mannheim, *Ideology and Utopia* (New York: Harcourt, Brace and World, 1936), 212.

9 Tawney, *Religion and the Rise of Capitalism*, 88.

10 Ibid., 92.

11 Ibid., 9.

12 Cohn, *The Pursuit of the Millennium*, 271.

13 Ibid., 283ff. For Karl Mannheim, "The moment in which Chiliasm [millenarianism] joins forces with the active demands of the oppressed strata of society comes with the . . . Anabaptists"; see *Ideology and Utopia*, 211.

14 Tawney, *Religion and the Rise of Capitalism*, 107.

15 "The Protestant Sects and the Spirit of Capitalism " in Gerth and Mills, eds., *From Max Weber: Essays in Sociology*, 306.

16 Tawney, *The Rise of Capitalism*, 114–15.

17 Campion, *The Great Year*, 385.

18 See Weber, "The Protestant Sects and the Spirit of Capitalism," 321.

19 J. Bronowski and Bruce Mazlisch, *The Western Intellectual Tradition* (New York: Harper and Row, 1960), 49 f.

20 Max Weber, "Politics as a Vocation," in H.H. Gerth and C. Wright Mills, eds., *From Max Weber: Essays in Sociology* (New York: Oxford University Press, 1949), 124.

21 Francis Bacon quoted in J.M. Roberts, *The Penguin History of the World* (London: Penguin, 1997), 655; see also Campion, *The Great Year*, 393.

22 Bertrand Russell, *A History of Western Philosophy* (New York: Simon and Schuster, 1945), 100.

23 Karl Mannheim, "Conservative Thought," in K.H. Wolf, ed., *Karl Mannheim* (London: Transaction Publishers, 1993), 235.

24 Ibid., 230–31.

25 H. James Billington, *Fire in the Minds of Men* (New York: Basic Books, 1980), 94, 117.

26 Carlos Fuentes, *Latin America: At War with the Past*, first delivered as the CBC Massey Lectures (Toronto: CBC Enterprises, 1984), 30.

27 Christopher Columbus, quoted in Tawney, *The Rise of Capitalism*, 89.

28 Fuentes, *Latin America*, 29.

29 Henry Parkes, *Gods and Men* (New York: Vintage, 1965), 115, note 5.

30 Deuteronomy 7: 1–5.

31 Parkes, *Gods and Men*, 116 and note 9.

32 Parkes holds that Deuteronomy is "The *fons et origo* of racist doctrine in the whole Western World." *Gods and Men*, 115.

33 W.J. Cash, *The Mind of the South* (New York: Alfred A. Knopf, 1962), 54.

34 Ibid., 89, 132.

35 Brown, *Strain of Violence*, 23.

36 Fuentes, *Latin America*, 8–10.

37 Ibid.

38 See William Krehm, *Democracies and Tyrannies of the Caribbean* (Westport, Conn.: Lawrence Hill, 1984), 111.

39 George Grant, *Philosophy in the Mass Age* (Toronto: Copp Clark, 1959), 85; Bob Goudzwaard, *Capitalism and Progress* (Toronto: Wedge Publishing, 1979), 66.

40 Grant, *Philosophy in the Mass Age*, 88.

41 See Goudzwaard, *Capitalism and Progress*, 138.

PART THREE   SEPARATION

Chapter 16   Culmination: Cold Wars and Witch Hunts

1 Seymour Martin Lipset, *Political Man: The Social Bases for Politics* (Garden City, New York: Doubleday, 1963), xxv.

2 J.M. Roberts, *The Penguin History of the World* (London: Penguin, 1992), 940.

3 Ibid., 1003.

4 David Caute, *The Left in Europe Since 1789* (London: Weidenfeld and Nicholson, 1966), 194.

5 Ibid., 185, 192.

6 Paul Johnson, *A History of the Modern World* (London: Weidenfeld and Nicholson, 1984), 443.

7 B.R. Iffmark, quoted in Lipset, *Political Man*, xxxi–xxxii.

8 Johnson, *A History of the Modern World*, 407.

9 Lipset, *Political Man*, 170.

10 Ibid., 172–73.

11 John Garraty and Peter Gay, *The Columbia History of the World* (New York: Harper and Row, 1972), 729.

12 Friedrich Engels, *The End of Classical German Philosophy*, in L.S. Feuer, ed., *Marx and Engels: Basic Writings on Politics and Philosophy* (New York: Doubleday, 1959), 240.

13 R.R. Palmer and Joel Coulton, *A History of the World to 1815* (New York: McGraw Hill, 1984), 230–31.

14 Barrington Moore, *Social Origins of Dictatorship and Democracy* (Boston: Beacon Press, 1966), 3ff.

15 Robert Nisbet, *History of the Idea of Progress* (New York: Basic Books, 1980), 126.

16 Emmanuel Todd, *The Explanation of Ideology* (Oxford: Basil Blackwell, 1985), 102.

17 The Diggers sought to return common land to people by digging it up, the Levellers wanted to level inequality, and the Fifth Monarchy Men wanted to bring about the utopian Fifth Monarchy predicted in the millenarian eschatology of Joachim Floris.

18 See Moore, *Social Origins of Dictatorship and Democracy*, 20.

19 Michael Curtis, *The Great Political Theories* (New York: Avon Books, 1962), vol. 1, 293.

20 Karl Marx, "The Ideology of Capitalism," in T.D. Bottomore, *Karl Marx: Selected Writings in Sociology and Social Philosophy* (Harmondsworth: Penguin, 1967), 169; and see Curtis, *Great Political Theories*, vol. I, 294.

21 R.H. Tawney, *Region and the Rise of Capitalism* (Toronto: Mentor, 1963), 111.

22 Ibid., 115.

23 Charles Taylor, *Sources of the Self* (Cambridge, Mass.: Harvard University Press, 1989), 131; and Bertrand Russell, *A History of Western Philosophy* (New York: Simon and Schuster, 1945), 565.

24 Ibid., 144.

25 George Steiner, *Heidegger* (London: Fontana, 1978), 56.

26 Julian Marias, *History of Philosophy* (New York: Dover, 1966), 222; see also Stuart Hampshire, *The Age of Reason* (New York: New American Library, 1956), 62.

27 Pascal, *Pensées* (Harmondsworth: Penguin, 1966), Series II, (The Wager) verse 418, 149.

28 Hans Jonas, *The Gnostic Religion* (Boston: Beacon Press, 1963), 322–23.

29 Ibid., 325.

30 Maurice Merleau-Ponty, *Humanism and Terror* (Boston: Beacon Press, 1969), 179.

31 Thelma Z. Lavine, *From Socrates to Sartre* (New York: Bantam, 1984), 340.

32 Anthony Flew, *An Introduction to Western Philosophy* (London: Thames and Hudson, 1989), 467.

33 See Jean-Paul Sartre's essay, "Existentialism" in *The Norton Reader* (New York: W.W. Norton, 1977), 1238.

34 Marias, *History of Philosophy*, 440.

35 Jean-Paul Sartre, quoted in Marias, *History of Philosophy*, 441.

36 Martin Jay, *The Dialectical Imagination* (Toronto: Little, Brown, 1973), 274.

37 Albert Camus, *The Rebel* (New York: Random House, 1956), 298.

38 Claude Lévi-Strauss, inaugural lecture at the Collège de France, quoted in Susan Sontag, *Against Interpretation* (New York: Delta, 1966), 81.

39 Baruch Spinoza, "The Foundations of the Moral Life," in Saxe Commins and Robert Linscott., eds., *The World's Great Thinkers: The Speculative Philosophers* (New York: Random House, 1947), 172.

40 See Spinoza, *Tractatus Theologico-Politicus and Tractatus Politicus*, in Curtis, *Great Political Theories*, 317.

41 Isaiah Berlin, *Karl Marx* (Oxford: Oxford University Press, 1996), 10.

42 John Passmore, *The Perfectibility of Man* (London: Cox and Wyman, 1972), 216.

43 Ibid., 215.

44 Jay, *The Dialectical Imagination*, 82; Berlin, *Karl Marx*, 35–36; and Nisbet, *History of the Idea of Progress*, 157.

45 See Taylor, *Sources of the Self*, 277.

46 See J. Needham, "Science and Civilization in China," in Fritjof Capra, "*The Tao of Physics* (London: Fontana, 1984), 320; and see Joseph Campbell, *The Masks of God: Creative Mythology* (New York: Penguin, 1976), 480–81.

47 Capra, *The Tao of Physics*, 329–30.

48 Felipe Fernandez-Armesto, *Millennium* (Toronto: Doubleday, 1995), 129–34. Armesto discusses the emergence and eclipse in the fourteenth

century of what seems to have been China's only indigenous millenarian movement.

49 Carl Jung, *Psychological Types*, Bollingen Series XX (Princeton, NJ: Princeton University Press, 1977), 194.

50 Moore, *Social Origins of Dictatorship and Democracy*, 162–63.

51 See Moore, *Social Origins of Dictatorship and Democracy*, 199.

52 Auguste Comte, "Catechism of Positivist Religion" in Johnson, *A History of the Modern World*, 75–76.

53 Karl Jaspers, *Socrates, Buddha, Confucius, Jesus* (New York: Harcourt, Brace, Jovanovitch, 1957), 50.

54 Herbert Muller, *The Uses of the Past* (New York: Oxford University Press, 1952), 365.

55 See Jung, *Psychological Types*, 307.

56 Nisbet, *History of the Idea of Progress*, 130.

57 Louise Brown and George Carson, *Men and Centuries of Civilization* (New York: Knopf, 1948), 436.

58 George Locke, "The Second Treatise of Civil Government," in Curtis, *The Great Political Theories*, vol. 1, 338–39.

59 Ibid., 341.

60 The charge of unfalsifiability could be brought against this book. And rightly so, if it were a theory. But theories usually have a certainty that extends to prophecy and I make no claim that politics will cease to be dualistic; I have only tried to say that political dualism looks as if it is declining and that if it doesn't it would be better if it did.

61 Joseph Campbell, *The Masks of God: Oriental Mythology* (Arkana, New York: Penguin, 1991), 506–7, 513.

62 Johnson, *A History of the Modern World*, 444.

63 Moore, *Social Origins of Dictatorship and Democracy*, 223.

64 Todd, *The Explanation of Ideology*, 2; see Johnson, *A History of the Modern World*, 444–45; and Moore, *Social Origins of Dictatorship and Democracy*, 89–90.

65 Moore, *Social Origins of Dictatorship and Democracy*, 227.

66 Johnson, *A History of the Modern World*, 195.

Chapter 17   Dissonance: Three Worlds or a Kantian Universe?

1 Raymond Boudon, *Ideology* (Cambridge: Polity Press, 1989), 174.

2 Ibid., 177–78.

3 Ibid., 187.

4 Ibid., 183–84.

5 Article on Montesquieu, *Encyclopedia Britannica*, vol. XVIII, 11th ed. (Cambridge: Cambridge University Press, 1912), 777.

6 Norman Hampson, *Will and Circumstance: Montesquieu, Rousseau and the French Revolution* (Oklahoma: University of Oklahoma Press, 1983), 18.

7 Ibid., 22.

8 Ibid., 10.

9 Emmanuel Todd, *The Explanation of Ideology* (Oxford: Basil Blackwell, 1985), 1.

10 Ibid., 5.

11 Paul Johnson, *A History of the Modern World* (London: Weidenfeld and Nicholson, 1984), 550.

12 Todd, *The Explanation of Ideology*, 46.

13 Ibid.

14 Ibid.

15 Ibid., 195.

16 John Garraty and Peter Gay, *The Columbia History of the World* (New York: Harper and Row, 1972), 1115.

17 For example, Lake Sagaris's comments on Mapuche Indians in Chile in her book, *After the First Death* (Toronto: Somerville House, 1996), 245, 247.

18 Todd, *The Explanation of Ideology*, 116.

19 Ibid., 195.

20 Carlos Fuentes, *Latin America* (Toronto: House of Anansi, 1998), 57.

21 George Woodcock, *Anarchism* (Kingston, Ontario: Quarry Press, 1995), 425–26.

22 Ibid., 427.

23 Seymour Martin Lipset, *Political Man: The Social Bases for Politics* (Garden City, New York: Doubleday, 1963), 176.

24 See Timothy Garton Ash, "Back Yards," *The New York Review of Books*, Nov. 22, 1984.

25 See Todd, *The Explanation of Ideology*, 115.

26 Bernard Dietrich, *Somoza* (New York: E.P. Dutton, 1981), 296–97.

27 See Christopher Dickey, *With the Contras* (New York: Simon and Schuster, 1985), 94–95.

28 This was the author's experience of the rebel groups of Pastora and Spadafora in Nicaragua and in exile in Costa Rica; two of Pastora's Commanders, under attack from the Sandinistas and harassment from the CIA, explicitly stated that their group was neither Left nor Right.

29 Robert S. Klein, "Nicaragua's Untold Stories," *New Republic*, Oct. 3, 1984.

30 See Anthony Flew, *Introduction to Western Philosophy* (London: Thames & Hudson, 1989), 95–96.

31 Christopher Dawson, *The Dynamics of World History* (New York: New American Library, 1962), 54, 277.

32 Robert Nisbet, *History of the Idea of Progress* (New York: Basic Books, 1980), 22.

33 Christian Lenhardt, "The Legacy of Critical Idealism," in Asher Horowitz and Terry Maley, eds., *The Barbarism of Reason: Max Weber and the Twilight of Enlightenment* (Toronto: University of Toronto Press, 1994), 32.

34 Isaiah Berlin, *Karl Marx* (Oxford: Oxford University Press, 1996), 113.

35 Ibid., 115–16.

36 See Mark Warren, "Nietzsche and Weber: When Does Reason Become Power?" in Horowitz and Maley, eds., *The Barbarism of Reason*, 69.

37 Hugh Thomas, *A History of the World* (New York: Harper and Row, 1979), 520.

38 See Stanley Ryerson, *The Founding of Canada* (Toronto: Progress Books, 1960), 232.

39 Edmund Burke, "Reflections on the Revolution in France," in Michael Curtis, *The Great Political Theories* (New York: Avon Books, 1962), vol. 2, 60.

40 Nisbet, *History of the Idea of Progress*, 282.

41 Ibid., 53.

42 The effect of America's sectarian heritage in seventeenth-century Puritan England upon American politics from the Revolution through the Civil War is the subject of Kevin Phillips's highly original *The Cousins' Wars* (New York: Basic Books, 1999).

43 Phillips, *The Cousins' Wars*, 165.

44 Ibid., 170.

45 Garraty and Gay, *The Columbia History of the World*, 755.

46 Phillips, *The Cousins' Wars*, 179.

47 Ibid., 165, 169.

48 Alexis de Tocqueville, *Democracy in America* (New York: Vintage, 1954), 277.

49 See Arthur Herman, *The Idea of Decline in Western History* (New York: The Free Press, 1997), 317–18.

50 Philip Slater, "The Old Culture and the New," in *The Pursuit of Loneliness* (Boston: Boston Beacon Press, 1970).

51 Herman, *The Idea of Decline*, 327.

52 See Saul Bellow, "Culture Now," *Intellectual Digest*, September 1971.

Chapter 18 Power: Beheading Marx, Decapitating Louis

1 Bernard-Henri Lévy, *Barbarism with a Human Face* (New York: Harper and Row, 1979), 15.

2 Michel Foucault, "Truth and Power," interview; in Colin Gordon, ed., *Power/Knowledge* (New York: Pantheon, 1980), 118.

3 Foucault, "Politics and Reason," in Kirtzman, ed., *Michel Foucault, Politics, Philosophy, Culture* (New York: Routledge, 1988), 67.

4 Foucault, "The Eye of Power," in Colin Gordon, *Power/Knowledge*, 159.

5 Crane Brinton, *A History of Western Morals* (New York: Paragon House, 1990), 294.

6 Voltaire, "Equality" in B.R. Redman, ed., *The Portable Voltaire* (New York: Viking Press, 1949), 113–14.

7 Ibid., 114.

8 Christopher Dawson, *The Dynamics of World History* (New York: New American Library, 1962), 277.

9 This is the thesis of John Ralston Saul's *Voltaire's Bastards* (Toronto: Penguin, 1992).

10 Charles Taylor, *Sources of the Self* (Cambridge, Mass.: Harvard University Press, 1989), 357, 361; J. Bronowski and Bruce Mazlisch, *The Western Intellectual Tradition* (New York: Harper and Row, 1960), 285.

11 Taylor, *Sources of the Self*, 361.

12 Bronowski and Mazlisch, *The Western Intellectual Tradition*, 303; and see Maurice Cranston, *Jean Jacques* (New York: W.W. Norton, 1983), 27. See also Patrice Higonnet, *Goodness Beyond Virtue: Jacobins During the French Revolution* (Cambridge, Mass.: Harvard University Press, 1998), 271, for Calvinist attraction to Jacobinism in the Protestant regions of the south of France. Higgonet also reports that anti-Jacobin regions were also anti-Protestant and that Jacobinism was seen as a force of the Reformation, 235–36.

13 Rousseau, "Social Contract," Book II, in Curtis, *The Great Political Theories*, vol. 2, 25.

14 Jean Matrat, *Robespierre* (New York: Scribner's, 1971), 63, 67, 69, 165.

15 Rousseau, "Social Contract," Book II, in Curtis, *The Great Political Theories*, vol. 2, 28.

16 See Jean-Jacques Rousseau, "The Social Contract," Book I in Michael Curtis, *The Great Political Theories* (New York: Avon Books, 1962), vol. 216–19.

17 Rousseau, "Social Contract," Book II, in Curtis, *The Great Political Theories*, vol. 2, 24; and see Norman Hampson, *Will and Circumstance: Montesquieu, Rousseau and the French Revolution* (Oklahoma: University of Oklahoma Press, 1983), 30.

18 See Taylor, *Sources of the Self*, 339.

19 See Hampson, *Will and Circumstance*, 37.

20 Rousseau, "Social Contract," in Curtis, *The Great Political Theories*, vol. 2, 27.

21 Ibid., 20–21.

22 Karl Marx, "Bruno Bauer, 'Die Judenfrage,'" in Tom Bottomore, ed., *Karl Marx, Early Writings* (New York: McGraw-Hill, 1964), 30–31.

23 The distinction is Brinton's, *A History of Western Morals*, 301.

24 See Bertrand Russell, *A History of Western Philosophy* (New York: Simon and Schuster, 1945), 684–85.

25 Foucault, "Social Security," in Kritzman, ed., *Michel Foucault*, 160–65.

26 See W.D. Burnham, "Why is the Right Ascendant?" in *Dissent*, fall 1983, 440.

27 This is partly the thesis of Francis Fukuyama in *The End of History and the Last Man* (Toronto: Macmillan, 1992), although he has not received due credit for questioning the lack of substance in Liberal Democracy and its Nietzschean "Last Man."

28 Discussion between Roy Medvedev, and Giuletto Chiesa, in "A Time of Change," *Dissent*, summer 1990, 325.

29 Ibid.

30 David Remnick, *Lenin's Tomb* (New York: Random House, 1993), 435.

31 Ibid., 439.

32 J. Lipski, "Poland, the State and Markets," *Dissent*, summer 1990, 358.

33 See Alberto Moravia, "The Pole of History and the Way of Peace," excerpted from "Novi Argumenti," *Harper's Magazine*, August 1984.

34 Herman, *The Idea of Decline*, 408.

35 A.L. Chickering, *Beyond Left and Right: Breaking the Political Stalemate* (San Francisco: ICS Press, 1993), 140.

36 Marshall McLuhan, *The Medium Is the Message* (Toronto: Bantam, 1967), 115. See David Bell, *The Cultural Contradictions of Capitalism* (New York: Basic Books, 1976), 107–8.

37 See Barrington Moore, *Social Origins of Dictatorship and Democracy* (Boston: Beacon Press, 1966), 228ff.

38 Ibid.

39 Bell, *The Coming of Post-Industrial Society* (New York: Basic Books, 1976), 244.

40 See George Soros, "The Capitalist Threat," *Atlantic Monthly*, Feb., 1997.

41 Ibid.

42 Bell, *The Coming of Post-Industrial Society*, 483.

43 Ibid., 119.

44 Bell, *The Cultural Contradictions of Capitalism*, 285.

45 See Dennis Wrong, "Sceptical Thoughts about a Fashionable Theory," *Dissent*, fall 1983, 497–99.

46 See Drucker, who favours technocracy, in "Beyond the Information Revolution," *Atlantic Monthly*, October 1999, 57; and George Steiner who opposes it in *Bluebeard's Castle* (London: Faber, 1971), 100–103.

47 See Bell, *The Cultural Contradictions of Capitalism*, 317.

48 Drucker, "Beyond the Information Revolution."

49 See, in general, Charles Taylor, *The Malaise of Modernity* (Concord, Ontario: Anansi, 1991).

50 Foucault, in "On Power," in Kritzman, ed., *Michel Foucault*, 103.

51 See Gilbert Germain, "The Revenge of the Sacred," in Asher Horowitz and Terry Maley, eds., *The Barbarism of Reason: Max Weber and the Twilight of Enlightenment* (Toronto: University of Toronto Press, 1994), 251.

52 Max Weber, "Politics as a Vocation," in H.H. Gerth and C. Wright Mills, eds., *From Max Weber: Essays in Sociology* (New York: Oxford University Press, 1946), 82.

53 Lévy, *Barbarism with a Human Face*, 149.

54 Foucault, "Truth and Power," in Gordon, ed., *Power/Knowledge*, 121.

Chapter 19   Fragmentation: The Deconstruction of Hiram

1 See Christopher Lasch, *The True and Only Heaven: Progress and Its Critics* (New York: W.W. Norton, 1991), 22.

2 Felipe Fernandez-Armesto, *Millennium* (New York: Simon and Schuster, 1996), 705.

3 Carlos Fuentes, *Latin America at War with the Past* (Toronto: CBC Enterprises, 1984), 69.

4 Boris Kapustin, "Russia as a Postmodern Society" in *Dissent*, winter 2000.

5 See Jacques Derrida, "The Ends of Man," in Kenneth Baynes, James Bohan, and Thomas McCarthy, *After Philosophy* (Cambridge, Mass.: MIT Press, 1989), 131, 141, 146.

6 In this book I've tried to do something similar (if not quite as esoteric) in "deconstructing" Western dualism into its cultural, historical, and intellectual parts.

7 Derrida, *The Ends of Man*, 132.

8 Jean-Jacques Lyotard, quoted in the introduction to "The Postmodern Condition," in Baynes, Bohan, McCarthy, *After Philosophy*, 70.

9 Lyotard, "The Postmodern Condition," 76.

10 Derrida, *The Ends of Man*, 151.

11 See Charles Taylor, *Sources of the Self* (Cambridge, Mass.: Harvard University Press, 1989), 487–89.

12 Jacques Derrida, "The Spectres of Marx," quoted in Mark Lilla, "The Politics of Jacques Derrida," *New York Review of Books*, June 25, 1998, 39.

13 Francis Fukuyama, *The End of History and the Last Man* (Toronto: Macmillan, 1992), 213ff.

14 Theodor Adorno, quoted in Edward Said, *Cultural Imperialism* (New York: Knopf, 1993), 258; see also 239.

15 See Vaclav Havel, "Six Asides About Culture," Paul Wilson, ed., *Open Letters: Selected Writings, 1965–1990* (New York: Knopf, 1991), 277.

16 Daniel Bell, *The Cultural Contradictions of Capitalism* (New York: Basic Books, 1996), 330–31.

17 Nicholas Campion, *The Great Year* (London: Penguin, 1994), 469.

18 A.L. Chickering, *Beyond Left and Right: Breaking the Political Stalemate* (San Francisco: ICS Press, 1993), 168.

19 David Trend, *Cultural Democracy, Politics, Media, New Technology* (Albany, New York: State University of New York Press, 1997), 22–24.

20 Bell, *The Cultural Contradictions of Capitalism*, 332.

21 Said, *Cultural Imperialism*, 193.

22 See Robert D. Kaplan, *The Ends of the Earth* (New York: Random House, 1996), 107.

23 Ibid., 108–9.

24 Said, *Cultural Imperialism*, 58.

25 See Lyotard, "The Postmodern Condition," 81.

26 See Bertrand Russell, *A History of Western Philosophy* (New York: Simon and Schuster, 1945), 600.

27 See Charles Taylor, *Multiculturalism* (Princeton, NJ: Princeton University Press, 1992), 44.

28 F.L. Pick and G.N. Knight, *The Pocket History of Freemasonry* (London: Hutchinson, 77).

29 See Alexander Piatigorsky, *Who's Afraid of Freemasons?* (London: The Harvill Press, 1997), 272–73.

30 Ibid., 301.

31 See Albert Mackey, *The History of Freemasonry* (Avenel, New Jersey: Random House, 1996), 41; and Pick and Knight, *Freemasonry*, 113.

32 Mackey, *Freemasonry*, 31.

33 Piatigorsky, *Who's Afraid of Freemasons?*, 280; 330–31.

34 The standard legend appears in Mackey, *Freemasonry*, 67.

35 I Kings, 7.

36 Piatigorsky, *Who's Afraid of Freemasons?*, 89.

37 See Mackey, *Freemasonry*, 421–26.

38 Piatigorsky, *Who's Afraid of Freemasons?*, 329.

39 Ibid., 88.

40 Ibid., 87.

41 See James H. Billington, *Fire in the Minds of Men* (New York: Basic Books, 1980), 96.

42 Ibid., 94–95.

43 Ibid., 6.

44 François Furet, *Interpreting the French Revolution* (Cambridge: Cambridge University Press, 1981), 184–85.

45 Patrice Higonnet, *Goodness Beyond Virtue: Jacobins During the French Revolution* (Cambridge, Mass.: Harvard University Press, 1998), 334.

46 See Mark Wigley, *The Architecture of Deconstruction: Derrida's Haunt* (Cambridge, Mass.: MIT Press, 1993).

47 William Phillips, "Sources of the Left," *Partisan Review*, spring 1998, 186.

48 Robert Nisbet, *History of the Idea of Progress* (New York: Basic Books, 1970), 337.

49 Christopher Lasch, *The Minimal Self* (New York: W.W. Norton, 1984), 19.

50 Ibid., 58–59.

51 Lasch, *The Minimal Self*, 197–99.

52 Lasch, *The True and Only Heaven*, 515.

53 Herman, *The Idea of Decline*, 386; Stephen Jones and Peter Israel, *Others Unknown: The Oklahoma City Bombing Case and Conspiracy* (New York: Public Affairs, 1998), 58.

54 Montana Militiaman Bob Fletcher, quoted in Michael Kelly, "The Road to Paranoia" in *The New Yorker*, June 19, 1995.

55 Lasch, *The True and Only Heaven*, 505.

56 Jones and Israel, *Others Unknown*, 60; and Kelly, "The Road to Paranoia," *The New Yorker*.

57 Timothy McVeigh, interviewed on *60 Minutes*, March 12, 2000.

58 Bernard-Henri Lévy, *Barbarism with a Human Face* (New York: Harper and Row, 1979), 189.

59 Chickering, *Beyond Left and Right*, 61.

60 Bob Rae, *The Three Questions* (Toronto: Viking, 1998), 20.

61 See Laponce, *Left and Right: The Topography of Political Perceptions* (Toronto: University of Toronto Press, 1981), 6–7.

62 Norberto Bobbio, *Left and Right: The Significance of a Political Distinction* (Chicago: The University of Chicago Press, 1996), 5.

63 Ibid., 32–33.

64 Ibid., 34.

65 Ibid., 59.

66 Allan Cameron in the introduction to Bobbio, *Left and Right*, xiii; and Samuel Brittan, *Capitalism with a Human Face* (Cambridge, Mass.: Harvard University Press, 236).

Chapter 20 Community: The City Block and the Cosmos

1 Charles Taylor, *The Malaise of Modernity* (Concord, Ontario: Anansi, 1991), 40-41.

2 Ibid., 95.

3 Ibid., 95-96.

4 Christopher Lasch, *The Revolt of the Elites* (New York: W.W. Norton, 1995), 112.

5 Ibid., 110-11.

6 Nicholas Campion, *The Great Year* (London: Penguin, 1994), 499.

7 Bob Goudzwaard, *Capitalism and Progress* (Toronto: Wedge Publishing, 1979), 186.

8 Campion, *The Great Year*, 500.

9 Hannah Arendt, *The Human Condition* (Chicago: The University of Chicago Press, 1958), 58.

10 Lasch, *The Revolt of the Elites*, 109.

11 James Chisholm, *Sex, Hope and Death* (Cambridge, UK: University Press, 1999), 48.

12 See Susan Sontag's essay, "Fascinating Fascism," in *Under the Sign of Saturn* (New York: Farrar, Straus, Giroux, 1980), 97.

13 See Eatwell, *Fascism: A History* (Harmondsworth: Penguin, 1996), 282.

14 Felipe Fernandez-Armesto, *Millennium* (New York: Simon and Schuster, 1996), 700.

15 See Francis Fukuyama, "The Great Disruption," *Atlantic Monthly*, May 1999, 56.

16 See Samuel Brittan, *Capitalism with a Human Face* (Cambridge, Mass.: Harvard University Press, 1996), 239; and Alan Wolfe, *Whose Keeper?* (Berkeley: University of California Press, 1989), 101.

17 Anthony Giddens, *Beyond Left and Right* (Stanford, CA: Stanford University Press, 1994), 8-9.

18 Ibid., 247-48.

19 Stephen Mulhall and Adam Swift, *Liberals and Communitarians* (Cambridge, Mass.: Blackwell, 1996), 165.

20 Robert N. Bellah, "Community Properly Understood" in R.N. Bellah, et al., *The Good Society* (New York: Knopf, 1991), 18; and Wolfe, *Whose Keeper?*, 258.

21 Lasch, *The Revolt of the Elites*, 106 and 114; Lasch, *The True and Only Heaven* (New York: W.W. Norton, 1991), 532.

22 Lasch, *The Revolt of the Elites*, 100.

23 A.L. Chickering, *Beyond Left and Right: Breaking the Political Stalemate* (San Francisco, CA: ICS Press, 1993), 35.

24 Jorge Castaneda, *Utopia Unarmed* (New York: Knopf, 1993), 367.

25 Frank Tannenbaum, *Ten Keys to Latin America* (New York: Random House, 1962), 68-69.

26 Castaneda, *Utopia Unarmed*, 366-67.

27 Ibid., 373-74.

28 Chickering, *Beyond Left and Right*, 37.

29 Hernando DeSoto, *The Other Path* (New York: Harper and Row, 1990), 239.

30 Benjamin Barber, *Strong Democracy* (Berkeley: University of California Press, 1984), 253.

31 Arendt, *The Human Condition*, 61; and see Tom Settle, *In Search of a Third Way* (Toronto: McClelland & Stewart, 1976), 185.

32 Arendt, *The Human Condition*, 69.

33 Ibid., 33, 44.

34 Ibid., 52–53.

35 A.R. Maryansky, "The Origin of Speech and Its Implications for Optimum Size of Human Groups," *Critical Review*, vol. 11, No. 2, 240.

36 Ibid., 240.

37 See George Simmel, quoted in Maryanski, "The Origin of Speech," 243.

38 John Garraty and Peter Gay, *The Columbia History of the World* (New York: Harper and Row, 1972), 329.

39 Charles Louis, Baron de Montesquieu, "The Spirit of Laws," Book VIII, in Michael Curtis, *The Great Political Theories*, vol. 1 (New York: Avon Books, 1962), 395–96.

40 Rousseau "The Social Contract," in Michael Curtis, *The Great Political Theories*, vol. 2, 27.

41 Maryansky, "The Origin of Speech," 241.

42 Arendt, *The Human Condition*, 76.

43 James Sennett, *The Conscience of the Eye* (New York: Knopf, 1990), xiii.

44 See Arendt, *The Human Condition*, 55.

45 Lasch, *The Revolt of the Elites*, 99.

46 See Wolfe, *Whose Keeper?*, 95, 256–57.

47 Barber, *Strong Democracy*, 101–2.

48 Bellah, "Community Properly Understood," in Bellah, et al., *The Good Society*, 127.

49 Barber, *Strong Democracy*, 252–53.

50 Jane Jacobs, *Cities and the Wealth of Nations* (New York: Random House, 1985), 42; Chaps. 2–4.

51 Ibid., 41.

52 Settle, *In Search of a Third Way*, 188.

53 See Bob Rae, *The Three Questions* (Toronto: Viking, 1998), 92, 97; Goudzwaard, *Capitalism and Progress*, 216–19; and Settle, *In Search of a Third Way*, 185.

54 See Rae, *The Three Questions*, 58.

55 Bellah, "Community Properly Understood," 135.

56 Barber, *Strong Democracy*, 152, 273; Lasch, *The Revolt of the Elites*, 110–11.

57 Barber, *Strong Democracy*, 151.

58 Rousseau, "The Social Contract," in Curtis, *The Great Political Theories*, vol. 2, 29–30.

59 See Lasch, *The Revolt of the Elites*, 100–101.

60 Charles Taylor, *The Malaise of Modernity*, 9–10; see also Chickering, *Beyond Left and Right*, 159.

61 Rousseau, "The Social Contract," in Curtis, *The Great Political Theories*, vol. 2, 29–30.

62 Charles Taylor, "The Dangers of Soft Despotism," 48.

63 See Asher Horowitz, "The Comedy of Enlightenment: Weber, Habermas, and the Critique of Reification," in Asher Horowitz and Terry Maley eds., *The Barbarism of Reason: Max Weber and the Twilight of Enlightenment* (Toronto: University of Toronto Press, 1994).

64 Rae, *The Three Questions*, 98.

65 Patrice Higonnet, *Goodness Beyond Virtue: Jacobins During the French Revolution* (Cambridge, Mass.: Harvard University Press 1998), 334.

Index